D1595368

God of the Dao

God of the Dao
Lord Lao in History and Myth

Livia Kohn

CENTER FOR CHINESE STUDIES
THE UNIVERSITY OF MICHIGAN
ANN ARBOR

Published by
Center for Chinese Studies
The University of Michigan
Ann Arbor, Michigan 48104-1608

© 1998 The Regents of the University of Michigan
All rights reserved

∞ The paper used in this publication meets the requirements
of the American National Standard for Information Sciences—
Permanence of Paper for Publications and Documents
in Libraries and Archives ANSI/NISO/Z39.48—1992.

Library of Congress Cataloging-in-Publication Data

Kohn, Livia, 1956–

God of the Dao : Lord Lao in history and myth / Livia Kohn.
p.   cm. —
(Michigan monographs in Chinese studies ; 84)
Includes bibliographical references and index.
ISBN 0-89264-128-2 (alk. paper)
ISBN 0-89264-133-9 (pbk) (alk. paper)
1. Lao-tzu. 2. Taoism—Relations. I. Title. II. Series.
BL1930.K58   1998
299'.5142113—dc21   98-37907
CIP

Contents

Apparatus

Acknowledgments

This study treats the various sources on Lord Lao, the divinized Laozi, in Daoist history, then presents a mythological analysis of the stories associated with this god. It draws on many years of involvement with the figure of Laozi and his myth, nurtured by my teachers Anna Seidel, Fukunaga Mitsuji, and Yoshikawa Tadao, and the works of Yoshioka Yoshitoyo and Kusuyama Haruki.

In addition, I am most grateful to my colleague Daud Rahbar, who encouraged me to write a longer study on the subject, and to the many friends and colleagues who read parts of the manuscript and helped with suggestions and ideas. Sarah Allan, Anne Birrell, Norman J. Girardot, Whalen Lai, John Strong, and Franciscus Verellen each looked at portions of the second part on the Laozi myth. Catherine Despeux, Ute Engelhardt, Patrick Hanan, Russell Kirkland, Terry Kleeman, Detlef Kohn, Michael LaFargue, Stephen Little, Isabelle Robinet, Robert Sharf, and Yamada Toshiakiō made valuable suggestions on Part One. I am deeply indebted to them all.

Among scholarly studies, moreover, I gained important insights and help from Judith Boltz's work on later Daoist texts (1987), Kristofer Schipper's studies of the Daoist body and forms of Daoist ritual (1978; 1985; 1994), and Masuo Shin'inchirō's examination of Daoist texts transmitted to Japan (1994; 1995).

Some ideas contained in this book were first presented at conferences: the mythological analysis of the transmission of the *Daode jing* at the First American-Japanese Conference on Taoist Studies (Tokyo, 1995) and the examination of the conversion of the barbarians in light of the myth of the hero at the 48th Annual Meeting of the Association for Asian Studies (Honolulu, 1996). Both conferences helped to clarify issues of analysis, and I am very grateful to the scholars present at those meetings, especially Suzanne Cahill, Peter Nickerson, Harold Roth, and Yamada Toshiaki, for their critical questions and insightful observations.

Illustrations

Tables

Abbreviations

DZ   Daozang (Daoist canon)[*]
P.   Pelliot collection of Dunhuang manuscripts
S.   Stein collection of Dunhuang manuscripts
SDZN   *Sandong zhunang*
T.   Taishō Tripitaka (Buddhist canon)[†]
YJQQ   *Yunji qiqian*

---

[*] Texts in the Daoist canon are cited according to Schipper 1975.
[†] Citations from the Buddhist canon give the serial number, the volume, and the page.

Preface

The classical hagiography of Lord Lao reads as follows:

> Laozi is the Highest Lord Lao [Taishang laojun]. For successive generations he continued to transform without ever manifesting himself by being born in a human body. Then, under the reign of King Yangjia of the Shang [1408–01 B.C.E.], he divided his spirit and transformed his energy to take refuge in the womb of the Jade Maiden of Mystery and Wonder [Xuanmiao yunü]. After eighty-one years, in the reign of King Wuding [1198–94] and with the year star in *gengchen*, on the fifteenth day of the second month, he was born in the hour of the rabbit [5–7 A.M.]. The event occurred in the southern state of Chu, in Hu district, Lai village, Quren hamlet.
>
> He emerged from his mother's left armpit. At that time she was standing under a plum tree. Pointing to the tree, he said: "This will be my surname [Li]." At birth, he had white hair, a yellow complexion, long ears, and big eyes. His nose had a double bridge and four nostrils, while his ears had three openings. He had beautiful whiskers, a broad forehead, and few teeth. On the soles of his feet he had the signs of the three [forces] and the five [phases]. His palms contained the character for the number ten. His last name was Li, his given name Er, his style Boyang. He was also called Laozi, or again, Lao Dan.
>
> When King Wen became Western Lord, he summoned him to court and made him an archive administrator. Under King Wu of the Zhou [1122–15], he moved and became an archivist. At this time he also wandered to the four ends of the world, to countries like Daqin [Rome] and Tianzhu [India]. There he became known as Master Gu [Buddha] and converted all these countries, only to return to China under King Kang [1078–52] and again become a historian of the Zhou.
>
> In the twenty-third year of the rule of King Zhao [1029], he climbed on a carriage drawn by a black ox and went across the Hangu Pass [in the Zhongnan Mountains]. The guardian of the pass, Yin Xi, recognized him and begged him to impart his teaching. In the twenty-fifth year, Lord Lao descended once more, this time in Shu [Sichuan]. There, in a shop selling black sheep, he met again with Yin Xi. Together they crossed the floating sands [Taklamakan Desert] into the countries of the barbarians.
>
> In the time of King Mu [1001–946], he returned to the Middle Kingdom. Then, in the seventeenth year of King Jing [502], Confucius came to ask him about the Dao; on leaving, he sighed and likened Lord Lao to a dragon. In the ninth year of King She [305], he [Lord Lao] left China again

via the pass and flew up to Mount Kunlun. Under the Qin dynasty [221–06], he descended to reside on the bank of the Yellow River. He was then known as the Master on the River [Heshang gong]. . . .

Lord Lao has continued to appear in all eras, joining the kalpas of the world and going along with all transformations, yet ultimately existing without limit and living on forever and ever. His appearances and withdrawals cannot be fathomed, his changes and transformations are without bounds. He goes utterly beyond heaven and humanity, and no one can do him justice with mere words.

This account of Lord Lao's divine career, found in both the *Zengxiang liexian zhuan* (Illustrated Immortals' Biographies, 1.1b)* of the Yuan and the *Xiaoyao xu jing* (Scripture of [Immortals] Wandering in the Void, DZ 1465, 1.3b–4b) of the Ming dynasty, summarizes the main events and activities in the god's life, emphasizing his divine nature and oneness with the Dao as well as his continued concern for the world and active manifestations within it. The story it presents is the result of a long process of development, which can be described as the historical unfolding of different roles the god played in successive dynasties; it also represents the mythological growth of episodes and motifs linked with his divinity as the belief system of Daoism changed over time.

To understand the immensely complex figure of Lord Lao, the dimensions of history and myth must both be considered carefully. Moreover, inquiry in these areas must address different issues, rely on different sources, and ask fundamentally different questions. The historical approach inquires about the when and where and what of the god; it considers his role or image in certain periods and for certain social groups, such as the government elite, the wider populace, individual seekers of long life, and even believers of other religions. Accordingly, it makes use not only of religious hagiographies but also of official and popular inscriptions, reports on miracles, texts on physical and meditative practices, Buddhist and popular tales, as well as works of art and literature.

The mythological approach, on the other hand, asks about the meaning of his life story as formulated in any period and tries to understand the relevance of specific episodes and mythical motifs in relation to the worldview and practice of Daoist followers. To elucidate their deeper significance, it further compares specific aspects of the overall myth to variant Daoist themes, to similar stories and symbols in the other religious traditions of China, and even to non-Chinese and Western patterns in myth and in religious thinking. Against the Daoist

---

* The text here follows a 1921 edition brought out by Dacheng shuju in Shanghai.

tradition confined largely to hagiographic sources, this inquiry compares materials from ancient Daoist texts, Confucian classics, Buddhist sūtras, and popular collections, then reaches out to general, theoretical studies of specific motifs and religious phenomena.

Where history remains within the limits of the time and space of traditional China, mythology goes beyond those boundaries and looks at underlying patterns of thought and imagery, often vague and almost always contradictory, that give an indication of the workings of the religious mind, as opposed to the outer manifestations of religious devotion or practice. Lord Lao as one of the key gods of traditional Daoism has an important function on both of these levels: He is prayed to as savior, depicted in statues and murals, and worshiped as the ancestor of emperors; at the same time he stands for the Dao and in his actions symbolizes the ideal Daoist way of life on earth.

Lord Lao in Daoist history and worldview cannot be understood by looking at history without myth or at myth without history. At the same time these two areas of inquiry are sufficiently different so that, despite an occasional overlap, they are not easily presented together. For this reason the present volume is divided into two parts, the first providing a historical discussion that addresses the role of Lord Lao in Chinese religious history, the second exploring mythological issues in particular, comparing the elemental nature of Daoist worship represented by Lord Lao to that of other traditions, both of China and beyond.

Part One: History

Introduction to Part One

Lord Lao (Laojun) is the divinized form of Laozi, the Old Master, who is known primarily as the alleged author of that oldest Daoist text, the *Daode jing* (Book of the Dao and Its Virtue). In introductions to its translations, he is commonly described as having lived in the sixth century B.C.E. as an official of the Zhou dynasty who had both eminent knowledge of the rites and strong reclusive tendencies. Confucius (551–479 B.C.E.) heard of him and went to learn his teaching. Later, when he felt that the dynasty was declining, Laozi left China for the western lands and on the road transmitted his ideas to the border guard Yin Xi who compiled them into the *Daode jing*.[1]

The traditional account of Laozi's life and person is largely based on his biography in chapter 63 of the *Shiji* (Historical Records) of 104 B.C.E., which in turn recounts stories told in the *Zhuangzi* (Writings of Master Zhuang) of the third century B.C.E. Written several centuries after the alleged lifetime of the philosopher, both sources are based on hearsay and exhibit a fair amount of insecurity about who or what the Old Master really was.[2] Vaguely identified with more than one person, in the

---

[1] Translations of the *Daode jing* are exceedingly numerous and vary greatly in scope, outlook, and quality. For a critical evaluation and list, see LaFargue and Pas 1998.

[2] The account in the *Shiji* is translated and discussed in Fung and Bodde 1952, 1:170; Kaltenmark 1969, 8; Lau 1982, X–XI; Graham 1990 (reprinted in Kohn and LaFargue 1998, 23–39). In the *Zhuangzi*, Laozi's meeting with Confucius appears in chapters 4, 12, 13, 14, 21, and 22. For a discussion, see Kimura 1959. See also Hurvitz 1961; Seidel 1969, 11–17; Graham 1990. First doubts about the historicity of the philosopher arose around the turn of the century (Giles 1906, 7). A debate among Western scholars on his identity and dates was also carried on by Homer Dubs and Derk Bodde in the 1940s. Discussion ranged from claiming him to be an aristocrat of the third century B.C.E. to believing him an ancient figure shrouded in mystery. See Dubs 1941; 1942; Bodde 1942a. Recently, Chinese

Former Han dynasty (206 B.C.E.–6 C.E.) Laozi was less important than the book associated with him, but his fame grew as the text was venerated with increasing devotion.[3]

Accordingly, as the legendary figure of Laozi continued to rise in public and cultic estimation, he did not remain a philosopher, however famous, but was soon elevated to an immortal of high magical powers who lived as long as heaven and earth. In the official state ritual of the Later Han, moreover, Laozi became the representative of the central harmony of the cosmos. With the emergence of the Daoist religion in the second century C.E., he grew further into a widely worshiped popular savior and harbinger of the new age of Great Peace who saved the faithful and condemned the wicked.[4]

As Daoism flourished, with new revelations and under the influence of Buddhism (300–500 C.E.),[5] Laozi, then increasingly called

scholarship has gone back to crediting the historicity of the early accounts. They place Laozi again in the lifetime of Confucius and make him indeed the author of the *Daode jing*. See Liu 1994; Huang 1996.

[3] Laozi's veneration has continued to be linked with the *Daode jing*. The *Daode jing* has continued, in a lively, long-lived, and fruitful commentary tradition in China as well as in numerous translations in the West, to be central to spreading Laozi's fame and making his ideas acceptable to an audience beyond Daoist communities. For studies of its commentaries, see Lin 1977; Robinet 1977; 1998; Chan 1991.

[4] The most detailed study of Laozi's divinization under the Han is found in Seidel 1969. Summaries are contained in Seidel 1978; 1978a; Kohn 1998. On Laozi as a representative of immortals and their powers, see Kohn 1996.

[5] The early Daoist movements of the second century, Great Peace (Taiping) and Celestial Masters (Tianshi), were the first to worship the divinized Laozi as a popular savior. While the Great Peace movement was eradicated after it rose in rebellion as the Yellow Turbans in 184, the Celestial Masters continued to flourish and gave rise to further movements. The most important among them is Highest Clarity (Shangqing), which began in the 360s with a series of visions by the medium Yang Xi in the Nanjing area. One of the key deities communicating with him was Wei Huacun, a former libationer of the Celestial Masters who had ascended to high rank in heaven (see Strickmann 1978). On the basis of the scriptures thus revealed, Ge Chaofu began the compilation of the Numinous Treasure (Lingbao) corpus in the 390s, which was continued and expanded by his disciples well into the fifth century under increased Buddhist influence (see Kobayashi 1990). In the meantime, the Celestial Masters survived and spread throughout China, giving rise to new developments in the fifth century. In the south, they reorganized themselves and wrote new scriptures, then began to gradually merge with Numinous Treasure (see Kobayashi 1990). In the north, Kou Qianzhi replaced the earlier Zhang lineage and founded a new lay, organized, and precepts-centered cult that became the state religion under the Toba-Wei (see Mather 1979). In his wake the northern Celestial Masters centered

Lord Lao, fulfilled new roles. He was visualized in meditation, identified with the Buddha, represented in statues, and encountered in trances as the giver of revelations. With the integration of the various Daoist schools into one organized system in the sixth century, his life story developed into a complex, integrated myth and he became the third and most popular member of the Daoist trinity. Next, the emperors of the Tang dynasty (618–906) claimed descent from him and recorded many numinous appearances of his divine form, through which he showed approval of their rule. He unfailingly protected the land and gave succor to the faithful.[6]

Under the Song (960–1280), Lord Lao received continued imperial honors, but was replaced as protector of the state by the Dark Warrior (Xuanwu). To maintain the claim to his central position, Daoists wrote extensive hagiographies of him that traced his cosmic life from the beginning of creation to miracles wrought in the eleventh century. At the same time, newly emerging Daoist sects venerated him as the giver of revelations and popular talismans.[7] The Yuan dynasty (1280–1368), under Mongol rule, saw first a major elevation, then the downfall of organized Daoism. Taking Lord Lao along, this development resulted in an overall decrease in his importance, both politically and in the cult.[8] Nevertheless, in the Ming (1368–1644) and Qing (1644–1911) dynasties he remained the central deity of the two leading Daoist schools, Orthodox

---

their activities at Louguan in the Zhongnan Mountains, which became a major center for Lord Lao worship (see Kohn 1997). In the sixth century, with the drive for political unification picking up, the various Daoist schools began to propose models for an integrated religion. The Three Caverns (*sandong*) system of the southern Celestial Masters emerged as dominant and remained so throughout the Tang dynasty. Major later schools that worshiped Lord Lao include Heavenly Heart (Tianxin) of the Song and Complete Perfection (Quanzhen) of the Yuan.

[6] Laozi's identification with the Buddha is documented in a series of texts known as the *Huahu jing* (Scripture of the Conversion of the Barbarians), examined in Wang 1934; Zürcher 1959; Kubo 1972; Seidel 1984; Reiter 1990; Kohn 1995. The unfolding of his medieval hagiography is studied in Liu 1934; Yoshioka 1959; Kusuyama 1979; Kohn 1989a; 1989d. On Lord Lao in Daoist art and as a member of the trinity, see Pontynen 1980; 1980a; 1983; James 1986; Kamitsuka 1993; 1998. For Lord Lao under the Tang, see Verellen 1992; 1994; Barrett 1996.

[7] For studies of Xuanwu, see Grootaers 1952; Lagerwey 1992; Seaman 1987. There are as yet no studies of Lord Lao in the Song or among new Daoist sects, but the key hagiographies are described in Boltz 1987, 131–36.

[8] Much of the Buddhist-Daoist debate under the Yuan focused on Lord Lao's conversion of the barbarians and his claim to the founding of Buddhism. See Thiel 1961; Kubo 1968; 1972; Reiter 1990.

Unity (Zhengyi) or Celestial Masters (Tianshi) and Complete Perfection (Quanzhen), and appeared in vernacular literature as a wondrous immortal and valiant fighter for the good. To the present day, statues of Lord Lao stand in Daoist monasteries, the main locations of his exploits are honored as holy places, and tales of his life are told in books and picture stories.[9]

Contemporary scholarship has paid most attention to the early divinization of Lord Lao and to the unfolding of his medieval hagiography as well as to his role as the embodiment of the Dao and his sponsorship of certain visualizations and alchemical methods.[10] However, there are numerous Daoist texts that describe the god or claim to originate from him that have never been examined, let alone placed in the context of his overall historical development and hagiographic unfolding.

Attempting a first step in this direction, the present study describes the materials found on Lord Lao in traditional China. In each case, I identify a specific aspect of the god: his status as cultic high god of the Celestial Masters and Complete Perfection in hagiographies; his veneration as a symbol of political unity and cosmic harmony in inscriptions found at the philosopher's birthplace of Bozhou (modern Luyi in Henan) but also at other places of divine importance; his role as revealer of Daoist community rules, works of wisdom, and practical instructions, transmitted through the ages and appearing in different sections of the Daoist canon; his relation to other gods in sacred traditions of China, as both a model for their hagiographies and for their roles in the pantheon; and, last but not least, his importance as a popular protector of life and wealth, documented in a variety of sources.

Through most of Chinese history these different aspects of Lord Lao coincided, and different groups of people expressed them in the medium most accessible to them. Thus hagiography can be described as the medium of the organized Daoist schools, notably the Celestial Masters

---

[9] On the Celestial Masters under the Yuan and Ming, see Sun 1981; Zhuang 1986. On Complete Perfection, see Yao 1980; Yokote 1990; Mori 1994. Lord Lao as the sponsor of popular gods is discussed in Boltz 1986; Kohn 1997a. For his contemporary role, see Li 1993a; Ren Farong 1983.

[10] The most fundamental studies are Yoshioka 1959; Seidel 1969; Kusuyama 1979. In addition, Laozi as the body of the Dao is discussed in Schipper 1978; 1994, 113–29; Kohn 1998. His role in Daoist visualization is mentioned in Lagerwey 1991, 57–61; in alchemy, in Baldrian-Hussein 1990. For a general summary, see also Boltz 1987. For modern Chinese discussions, see Wang 1991; Wang Ming 1984, 4–7; Li 1993, 19–43.

and Complete Perfection, who paid high worship to the god. Official inscriptions carved on stone stelae and placed at important sanctuaries expressed the imperial court's veneration of Lord Lao; they were as much a means of political propaganda as a medium of religious sentiment. Community rules were again part of the organized religion, but both meditation instructions and philosophical texts associated with Lord Lao gave expression to views held by various practitioners. Some practitioners can be located and identified as followers of well-known patriarchs or schools, while others remain shrouded in mystery. The impact Lord Lao had on the hagiographies of other deities again points to an organized religious environment, but his influence was also increasingly sponsored and guided by the government, especially in later ages. Only the popular image of the god offers a sense of his worship among wider segments of the population. This is documented in various sources such as art works, talismanic scriptures, and novels that appear only sporadically in history and unfortunately provide no more than tantalizing glimpses of his career in this area.

Despite the great variety and uneven distribution of the sources, it may be assumed that Lord Lao, after he had been elevated to master immortal, representative of cosmic harmony, and popular savior in the Later Han dynasty, continued to play his various roles in different forms throughout the ages. Still, the sources do not provide a complete picture, and our conclusions are limited by what they tell us. Lord Lao emerges as a multifaceted god of the Dao, who like the Dao itself meant different things to different people and had something to offer everyone. The major changes in how he is perceived, on the other hand, coincide with important developments in the religion as a whole, allowing further examination and even reconfirmation of the periodization models established in recent scholarship.

1

Daoist Hagiographies
Lord Lao as High God of the Dao

H agiography as a genre belongs to the class of religious or sacred biography which, located between mythology and biography, makes use of biographical data or legendary stories about a saintly person to express the "emerging mythical ideals" of a given religion or tradition. The life of such a person—whose birth and death are marked by supernatural signs—in the unfolding of a hagiography becomes a metaphor for the key concepts and ideals of the religious community. Through this process, the original person and his deeds are increasingly "dissolved in an image," a mythical way of expressing "the unresolved tensions experienced both by the leaders and the society as a whole."[1]

Subjects of hagiography are thus less real people or even specific deities than reflections of specific cultural contexts and expressions of what a given religion and/or society values at certain moments in history. This holds true for Lord Lao as much as for Christ or the Buddha, all figures whose life stories have become paradigmatic for the development of their cults and whose hagiographies are rewritten and reinterpreted as part of the continued interaction of myth and history in their respective traditions.[2]

---

[1] A concise summary of the key features of sacred biography is found in LaFleur 1987. Collections of essays on the topic of religious biography are Williams 1982; Reynolds and Capps 1976. The quotations are taken from pages 2, 10, and 13 of the latter.

[2] For comparative accounts of these two founders' lives, see Dibelius 1935; Jaspers 1962. Studies of the Buddha's life as sacred biography are found in Reynolds 1976; Pyysiainen 1987.

The Ancient Philosopher

True to type, in his religious biography Laozi is a legendary figure from the beginning, when he appears in the *Zhuangzi* and several other early texts[3] as an ancient philosopher called Lao Dan. In these accounts he serves the Zhou court as an archivist and becomes the teacher of Confucius. The *Zhuangzi*, in particular, has a total of sixteen passages featuring Lao Dan, three of which are in the "Inner Chapters," the oldest and most authentic layer of the text (Graham 1980; Liu 1994). Here he appears as a famous sage who possesses extraordinary insight into the affairs of "the government of the enlightened king" (ch. 7) and proclaims Confucius' dire need for instruction because "[he] certainly hasn't yet reached the state of a perfect man" (ch. 5). Then Lao Dan himself is described as having died a natural death, a detail that unmasks him as a failed "perfected" (ch. 3).[4] Other passages describe not only Lao Dan's instruction of Confucius but also his analysis of the human mind (ch. 11), his rejection of artificiality (ch. 13), his definition of the ubiquity of the Dao (ch. 22), his teaching of life-preservation by acting without conscious knowledge (ch. 23), his criticism of the world's cruelties (ch. 25), and his favoring of purity and humility (ch. 27).[5]

The very first image developed of the sage thus shows him as a personage of great age, who has sharp words for anyone with foolish ideas and who never tires of extolling the value of the Dao's simplicity, nonaction in government and self-cultivation in life, and the need to remain in seclusion. Laozi the philosopher is an inspired teacher, seeing the shortcomings of his students with a penetrating eye and lecturing in clear, cutting statements. Yet with all this he also retains a dignified demeanor and exerts tremendous influence.

In contrast to the image created in the *Zhuangzi*, the Laozi in the anecdotes of other Warring States philosophers remains rather vague and "is probably to be regarded as the product of conflicting traditions that circulated about him" (Hurvitz 1961, 318). Still, most sources agree that his position at the Zhou court was that of an "archive administrator" (*shouzang shi*), which later hagiographies sometimes describe as an

---

[3] The philosopher Laozi is also mentioned in the *Guanzi* (Writings of Master Guan), the *Zhanguo ce* (Record of the Warring States), the *Xunzi* (Writings of Master Xun), the *Hanfeizi* (Writings of Master Han Fei), and the *Lüshi chunqiu* (Spring and Autumn Annals of Mr. Lü), all philosophical texts prior to the Han. See Kimura 1959, 41–164.

[4] The passages on Laozi are collected and studied in Kimura 1959, 43–50. For those in the "Inner Chapters," see Watson 1968, 94, 71, and 52.

[5] In English translation, these are found in Watson 1968, 116, 150, 241, 253, 287, and 307.

"archivist" (*zhuxia shi*). Both terms indicate lesser positions in the office of the Grand Scribe or Grand Historian (*taishi*), who under the Zhou was an observer of the times and their faithful recorder. Under the Han, the role of the *taishi* shifted to include "the recording and interpreting of celestial and other remarkable natural phenomena, weather forecasting, and various esoteric aspects of astronomy" (Hucker 1985, 481). The Grand Scribe became the Grand Astrologer, and with this shift Laozi too advanced from a petty clerk to one who knew heaven and earth and could forecast their movements.

Laozi's meeting with Confucius has been the subject of a detailed study by A. C. Graham (1990), who examines his biography in the *Shiji*. Comparing it with similar tales in Confucian texts, such as the *Zengzi wen* (Questions of Master Zeng) and the *Kongzi jiayu* (Kong Family Annals), Graham concludes that the story probably goes back to an originally Confucian tale meant to highlight Confucius's humility and continued willingness to learn, so that he even traveled to the Zhou capital to gain some minor official's insights into the proper performance of funeral rites. This story was used to claim Lao Dan as archetypal master of Daoism in the fourth century B.C.E. when the *Daode jing* was first compiled[6] and the growing Daoist school found itself in need of a properly hoary founding figure.

Next, according to Graham, when the Qin gained supremacy in the second century B.C.E., Laozi was presented to the first emperor as a powerful political thinker and was linked with Grand Astrologer Dan (written differently), who in 374 B.C.E. had predicted the rise of Qin. This presumed an unusual longevity for the philosopher, who was, as the *Shiji* reports, said to have lived 160 or 200 years. After the Qin had come to power, however, this longevity became a liability because Laozi was no longer around to advise the emperor in person. As a result, so Graham speculates, the story of Laozi's western emigration was invented, a convenient way not only of "disposing of the body" but also of accounting for the compilation of the *Daode jing*, allegedly transmitted under duress to the border guard Yin Xi (*Shiji* 63). Finally, under the

---

[6] The compilation of the *Daode jing* has been variously placed between 500 and 250 B.C.E. The dominant view until recently favored a late date (Waley 1934; Dubs 1941; Lau 1963), apparently confirmed by the findings of the manuscripts at Mawangdui (Lau 1982; Henricks 1989; Möller 1996). However, the newest Chinese scholarship argues for the credibility of the old sources and places the text in the 500s (Liu 1994, 172–86). Linguistic analysis dates it to around 350 (Baxter 1998) as does a new find, the so-called Bamboo *Laozi* discovered at Guodian, Hunan (Kohn and LaFargue 1998, 16).

Han, when the close connection to the Qin turned problematic, Laozi's birthplace was relocated to Bozhou near the Han rulers' homeland of Pei, and he was linked with the Li clan, a family of faithful retainers of the Han house.[7]

Even in the very beginning, and for a long time before his divinization as Lord Lao, Laozi was thus a legendary figure whose story developed in accordance with the needs of the time. He was known for two key episodes: his service as an archivist and reclusive thinker under the Zhou, who also taught Confucius; and his western emigration and transmission of the *Daode jing* to Yin Xi. A number of added details also became part of the story's central core: his birthplace in Bozhou, his family name, Li, his personal name, Dan, and his lifetime in the sixth century B.C.E.

The Early Myth

This nucleus of the Laozi story, which in the early Han can still be described as a legend since it dealt with a human being and alleged historical facts, evolved gradually into a myth that focused on an entirely divine protagonist. In the Han dynasty three separate groups picked up the already stylized figure and expanded his life and deeds in accordance with their own vested interests. Among them there were first the so-called magical practitioners (*fangshi*), individual seekers of immortality, who adopted Laozi as their patriarch and idealized him as an immortal, a particularly gifted human being who had, by his own initiative and efforts, attained the purity and power of the celestials.

Second, there was the political elite, the imperial family and court officials, who saw in Laozi the personification of the Dao and worshiped him as a representative of their ideal of cosmic and political unity alongside the Yellow Emperor (Huangdi) and the Buddha. Here Laozi became the object of formal imperial sacrifices and inscriptions.

Third, there were popular religious cults, millenarian in nature,[8] which identified Laozi as a god who had become manifest repeatedly over the ages and saved the world time and again. He would, they believed, come yet again as the messiah and bring about a new age of Great Peace (*taiping*). This deified Laozi, then, was like the personi-

---

[7] This discussion summarizes Graham 1990, also reprinted in Kohn and LaFargue 1998, 23–38. For details of Laozi's position in the early Han, see also Seidel 1969, 18; 1969a, 222.

[8] For more details on millenarianism and its role in the myth of Lord Lao, see chapter 13.

fication of cosmic harmony worshiped by the court but equipped with tremendous revolutionary power. As a messiah, he could overturn the present and reorganize the world, leading the faithful to a new state of heavenly bliss in this life on earth.[9]

The key texts of these groups describing Laozi were, first, Liu Xiang's *Liexian zhuan* (Immortals' Biographies, DZ 294) and Ge Hong's *Shenxian zhuan* (Biographies of Spirit Immortals, dated 320); second, the *Laozi ming* (Inscription for Laozi) by Bian Shao of 165 and the *Shengmu bei* (Stele for the Holy Mother), dated to 153; and third, the *Laozi bianhua jing* (Scripture of the Transformations of Laozi), a Dunhuang manuscript (S. 2295) dated to around 185. They all add new information to the two key episodes of the Laozi legend.

First, the immortal's biographies make him a long-lived master of magic and longevity techniques who has powers over life and death and, like the ancient immortal Pengzu, goes on living forever and ever.[10] In addition, both texts describe him as not only transmitting the *Daode jing* to Yin Xi but also taking him along on his journey, which leads due west and results in the conversion of the barbarians to his teaching, then known as "Buddhism." The immortals' biographies thus expand the life power of the philosopher according to their vision of immortality and mythically change the end of his life, left unspecified in the *Shiji* ("Nobody knows what became of him") to explain the arrival of the new religion from the west.[11]

Next, the two imperial Han inscriptions identify Laozi with the Dao and make him the creator of the universe. No longer a mere human

---

[9] This description follows Kohn 1998. The key study of the official and messianic adoptions of Laozi is Seidel 1969; a German summary of the latter is found in Seidel 1978 and 1978a. A general survey of Laozi and his hagiography is found in Kaltenmark 1980, 63–66; Boltz 1987a.

[10] Pengzu, too, lived under the Shang, served in government office, and attained the ripe old age of 800 years (see Sakade 1985). According to later stories that emphasize his supernatural birth, he, like Lord Lao, emerged from his mother's left armpit and emigrated to the west to wander through the "floating sands," the Taklamakan Desert (Liu 1934, 69).

[11] Translations of immortal biographies are found in Kaltenmark 1953; Güntsch 1988; Kohn 1996. For discussions of the date and history of the *Shenxian zhuan*, see Fukui 1951; Kominami 1974; Shimomi 1974; Yamada 1974. On Ge Hong (261–341) and his major work, the *Baopuzi* (Book of the Master Who Embraces Simplicity, DZ 1185), see Ware 1966; Sailey 1978; Sivin 1969. Early records of Laozi's western journey are also found in citations from the *Xiyu zhuan* (Chronicle of Western Regions) and the first version of the *Huahu jing*. For studies, see Wang 1934; Zürcher 1959, 298–320.

philosopher or even a gifted immortal, he is now the root of the entire world, the personification of the order and inherent creativity of the cosmos. Laozi creates the world and has grown into the god Lord Lao; the beginning of his life is extended back to the dawn of the universe, and his entire career is transformed into a celestial myth.[12]

The same motif is also present in the key text of the popular cults, the *Laozi bianhua jing*, which can be described as the first full formulation of the Laozi story as myth and thus the first real hagiography of the god.[13] Aside from a eulogy on Laozi as the Dao and his powers before and during creation, it also contains a description of his repeated descents as the teacher of dynasties who gives guidance to all the major rulers, from Fu Xi on down to the Zhou dynasty. This account develops Laozi's early life mythically to parallel the unfolding of Chinese history and culture. Moreover, it also transforms his birth under the Zhou into a supernatural event, involving a pregnancy of seventy-two years and numerous marvelous signs of sagely physiognomy.

As to the end of his life, the text describes Laozi as ascending back to heaven after transmitting the *Daode jing* to Yin Xi. From there he makes repeated descents as teacher and savior of the world. He comes to the barbarians as the Buddha and gives the Dao to various early Daoists, notably those of Sichuan. The text ends with a descent in 155, during which he reveals instructions on Daoist meditation and recitation of the *Daode jing*. It concludes on a slightly apocalyptic note, admonishing believers to "hurry and follow" Lord Lao "when Venus fails in its course five or six times," to be thus saved from danger (Seidel 1969, 73).

Although these texts represent different groups and provide some-what different developments of the legend—the major discrepancy being Laozi's founding of Buddhism through divine descent rather than the journey west —their additions and expansions all became firmly part of the complex myth. Embedding the two key episodes of the early legend in a tightly knit network of mythological expansions, they create the basic structure of the myth, which at this point can be described as consisting of six distinct parts:

---

[12] For more details on these texts, see chapter 2.

[13] The text is dated to 185 C.E. on the basis of internal evidence, but its current edition goes back to the year 612. It gives expression to the beliefs of a popular messianic cult, located in southwest China, where the Celestial Masters were also active at the same time. The manuscript (S. 2295) is reprinted in Seidel 1969, 131–36; Ōfuchi 1979, 686–88. For a French translation see Seidel 1969, 60–73. See also Robinet 1997, 51–52.

1. Laozi as the Dao creates the universe (creation);
2. Laozi descends as the teacher of dynasties (transformations);
3. Laozi is born on earth and serves as an archivist for the Zhou (birth);
4. Laozi emigrates and transmits the *Daode jing* to Yin Xi (transmission);
5. Laozi and Yin Xi go west and convert the barbarians to Buddhism (conversion);
6. Laozi ascends to heaven and comes back again to give revelations to Chinese seekers, founding Daoist schools (revelations).

Medieval Developments

This basic structure remains the same in the many Daoist texts that describe the life of Lord Lao (see Table 1), but later hagiographies expand both its depth of content through additional motifs and its structure through further episodes. First, among the fourth-century Celestial Masters in north China, the god is described as both master practitioner of immortality techniques and savior of the people. This is expressed in the *Laojun bianhua wuji jing* (Scripture of Lord Lao's Infinite Transformations, DZ 1195), a text dated to the Eastern Jin. A short but powerful document, it is written in seven-character verses like the contemporaneous meditation manual *Huangting jing* (Yellow Court Scripture), also ascribed to Laozi. In the wake of the *Laozi bianhua jing*, the *Laojun bianhua wuji jing* takes up the notion of Lord Lao's transformations and his continued willingness to save the world.[14]

In content, the *Laojun bianhua wuji jing* outlines the exploits of the god and describes his attempt to civilize the barbarians, then appeals to the chosen people of the Dao (*zhongmin*) to take up certain physiological and ritual techniques in expectation of the True Lord of Great Peace (Taiping zhenjun), whom Lord Lao will send to bring harmony to the world (3b).

---

[14] For the historical situation in fourth-century north China, see Kohn 1995, 10. On the text, see Ren and Zhong 1991, 943. It has not been studied in any detail, but is mentioned in connection with the conversion (Schipper 1994a, 70) and with alchemical practices (Baldrian-Hussein 1990, 175). Scholars date it differently: Eastern Jin in Baldrian-Hussein 1990, 175; late fourth to early fifth centuries in Seidel 1969a, 237; late sixth century in Seidel 1969, 60 n. 1.

Table 1
Extant hagiographic works on Laozi/Lord Lao

Date	Text	English title
B.C.E.		
250	*Zhuangzi*	Writings of Master Zhuang
104	*Shiji*	Historical Records
	Zengzi wen	Questions of Master Zeng
	Kongzi jiayu	Kong Family Annals (300 C.E.)
C.E.		
100	*Liexian zhuan*	Immortals' Biographies
185	*Laozi bianhua jing*	Scripture of the Transformations of Laozi
200	*Xiyu zhuan*	Chronicle of Western Regions
300	*Huahu jing (1)*	Scripture of the Conversion of the Barbarians
320	*Shenxian zhuan*	Biographies of Spirit Immortals
330	*Laojun bianhua wuji jing*	Scripture of Lord Lao's Infinite Transformations
420	*Santian neijie jing*	Inner Explanation of the Three Heavens
	Dadao jialing jie	Community Rules of the Great Dao
	Miaoshi jing	Scripture of Wondrous Beginning
	Xuanmiao neipian	Essential Record of Mystery and Wonder
480	*Daode zhenjing xujue*	Introductory Explanation to the *Daode jing*
	Lingbao sanbu bajing jing	Numinous Treasure Scripture on the Eight Luminants in Three Divisions
	Falun jing	Scripture of the Wheel of Law
530	*Kaitian jing*	Scripture of Opening the Cosmos
	Wenshi neizhuan	Essential Biography of Master Wenshi
	Huahu jing (2)	Scripture of the Conversion of the Barbarians
570	*Xiaodao lun*	Laughing at the Dao
622	*Bianzheng lun*	In Defense of What Is Right
670	*Hunyuan zhenlu*	Perfect Account of Chaos Prime
713	*Miaomen youqi*	Entrance to the Gate of All Wonders
	Huahu jing (3)	Scripture of the Conversion of the Barbarians
885	*Lidai chongdao ji*	Record of Reverence for the Dao over Successive Generations
901	*Daojiao lingyan ji*	Record of Daoist Miracles
	Daode zhenjing Guangsheng yi	Wide Sage Meaning of the Perfect Scripture of the *Daode jing*
905	*Yongcheng jixian lu*	Record of the Assembled Immortals in the Heavenly Walled City
921	*Xianyuan bianzhu*	A String of Pearls from a Forest of Immortals
978	*Taiping guangji*	Expansive Record of the Taiping Era
1023	*Hunyuan huangdi shengji*	Sage Record of the Sovereign of Chaos Prime
1086	*Youlong zhuan*	Like unto a Dragon
1100	*Laojun jinshu neixu*	Preface to the Golden Book of Lord Lao
1145	*Sandong qunxian lu*	Record of the Host of Immortals of the Three Caverns
1191	*Hunyuan shengji*	Sage Record of Chaos Prime
	Laojun nianpu yaolüe	Essential Chronology of Lord Lao
	Laozi shilüe	Brief History of Laozi
1200	*Xuanmiao yunü zichuan xiandao*	Ways of Immortality Transmitted by the Jade Maiden of Mystery and Wonder

Table 1—*continued*

Date	Text	English title
1250	*Laojun bashiyi hua tushuo*	Illustrated Explanations of the Eighty-one Transformations of the Venerable Lord
1300	*Zengxiang liexian zhuan*	Illustrated Immortals' Biographies
1326	*Jinlian zhenzong xianyuan xiangzhuan*	Illustrated Record of the Immortal Origins of the True Lineage of the Golden Lotus
1335	*Xuanpin lu*	Record of the Mystery Ranks
1400	*Lishi tongjian zhenxian tidao houji*	Supplement to the Comprehensive Mirror of Perfected Immortals
	Xiaoyao xu jing	Scripture of [Immortals] Wandering in the Void
1593	*Soushen ji*	In Search of the Supernatural
1652	*Liexian quanzhuan*	Complete Immortals' Biographies

The various methods, including energy circulation and sexual techniques (5ab) as well as alchemical concoctions (8ab), will not pacify the world but allow people to ascend to the heavens of the immortals. Thereby they will overcome the present disastrous state, in which "barbarian horses are neighing in Chang'an" (6a) and the unkempt Central Asians have settled themselves firmly in Ye (6b). Laozi, as before, comes to rescue his creation.[15]

In south China at the same time, the *Santian neijie jing* (Inner Explanation of the Three Heavens, DZ 1205), a mythical outline of Celestial Masters' history, adds new motifs that increase the depth of all key episodes of the hagiography.[16]

The creation story, to give an example, begins with the Dao as the underlying creative power of the world, "dark and obscure, vast and open, and without prior cause" (1.2a). Revolving in emptiness and spontaneity, it "transforms and brings forth the Elder of the Dao and the Virtue," followed by the three highest heavens with their numerous gods and divine functionaries (1.2a). Once they exist, the Dao as Great Nonbeing creates the three basic energies, mysterious, primordial, and beginning,

---

[15] This same understanding of the god is manifest in the major revelation of rules and precepts granted to Kou Qianzhi (365–448) in 415, and leads to the establishment of the Daoist theocracy under the Northern Wei. The revelation is recorded in ch. 114 of the *Weishu* (History of the Northern Wei; trans. in Ware 1933) and discussed in Mather 1979. See also Tang and Tang 1961; Ōzaki 1979; Yamada 1995. For the precepts revealed, see chapter 3.

[16] Primarily, it integrates the conversion with the revelations by having Lord Lao and Yin Xi first convert the barbarians, then having Yin Xi born as the Buddha while the god returns to China to reveal the Dao to Zhang Daoling and others (see Fig. 1). On the text, see Schipper 1978; Kobayashi 1990; Maeda 1995; Robinet 1997, 68–69; Bokenkamp 1997, 186–229.

which "intermingle in chaos, following each other, then transform to bring forth the Jade Maiden of Mystery and Wonder" (1.2b). She, then, is the one who gives birth to the celestial Laozi through her left armpit. The god in this version is not the Dao *per se* but its direct product, mediated through a series of transformations that bring forth heavens, spiritual powers, pure energies, and a mother figure. He is born supernaturally even in heaven. His emergence from the left armpit borrows on the story of the birth of the Buddha, who leaves his mother through her right hip.[17]

Next, Lord Lao creates the world. Under his guidance, mysterious energy rises up to form heaven, beginning energy sinks down and becomes earth, while primordial energy flows everywhere and turns into water—thus forming the three basic realms of the Celestial Masters' universe. In addition, the god creates three major continents with three countries each, where he places people and religions: Daoism in the center (China), Buddhism in the west, and the "Way of Clear Harmony" in the south (1.3b).[18] Thus the world with its main continents and religions comes into existence. The creation in the *Santian neijie jing* is much more detailed than earlier creations associated with Lord Lao, such as those found in the *Laozi ming* and *Laozi bianhua jing*. It accounts not only for the existence of the heavens and the world but also for the distribution of major religious systems. Similar changes also apply to other parts of the myth, which show how the deity plans the unfolding of Chinese culture and the development of Daoism, providing a history of the Celestial Masters and their first leader, Zhang Daoling (see Fig. 2).[19]

Concluding its hagiographic account, the *Santian neijie jing* rewrites the conversion to include the full story of Yin Xi's birth as the Buddha, integrating, almost verbatim, the description in the Buddhist source *Taizi ruiying benqi jing* (Sūtra of the Origins and Deeds of the Prince in Accordance with All Good Omens; T. 185; 3.471–83), translated by Zhi Qian in the third century (see Karetzky 1992). Like the Buddha, Yin Xi enters the

---

[17] The biography of the Buddha was stylized early on. See Thomas 1927; Lamotte 1987. For a discussion of its various Chinese texts and sculptural expressions, see Karetzky 1992. The birth story is analyzed in Karetzky 1992, 15.

[18] The discrimination of Daoists against other believers is the subject of Schipper 1994a, 72. A survey of the different attitudes is also found in Kohn 1995, 8–24. A chart of the cosmology of the *Santian neijie jing* is found in Bokenkamp 1997, 192.

[19] A similar, slightly shorter history of the Celestial Masters is also found in the *Dadao jialing jie* (Community Rules of the Great Dao), a document contained in the *Tianshi kejing* (Scripture of Celestial Masters' Observances; DZ 789), dated variously

Fig. 2. Lord Lao, surrounded by a celestial entourage, reveals the Dao to Zhang Daoling.
Source: Detail of a Southern Song painting owned by Wan-go H. C. Weng.
Used with the kind permission of the owner.

queen's womb while she naps, steps out from her side, takes a number of steps, loudly proclaims his superiority in heaven and on earth, and is bathed by a group of divine dragons. Elsewhere, Lord Lao himself is described in this role, notably in the *Miaoshi jing* (Scripture of Wondrous Beginning, DZ 658, 6b), an otherwise cosmological text on heaven and hell that relates the conversion in a first-person narrative and has Yin Xi appearing as Ānanda. In addition, the god's birth as the Buddha is described in the *Xuanmiao neipian* (Essential Record of Mystery and Wonder), which survives in citations.[20]

Supplementing the *Santian neijie jing* are several texts that can also be placed in the fifth century. First, a short summary of the Buddha's birth, together with an account of major commentaries and ritual visualization instructions, appears in the *Daode zhenjing xujue* (Introductory Explanation to the *Daode jing*). This is a Dunhuang manuscript dated to the late fifth century that served as a formal religious introduction to the *Daode jing*.[21]

In addition, two hagiographic texts of Numinous Treasure (Lingbao) and Celestial Masters origin present a detailed description of Lord Lao's eighty-one divine bodily marks. The first, the *Lingbao sanbu bajing jing* (Numinous Treasure Scripture on the Eight Luminants in Three Divisions, SDZN 8.10b–12b),[22] presents a set of marks that indicate his

---

to the third or fifth centuries. Here the ground of the cosmos and originator of the teaching is not named Laozi or Lord Lao but simply "the Dao," indicating a pre-fifth-century usage among the Celestial Masters (Kobayashi 1995, 24). Still, all major events of the god's hagiography, including five sets of revelations, are attributed to this Dao, including the transmission of the *Daode jing* to Yin Xi and the conversion of the barbarians (12a–13b). Only when "the Dao" appears to Zhang Daoling is it given a formal title "Lord Lao Newly Arisen" (Xinchu Laojun, 14a). For a discussion of that text, see Kobayashi 1990, 329; Schipper 1994a, 68–69. A complete translation is found in Bokenkamp 1997, 165–85. The new title of Lord Lao also appears in tomb contracts of the same period. See Nickerson 1996, 194–95.

[20] On the *Miaoshi jing*, see Ren and Zhong 1991, 469. Citations of the *Xuanmiao neipian* are found in Gu Huan's *Yixia lun* (On Barbarians and Chinese) of 467 (*Nanshi* 75), *Xiaodao lun* 18 (T. 52.154c), *Sandong zhunang* (A Bag of Pearls from the Three Caverns; DZ 1139) 8.4a, *Miaomen youqi* 7b, *Yongcheng jixian lu* 1.2ab (DZ 783), *Guangsheng yi* 2.20b (DZ 725), and *Youlong zhuan* 3.7b (DZ 774). See Fukui 1964; Zürcher 1959, 301–03; Kobayashi 1990, 382–85; Kohn 1995, 219.

[21] S. 75; P. 2370; reprinted in Yoshioka 1959, 40–45; Ōfuchi 1979, 509–11. For discussions, see Ōfuchi 1964, 344–434; Takeuchi 1978, 6:220; Kusuyama 1979, 134–37; Kobayashi 1990, 269–95; Kohn 1995, 202–3; 1998a, 152–53.

[22] *SDZN* (*Sandong zhunang*) is a seventh-century encyclopedia by Wang Xuanhe. For a summary and discussion, see Reiter 1990a.

heavenly nature and matches them with constellations in the sky.[23] The second, the *Falun jing* (Scripture of the Wheel of Law, *SDZN* 8.13b–15a), gives a different list, showing his unusual longevity, the characteristics of his earthly existence, and various physical manifestations of celestial good fortune. Besides matching the physical attributes of the Buddha, this latter set looks back to ancient physiognomy lore and physical signs associated with early immortals, signs also cited as divine marks of the sage kings in Confucian myth.[24]

The Northern Celestial Masters

The next major hagiography of Lord Lao was compiled in the early sixth century by the northern Celestial Masters at their center Louguan in the foothills of the Zhongnan Mountains.[25] Known as the *Kaitian jing* (Scripture of Opening the Cosmos), it purported to describe the creation of the world and of culture through the god, but was unmasked as a forgery, as opposed to an ancient or revealed text. This unmasking occurred in a debate with the Buddhists in 520 at the Northern Wei court, and focused on the relative antiquity of the two religions. In terms of the hagiography, this text pushed Lord Lao's dates back into the Shang dynasty, a feature of his myth that persisted even though its primary Daoist text was destroyed.[26] To replace this text, three new scriptures were written in the sixth century that greatly expanded the myth of Lord Lao. They are:

— the extant *Kaitian jing* (DZ 1437), which describes events from creation to the early Zhou, giving detailed stages of the unfolding of the cosmos and providing titles the of scriptures the god taught to various

---

[23] This text is related to the *Ershisi shengtu* (Charts of the Twenty-four [Gods of] Life, DZ 1407), an early Numinous Treasure text. For a discussion of the Eight Luminants, which appear first in the *Huangting jing*, see Mugitani 1982, 48. Lord Lao plays only a minor role in the Numinous Treasure scriptures, of which he reveals only one text. See Bokenkamp 1997, 63. He occurs here, however, as the Lord of the Dao. See chapter 5 below.

[24] The second list, with some variation, becomes standard in all later hagiographies. A comparative list is found in Yoshioka 1959, 142–48. For a study, see Kohn 1996a.

[25] On the history and beliefs of this group, see Qing 1988, 430–44; Ren 1990, 219–35; Zhang 1991. For an English discussion, see Kohn 1997.

[26] For details on this debate and its impact on the myth, see chapter 10 in Part Two. A general history of the Northern Wei is found in Eberhard 1949.

emperors during his transformations, and its variant, the lost *Chuji* (Record of Beginnings);[27]

— the *Wenshi neizhuan* (Essential Biography of the Master Wenshi, *SDZN* 9.8b–14b), detailing the transmission of the *Daode jing* and training of Yin Xi. It includes a long narrative on the interaction of Laozi and Yin Xi on the pass, their second meeting in Sichuan (with a black sheep as the agreed upon sign), and their joint ecstatic excursion to the heavens;

— and the sixth-century version of the *Huahu jing* (Scripture of the Conversion of the Barbarians, *SDZN* 9.14b–20b), a lengthy retelling of the two sages' western travels that includes a dialogue with the barbarian king, mutual banquet invitations, and ordeals the Daoists have to undergo before the barbarians admit defeat.[28]

As part of the tradition of the northern Celestial Masters or Louguan school, which played an important role under the northern dynasties and in the early Tang, these texts represented the group's beliefs. They centered on the divinized Laozi and called for his veneration as creator, savior, and bringer of sacred scriptures, practical teachings, and organizational rules. In addition, the transmission of the highly honored *Daode jing* had by then been relocated to Louguan, as opposed to its earlier location on the Hangu Pass, east of Mount Hua. The school worshiped Yin Xi as its first patriarch and created several devotional scriptures around Yin Xi's encounter with Lord Lao.[29] Its

---

[27] The *Kaitian jing* is also found in *YJQQ* 2; trans. Kohn 1993, 35–43; Schafer 1997. The text integrates the creation story according to the school of the Three Sovereigns (Sanhuang), as is evident from citations of the *Sanhuang wen* (Texts of the Three Sovereigns) in the *Xiaodao lun* (sect. 17; see Kohn 1995, 91). The *Chuji* is cited in the *Xiaodao lun* (sect. 1, Kohn 1995, 54–55) and integrates the popular Pangu story into the Laozi myth. According to the latter, the world grew from the body of a cosmic giant; this story represents a Chinese version of the Indo-European myth of creation through sacrifice. See Liu 1993, 25–27; Lincoln 1975, 124. A Highest Clarity variant is found in the *Zhongxian ji* (Record of the Host of Immortals, DZ 166). See Wang Ka 1989, 61.

[28] The *Wenshi neizhuan* survives in fragments found in *Xiaodao lun* (Kohn 1995, 215); Cheng Xuanying's *Daode jing kaiti xujue yishu* (Supplementary Commentary and Topical Introduction to the Scripture of the Dao and Its Virtue, P. 2353, reprinted in Ōfuchi 1979, 461–66); *Shangqing daolei shixiang* (Daoist Affairs of Highest Clarity, DZ 1132); *Yiwen leiju* (Classified Collection of Artistic Writings); *Chuxue ji* (Record of Initial Learning); and *Taiping yulan* (Imperial Encyclopedia of the Taiping Era). See Ōfuchi and Ishii 1988, 665. Discussions of the text are found in Fukui 1962; Yamada 1982; Kohn 1998b. On the *Huahu jing*, see Zürcher 1959, 298–320; Kohn 1995, 195–97.

[29] These include the precepts text *Laojun jiejing* (Precepts of the Venerable Lord, DZ 784; see Kohn 1994); the mystical *Xisheng jing* (Scripture of Western

expansion of the god's myth reflects the growth of the northern Daoists as an organized religion, and defines the self-understanding of the Louguan group in the late Six Dynasties period.

Taken together the three texts change Lord Lao's hagiography in several important ways, providing extensive details on the creation and on his service as the teacher of dynasties. They push his birth back to the Shang dynasty and expand the story of his exploits on earth in a highly literary fashion. In addition, they significantly develop his first meeting with Yin Xi, relating a series of tests Yin Xi must undergo and increasing the number of scriptures and teachings he receives. They also supplement the key encounter between the two sages with two entirely new episodes. In one they meet again in Chengdu, Sichuan, with the help of a black sheep (*qingyang*); and in the second, after Lord Lao's formal approval of Yin Xi as an accomplished immortal, they go together on an ecstatic journey around the world and through the heavens. This expansion of the myth reflects the ordination procedures of the Celestial Masters in this period, and also integrates teachings and ordination ranks of the southern schools.[30]

Another function of Lord Lao's hagiography in this period was to establish him as the key deity, and through him, the Louguan school as the locus of the unification of Daoist teachings—a consolidation desired by the northern rulers and pursued by various Daoists. Lord Lao was thus styled as an eminently powerful figure, a god who created the world, a model teacher and instructor in the Dao, and a missionary savior who never tired in his worldwide travels and salvific efforts. He was thereby proposed as the deity of all China, the god who would provide an encompassing umbrella for the many schools and teachings current at the time.

This bid for power, however, was severely criticized in the Buddhist-Daoist debates and did not succeed. Instead, over the course of the sixth century Daoist teachings were integrated on the model of the southern system of the Three Caverns (*sandong*). In imitation of the Buddhist ranking system of the Three Vehicles (*sancheng*), the Three Caverns placed the Highest Clarity (Shangqing) school first, the Numinous Treasure school second, and the Three Sovereigns (Sanhuang)

Ascension, DZ 726; see Kohn 1991); and the ordination work *Chuanshou jingjie yi zhujue* (Annotated Explanation of the Transmission Formalities of Scriptures and Precepts, DZ 1238). For more on Louguan history and worldview, see Kohn 1997.

[30] The black sheep story, too, appears first in the *Chuji* as cited in the *Xiaodao lun*. See Kohn 1995, 52–53. For my discussion of the meaning of the myth in Daoist ordination, see Part Two.

and Celestial Masters third, thus joining the major schools of medieval Daoism into one integrated structure. Lord Lao, representative of the Celestial Masters, was merged with the Highest Lord of the Three Sovereigns and placed third to occupy the lowest position of a new trinity, preceded by the Heavenly Worthy of Primordial Beginning (Yuanshi tianzun)—a Daoist adaptation of the Buddha—and a bodhisattva-style deity called the Highest Lord of the Dao (Taishang daojun).[31]

In this third position, Lord Lao became the incarnate, living representative of the Dao who brought salvation to the world and interacted most directly with humanity through visions and miraculous manifestations.[32] After the reunification of the empire and the rise of the Tang dynasty, this closeness increased even more when Lord Lao became the ancestor of the ruling house—also surnamed Li—and the official sponsor of political harmony. Louguan Daoists were particularly fond of this role of the god and actively supported the rise of Tang, who came to power in 618 with the help of messianic Daoist prophecies.[33] As a result, in 620, Louguan was renamed Zongsheng guan (Monastery of the Ancestral Sage) in honor of the ancestral Lord Lao enshrined there. One of its abbots, Yin Wencao (622–688), a self-styled descendant of Yin Xi, became a prominent Daoist figure at court and the next major hagiographer of the god. As he celebrated Daoist rites in the eastern capital of Luoyang in 679, Yin's performance was blessed with a vision of the god surrounded by celestial officers and riding on a white horse that appeared before the assembled court. The emperor was so taken with this sign of celestial goodwill that he asked Yin to write a formal account of the deity's exploits.[34]

---

[31] On the emergence and structure of this model, see Ōfuchi 1979a, 261. On the trinity, see Jing 1994, 154–67.

[32] The structure of the trinity follows Buddhist doctrine in imitating the three bodies of the Buddha (*trikāya*) and the Mahāyāna system of having (1) a dhyāni-buddha, the abstract form of perfect purity who dwells quiescent in the heavens; (2) a dhyāni-bodhisattva, brought forth by the buddha and serving as creator of the world; and (3) the incarnated buddha, a human-born form of divine power, a teacher on earth who lives among people (see Getty 1988, 28, 45).

[33] See Bokenkamp 1994; Hendrischke 1993, 113; Barrett 1996; Robinet 1997, 184. For details of the campaign in relation to Daoist signs and places, see Bingham 1970, 95–96; Wechsler 1985, 69.

[34] This is mentioned in the *Da Tang Yin zunshi bei* (Inscription for the Venerable Master Yin of the Great Tang Dynasty), a tomb memorial for Yin Wencao by Yuan Banqian of the year 717. The text is contained in the *Gu Louguan ziyun yanqing ji* (Collection of the Abundant Blessings of the Purple Clouds at the Old

The resulting text, the *Xuanyuan huangdi shengji* (Sage Record of the Emperor of Mystery Prime), making use of the new title given to the deity in 666, was unfortunately lost and only survives in fragments. These are found in a text cited as *Benji* (Original Record) under the Tang and *Tangji* (Tang Record) under the Song. They also appear in Yue Penggui's *Xichuan qingyang gong beiming* (Inscription at the Black Sheep Temple of Sichuan, DZ 964) of the year 884 and in Xie Shouhao's *Hunyuan shengji* (Sage Record of Chaos Prime, DZ 770), dated to 1191.[35] As best can be gleaned from these citations, the text had a section on Lord Lao's transformations as a teacher of dynasties, contained a theoretical discussion of his elementary nature, and described his transmission of the Dao to Yin Xi. In addition, a large section also survives as a separate scripture under the title *Hunyuan zhenlu* (Perfect Account of Chaos Prime, DZ 954). It details in hitherto unknown depth the transmission of texts to Yin Xi, listing a large number presented in addition to the *Daode jing*, and recounting Lord Lao's concrete instructions on the practice of alchemy, visualization, and breathing exercises.[36]

Yin Wencao's hagiography probably also contained a section on Lord Lao's family tree and his relation to Yin Xi. He was most likely responsible for relocating Yin Xi's family home to Tianshui in Gansu—Yin Wencao's own hometown—and linking his lineage to Lord Lao through the female—either through Laozi's mother or wife—thus making himself a relative of both the god and the imperial family. As a result, in the eighth century Lord Lao was equipped with a full genealogy, and in 743 his father and mother were given formal titles and positions in the Tang ancestral temple (Xiong 1996, 281). Records of the relevant names and details of descent are found in texts cited by Du Guangting (850–933) in the second chapter of his *Daode zhenjing guangsheng yi* (Wide Sage Meaning of the Perfect Scripture of the *Daode*

Lookout Tower, DZ 957, 1.4b–9b) and in Chen et al. 1988, 102–4. A note here describes the physical stele as still extant in Louguan, 1.11 m high and 0.5 m wide, containing 26 lines of 70 characters each. A description of the flourishing Louguan center under the Tang is found in Du Guangting's *Daojiao lingyan ji* (Record of Daoist Miracles, DZ 590, 3.9b). See also Reiter 1983, 375.

[35] The latter contains numerous quotations, notably on Lord Lao's transformations (1.2b–3a, 1.7a–8a, 1.10a–11b, 1.14b), his philosophy of the Dao (1.20b), his manifestation at the Black Sheep Palace (1.32b), his identity with the Dao (2.37a), and his transmission of alchemical recipes (3.12ab). See also Kusuyama 1979, 429.

[36] These various fragments and their role in Laozi's hagiography are considered in Kusuyama 1977; 1979, 403, 428.

jing, DZ 725).[37] Again, the circumstances of the time and the needs of the believers determined the direction the hagiography took; the Lord Lao myth continued to serve as a flexible blueprint for the expression of religious and social concerns.

Yin Wencao's work, moreover, was not the only hagiography of the god popular in the Tang. Several others are cited in the *Miaomen youqi* (Entrance to the Gate of All Wonders, DZ 1123), a summary of Daoist teachings compiled on Emperor Xuanzong's orders in 713. Of the twelve texts it refers to in connection with Lord Lao's exploits, half are extant and have been mentioned above (*Santian neijie jing*, *Daode zhenjing xujue*, *Wenshi neizhuan*). The other six include *Louguan benji* (A Basic Record of Louguan, 7a) together with various other hagiographies, such as the *Gaoshang Laozi neizhuan* (Essential Biography of His Eminence Laozi, 8ab), the *Laozi jing* (Scripture of Laozi, 8b), and the *Laozi jindai jing* (Scripture of Laozi's Gown and Belt, 6b). The information in these texts, as far as can be judged from their citations, conforms to what is known from other sources, adding occasional details, for example, the god's ten titles from the *Baoxuan jing* (Scripture of Treasured Mystery).[38]

The Conversion of the Barbarians

While the main strand of Lord Lao's hagiography evolved in a fairly straightforward way from the Six Dynasties into the Tang, the story of the conversion of the barbarians underwent a more complex development. Written up extensively in the sixth century *Wenshi neizhuan* and in the second version of the *Huahu jing*—the first having been compiled by Wang Fu around the year 300 (see Zürcher 1959, 293)—it was criticized extensively by Buddhists using various means, including so-called counter-conversion scriptures and anti-Daoist polemics. Counter-conversion texts, such as the *Qingjing faxing jing* (Sūtra of Practicing the Dharma in Purity and Clarity), tend to reverse the claim of Daoist doctrine and declare that all major spiritual figures of ancient China were originally bodhisattvas sent by the Buddha to awaken the Chinese people. Thus Laozi was the Elder Kāśyapa, Confucius was Mānava, and Yan Hui was the bodhisattva Guangjing. Together they

---

[37] This work has a preface dated 30 October 901 (Verellen 1989, 137–38). The texts cited are *Xuanzhong ji* (Record of the Mysterious Center) and the *Lishi dazong pu* (Record of the Great Lineage of the Li Family; 2.19a–21a).

[38] For a reprint of the citations and a discussion, see Yoshioka 1959, 116–18.

successfully accomplished their mission to civilize the Chinese, then Laozi returned west to report to his master, the Buddha.[39]

Anti-Daoist polemics also cite counter-conversion theories and in addition try to show the absurdity of the Daoist story by placing several different versions of it side by side. Thus Zhen Luan's *Xiaodao lun* (Laughing at the Dao, T. 2103, 52.143c–52c; trans. in Kohn 1995), a polemical treatise in thirty-six sections dated to 570, shows that Daoist texts claim the emergence of five different Buddha figures at approximately the same time, some being identified with Laozi, others with Yin Xi, still others with Laozi's former wife, and some even with Śākyamuni himself. Similarly the *Bianzheng lun* (In Defense of What Is Right, T. 2110, 52.489c–550c), a summary of various debates compiled in 622, has numerous citations from the *Huahu jing* and related texts and painstakingly and acrimoniously refutes their claims.[40]

As a result, the conversion theory became *non grata* and texts like the state-sponsored Daoist encyclopedia *Wushang biyao* (Esoteric Essentials of the Most High, DZ 1138) of the year 574 do not mention it at all.[41] The Tang government, after several more debates, even went so far as to proscribe the *Huahu jing* completely in 668 and 705. Only under the reign of Xuanzong did the Daoists feel strong enough to produce a new version of the text, the third in its history. This consisted of a total of ten scrolls, of which four (chs. 1, 2, 8, and 10) have survived in Dunhuang.[42]

The principal rewriting of the conversion story is contained in the first scroll; it relates the events from an intensified mythological aspect. Here Lord Lao has no need to give banquets or undergo ordeals in order to subdue a recalcitrant barbarian king. Instead, he simply sets himself

---

[39] The *Qingjing faxing jing* was lost and only recently rediscovered in Japan. See Ochiai 1991. For a discussion of its counter-conversion theories, see Ishibashi 1991. Other texts featuring similar tales, such as the *Guangshuo pin* (Chapter of Broad Explanations), are cited at length in the *Xiaodao lun*. See Kohn 1995, 71–72; Zürcher 1959, 317–18.

[40] The *Xiaodao lun* discusses conversion doctrines especially in sects. 5, 8, 18, and 19 (see Kohn 1995). The *Bianzheng lun* focuses on them particularly in its sixth chapter (52.524c–37b).

[41] See Lagerwey 1981, 32. The *Wushang biyao* generally has very little information on Lord Lao, mentioning him only as the revealing deity of the early Celestial Masters and as the ruler of the Great Clarity heaven, and citing him in various prayer invocations. See Lagerwey 1981, 103, 126, 153, 165, 161, 183.

[42] Chapter editions and translations are as follows: Ch. 1 is S. 1857, T. 2139, 54.1266b–67b, trans. in Kohn 1993, 71–80; ch. 2 is S. 6963, Yoshioka 1959, 473–81; ch. 8 is P. 3404, Yoshioka 1959, 484–90; ch. 10 is P. 2004; T. 2139, 54.1267c–70b; also S. 2081, trans. in Seidel 1984.

up in Khotan and raises his divine staff to summon the celestial host and the barbarian peoples. They all come, to the wafting of incense and the sound of heavenly music, to listen to his gracious sermon, which condemns the barbarians' hygienic and social habits, and orders them to cultivate the Dao with the help of Buddhist precepts and shaving practices.

This concluded, the god leaves Khotan to work miracles and spread the Dao in other parts of Central Asia. Reaching India, he becomes the Buddha of Purity, a precursor of the Buddha Śākyamuni. Traveling back to China, he visits the immortal paradise islands of Penglai and organizes the ranks of the immortals. Then he goes west again under King You and orders Yin Xi to be born as the Buddha, only to return east once more and become the teacher of Confucius. Taking a well-earned rest in the heavenly realm of Kunlun for a few centuries, he presents various revelations to religious Daoists, then appears again in the west as Mani, the founder of Manichaeism—which reached China in 694, just prior to the compilation of this text. The text ends with the prophecy that all religions, which are ultimately and originally one, will eventually return to unity, thus creating harmony on earth. "All three teachings will find a great reunion and be equal," Lord Lao says, "as all people will be joined in me, worshiping me in the chambers of silence."[43]

This version of the conversion is far removed from its original appearance in the third century. No longer an explanation for the development of Buddhism or a powerful polemical statement about its inferiority, it is a largely mythical depiction of the Dao, showing its universality, ubiquity, and encompassing powers of creation and civilization. Buddhism is coincidental to the continuous appearances of the god, who never seems to stand still, always moving either up and down between heaven and earth or east and west between China and the barbarian countries. The conversion, originally developed as a supplement to Laozi's biography in the *Shiji*, here has grown to a full mythical statement, showing in narrative form the celestial powers and universal impact of the deity.

Moreover, the almost frantic pace of the god's movements, as well as his new identification with the Persian prophet Mani (216–276), who created a teaching that combined Zoroastrianism, Gnosticism, and Christianity, adds a new element to the story. Lord Lao's travels, in particular the frequent back-and-forth movements through different spheres and countries, closely follow the biography of the prophet. Mani,

---

[43] Kohn 1993, 79. On the arrival of Manichaeism in China, see Lieu 1985, 189; Forte 1973; 1992, 226.

supported by the Persian ruler Shāpur (r. 242–273), traveled widely all over Western, Central, and South Asia to spread his teaching and convert the people—a life story that may have inspired the increased missionary activity of Lord Lao in the growing Daoist myth.[44]

Besides being a religious effort, however, the adaptation of Manichaeism into Daoism was also a political move in that it substantiated Uighur dependence, at least ideologically, on the Chinese state. The Uighurs, having helped the Tang in their restoration after the 755 rebellion of An Lushan, discovered Manichaeism at the Chinese court and invited four missionaries to their country. Soon they converted to the new creed and made it their state religion, giving a great boost to Manichaeism in Central Asia (Forte 1992, 226–27). The Daoist claim to Lord Lao's identity with Mani thus had the political effect of making the Uighurs seem second-hand Daoists, and establishing them as lesser subjects of the Chinese throne.

Unlike Buddhists who vigorously rejected subsummation under an indigenous Chinese religion, protested against the Huahu jing, and created counter-conversion theories, the followers of Mani responded positively and used Daoism to gain "a much-needed foothold in the mainstream of Chinese religious life."[45] As a result, Daoists and Manichaeans alternated in the use of the same temple buildings and one Manichaean text even appeared in the Song edition of the Daoist canon.[46] In general the new religion prospered greatly through its close relation with Daoism until it faded in the seventeenth century.

To return to the conversion of the barbarians, by the eighth century this narrative had developed from a crude polemical attempt to subdue and ridicule a foreign religion into a highly potent part of the Laozi myth and a useful vehicle for the integration of Manichaeism into China. It attributed to Lord Lao certain characteristics of Mani and created a legitimate place for the foreign creed on Chinese soil. This less offensive version of the conversion, however, did not remain dominant, and yet

---

[44] For a discussion of the biography of Mani, see Widengren 1961, 30–35; Lieu 1985, 54–59.

[45] Lieu 1985, 207. The Manichaeans even cite the Huahu jing in one of their texts, the Moni guangfo jiaofa yilüe (Compendium of Doctrines and Styles of the Teaching of Mani, Buddha of Light, S. 3969). See Haloun and Henning 1953, 192.

[46] Lieu also reports on the case of the Daoist abbot Zhang Xisheng, who felt it necessary to record the architectural changes he made from 1234 to 1264 on buildings originally dedicated to the worship of Mani, lest he desecrate them (1985, 252–53). The Manichaean text included in the canon of 1116 is the Erzong sanji jing (Scripture of Two Principles and Three Time Periods). See Lieu 1985, 226.

another, more hostile presentation of the story appeared under the Yuan. This was the illustrated *Laojun bashiyi hua tushuo* (Illustrated Explanations of the Eighty-one Transformations of Lord Lao; Reiter 1990) of about the year 1250, which led not only to massive debates between Buddhists and Daoists but also to a proscription of all Daoist texts except the *Daode jing* in 1281.[47]

Systematic Hagiographies

While sources on Lord Lao's exploits up to the high Tang were varied in nature and have to a large extent been lost, a number of systematic hagiographies emerged in the late Tang and Song. These works were scholastic in method, comprehensive in scope, systematic in organization, and universal in outlook.

The first to present such a work was Du Guangting (850–933), the leading Daoist writer and ritualist of the late Tang, who served as an editor of court memoranda, imperial counselor, and participant in controversies with Buddhists. He compiled numerous Daoist texts and liturgies, both at the Tang imperial court and under the king of Sichuan, and discusses Lord Lao in four works. The first is the *Lidai chongdao ji* (Record of Reverence for the Dao over Successive Generations, DZ 593), a chronicle of Daoist dynastic signs in Chinese history, written specifically to encourage and legitimate the Tang restoration under Emperor Xizong in 885, which focuses on Lord Lao's political role. Second, on a more popular level, Du described numerous miracles and supernatural occurrences of the god in chapters 5 and 6 of his *Daojiao lingyan ji* (Record of Daoist Miracles, DZ 590), a general account of wondrous events or miracles associated with Daoist gods and institutions.[48]

Third, Du created a mythical account of Lord Lao's birth and the teaching he receives from his divine mother, the Holy Mother Goddess (Shengmu yuanjun), in his *Yongcheng jixian lu* (Record of the Assembled Immortals in the Heavenly Walled City, DZ 783). It depicts the god as a quasi-human seeker of transcendence, bent on recovering the vision of

---

[47] Another conversion offshoot also appeared under the Yuan, the *Jieshi zhouzu jing* (Scripture on Neutralizing Curses, DZ 652), but there the story is merely the framework narrative of a story in which Lord Lao teaches Yin Xi technical methods of neutralizing curses and countering demonic influences. For more on the conversion text and debates of the Yuan, see ch. 2 below.

[48] Both these works have been studied by Verellen (1992; 1994). For details of Du's biography, see Verellen 1989; Cahill 1986; Li 1985.

immortality seekers and magic practitioners.[49] Last but not least, Du also wrote the first formal hagiographic analysis of Lord Lao as part of his *Daode zhenjing guangsheng yi*, a fifty-scroll collection of commentaries to the *Daode jing* that begins with an extensive introduction on the god and his exploits. In the second scroll, Du analyzes the god's deeds in a total of thirty items, with an additional seventeen items specifically on his birth. He begins with the god's identity with the Dao as part of the creative process and natural spontaneity of the cosmos (nos. 1–2), then points out that his true body is the perfect essence of nonarising and takes form in utter emptiness (3–4). Once born, Lord Lao initiates the great teaching of the Dao, always moving along with the kalpas (5–6). He is not only the root cause of the universe, the ultimate source of the myriad beings (7), but also establishes the immortal hierarchy (8), descends to serve as the teacher of dynasties (9), and creates the texts of the different Daoist schools (10–12).

In addition to creating the basic Daoist teachings, Lord Lao inspires the sage-ruler Fu Xi to create the trigrams of the *Yijing* (Book of Changes), teaches Shennong the basics of agriculture and Zhurong the making of pottery (13–15). He organizes a legal system in High Antiquity and creates utensils and material objects (16–17). He instructs various ancient emperors in the Dao, including the Yellow Emperor on Mount Kong-tong, Emperor Zhuanxu on Mount Heng, Emperor Ku on the banks of the Jiang River, Emperor Yao on Mount Gushe, and Emperor Shun in Heyang (18–22). He is the one to teach Yu how to control the floods and sees that Tang, the first emperor of the Shang, establishes a righteous reign (23–24). Then, having set up the world and its basic culture, Laozi decides to take human form, enters his mother's womb under King Yangjia of Shang, and emerges eighty-one years later (25–26). The events of his birth are further subdivided:

Lord Lao (1) emerges supernaturally through his mother's armpit; (2) takes nine steps; (3) is supported by immortals and (4) bathed by nine dragons; (5) he declares his nobility and (6) his intention to save humanity. Through this birth the deity (7) makes people see the perfect Dao; (8) shows that the Dao can be reached through personal practice; (9) reveals the possibility of attaining perfection through energy cultivation; and (10) demonstrates the feasibility of immortality through his own ascension. More specifically, the deity (11) is born on the fifteenth of the second month (12) in Bozhou, known as Quren hamlet in the community

---

[49] This vision is described again in various later texts focusing on the Mother Goddess. See the description of shorter biographies below in this chapter.

of Lai in the state of Chu. After his birth, he (13) undergoes nine transformations and exhibits seventy-two divine signs. Having received the true teachings from his mother, he (14) allows her to ascend to heaven and has her honored as Great Queen of Former Heaven (Xuantian taihou). After his own successful ascension, he (15) receives the worship of various emperors, (16) actively supports his descendants in the Tang imperial house by making an ancient cypress blossom again and (17) showering miraculous signs on his birthplace.

These events eventually lead to the original subject of Du's discourse: the elucidation of a comment by Emperor Xuanzong that "Laozi is the esoteric name of the Highest Sovereign Emperor of Mystery Prime" (2.1a). In effect they set up the explanation of why Laozi is called Laozi and culminate in a sophisticated interpretation of this name. Du's systematization is not a hagiographic enterprise *per se* but part of a scholastic undertaking to correctly understand the deity's name and role in the universe (see Kohn 1998e, 133–35). Nevertheless, Du's account served as the model for later hagiographies that often integrate its descriptions verbatim.[50]

The second systematic hagiography, and a direct heir to Du Guangting's work, is the *Youlong zhuan* (Like unto a Dragon, DZ 774). Dated to 1086 and consisting of six scrolls, it was written by Jia Shanxiang, a Daoist serving at the Taiqing gong (Great Clarity Temple) in Lord Lao's birthplace of Bozhou. Originally from Pengzhou in Shandong, Jia was a friend of the statesman Su Dongpo (1037–1101) and wrote various Daoist works, including the *Taishang chujia chuandu yi* (Highest Observances for Recluse Ordination, DZ 1237), a technical manual detailing ordination procedures. The highlight of his Daoist career, as recorded in Zhao Daoyi's *Lishi zhenxian tidao tongjian* (Comprehensive Mirror Through the Ages of Perfected Immortals and Those Who Have Embodied the Dao, DZ 296, 51.16a), was his experience of a miracle, when during a lecture of his that mentioned healing the blind, an old lady who had been blind for thirty-one years suddenly regained her eyesight. In addition, Jia anticipated his own death in a dream in which he was endowed with celestial honors and served as head of the celestial Palace of Great Clarity.[51]

---

[50] In addition, Du also wrote other encomia and records of Laozi, but these have not been preserved. See Verellen 1989, 206. For more on the *Yongcheng jixian lu*, see Cahill 1993.

[51] For a brief description of Jia's life and work, see Boltz 1987, 131–32. On his ordination text, see Ren and Zhong 1991, 977.

Jia's presentation of Lord Lao's deeds describes the exploits of the god in thirty sections. He gives a complete account of all his supernatural abilities and actions: how he existed prior to all and created the world; how he descended to be the teacher of dynasties and was born supernaturally to serve as an archivist under the Zhou; how he transmitted the *Daode jing* to Yin Xi and made him his partner; how he emigrated to the west to convert the barbarians; and finally, how he came back to provide revelations of the Dao and be manifest in visions and miracles in China all the way down to the Tang and Song dynasties.

The date of the *Youlong zhuan*, 1086, coincides with that of Sima Guang's *Zizhi tongjian* (Comprehensive Mirror to Aid in Government), which indicates that the text, within its own tradition, responds to the overarching historiographic concerns of the Song. In this it is also similar to the Buddhist *Fozu tongji* (Comprehensive Record of Buddhist Patriarchs, T. 2035, 49.129–477) of the year 1250.[52] The *Youlong zhuan* is thus not merely a devout account of Lord Lao's deeds but also a universal history of the Dao, proposing a Daoist view of how and why the world came into being and history unfolded as it did. In turn, it serves as a key source and general model for the voluminous *Hunyuan shengji* of a century later, and is also the key source for the discussion of the Laozi myth in Part Two of this volume.

The *Hunyuan shengji* dates from 1191. Its author Xie Shouhao (1134–1212) came from Yongjia (Zhejiang) and was a classical scholar who became an active Daoist at the Wanshou gong (Monastery of Eternal Life) of Xishan (Jiangxi) in his later years. Apparently he closely identified with his hagiographic work, sporting "hair and beard white and hoary, so that many people said he looked like a living Laozi come to earth" (*Lishi zhenxian tidao tongjian xubian*, DZ 297, 5.8a). He took great pride in this work, to the point of refusing to change even "a single word" (5.8a). He also seems to have had every intention of continuing his writing in the otherworld, dreaming before his death that a divine personage summoned him to heaven so he could "compile a historical record of the perfected immortals" (5.8b).[53]

Xie's *Hunyuan shengji* is the longest and most extensive of all the hagiographies, consisting of nine scrolls that begin with a general chronological survey (*nianpu*), then describe the events of the deity's life from the creation of the world through his transformations, birth,

---

[52] For a detailed study of this text and its relevance as a universal history of Buddhism, see Schmidt-Glintzer 1986.

[53] For a basic description of Xie's life and work, see Boltz 1987, 133.

emigration, and conversion of the barbarians, to the revelations and miracles he worked in Daoist history, ending with the reign of Emperor Zhenzong in the late eleventh century. Outside of the *Hunyuan shengji* proper, parts of Xie's work also appear in two other texts: its first scroll, the chronology, is found also in the *Laojun nianpu yaolüe* (Brief History of the Lord Lao, DZ 771), a text that also has a Yuan dynasty commentary by Li Zhidao. Parts of scrolls 1–3, an earlier draft of the main opus, appear also in the *Laozi shilüe* (Historical Summary of Laozi, DZ 773). This redundancy shows, as Judith Boltz points out, "not only that Xie Shouhao's work was widely used but also that it was highly regarded."[54]

In addition to these major hagiographies, a number of shorter Laozi biographies survive from the tenth century. First, there are Wang Songnian's *Xianyuan bianzhu* (A String of Pearls from a Forest of Immortals, DZ 596, 1.4ab) of the year 921 and the imperially sponsored encyclopedia *Taiping guangji* (Expansive Record of the Taiping Era, 1.1a) of 978, both of which style Laozi as an immortal in imitation of the ancient *Shenxian zhuan*.[55] Next, the Daoist encyclopedia *Yunji qiqian* (Seven Tablets from a Cloudy Satchel, DZ 1032) of 1023 gives an account of his activities as creator and savior (102.1a–6b).[56] After the appearance of the *Youlong zhuan*, when Lord Lao's hagiography was standardized, it appeared in several summaries, including the anonymous *Laojun jinshu neixu* (Preface to the Golden Book of the Lord Lao, DZ 772) of about 1100; Chen Baoguang's *Sandong qunxian lu* (Record of the Host of Immortals of the Three Caverns, DZ 1248, 1.4ab) of 1154; the *Zengxiang liexian zhuan* of the Yuan; Hong Zicheng's *Xiaoyao xu jing* of the early Ming; and Wang Shizhen's *Liexian quanzhuan* (Complete Immortals' Biographies, 1.9–10) of 1652.

In addition there are four short hagiographies that do not follow the *Youlong zhuan* model. First is Liu Zhixuan's *Jinlian zhenzong xianyuan xiangzhuan* (Illustrated Record of the Immortal Origins of the True Lineage of the Golden Lotus, DZ 174, 11a–13a) of 1326, an account of the patriarchs of Complete Perfection, the leading Daoist school since the

---

[54] On Xie's other works, see Boltz 1987, 135 and 306 n. 330; Chen 1975, 271. Her comment on the importance of his work is found in Boltz 1987, 135.

[55] The account appears on pp. 1–4 of the *Taiping guangji* in the Renmin wenxue edition (Beijing, 1959).

[56] In addition to this, the *Hunyuan huangdi shengji* in the *Yunji qiqian* also mentions Lord Lao as the dispenser of major philosophical texts, such as the *Qingjing jing* (Scripture of Purity and Tranquility; 17.13b) and the *Wuchu jing* (Scripture on the Five Pantries, 61.6b, 119.24a), as well as the teacher of visualizations (45.11b), inner alchemy (70.1a), and talismans (11.53a).

Song. It begins by outlining Lord Lao's traditional hagiography, then emphasizes his political importance, lists his official titles, and presents him in an almost monkish portrait (see Fig. 3).[57]

Second, Lord Lao figures in the *Xuanmiao yunü zichuan xiandao* (Ways of Immortality Transmitted by the Jade Maiden of Mystery and Wonder, DZ 868), a text closely related to the *Hunyuan shengji* of the year 1191. It describes him as a seeker of immortality. The same image of the god appears as well in the hagiographies of Laozi's mother (Wushang yuanjun) and the Goddess of the Great One (Taiyi yuanjun) in the *Lishi tongjian houji* (Supplement to the Comprehensive Mirror of Perfected Immortals, DZ 298, 1.1a–9a).[58] Both accounts contain a variant in which Lord Lao receives basic teachings then wanders widely in search of the Dao and encounters the Goddess of the Great One. She refuses to teach him easy methods and leaves him to his own devices, and so he becomes a hard-working practitioner himself.

A third version of Lord Lao's hagiography is contained in Zhang Tianyu's *Xuanpin lu* (Record of the Mystery Ranks, DZ 781, 1ab) of 1335, which focuses mainly on his meeting with Yin Xi. Fourth and finally, there is Zhang Guoxiang's *Soushen ji* (In Search of the Supernatural, DZ 1470, 1.6b–9a) of 1593, which has not only the standard information on the god, but also a description of his identification with Lord Goldtower (Jinque dijun) and his interaction with the Heavenly Worthy (Tianzun) and the Lord of the Dao.

* * * * *

From 250 B.C.E. to 1650 C.E., numerous texts present the nature and deeds of Laozi or Lord Lao, first philosopher, then master of immortality, later high god of the Dao. While early documents establish some of the basic episodes of the later myth and later summaries provide a general outline of his deeds, all the major religious accounts of his life describe him in cosmic dimensions as a mythical figure. They are typically products of organized Daoist schools, from the communal cult in southwest China that brought forth the *Laozi bianhua jing* in the late second century through the Celestial Masters in both north and south

---

[57] On this text, see Boltz 1987, 64–65. For more on Lord Lao in Complete Perfection texts, see chapter 4 below.

[58] On the first text, see Ren and Zhong 1991, 631; Baldrian-Hussein 1990, 177.

Fig. 3. A Lord Lao portrait of the Complete Perfection school.
Source: Jinlian xiangzhuan 11b

China and their successors at the Tang court, to Daoists associated with the grand temple at Bozhou and the followers of Complete Perfection. With each rewriting of the god's tale, the particular concerns of each group and its needs, as defined by its specific historical situation, are expressed in the new episodes and mythical motifs attached to the god.

The very first religious hagiography, the *Laozi bianhua jing*, describes Laozi's role as creator and teacher of dynasties, including his manifestations in Sichuan, thus serving to legitimate the group's particular teachings. The *Santian neijie jing* gives an account of the god's activity in heaven and on earth to present an integrated history of the southern Celestial Masters and prove their superiority vis-à-vis the Buddhists. The *Wenshi neizhuan* and related texts of the sixth century similarly propose Lord Lao, and through him the Louguan teaching, as the key unifying force of all Daoist schools, at the same time providing a mythical model for integrated ordination as envisioned by the northern Celestial Masters. Tang hagiographies place more emphasis on the political role of the god and equip him with a complete family history, extending his genealogy back to the Yellow Emperor and forward to living members of the Li and Yin clans. At the same time, the conversion story, always both a religious and political tale, is transformed into a mythical documentation of the universal power of the Dao and serves as a vehicle for the integration of Manichaeism.

After the high Tang, the systematic hagiographies of Du Guangting, Jia Shanxiang, and Xie Shouhou present either a complete account of the nature of Lord Lao or a systematized universal history from a Daoist perspective, proving the continued importance and underlying power of the Dao on earth at a time when imperial favor has shifted elsewhere. The Yuan version of the conversion story, highly propagandistic with its numerous illustrations, represents an all-out effort of Daoists to bring the Buddhists completely under their control. In this they were encouraged by Chinggis Khan's appointment of the Daoist Qiu Chuji (1148–1227) as head of all Chinese religions. In accordance with this effort, the account of Lord Lao by Complete Perfection followers emphasizes his political role, in contrast to later biographies by Celestial Masters that focus on the god's powers of salvation or his interaction with the high gods of other Daoist schools.

All these different schools and traditions created their own image of the god, but this image is more than mere fantasy or theory. It comes alive for believers on two levels: as a representation of the central doctrines that shape their worldview, be they the continued benevolent presence of the Dao on earth or the importance of Daoist worship for political harmony; and through the sensually perceived presence of the deity in visions, miracles, and meditative visualization. Thus as believers of the *Laozi bianhua jing* cult personally experienced several descents of the deity in Sichuan, followers of the Celestial Masters in the south recited the *Daode jing* and visualized Lord Lao among the stars. Kou Qianzhi in the north encountered him in person, while Louguan Daoists received key scriptures from him. Throughout the Tang he manifested himself in visions and miraculous finds, and certain Complete Perfection Daoists were personally guided to heaven by him.

The god, however artificial his hagiographic stylization may appear, thus remained an active participant in his devotees' lives. He was venerated formally in prayer services and during birthday celebrations at his sanctuary in Bozhou but also appeared to help people or take devout followers with him to the heavens of the immortals. As high god of the Celestial Masters and Complete Perfection schools, Lord Lao was thus a divine shield, guarding Daoists on earth and giving them a sense of purpose and protection, of rightness and cosmic power.

2

Official Inscriptions
Lord Lao as the Symbol of Political Stability

Political stability in traditional China was seen not only as the result of social peace and economic prosperity but as a part of cosmic harmony. For this reason, from an early period rulers performed a variety of rituals to ensure that their reign would be blessed by the heavenly forces and gods of the universe and that the Dao would flow smoothly through their realm. Besides performing regular imperial and state sacrifices, they also built a temple complex known as Mingtang (Hall of Light) specifically for cosmic rituals. Square in layout, it was divided into nine chambers of equal size, eight of them placed around the ninth in the center, which was marked by a round lookout tower, the Lingtai (Numinous Terrace). It was used as a technical observatory especially for the Northern Dipper (*beidou*) or Pole Star (*beiji*), the central constellation and key symbol of heaven and the ruler.

The position of the center stood for the balancing power of the universe and was considered crucial in any effort to maintain cosmic, and therefore political and social, stability. Deities of the center were of essential importance; they included the Dipper or Pole Star among the constellations, and various gods on earth. The Yellow Emperor, yellow being the color of the center, was venerated in this function for some time, but under the Han he was replaced by Great Unity (Taiyi). In due course, Lord Lao as the personified representative of the Dao on earth was also associated with the center and worshiped formally in imperial sacrifices, as well as offered honors in various official inscriptions (see Table 2).[1]

---

[1] For descriptions of the old Mingtang, see Maspero 1951; Soothill 1952, 117; Mikami 1966; Bilsky 1975, 292. Later attempts at construction are discussed in Forte 1988. On shifts in the Han pantheon, see Seidel 1969, 35.

37

Table 2
Official inscriptions on Lord Lao

Date	Text	English title
Han		
153	*Shengmu bei*	Stele for the Holy Mother
165	*Laozi ming*	Inscription for Laozi
Sui		
591	*Laoshi bei*	Stele for Sir Lao
	Xiu Laozi miao bei	Stele on the Restoration of the Laozi Temple
Tang		
625	*Zongsheng guan ji*	Record of the Monastery of the Ancestral Sage
723	*Laozi Kongzi Yan Hui zan*	Encomium for Laozi, Confucius, and Yan Hui
729	*Xuanyuan lingying song*	Praise for the Miracles of Mystery Prime
742	*Qingtang guan ji shengming*	Sage Inscription and Record of the Tang Blessings Monastery
	Meng zhenrong chi	Imperial Orders upon Dreaming of the Perfected Image
826	*Sansheng jibei*	Stele for the Three Sages
884	*Xichuan qingyang gong beiming*	Stele Inscription at the Black Sheep Palace
Song		
1008	*Qingtang guan beiming*	Stele Inscription at the Tang Blessings Monastery
1011	*Laozi duguan ming*	Inscription on Laozi Going Through the Pass
1014	*Laojun zan*	Encomium for Lord Lao
1272	*Laozi xiangzan*	Praise and Portrait of Laozi
Yuan		
1262	*Chongxiu zongsheng guan ji*	Record of Restoring the Monastery of the Ancestral Sage
1265	*Zongsheng gongtu bawen*	Supplement to the Structure of the Palace of the Ancestral Sage
1284	*Chongxiu shuojing tai ji*	Record of Reconstructing the Terrace of Scripture Revelation
1293	*Louguan xianshi zhuan bei*	Inscription on Early Louguan Masters
1295	*Gu Louguan xiniu bo ji*	Record of the Cypress to Which the Ox Was Tethered at Old Louguan
1300	*Chongxiu taichu gong bei*	Inscription on the Reconstruction of the Palace of Grand Initiation
1303	*Chongjian wenshi dian ji*	Record of Rebuilding the Hall to Yin Xi

These inscriptions share the same characteristics as temple inscriptions in general. They were typically composed by scholar-officials, members of the elite, or educated religious specialists and were addressed to the same kind of people, reflecting not only the mentality of the upper classes but also serving a particular political purpose—commonly to demonstrate the orthodoxy and socially beneficent role of a given deity. Written in highly stylized language and often full of clichés, inscriptions rendered a cult official and emphasized its object's accordance with state norms, turning the temple at which they were placed into a location of political power and influence.[2]

Just as inscriptions in general tell us more about the government's view of certain cults than about their religious significance or role among the wider populace, so inscriptions on Lord Lao reflect the political importance attached to the deity and his stylization as a central divinity of cosmic harmony. They were typically placed at the temples most sacred to him, but these changed as new centers of religio-political power emerged. Thus, while the early inscriptions of the Han and Sui are at the god's birthplace in Bozhou, those of the Tang are also found at Louguan, the official sanctuary of the "ancestral sage," on Mount Longjiao, where he appeared in a vision to announce the Tang ascent, and in Sichuan, where he met Yin Xi for a second time. The Song continued the Tang pattern, but under the Yuan, Louguan was again favored over all other locations since by then it had become a center of the Complete Perfection school and part of that school's bid for political influence.

Laozi Under the Han

The first inscription to describe the official view of Laozi under the Han is a stele erected at his birthplace in Bozhou in honor of his mother. The *Shengmu bei*, dated to 153 C.E., praises Laozi as identical with Dao.[3] It says:

Laozi, the Dao:
Born prior to the Shapeless,
Grown before the Great Beginning,
He lives in the prime of the Great Immaculate,
And floats freely through the Six Voids.

---

[2] A comprehensive discussion of the role and characteristics of temple inscriptions is found in Katz 1997. Their official role and purpose are also emphasized in Duara 1988; Hansen 1990; Kleeman 1993.

[3] The stele is mentioned in Li Daoyuan's *Shuijing zhu* (Annotated River Classic) of the sixth century (23.11a). It describes its location and gives its date as "Yongxing 1," referring to an unfortunately rather popular reign title, which dates the stele to either 153, 305, 350, 357, or even 409 C.E. Scholars have argued variously in favor or against one or the other, but, due to the text's closeness in outlook and style to the *Laozi ming* of 165, have tentatively settled for 153 (Seidel 1969, 37; Kusuyama 1979, 317).

> He passes in and out of darkness and confusion,
> Contemplating chaos as yet undifferentiated,
> Viewing the clear and turbid in primordial union.

This description is closely echoed by the second major inscription of the period, the *Laozi ming*, which is dated to 24 September 165.[4] It contains a record of the imperial sacrifices to the divine Laozi undertaken by Emperor Huan at the sage's birthplace and begins with a summary of the facts known about the ancient philosopher. It repeats the account in the *Shiji*, gives a concrete description of the birthplace, and cites the *Daode jing* as the major expression of his ideas. In addition, this inscription praises Laozi as the central deity of the cosmos, who was born from primordial energy, came down to earth, and eventually ascended back to the heavenly realm as an immortal. It says:

> Laozi was created from primordial chaos and lived as long as the three luminants [sun, moon, stars]. He observed the skies and made prophecies, freely came and went to the stars. Following the course of the sun, he transformed nine times; he waxed and waned with the seasons. He regulated the three luminants and had the four numinous animals by his side. He concentrated his thinking on the Cinnabar Field, saw Great Unity in his Purple Chamber, became one with the Dao, and transformed into an immortal. (Seidel 1969, 123)

Laozi here is a celestial deity who moves freely among the stars and planets. Even when incarnate in a human body, he sees his physical form as something celestial, finding heavenly palaces (the Cinnabar Field) and deities (Great Unity) within.

Next, the inscription recounts the concrete circumstances that led Emperor Huan to make the sacrifice, mentioning a dream the emperor had of the deity and listing the credentials of the text's author, an official named Bian Shao. All this is still by way of introduction to the actual praise offered to the deity, which combines the Laozi vision of the immortality seekers with the understanding of Laozi as a personification of the Dao and cosmic harmony. It says,

> Laozi joins the movements of the sun and the moon, is at one with the five planets. He freely comes and goes from the Cinnabar Field; easily travels up and down the Yellow Court. He rejects ordinary customs, conceals his light, and hides himself. Embracing the prime, he transforms like a spirit and breathes the essence of perfection.

---

[4] For discussions of this inscription, see Yoshioka 1959, 21–31; Seidel 1969, 37; Kusuyama 1979, 303–15; Maspero 1981, 394.

None in the world can approach his depth; we can only look up to his eternal life. Thus our divine emperor offers a sacrifice to Laozi to document his holy spirituality. I, this humble servant, in my turn strive to ensure his continued fame and thus engrave this stone to his greater glory. (Seidel 1969, 128)

The divine Laozi was thus venerated as the representative of cosmic harmony by the elite of the Han dynasty, identified with the Dao, and worshiped in formal imperial sacrifices. This vision of the god perpetuates a Former Han teaching known as "Huang-Lao" after the two senior representatives of its ideas, the Yellow Emperor (Huangdi) and Laozi. As documented both in the *Huainanzi* (Writings of the Master of Huainan, DZ 1184) and in silk manuscripts found in Han tombs,[5] this teaching was syncretic in that it combined Legalist statecraft with Daoist *laissez-faire* and yin-yang cosmology. It had its own particular vision of the Dao, seeing it as the most elementary force of creation at the root of all existence, ordering both the human world and the universe at large. The Dao, the power of cosmic harmony, then pervades all to the effect that there is no significant qualitative difference between the different levels of cosmos, nature, state, and the human body.

Laozi in Huang-Lao Daoism was venerated as the author of *Daode jing*, which was recited by the followers of that teaching, and appeared as the teacher of the Yellow Emperor, then associated with the veneration of the center. The Yellow Emperor was sage, ruler, and god, a culture hero and an immortal. He defeated Chiyou, "the Wormy Rebel," created culture, and ascended to heaven on the back of a long-whiskered dragon. A mighty hero on his own, Huangdi was nonetheless represented as an ignorant fool in comparison to Laozi,[6] who was at one with the Dao and resided at the source of creation, the true representative of the underlying power of the cosmos. While the Yellow Emperor stood for the practical Dao of politics and culture, for its active, outgoing, visible aspect, Laozi represented it at the center of all, as the cosmic harmony later venerated in sacrifices and praised in inscriptions.

---

[5] The *Huainanzi* has recently been studied in Le Blanc and Mathieu 1992; Major 1993; a partial English translation is found in Morgan 1934. On a philosophical analysis of the silk manuscripts, see Peerenboom 1991.

[6] On myths surrounding the Yellow Emperor, see Tetsui 1970; 1972; Lewis 1990, 174; Yü 1964, 103. On the contrast between him and Laozi, see Seidel 1969, 51; 1969a, 228.

The Sui Inscription

The Sui rulers, after uniting the empire in 589, followed the Han model and similarly performed formal worship of Lord Lao as a representative of the Dao and cosmic harmony.[7] Although tending more towards Buddhism and engaging in the establishment of Buddhist state monasteries to support their rule, the Sui did not suppress other creeds and gave token support to Daoism. They therefore did not destroy the state-sponsored Daoist center of the Northern Zhou, the Tongdao guan (Monastery of Reaching to the Dao), but transformed it into an ordinary monastery while also sanctioning other Daoist establishments and welcoming Daoist reports on favorable portents and calendar calculations. In addition, the Sui period saw the creation of numerous icons dedicated to Lord Lao and the depiction of his conversion of the barbarians in temple frescoes.[8]

Emperor Wen of the Sui was the first ruler since the Han to officially honor Lord Lao at his birthplace. He had the god's temple, long established and the center of a flourishing cult, refurbished, an event documented in the *Xiu Laozi miao bei* (Stele on the Restoration of the Laozi Temple; Chen et al. 1988, 43–44), dated to 591. In addition, in 586, he ordered Xue Daoheng, "the greatest literary figure of his time to compose an elegant commemorative piece that was engraved on a stone set up at the site."[9]

This inscription is known as the *Laoshi bei* (Stele for Sir Lao) and today may be found in the *Wenyuan yinghua* (Radiant Blossoms from a Garden of Literature, 848.1a–5a; see Chen et al. 1988, 42–43). It begins with general observations on the cosmology of heaven and earth and the rhythm of the cosmic energies. Next, it praises the government of ancient sage rulers and bemoans its decline, which resulted in the squabbles of

---

[7] Before the Sui, Daoism had played a strong state-supporting role for the Northern Wei, who not only sponsored a Daoist theocracy in the early fifth century but many of whose rulers also accepted Daoist initiation. See Seidel 1983. They did not, however, leave any official inscriptions to the god.

[8] On the Sui, their policies and religious preferences, see Wright 1978. On their use of Buddhist monasteries for state purposes, see Forte 1992, 217. Statues of Lord Lao of the time are studied in Pontynen 1983, 49–54; 1980, 308. On evidence for murals of the conversion, see Ch'en 1945, 1.

[9] Xue Daoheng was originally from Fenyin. He was an official under the Northern Qi and the Northern Zhou, rising in rank as the dynasties changed. He was highly esteemed by Emperor Wen, whose posthumous eulogy he also wrote. His biography is contained in *Suishu* (History of the Sui) 57 and *Beishi* (History of the Northern Dynasties) 36. For a Western description and the citation, see Wright 1978, 137.

various philosophical schools in the Warring States period. "Even the three hundred rules of the ritual classics could not harmonize their inner feelings; even the three thousand laws in the legal codes could not still their jealousies" (1b). Xue Daoheng concludes this first part by stating that tradition and political rule, to be harmonious and pure, have to be firmly linked with their true source and origin, that is, with the Dao.

In a second major section, Xue describes the biography of Lord Lao in three parts and twelve items:

I. Lord Lao's life:
1. his supernatural stature and identity with the Dao;
2. his wondrous birth and bodily marks;
3. his transformations and repeated service to ancient rulers;
4. his meeting with Confucius as an archivist of Zhou;
5. his meeting with Yin Xi and transmission of the *Daode jing*;
6. the profundity of the text and the essence of Lord Lao's teaching; "cultivating the self to purify the spirit" and "ordering the country to establish harmony" (1b).

II. Lord Lao's immortality:
7. his ecstatic journeys through the heavens and feasts with the immortals;
8. his marvelous powers and eternal life;
9. his death as the shedding of the cicada's skin.

III. The Dao in the world:
10. its continued support for rulers, for example, helping the Yellow Emperor against the Wormy Rebel;
11. its active protection of the people and promotion of Great Peace;
12. its manifestation in human form as Laozi, who reappeared frequently to help humanity (*Laoshi bei* 1b–2b).

The second section of the stele relates that the Great Dao is incorporated in the figure of Lord Lao, who teaches the parallel cultivation of body and state. To the individual this brings supernatural power and eternal life, while the state attains Great Peace: no more evil omens in the sky, no more bad harvests on earth, perfect harmony for mountains and rivers, rites and music. More than that, historically the Dao has continuously assisted virtuous rulers and always supported righteous causes, such as the Yellow Emperor's fight against the Wormy Rebel. In every age the Dao has been there, a pure transformation of spirit, bestowing good fortune. But to ensure the presence of the Dao, it must be venerated and cared for. The ruler's failure to do so caused the barbarians to descend upon China in the Jin dynasty and brought a time of great misery for the country.

The third and longest section of the *Laoshi bei* is, as Arthur Wright has already noted, "devoted to elegant praise of the advent of Sui rule" (1978, 137). Xue Daoheng states that the empire is unified again and the virtuous great Sui have taken over the mandate of heaven in harmony with the divine Dao. Wondrous omens signify the arrival of a new beginning, springs bring forth sweet wine, and heavenly dew collects in large quantities. Soon the emperor will make a formal announcement to Heaven on Mount Tai, but for now he takes a first step toward cosmic harmony by declaring his delight and duty to the Dao, restoring the Laozi temple to great splendor, and building the deity a new hall in a compound that is in every detail the earthly counterpart of the Jade Capital (*yujing*) in heaven. Statues are being made, murals painted, and a great *jiao* offering is held in the god's honor.

The *Laoshi bei* culminates in a poem that extols the virtues and powers of the Dao and again praises Lord Lao and his protective qualities. Simultaneously an announcement of success and a prayer for protection, it shows the renewed role of the god as the personification of cosmic harmony on the political level and the importance of Daoism in the legitimization of dynasties.

Louguan Support of the Tang

In the early decades of the seventh century, widespread rebellions rose against Sui rule. Many of the rebels' leaders had the family name Li or at least put someone with this name in the foreground, drawing unabashedly on messianic predictions surrounding the Daoist messiah Li Hong. The Tang rulers, whose family name was also Li, rose to power on this popular wave, legitimizing their effort with signs of supernatural support given by the divine Laozi in acknowledgment of his descendants as the rightful new rulers.[10]

The first such sign was given in 617, just about the time when Li Yuan took first steps toward independent military action and established himself as a new leader. An old rustic who identified himself as an emissary of Mount Huotai called upon Li Yuan to give him advice on

---

[10] For studies of the omens, see Hendrischke 1993, 113; Bokenkamp 1994; Barrett 1996, 20. On Li Hong, see Seidel 1969a.

how to take the strategically important town of Huoyi.[11] Originally, in Wen Daya's eyewitness account, the *Da Tang chuangye qiju zhu* (Annotated Report on the Arising of the Great Tang, 2.5a), this figure is identified only as a local deity. But later Daoist sources such as Du Guangting's (850–933) *Lidai chongdao ji* (4a) and Xie Shouhao's *Hunyuan shengji* (8.3b), specify that he was an emissary of Lord Lao, drawing on the fact that the gods of Mount Huotai were identified as Daoist deities and transforming the old man's appearance into a visitation of Lord Lao.

Around the same time, the abbot of Louguan, Qi Hui (558–630), supported the Li family's campaign by giving provisions to a branch of the army led by Li Yuan's daughter, Princess Pingyang, the wife of Chai Shao. When the future emperor came to the area, Qi took one look at him and said: "Now a true lord has come. He will bring peace to the four quarters" (*Hunyuan shengji* 8.2b). With this, the Daoist community of Louguan pledged its support to the new rulers (Wechsler 1985, 70). This course was greatly blessed even as early as the eleventh month of 617, when during a local *jiao* offering auspicious white clouds crowded around the altar and a pair of white deer appeared as tokens of celestial favor (*Hunyuan shengji* 8.3b).

Soon after the establishment of the dynasty in 618, the Tang rulers acknowledged their debt to Lord Lao by honoring him officially as the ancestor of their house and bestowed primary care for his worship on the supportive community at Louguan, renaming the institution Zong-sheng guan. This is recorded in the first Tang inscription, the *Zongsheng guan ji* (Record of the Monastery of the Ancestral Sage), which was set up at Louguan in 625.[12] It records briefly the history of Louguan, mentioning temples erected there by the emperors Qin Shihuang and Han Wudi, then praises its role as the earthly home of numerous immortals and gives special recognition to the Louguan masters Chen Baochi and Wang Yan. According to the text, during the wars of unification Louguan suffered greatly, but during the ascendancy of the Tang it was a center of auspicious signs. For this reason, in 620, the monastery was renamed and refurbished, and a great *jiao* offering was held there.

---

[11] On the progress of the Tang campaign and the official report on this prophecy, see Bingham 1970, 95–96; Wechsler 1985, 69.

[12] Contained in the *Gu Louguan ziyun yanqing ji* 1.1a–4b. On this work, see Boltz 1987, 126. Also reprinted in Chen et al. 1988, 46–47.

Louguan continued to be a center of divine attention and under Xuanzong was the site of a major Daoist find, to which Lord Lao directed the emperor by appearing to him in a dream in 741. This is described in the inscription *Meng zhenrong chi* (Imperial Orders upon Dreaming of the Perfected Image).[13] According to this, the deity addressed the emperor saying:

> I am your original ancestor. An image of me, over three feet tall, has been hidden over one hundred miles southwest of the capital for longer than people today can imagine. If you send someone out to search for it, I will give signs for its discovery. It will give you blessings for thousands of years and good fortune without toil. I myself grant salvation to this era, and my meeting with you today in this hall grants you great blessings. (Verellen 1994, 131)

Following instructions, the emperor sent out officials to search for the promised signs. Guided by a purple cloud just as Yin Xi had been at the *Daode jing* transmission, they were led to Louguan, where a beam of light pointed them to a specific spot. Digging there, they unearthed a three-foot statue of Lord Lao, which the emperor installed in the palace for imperial worship. Copies were distributed to the country's official temples.[14]

Another memorial on the event was composed by Liu Tongsheng and similarly placed at Louguan in 742. It is called *Xuanyuan lingying song* (Praise for the Miracles of Mystery Prime) and contains a formal encomium for the god full of traditional clichés and lofty phrases.[15]

Further Blessings for the Tang

Another stele offering praise for Lord Lao, this time in conjunction with Confucius and Yan Hui, is the *Laozi Kongzi Yan Hui zan* (Encomium

---

[13] This was carved first for Louguan, then distributed all over the empire. It is reprinted in Chen et al. 1988, 126–27. On Xuanzong's inspired dreams, see also Duyvendak 1947; Barrett 1996, 62.

[14] One result of this find was the granting of a new title to Lord Lao: "Sovereign Emperor of Mystery Prime, Sage Ancestor and Great Dao" (Shengzu dadao xuanyuan huangdi) in 749. A still longer version was conferred in 754 after the god appeared in the Taiqing gong and voiced his approval of Xuanzong's reign: Great Sovereign, Celestial Emperor of Mystery Prime, Sage Ancestor and Great Dao of the Golden Towers (Da shengzu gaoshang dadao jinque xuanyuan tianhuang dadi). See Schafer 1987, 50; Barrett 1996, 63.

[15] The text is found in the *Gu Louguan ziyun yanqing ji* (1.9b–13a); reprinted in Chen et al. 1988, 132–33.

for Laozi, Confucius, and Yan Hui; Chen et al. 1988, 109), dated to 723 and probably located in the capital. In addition, there are two further Tang inscriptions that honored numinous appearances of the god. The first, the *Qingtang guan ji shengming* (Sage Inscription and Record of the Tang Blessings Monastery), recounts mysterious events that occurred shortly after the founding of the dynasty and during the struggle for its consolidation.[16] It was engraved in 729 at the Qingtang guan (Tang Blessings Monastery) and erected in honor of Lord Lao's visitation at Mount Yangjiao (Ramhorn), which by then had been formally renamed Longjiao (Dragonhorn). Located in Jiangzhou (Shanxi), this mountain overlooked the site of a battle between Li Yuan's son Shimin, Prince of Qin, and a rival force under Liu Wuzhou and Song Jingang in 620. Curious about the military action, the commoner Ji Shanxing climbed the mountain to observe it, when he was suddenly confronted by a man with white hair and clad in a white robe, riding on a white horse with a red mane and red hooves (see Fig. 4).

This was Lord Lao clad in Gaozu's colors. After identifying himself as the ancestor of the new emperor, he gave Ji the order to assure Li Yuan of his success and of the deity's continued support. When Ji, being shy of authority, did nothing, Lord Lao appeared again and promised him a numinous sign upon arrival at headquarters. Thus prompted, Ji went to see the local governor, Heruo Xiaoyi, who presented him to Li Shimin, who in turn sent him on to the capital. Ji's arrival there coincided with that of a man from Xunzhou in Shaanxi who presented a stone turtle with an auspicious inscription, saying: "The empire will be at peace for thousands and ten thousands of years." Simultaneously, the enemy forces were defeated, thus fulfilling the deity's words. The inscription also records another early blessing, i.e., the deity's prediction that an old, withered cypress at Bozhou would flourish again as soon as the Tang were secure in their rule. The tree, so the record relates, indeed burst into new bloom as soon as all internal resistance was wiped out and Tang rule firmly established (Chen et al. 1988, 112).

The other Tang inscription was placed at the location of the god's second meeting with Yin Xi in Chengdu, Sichuan, and tells of a major Laozi miracle that occurred there. Written in 884 by the scholar-official

---

[16] Chen et al. 1988, 111–13. This text also has a supplementary inscription, dated to 823 (Chen et al. 1988, 113–14). For a collection of documents on Lord Lao in the early Tang, see also the *Longjiao shanji* (Record of Dragonhorn Mountain, DZ 968).

Fig. 4. Lord Lao appears to Ji Shanxing on Mount Yangjiao.
Source: Laojun bashiyi hua tushuo, no. 65

Yue Penggui, this lengthy document is entitled *Xichuan qingyang gong beiming* (Stele Inscription at the Black Sheep Palace, DZ 964). It begins with an outline of Lord Lao's life, then describes how, in October 883, a *jiao* offering was made in the Zhongxuan guan (Monastery of Central Mystery) at Black Sheep Market in Chengdu city. Suddenly a red glow illuminated the area, culminating in a purple hue near a plum tree. Bowing, the officiating priest advanced and had the indicated spot excavated to uncover a solid square brick. It bore six characters in ancient seal script, saying: "The Highest Lord brings peace to the upheaval of [the reign period] Central Harmony." Not only was this wondrous text written in a seal script unpracticed for a millennium, but the brick itself was like an ancient lithophone, making marvelous sounds when struck and looking luminous like jade when examined closely (12b; Verellen 1994, 144).

After an exchange of several memorials and formal orders, all faithfully recorded in the inscription, the temple was formally renamed Qingyang gong (Black Sheep Palace). It received several new halls, was deeded a large piece of land, and honored with gifts in cash and valuables.[17] The officiating priest was promoted in rank and given high emoluments. In addition, great festivals were held at Daoist institutions throughout the empire, and Yue Penggui was entrusted with writing the inscription. His work, in addition to recounting the specific miracle, also contains an outline of Lord Lao's life based on Yin Wencao's work. It begins with the creation and includes the god's transformations through the kalpas down to his birth, the transmission of the *Daode jing*, his emigration, and the conversion of the barbarians (1a–11b). It culminates in a long poem, giving praise to the deity (21a–23b).

Not only were Louguan, Mount Longjiao, and Chengdu sites of divine manifestations of Lord Lao, the two capitals where the Tang instituted the god as part of the imperial ancestral cult also received visitations. Other holy locations were the god's birthplace at Bozhou, where regular sacrifices were held, especially on his birthday, and the Hangu Pass, where he first met Yin Xi.

The ancestral temples, the Taiqing gong in Chang'an and the Taiwei gong (Great Tenuity Temple) in Luoyang, were both impressive complexes with special halls to Lord Lao that figured not only in imperial sacrifices but also housed Daoist academies and training centers for Daoist officials. The former contained a large statue of the god,

---

[17] See Verellen 1994, 145–48. On the present state of this important Daoist sanctuary, see Yūsa 1986.

sculpted from precious jade by Yang Huizhi and dressed in ornate garb studded with pearls, facing south like the emperor of heaven.[18]

Other statues of the god have also survived from this period, such as the stone engraving of 726 that shows him surrounded by a flaming mandorla, the image of the trinity surrounded by twenty-three attendants dated to 742 and found in a cave in Sichuan, and the 748 stele showing Lord Lao at the Xuanmiao guan (Monastery of Mystery and Wonder) in Sichuan.[19] The god's exploits, moreover, were depicted in colorful murals, the most famous of which were those executed by the court painter Wu Daozi (ca. 689–758). Located in the god's temple on Mount Beimang north of Luoyang, they were so beautiful that they inspired a poem by Du Fu and were restored and even expanded under the following dynasties.[20]

The god's birthplace at Bozhou, too, was honored greatly as the site where he had given the sign of the revitalized cypress. Both Xuanzong and his successors visited the Taiqing gong there on a number of occasions to personally offer prayers for the wellbeing of country, state, and people (Ding 1980, 201–06). Xuanzong in particular honored the institution with the erection of a *Daode jing* stele before the main hall, granted it renovations and enlargements, and installed a state-trained official as its abbot. The institution's holdings, as Benn says, "grew to mammoth proportions, eventually embracing more than seven hundred *jian* [bays]" (1987, 131).[21] In response to the imperial favor, the god descended there more than once: In 841 he came to decree that his birthday be honored throughout the empire and to arrange for a great three-day *jiao* offering; in 880 he appeared with clouds of black smoke

---

[18] On the layout and functions of the temples, see Ding 1979, 288–95; 1980. On the statue, see Ding 1979, 296; Jing 1994, 176.

[19] On these objects, see Pontynen 1983, 84; Jing 1994, 172, 176.

[20] On Wu Daozi, see Huang 1991. On the Du Fu poem, see Ding 1979, 293. On the temple, see *Taiping guangji* 212.397. The painting is described in Sickman 1980; its later restoration, in Jing 1994, 186. Other murals, such as Yan Liben's "Painting of the Western Ascension" are mentioned in the literature as showing Lord Lao converting the barbarians. For references, see Ch'en 1945, 1–2.

[21] A *jian* is a "bay," measuring the space between two pillars in a traditional building, about three meters wide (Liu 1989, 27–28). A small local temple might have only three bays, while a major sanctuary would have at least seven. Seven hundred means a huge complex of buildings.

and thunderous heavenly drums to frighten off rebels who were attacking the sanctuary.[22]

Last but not least, in 741 the monastery on the Hangu Pass, where Laozi first met Yin Xi, was the site of the momentous find of a celestial talisman, known as the "Heavenly Treasure." To point to it, Lord Lao appeared to the palace guard Tian Tongxiu. Tian was on duty at the Danfeng men (Red Phoenix Gate) in the capital when he saw a purple cloud advancing from the northwest that contained Lord Lao on a white horse with two attendants. The deity addressed him, "Long ago, when I left with Yin Xi for the floating sands, I hid a golden casket with a numinous talisman at Yin Xi's old border post in Taolin District. Ask the emperor to get it." Tian duly reported the incident and, together with several officers, was sent to the pass, where they indeed found a stone container with a golden box and several jade plates that were inscribed with red characters in old seal script. In response to this sign, the emperor changed the reign title to Tianbao (Heavenly Treasure) and honored the Daoist institution on the pass with an imperial stele and generous gifts.[23]

These numerous manifestations and visions of the deity recorded in official inscriptions under the Tang were not only placed in various, often newly emerging, places of sacred impact but also show a completely different Lord Lao. No longer the far-distant cosmic creator and abstract symbol of cosmic harmony and state protection, he has become the concerned ancestor of the ruler of the new dynasty, a deity who is close to humanity both as the third god of the trinity (and thus the teaching aspect of the Dao) and because he has active family ties on earth and is a responsible and caring ancestor to his descendants. This new Lord Lao is closer to the people, more human, and more accessible. His manifestations, formerly granted only to a select few or occurring as momentous revelations that sparked whole Daoist movements, now are widespread and popular. He appears to ordinary people and speaks in clear ordinary language, politely identifying himself to his human partner and giving almost trivial sounding messages to farmers, commoners, and other people. He becomes manifest in visions and dreams for the sake of his descendants and plants various signs of divine approval at

---

[22] The manifestation of 841 is described in *Youlong zhuan* 6.4b. His efforts against the rebels are found in *Guangsheng yi* 2.15ab; *Daojiao lingyan ji* 1.9ab. See also Reiter 1983, 372–73; Verellen 1994, 139.

[23] *Daojiao lingyan ji* 6.2b–3b; Verellen 1994, 130–31.

strategic supernatural locations, often those associated with his life on earth, such as Bozhou, Louguan, the Hangu Pass, and Chengdu.

In the political vision of the Tang, Lord Lao, the personification of the ineffable Dao, the distant creator god and granter of obscure revelations, is thus transformed into a practical and accessible deity, whose appearances and activities have a direct impact on the state and its fortunes. This new image of the god goes hand in hand with the redefinition of the role of Daoist religion at this time. No longer primarily focused on the otherworld, on immortality practices, or on oneness with the Dao, it sees its main role as supporting the state and creating a society of Great Peace, giving support to rulers even in war and advising them to the greater benefit of all. The political and socially active dimensions of Daoism, never absent even in the earliest movements, have come to the fore to be fully embraced by a ruling dynasty; the Dao is even actively linked with the dynasty by family relation, the strongest of all Chinese ties. Lord Lao, the god personifying the Dao, has matured into a political symbol of great immediacy and personal impact.

Song Imperial Worship

The Song came to power in 960, and because their family name was Zhao, not Li, they did not have the same ancestral ties to Lord Lao. As a result, the political importance of the god and his immediate impact on the fortunes of the state diminished. Nevertheless he continued to be officially honored both scripturally and ritually, especially in the early years of the dynasty. Then increasingly he was replaced by the Dark Warrior as the cosmic power of the center and the key protector of the state. Lord Lao's scriptural worship was apparent in the Song rulers' high esteem for the *Daode jing*, which they cited in edicts and inscriptions, examined for political advice, and occasionally even wrote commentaries on (e.g., Emperor Huizong, r. 1101–1126). They also sponsored various editions and printings of the Daoist canon, for which they had materials collected from all over the empire.

In terms of ritual, the Song house continued the imperial sponsorship of Lord Lao's major sacred places, especially his birthplace in Bozhou, where annual ceremonies were held on the god's birthday. They honored him in several formal inscriptions, and bestowed yet a new title upon him. This general pattern, described in the *Hunyuan shengji*, was established from the very beginning of the dynasty, with Taizu sacrificing at Bozhou in 960 (9.29b) and Taizong lauding the *Daode jing* in 982 and drawing on its political doctrines in 984 (9.30a). In 991 Taizong also offered sacrifice at Bozhou and had the temple and its grounds renovated. He further expanded them in 993 and instituted regular sacrifices there in 995 (9.30b–31a). In addition, he ordered the first compilation of Daoist scriptures, demonstrating his deep appreciation of the Dao.[24]

These various forms of veneration were most actively continued under Zhenzong (r. 998–1022), who generally paid much attention to divine signs and manifestations, as documented in the so-called Heavenly Text Affair (see Cahill 1980). He put Wang Qinruo (962–1025) in charge of a scripture collection project and compiled a personal preface to the canon when it was completed in 1019, under the title *Da Song tiangong baozang* (Precious Canon of the Celestial Palace of the Great Song). In it he lauds Lord Lao as an important auspicious sign for every ruling Chinese dynasty and a great representative of cosmic harmony.[25]

In addition, Zhenzong also paid homage to the god personally by worshiping at the temple honoring the Tang on Mount Longjiao and having an inscription placed there in 1008. In this work, the *Qingtang guan beiming* (Stele Inscription at the Tang Blessings Monastery), he cites the *Daode jing* and emphasizes Lord Lao's celestial nature and identity with the Dao. In 1011, when passing the Hangu Pass on his return from performing earth sacrifices in Fenyin, he had yet another Laozi inscription erected. This text, entitled *Laozi duguan ming* (Inscription on Laozi Going Through the Pass), praises the god's spiritual powers, summarizes his biography as described in the *Shiji*, and ends with a prayer for a peaceful and prosperous reign.[26] In 1014, moreover, after a visit to Bozhou where he personally worshiped at the Taiqing gong, Zhenzong issued an edict called the *Laojun zan* (Encomium for Lord Lao), in which he praises the god's powerful stature in nature and among humanity, calling him "the energy of chaos and essence of the obscure, who initiates the primordial transformations yet is himself without root, who crowns all life and creation yet represents the beginning of all" (*Hunyuan shengji* 9.35b). He then formally honored the deity with the title "Highest Lord Lao, Supreme Virtuous Sovereign Emperor of Chaos Prime" (Taishang laojun hunyuan shangde huangdi),

---

[24] On the continued importance of Bozhou, see Ding 1979, 285–86. For the Song compilations of Daoist canons, see Boltz 1987, 5.

[25] So described in *Hunyuan shengji* 9.32ab. For discussions of Zhenzong's efforts, see also Boltz 1987, 5; Yoshioka 1955, 141.

[26] The two inscriptions are found in Chen et al. 1988, 238–39 and 245. The second also appears in *Hunyuan shengji* 9.34ab.

elaborating on the Tang title "Mystery Prime" (Xuanyuan) while also observing the taboo on the character *xuan* and replacing it with *hun*. This new appellation "Chaos Prime" had a significant impact on the later tradition and became the god's standard name.

Further Laozi-related activities of Zhenzong mentioned in the *Hunyuan shengji* include an encomium written as an inscription on a statue of the god (9.38b), a poem praising the miraculous cypress in Bozhou, now advanced to "Imperially Beloved Cypress" (9.39ab), and a preface to the *Huming jing* (Scripture on Protecting Life, DZ 632), a talismanic healing scripture associated with the god. In addition, the emperor sponsored the recovery of the Wu Daozi frescoes in the god's temple on Mount Beimang by having them sketched on handscrolls by the artist Wu Zongyuan (d. 1050). They survive today in two scrolls and show a lengthy procession of eighty-seven divinities "wearing elaborate headdresses and long gowns with flying sashes" (Jing 1994, 189).

The same pattern of activity continued under Zhenzong's successors, who variously lauded the *Daode jing*, sponsored Daoist compilations, and worshiped at Bozhou. A few incidents stand out, such as the active appearance of the god in a powerful vision that gave forth a blinding radiance during celebrations for his birthday at Bozhou in 1098 (*Hunyuan shengji* 9.43a); the healing of Liang Guangying's leprosy in 1112, when Lord Lao appeared and bestowed the *Huming jing* upon him (9.45b); the imperial compilation of a *Daode jing* commentary by Huizong in 1116 (9.46b); the formal sponsoring of a handscroll on the god under Emperor Gaozong (r. 1127–1162), in which the painter Wang Liyong (fl. 1120–1145) shows him in ten images as dynastic teacher from the Three Sovereigns to King Tang of Shang; the erection of statues of the Song pantheon around 1150, including Lord Lao as a member of the Daoist trinity; and the sponsoring of the *Laozi xiangzan* (Praise and Portrait of Laozi) in 1272.[27]

Taken together, Song imperial worship of the god thus followed basic Tang patterns, but without the strong ancestral overtones and without placing Lord Lao at the center of universal harmony and political stability. The Dark Warrior and his military assistants played a much more important role in the Song, but the Dao as represented by Lord Lao was not neglected. Its tradition was honored and official veneration of the deity continued. Although somewhat less intensive

---

[27] On Wang Liyong's handscroll, see Boltz 1987, 304n 320; with illustrations, Sickman 1980, 30–33. For more on the Song pantheon, see Jing 1994, 234. The inscription is found in Chen et al. 1988, 419; praising the god's cosmic qualities, it was set up at the Laozi Cavern in Rong District, Guangxi.

and less immediate than under the Tang, worship of Lord Lao remained an important part of the imperial state cult.

Rise and Fall Under the Yuan

The Yuan dynasty saw a new intensification of Lord Lao's worship and was another highpoint in his political career. Unlike the Tang, however, the rulers, who were Mongols and Tantric Buddhists, did not themselves venerate him in any particular way. Nevertheless he played a political role as the senior deity of Complete Perfection Daoism, whose leader Qiu Chuji served as the official Daoist envoy to Chinggis Khan in 1219 and was, in 1223, appointed head of all religions of China by the foreign ruler.[28] This decree allowed Daoists to offer sanctuary to the population and thus saved thousands of people from Mongolian atrocities. But because it also placed Buddhists under Daoist supremacy, it encouraged the takeover of Buddhist institutions and artifacts, sometimes in a most aggressive manner. When the Buddhists complained about this abuse, the Daoists countered by discrediting Buddhist teachings and publicizing the supremacy of Lord Lao in propagandistic pictures both on temple walls and in print.[29]

Lord Lao was represented, for instance, in the murals in the Yongle gong (Palace of Eternal Happiness), the temple dedicated to Lü Dongbin in Ruichang (Shanxi). Consisting of three halls dedicated to the trinity, the patriarch Lü,[30] and the Complete Perfection founder Wang Chongyang, the temple was first completed in 1252, then renovated over the course of the fourteenth century. The Sanqing dian (Hall to the Three Pure Ones) in particular contained extensive murals, showing 290 deities on a total wall space of ninety-four meters. The murals are still extant

---

[28] The long journey to the Khan's camp is described in the *Xiyou ji* (Record of the Western Journey; trans. in Waley 1963). On the meeting, see Jagchid 1980, 65; Yao 1986, 212. The school of Complete Perfection began in the late twelfth century in north China under the leadership of Wang Chongyang (1112–1170). It was ascetic in outlook and monastic in organization and integrated both Buddhist and Confucian values. On its early history, see Yao 1980; for later developments, see Tsui 1991; on its major doctrines, see Chen 1962; the school's texts are discussed in Boltz 1987.

[29] On the decree, see Yao 1986, 217. On Daoist aggression, see Thiel 1961, 20; Yao 1980, 152. For the role of the *Laojun bashiyi hua tushuo*, see Kubo 1968, 58.

[30] Lü Dongbin emerges in the Song dynasty as a popular immortal, transmitter of teachings, and member of the Eight Immortals. See Yetts 1916; Baldrian-Hussein 1986; Katz 1996.

and some figures have been preserved; they include a formal image of Lord Lao in his celestial position.[31]

In print, Lord Lao is styled as high god in the fourth version of the conversion story, the *Laojun bashiyi hua tushuo* (or *Tushuo*), which retells his exploits in eighty-one drawings with brief explanations.[32] Although we know that this work was prominent around the year 1250 and was a direct product of the political power struggle between the two religions, the exact circumstances of its compilation, the controversy around it, and its eventual destruction are not clear. The text is not mentioned in any official records and only features in the Buddhist polemic *Bianwei lu* (To Refute Heresies; T. 2116, 52.751a–81a). That text examines and refutes it, then presents an account of Daoist deeds of violence, and concludes with the imperial decree on the burning of Daoist books in 1281. As described in the *Bianwei lu*, the *Tushuo* was compiled under the leadership of Li Zhichang, a disciple of Qiu Chuji, in 1232. It caused several massive debates under Möngke Khan (Emperor Xianzong) in the 1250s and led to the Daoist persecution of 1281. This sequence of events is historically unfeasible, and—as Kubo has shown in detail—the *Bianwei lu* is riddled with mistakes, errors, and non sequiturs that render its account wholly unreliable.[33]

It is more likely that, as Kubo concludes, the *Tushuo* was compiled in the 1250s and became the object of debates that were considerably less grand in scale and less harmful to the Daoists than claimed in the *Bianwei lu* (1968, 60). The one real proscription of Daoism occurred only in 1281, thirty years after the *Tushuo* debates, and practically nothing is known about the events leading up to it. Scholars have offered different explanations: Ten Broeck and Yiu ascribe it to increased conflict and more heated disputes; Thiel speculates that the emperor was furious because the Daoists failed to secure favorable winds for his invasion of Japan; and Jing even holds the manipulations of a single Tibetan monk responsible.[34]

---

[31] On the murals and their history, see White 1940; Jing 1994, 289–306; Katz 1993; 1994; 1997; Lu 1982.

[32] The *Laojun bashiyi hua tushuo* survives in two editions, a Ming dynasty manuscript of 1532 that is reprinted with a German translation in Reiter 1990; and a 1930 Manchu-kuo edition, now at Tokyo University. A description of the first is found in Lu 1982, and English translations of sections 10, 34, and 42 of the text are contained in Ch'en 1945. A copy of the 1930 edition was made available to me by Yamada Toshiaki and is the source for the illustrations in Part 2 of this volume.

[33] See Kubo 1968, 50–51; cf. also Yoshioka 1959, 199–246.

[34] See Ten Broeck and Yiu 1950, 68 (also Jagchid 1980, 86); Thiel 1961, 52; Jing 1994, 60.

In any case, there was a serious struggle for power between the two religions in the middle of the century, in which Lord Lao took center stage. According to the *Bianwei lu*, Daoists presented him as the key god of the cosmos and root of all creative and political power, while Buddhists countered this understanding by going back to the ancient philosophers and histories and showing that he was merely an impressive thinker who had in fact died and left behind only one work worthy of consideration (Thiel 1961, 44). Demanding a serious dismantling of Lord Lao's divine position, they proposed the banishment of thirty-nine Daoist texts (T. 52.764b), among which, besides obviously anti-Buddhist treatises such as the *Huahu jing* and the *Sanpo lun* (On the Threefold Destruction Caused by Buddhism), were a large number of Lord Lao hagiographies. This again indicates the key role the god played in the fight for power.

Neither this proposed banishment of Daoist texts nor the actual proscription of the religion in 1281 had a serious impact on the activities of Complete Perfection Daoists, however. They continued to consolidate both their position and Lord Lao's status. One way they accomplished this was by rebuilding numerous halls at Louguan, including the old Zongsheng guan, the Shuojing tai (Terrace of Scripture Revelation), the location of the *Daode jing* transmission, and the Wenshi dian (Hall to Yin Xi). These architectural efforts, undertaken certainly with imperial consent if not actual support, are recorded in a number of inscriptions dated to the late thirteenth and early fourteenth centuries. About half of them, such as the *Chongxiu zongsheng guan ji* (Record of Restoring the Monastery of the Ancestral Sage, dat. 1262), the *Zongsheng gongtu bawen* (Supplement to the Structure of the Palace of the Ancestral Sage, dat. 1265), and the *Louguan xianshi zhuan bei* (Inscription on Early Louguan Masters, dat. 1293) make only brief mention of Lord Lao's transmission of the *Daode jing* to Yin Xi at Louguan. They concentrate more extensively on the construction and other activities going on at the time of their composition.[35]

Other inscriptions are more detailed in their recounting of the god's activities. Thus, the *Chongxiu shuojing tai ji* (Record of Reconstructing the Terrace of Scripture Revelation, dated 1284) describes Lord Lao's encounter with Yin Xi and offers high praise for the *Daode jing*. The *Gu Louguan xiniu bo ji* (Record of the Cypress to Which the Ox Was Tethered at Old Louguan, dat. 1295) describes the cypress to which Lord Lao had 2,400 years earlier tethered his ox upon arrival at Louguan and praises it for its continued existence, growth, and flourishing. Although many

---

[35] These texts are found in Chen et al. 1988, 549–52, 576–77, and 674–75.

generations were born and died in the meantime, the text exclaims, "this green palace [to the deity] has stood alone and never changed nor declined," remaining solid although "dynasties came and went and even mountains and rivers, hills and valleys moved and changed."[36] The *Chongxiu taichu gong bei* (Inscription on the Reconstruction of the Palace of Grand Initiation, dat. 1300), moreover, recounts not only the events at Louguan but also at the Hangu Pass and focuses on Yin Xi's talents and activities. In addition, it describes Lord Lao's divine manifestation at the pass under the Tang in 741. Last but not least, the *Chongjian wenshi dian ji* (Record of Rebuilding the Hall to Yin Xi, dat. 1303) relates the same events but adds the second meeting of the two sages at the Qingyang gong in Sichuan and identifies Yin Xi with the ancient philosopher Guanyinzi, citing the recovered *Wenshi zhenjing* (Perfect Scripture of Master Wenshi) to explain his thought.[37]

* * * * *

From the time of his first divinization in the Han until the Complete Perfection campaign for power under the Yuan, the divine Laozi was represented in official inscriptions under various dynasties. First in the early middle ages he was identified not only with the Dao, but through the Dao became the god of the center and the representative of cosmic harmony. As such he was offered formal imperial sacrifices at his birthplace in Bozhou and lauded as the protector of the state and supporter of righteous government. Then, claimed as the ancestor of the ruling Tang house, he was perceived as much more directly concerned with, and taking a more active interest in, the fate of the dynasty; at this point he manifested his benevolence in visions and miraculous signs. While his birthplace, which had evolved into a major cult center, underwent a significant expansion and continued to be the location of imperial worship, several new locations also became important in the official veneration of Lord Lao. Among them are the other three places most important in his earthly career: the Hangu Pass, where he first met Yin Xi, Louguan, where he transmitted the *Daode jing*, and Qingyang gong in Chengdu, where he met Yin Xi a second time to raise him to the status of full immortal. In addition, the location of the god's first major visitation

---

[36] Citations taken from Chen et al. 1988, 684. The *Chongxiu shuojing tai ji* is found in Chen et al. 1988, 642–44.

[37] These texts are found in Chen et al. 1988, 703–5 and 710–11.

at the beginning of the dynasty, Mount Longjiao, also became a cult center, and a monastery was established there to ensure "blessings for the Tang."

By making all these places into sacred centers of the god, the Tang essentially institutionalized Lord Lao's divine presence and used Daoist veneration as a vehicle for political stability and governmental control. This trend was especially pronounced under Emperor Xuanzong, who in addition to supporting the key sacred centers also set up Daoist establishments throughout the empire called Xuanyuan huangdi miao (Temples for the Sovereign Emperor of Mystery Prime) that were dedicated foremost to Lord Lao. He furthermore placed all Daoist clerics under the jurisdiction of the Bureau of Imperial Family Affairs, and in 742 changed the name of all Daoist institutions from "monastery" (*guan*) to "palace" (*gong*).[38] In addition, he had temples to Lord Lao set up on the five sacred mountains, restructured the two major ancestral temples in the capitals in accordance with Daoist ritual and cosmology, and instituted a completely new, Daoist-based liturgy in court ritual.[39]

With these changes the divine Laozi and Daoist cultic practice were turned into a vehicle of political unity and a means of furthering imperial rule, making the god an object of political propaganda at least as much as one of worship and veneration. This is not to say that the Tang did not in fact believe in the divine sponsorship of their dynasty, that people did not really experience the visions and miracles described in the inscriptions, or that the common people were not actually impressed by the cult and devout followers of it. All this probably occurred in fact and is, moreover, entirely in line not only with traditional Chinese ways of dynastic legitimization through prophecies, holy men, and auspicious signs, but also with religious experiences common in the middle ages,

---

[38] On the establishment of temples to Lord Lao and the renaming of Daoist monasteries, see Benn 1977; 1987, 128, 133–34; Barrett 1996. The Bureau of Imperial Family Affairs is the third of four major ritual divisions in the Kaiyuan ritual code, the other three being sacrifices, imperial banquets, and ceremonies for foreigners (McMullen 1987, 208). Offerings for Lord Lao, moreover, belonged among "propitious rituals," the first among five types of rites, the others being guest, army, felicitation, and ill omen rituals (McMullen 1987, 195). For more on Xuanzang's Daoist rule, see Kirkland 1986; on his ritual changes, see Schafer 1987; Xiong 1996.

[39] The Daoist transformation of the five sacred mountains follows an initiative of the Sui, which had placed Buddhist monasteries at their base, setting up "Buddhist establishments in key centers throughout the empire, thus associating Buddhism with the most important and enduring nature divinities" (Forte 1992, 217).

and not only in China.[40] Still, the transformation of the god in the official inscriptions of the Han, Sui, and Tang was conditioned entirely by the changes in the political situation and had little or no religious basis; thus these texts must be read more as political than religious statements.

The same holds true for documents surviving from later times, from the Song and the Yuan. The Song, inheriting the Tang cult, changed it by shifting their sacred locations to different sites and by focusing more on the Dark Warrior as representative of the cosmic center and protector of the state. Yet they also maintained the Lord Lao's cult by sponsoring ceremonies and stelae at Bozhou, Mount Longjiao, and on the Hangu Pass, as well as by giving generally benevolent support to Daoist organizations and scriptural collection projects

The Yuan, on the other hand, as foreign rulers not dependent on traditional Chinese forms of legitimization and thus able to break with the past, were still caught in the same quandary as the Northern Wei before them. To rule an empire as large and as bureaucratically structured as China, they had to rely on native collaborators, and where better to find them than in organizations that were traditionally secondary yet equipped with powerful structures—the indigenous organized religions? As a result, both dynasties, the Wei in the middle ages and the Yuan later, saw an outbreak of aggressive debates between Daoists and Buddhists, accompanied by strident polemics, often absurd claims of superiority, and the sometimes violent takeover of each other's religious centers. During both periods the *Huahu jing* flourished. Although grounded in the background of the cult and the hagiography of the god, it was, like the official inscriptions, first and foremost dedicated to political aims. Lord Lao under the Yuan thus appeared as he had under the Northern Wei, as a symbol of an aggressive Daoist universalism; he was instrumental in the Daoists' all-encompassing quest for political influence. But once they had succeeded in that quest, he again became a stately senior deity, worshiped by followers of all the Daoist schools and appearing increasingly in the roles of sponsor for other gods and popular protector.

---

[40] A discussion of comparative ideas and practices in the medieval West is found in chapter 14 below.

3

Revealed Instructions
Lord Lao as the Source of Wisdom and Long Life

Daoism is a scriptural religion, and its major teachings are claimed to be originally contained in sacred writings based in the various heavens, from which they are revealed by the gods to human beings on earth. Scriptures in Daoism, as the *Suling jing* (Scripture of Immaculate Numen, DZ 1314) has it, "originally existed with the Primordial Energy, the source of all life, and were produced at the Grand Initiation of the universe" (6b).[1] They formed through the coagulation of original energy and existed before the world came into being. The Dao itself, in the time of cosmic chaos, was manifest only in the shape of Lord Lao and in the form of the scriptures.

Nothing but rays of pure light in the beginning, the scriptures condensed to form written heavenly symbols. Made of jade, they were inscribed on tablets of gold in the highest of the thirty-six heavens, to which only the heavenly host have access. They were ranked according to their inherent power, time of origination, and their duration. The highest of all scriptures, those associated with the school of Highest Clarity, were said to be stored in the heaven of that name, and were revealed in the first of the cosmic kalpas by the Heavenly Worthy. They are found in the first of the Three Caverns, the Perfection Cavern (*dongzhen*). The second group, those of Numinous Treasure, based in the heaven of Jade Clarity (*yuqing*), were revealed by the Lord of the Dao in the second major kalpa, and survive in the Mystery Cavern (*dongxuan*). The third type, those spoken by Lord Lao in the third kalpa, originated in the heaven of Great Clarity (*taiqing*) and make up the Spirit Cavern (*dongshen*). In terms of contents, the first group contains texts that describe the highest heavens and give

---

[1] For a discussion of the sacrality and nature of Daoist texts, see Robinet 1993, 21; Bumbacher 1995. On sacred writing in mainstream Chinese culture, see Ching 1997, 134–53.

instructions on ecstatic excursions; the second has tales of gods, works on rituals, and scriptures on universal salvation; and the third, linked with Lord Lao, has practical methods of observation, visualization, physical practices, and alchemy.

Just as these scriptures were said to originate at different cosmic times, so they survive for different lengths of time. As the *Duming miaojing* (Wondrous Scripture on the Salvation of Life, DZ 23), one of the early Numinous Treasure texts, says:

> When a great kalpa comes to an end... all writings on the various methods, on techniques such as gymnastics and nourishing life, change with the kalpa and are scattered among ordinary folk. They are tied to the six lower heavens, the World of Desire, and so even when a lesser kalpa ends they perish along with everything else and vanish completely. (14b; Kohn 1995, 126 n. 7)

The *Duming miaojing* claims limited powers of survival for Highest Clarity talismans and permanent security only for Numinous Treasure and Highest Clarity scriptures, which "rest above the twenty-eight heavens, beyond even the World of Formlessness" (15a). Its basic system matches the later integrated version, where texts associated with Lord Lao are predominantly practical, of the lowest rank, and thought to have only limited powers of survival.[2]

Those texts are all found in the Spirit Cavern or its related supplements of the canon and can be divided into several major types. They contain first of all philosophical and meditational words of wisdom for individual seekers of mental peace as well as practical instructions on techniques of visualization, longevity, and inner alchemy for adepts of immortality (see Table 3). But there are also community rules for organized Daoist groups and ritual visualizations and incantations for masters of the Dipper or thunder rites (see chapter 4).

Among the texts on wisdom and long life, only a few have a specific revelation story, such as the old tale of Laozi transmitting the *Daode jing* to Yin Xi on the pass. Still, several can be linked to visualization practice, in which Lord Lao becomes not only the revealer of methods but also the object of the technique, and thus may go back to actual visions, consciously induced in meditation and then transformed into a personal revelation. If this is the case, the texts remain silent about it and many of them can only be linked tentatively to certain periods and/or practitioners.

---

[2] A similar description of the powers of the scriptures is also found in *Wushang biyao* 21.1a.

Table 3
Works on wisdom and long life revealed by Lord Lao

Text	English title, Source
Wisdom Scriptures	
Taisu jing	Scripture of Great Simplicity, DZ 1424
Xisheng jing	Scripture of Western Ascension, DZ 726
Qingjing jing	Scripture of Purity and Tranquility, DZ 620
Qingjing xinjing	Heart Scripture of Purity and Tranquility, DZ 1169
Wuchu jing	Scripture on the Five Pantries, DZ 763
Dushi jing	Scripture on Going Beyond the World, DZ 648
Liaoxin jing	Scripture on Perfecting the Mind, DZ 642
Neiguan jing	Scripture on Inner Observation, DZ 641
Xuantong jing	Scripture of Mysterious Pervasion, Dunhuang ms., Shinsōdō collection
Xuwu benqi jing	Scripture on the Origins and Deeds of Emptiness and Nonbeing, DZ 1438
Early Visualization	
Huangting jing	Yellow Court Scripture, DZ 403
Laozi zhongjing	Central Scripture of Laozi, DZ 1168
Mingjian jing	Scripture of Magical Mirrors, DZ 1207
Tang Visualization	
Cunsi tujue	Illustrated Visualization Instruction, DZ 875
Haoyuan jing	Scripture of the Vast Prime, DZ 659
Huangting jing zhu	Commentary to the Yellow Court Scripture, DZ 263
Huangting neijing wuzang liufu tu	Diagrams of the Five Organs and Six Viscera According to the *Huangting jing*, DZ 432; DZ 263, ch. 54
Zhenzhong jing	Pillowbook Scripture, DZ 1422
Zhenzhong shenzhou jing	Divine Spells of the Pillowbook, DZ 872
Longevity Techniques	
Zhenren neili daojia neishi lü	Esoteric Rites of the Perfected and Rules for Daoists in Attendance in the Inner Chamber
Yangsheng jue	Instructions on Nourishing Life, DZ 821
Zhiyan zong	Comprehensive Perfect Words, DZ 1033
Inner Alchemy	
Nei riyong miaojing	Wondrous Scripture of Inner Daily Practice, DZ 645
Wai riyong miaojing	Wondrous Scripture of Outer Daily Practice, DZ 646
Neidan jing	Scripture on Inner Alchemy, DZ 643
Neidan shouyi jing	Scripture of Guarding the One in Inner Alchemy, DZ 644
Qi Exercises	
Laojun shuo shisizi yangsheng jue	Formula on Nourishing Life in Fourteen Characters Revealed by Lord Lao
Laozi quanzhen qigong	Laozi's Qi Exercises of Complete Perfection

Still, the early meditation texts, found in materials linked with Ge Hong and the precursors of Highest Clarity, can be placed fairly securely in the tradition of the magical practitioners and alchemists of south China in the fourth century. Unlike these works, many later materials can only be related vaguely to certain groups, and only a few names of individual adepts or known historical figures provide some clue to the social and religious standing of their compilers. Nevertheless, one can say that Lord Lao as the source of philosophical wisdom and methods of cultivation was a key figure in religious Daoism, who, through unfolding scriptural developments, gave expression to changing modes of devout practice and emerging forms of religious thought.

Wisdom Scriptures

Laozi, even as ancient philosopher, was most closely associated with the *Daode jing*, a scripture representing the lofty wisdom of the Dao. In continuation of this association, he later appeared as the source of semi-philosophical texts that were often short and cryptic, sometimes associated with specific practices such as insight meditation, yet always closely connected to the *Daode jing* whose phrasing and terminology they used.

The first such text is the *Taisu jing* (Scripture of Great Simplicity, DZ 1424), a short, verse-style treatise that combines *Daode jing* thought with *Yijing* cosmology and was composed in the Later Han. Revealed by Lord Lao, this text links the philosophy of simplicity and harmony with the stages of cosmic evolution, which begin with Great Simplicity at the origin of all.[3] It says,

> The Great Simplicity is luminous and brilliant—we call it Dao.
> At the time of Great Simplicity, spirit came and managed it,
> Then Dao gave birth to it, gave birth to it and gave it form.
> Then Dao gave it a name, and went on to complete it.
>
> Therefore, heaven and earth are manifest in physical shape,
> Dao and virtue are manifest in the sacred scripture:
> In Dao, none is greater than spontaneity;
> In virtue, none is greater than long life.

Going on to cite the section on creation from the One to the Two in *Daode jing* 42, the text praises union with the One and recommends the practice of the Dao as performed by the sages, emphasizing the ultimate identity of every being with the Dao and stressing the usefulness of longevity

---

[3] The text's title is listed in *Baopuzi* 19; Du Guangting in his *Taishang huanglu zhai yi* (Highest Observances for the Yellow Register Rite, DZ 597) claims it was Lord Lao's revelation to the middle Three Sovereigns at the dawn of history. See Ren and Zhong 1991, 1128.

techniques. It praises the delights of virtue and the power of the human mind and ends with references to the cosmology of the *Yijing* and the creation in the *Huainanzi*.

Another philosophical text that followed the *Daode jing* is the fifth-century *Xisheng jing* (Scripture of Western Ascension, DZ 726; trans. Kohn 1991). Set at the encounter with Yin Xi on the pass, it was written by the Louguan group and, as can be gleaned from the (legendary) biography of its first commentator Wei Jie (*Zhenxian tongjian* 29.4a–5b), reflected the mystical endeavors of well-educated, upper-class eremitic practitioners.

The *Xisheng jing* consists of thirty-nine sections, many of which take a line from the *Daode jing* as their base and show the progress of the adept toward union with the Dao. Each section begins with the words "Laozi said," and the text, like the *Daode jing*, urges its readers to overcome deliberate, classificatory thinking and become one with the Dao in a state of no-mind, no-body, and no-intention. Still, organized practice also plays a role, and scriptures and precepts are emphasized as important initially, but are increasingly replaced by the growing inner intuition of the Dao. As the text proceeds, all discriminating categories and conscious intentions are gradually overcome in favor of an increasingly cosmic sense of self and world, resulting in the ideal figure of the sage who is part of the Dao yet also active in the world as teacher, helper, and ruler. Even he, however, will finally return to the Dao, joining his human mind and body with the inner flow of the cosmos (see Kohn 1991).

A still more important and influential text of the same type emerged in the late Tang dynasty under the influence of Buddhist insight meditation; it expresses a somewhat different form of wisdom based on the practice of observation (*guan*). This is the *Qingjing xinjing* (Heart Scripture of Purity and Tranquility, DZ 1169), joined by its shorter and more famous version, the *Qingjing jing* (Scripture of Purity and Tranquility, DZ 620).[4] Phrased in verses of four characters, the text combines the ideas of the *Daode jing* with the practice of Daoist observation and the structure of the Buddhist *Panruo xinjing* (Heart Sūtra of Perfect Wisdom, T.250–57). The latter was compiled on the basis of the *Prajñāpāramitāsūtra* (Perfection of Wisdom Sūtra), probably in China in the early seventh century, and

---

[4] For a brief description of these texts, see Ren and Zhong 1991, 925, 447, and 460; Li Yuanguo 1991, 1822, 1825, and 1816. On the *Qingjing jing*, see also Ishida 1987; Mitamura 1994. Kamata lists it among his collection of "Buddhist texts in the Taoist canon" (1986, 280). The notion of "purity and tranquility" is already found in the *Xianger* commentary to the *Daode jing*. See Bokenkamp 1997, 51, who translates the terms as "clarity and stillness."

taken to India by Xuanzang where it was translated into Sanskrit together with the *Daode jing* (Nattier 1992, 169). Like the *Qingjing xinjing*—and also like its earlier Daoist adaptation, the seventh-century *Shengxuan huming jing* (Scripture of Protecting Life and Ascending to the Mystery, DZ 19; see Fukui 1987, 282)—the "Heart Sūtra" does not conform to the standard format of classical religious texts but is a collection of essential ("heart") passages and spells from a longer scripture that is used for ritual and magical recitation.[5]

The *Qingjing xinjing* follows this pattern, giving short, mantra-like verses that emphasize the need to eliminate ordinary perception in favor of purity and tranquility—the "perfect wisdom" of the Dao. In content, it first describes the nature of the Dao as divided into yin and yang, turbid and pure, tranquil and moving, then stresses the importance of the mind in the creation of desires and worldly entanglements. It recommends the practice of observation to counteract this, i.e., the observation of other beings, the self, and the mind, which results in the realization that none of these really exist. Completing this, practitioners reach the observation of emptiness, which brings them into a state of complete purity and tranquility or oneness with the Dao. The latter part of the work reverses direction and outlines the decline from pure spirit to the fall into hell. Spirit develops consciousness or mind, mind recognizes a body or self, the self sees the myriad beings and develops greed and attachment toward them. Greed then leads to involvement, illusory imaginings, and erroneous ways, which tie people to the chain of rebirth and, as they sink deeper into the quagmire of desire, makes them fall into hell.

The *Qingjing jing* is a shorter version of this text that became enormously influential. It has a first commentary by the famous master Du Guangting (850–933; DZ 759),[6] and rose to great prominence in the Song dynasty, when it was used in the so-called Southern School around Bai Yuchan (fl. 1209–1224) and his disciples Li Daochun (fl. 1288–1290) and Wang Jie (fl. 1310; see Boltz 1987, 179–83). These men, experts in thunder rites and inner alchemy, each wrote a commentary to the text, reading it allegorically and in an alchemical context (DZ 755, 757, 760).[7]

---

[5] For this definition, see Nattier 1992, 175, citing Fukui 1987, 201–07.

[6] Verellen, studying Du's biography, finds the attribution of authorship erroneous (1989, xii). A close study of its content and phrasing by Mitamura, however, reconfirms the closeness of the work to Du's thought and style (1994, 84).

[7] A translation of the text is found in Kohn 1993, 24–29. For a variant rendering with a contemporary inner-alchemical commentary, see Wong 1992. Ishida gives a list of commentaries and early translations (1987, 99). On the representatives of the Southern School and their practices, see Skar 1997.

Later the *Qingjing jing* became a central scripture of the school of Complete Perfection, in whose monasteries it is recited to the present day as part of the daily services. It is first among an entire branch of wisdom literature associated with Lord Lao that can be described as the "purity and tranquility" type.

Another text similar to the *Qingjing jing*, though dated slightly earlier, is the *Wuchu jing* (Scripture on the Five Pantries, DZ 763), so called because it emphasizes the need to replenish the energy in the five inner organs as one would replenish food in a pantry (1a). It is a short text that consists of five stanzas or twenty lines of five-character verse and survives in an edition with commentary by Yin An, a Daoist adept and official under Emperor Xuanzong.[8]

It begins with the traditional notion that the "one Original Energy [divides and] joins to form Great Harmony" (1a), then emphasizes that attaining this harmony in oneself will lead to longevity within and a peaceful life without, which in turn helps adepts to find oneness of inner nature with "the Mystery" (2a). Moving on to contrast illusory imaginings and true wisdom (2b), the text recommends the utter emptying of the mind (3a) to the point where it is "a clear mirror, on which no dust will collect" (3b, commentary). Like its Chan Buddhist counterpart, this image of the mirror stands for a gradual approach to realization, a tendency typical of Daoist texts at the time.[9] Gradual attainment is explicitly favored in the *Wuchu jing* (5a, commentary), reflecting similar statements in Sima Chengzhen's (647–753) *Tianyinzi* (Writings of the Master of Heavenly Seclusion, DZ 1026; trans. Kohn 1987a). After admonishing people to maintain a balance, neither getting involved with entanglements nor pushing hard to cut them off (3b), working on cultivation but not overdoing it (4b), the text concludes with the triumphant return to Original Energy (5b), the attainment of mystical union with the Dao.[10]

---

[8] On this text, see Li Yuanguo 1991, 1876. Yin An was a Daoist practitioner at the Suming guan (Monastery of Majestic Light) whom Xuanzong offered a post as official and academician and eventually persuaded to become supervisor of the imperial archives. See *Tangshu* (History of the Tang) 200.

[9] The symbolic role of the mirror in medieval China is discussed in Lai 1979; Ching 1983; Demiéville 1987.

[10] The need to strike a balance is also clearly formulated in the *Dingguan jing* (Scripture on Concentration and Observation, YJQQ 17), another text linked with Sima Chengzhen. See Kohn 1987, 135.

Five further texts belong to the same Tang Daoist milieu and equally relate Lord Lao's words on purity and personal wisdom. To describe them briefly, the *Neiguan jing* (Scripture on Inner Observation, DZ 641; trans. Kohn 1989b) of the eighth century consists of thirteen sections that describe the growth of the human embryo as a spiritual entity, admonishing people to reduce their desires and cultivate emptiness and tranquility. In the *Liaoxin jing* (Scripture on Perfecting the Mind, DZ 642), Lord Lao describes the central role of the mind as the origin of both good and evil, salvation and sin, and encourages practitioners to begin their career in the Dao by observing it carefully and working toward its purification. The Dunhuang manuscript, *Xuantong jing* (Scripture of Mysterious Pervasion), also known as *Tianying jing* (Scripture of Alignment with Heaven), similarly has Lord Lao emphasize the need for inner observation of all beings, because they tend to lose the Dao by scattering their minds and spirits. The Dao, however, never loses them and is always there to be recovered.[11]

In addition, there is the *Xuwu benqi jing* (Scripture on the Origins and Deeds of Emptiness and Nonbeing, DZ 1438), in which Lord Lao outlines the three energies (primordial, mysterious, and beginning) and relates their creation of the world. He describes their spiritual parallel in the states of emptiness, nonbeing, and serenity, which can be attained through the perfection of physical essence, vital energy, and spontaneous nature. And, last but not least, there is the *Dushi jing* (Scripture on Going Beyond the World, DZ 648), which has three sections, "Mutations of the Dao," "The Five Phases," and "Systems of Mystery," and discusses the purity of the Dao, its manifestation in the world, and various concrete ways (diets, breathing, alchemy) of attaining it.[12]

All these observation-based texts of the Tang dynasty, and also the earlier *Taisu jing* and *Xisheng jing*, focus on the mind as the central agent of human perfection or decline and place the highest emphasis on the need to eliminate desires and sensory entertainments in favor of an all-pervading purity and tranquility. They reflect the kind of Daoist concerns typical of educated followers of the *Daode jing*, depicting Lord Lao as the archetypal Daoist master of the mind and thoughts and his teaching as one of tranquility, serenity, and sensory withdrawal. Rather than a divine revealer of community rules or specific practices, he here appears

---

[11] The *Liaoxin jing* is described briefly in Li Yuanguo 1991, 1819. The *Xuantong jing* is contained in the Teisōdō Collection and edited in Ōfuchi 1979, 694–96.

[12] The *Xuwu benqi jing* is also contained in YJQQ 10. It is briefly discussed in Li Yuanguo 1991, 1825 and 1877; Ren and Zhong 1991, 1137. On the *Dushi jing*, see Ren and Zhong 1991, 463; Li 1991, 1825.

as a wondrous teacher of wisdom who—almost like a bodhisattva—has followed the path himself and, once liberated, discovered compassion so strong that he could not stay away and let people fend for themselves. He gives an analysis of body, mind, and spirit, and shows the way to purity, tranquility, and serenity of mind, thus leading his followers to salvation and heavenly bliss. Less a high god of an organized community, the Lord Lao of the revealed wisdom scriptures is a model for individual and philosophically minded seekers of personal peace and heavenly delights.

Early Visualization

Yet another persona of the god is present in visualization texts of the early middle ages associated with Ge Hong (261–341) and the southern alchemical tradition. The first of these is the *Mingjian jing* (Scripture of Magical Mirrors, DZ 1207), a text related to Ge Hong's *Baopuzi* (Book of the Master Who Embraces Simplicity, DZ 1185) that is divided into twenty sections, each beginning with "Laozi said."[13] It claims to be revealed by the god as a set of instructions for immortality practitioners and describes the wondrous powers to be gained:

> Anyone mastering this method can multiply himself and spread out his body, take one and turn it into ten thousand, set up the six armies, or place himself a million miles away. By simply inhaling and exhaling he can come and go to distant places, ride on the clouds and walk on water, merge in and out of the spaceless, and render visible the divinities of heaven, gods of earth, evil demons, ancient sprites, and all sorts of hidden dead. By mere concentration he can see ahead and predict the future—mastering this, anyone can become a king among immortals. (1a)

The text next describes various methods involving mirrors, beginning with the basic requirements of purification and the establishment of a secluded chamber where "you won't hear the rumblings of carriages, the clanging of bells, or even the chirping of birds" (1ab). Then a set of clear mirrors must be obtained, ideally with few ornaments and no bumps or scratches (2a). As adepts gaze into them, a plethora of gods will appear in the four directions, not the least of whom is the divine Laozi in his nine transformations.

---

[13] On the *Mingjian jing*, see Ren and Zhong 1991, 953. For a translation of the *Baopuzi*, see Ware 1966.

> There is a personage six feet five inches tall, wearing an angled cap and a white robe with a red collar, embroidered with tiger script and phoenix seals. His surname is Li, first name Er, also called Boyang. You will see him at the break of day. (3b)

In each transformation, the god appears in a different size and garb, is called by a different name, and manifests at a different time of day, all the way to the ninth, when he is "nine feet five inches tall, wears a spontaneity cap and a green and purple robe, is called Li Yuan, also Bowen, and appears at dusk" (4b). Through the figure of the god, adepts participate in the rhythm of the day, creating a tangible image of the energies of yin and yang as they transform in regular cycles and approach the wholeness of the Dao.

The contents of this text match Ge Hong's description of a similar method in the *Baopuzi*.[14] In Ge Hong's version, adepts gaze at themselves steadily in one or several mirrors over an extended period of time and as a result gain powers of omniscience, multilocation, and communication with the gods. As in the *Mingjian jing*, the central deity in the exercise is Laozi, who is here described as appearing surrounded by a divine entourage of fierce protectors and residing in celestial splendor, with

> a body nine feet tall and of yellow coloring; his face is bird-mouthed and has an arched nose. His bushy eyebrows are five inches long, his ears measure seven inches. There are three vertical lines on his forehead, his feet are marked with the eight trigrams, and his back shows the golden turtle. . .
>
> Laozi is attended by 120 yellow divine lads. To his left are twelve blue dragons, to his right thirty-six white tigers; before him go twenty-four vermilion birds, to his rear follow seventy-two dark warriors. His vanguard consists of twelve heavenly beasts; his rear guard, of thirty-six evil-dispellers. Above him hover thunder and lightning in brilliant flashes. (ch. 15; see Ware 1966, 256–57; Yamada 1995a, 23)[15]

---

[14] A forerunner of the practice is also found in a Han dynasty text, the *Xijing zaji* (Miscellanea from the Western Capital), which describes a magical mirror that would show a person's intestines and indicate both diseases and bad humors within. For example, "If a woman had an evil heart the mirror would reflect her gall bladder elongated and her heart in movement" (ch. 3). For a study of mirrors in Daoism, see Fukunaga 1973.

[15] The blue dragon, white tiger, vermilion bird, and dark warrior (turtle and snake) are the heraldic animals of the four directions. See Major 1986, 65; Staal 1984. The heavenly beast (*qiongqi*), an ox-like creature covered with bristles, and the evil-dispeller (*bixie*), a one-horned furry deer with a long tail, are baleful constellations associated with demonic powers.

A classic example of basic Daoist visualization practice and also an early case of Three Sovereign ecstatic divination (Andersen 1994, 12), the passage names and describes the god with precision and lists the numinous beasts of his entourage, all starry constellations of demon-dispelling nature. The deity thus visualized protects the practitioner, granting longevity, clear insight, omniscience, and eternal life. He has particular power over time and space, as represented by the cyclical Jia and Ding gods of time whom he can send out as messengers to protect and assist the adept.[16]

Another visualization scripture ascribed to the deified Laozi is the *Huangting jing*, also of the fourth century.[17] Its outer version begins with the words: "Laozi, living in seclusion, composed the seven-word text, explaining clearly the human body and its relation to the gods." It describes Laozi as the embodiment of the Dao, the ruler of gods and immortals, and the central moving power of the universe (DZ 263, 58.1a), whose active presence in the human body is essential for good health, vitality, and the prolongation of life.

Laozi resides in the Yellow Court, which is located variously at three points in the body: the spleen or stomach, the point between the eyebrows, and the lower cinnabar field. The color associated with these centers is yellow; they each function as mediating points between

---

[16] The Jia and Ding gods go back to designations of days within the sixty-day cycle and were first applied in fortune-telling with the help of the diviner's compass under the Han (see Harper 1978; Kalinowski 1983). Deified in early Daoist scriptures (Inoue 1992, 19), they rose in importance over the centuries, especially as divination was increasingly incorporated into organized Daoist practice (see Kalinowski 1990; Andersen 1994; Nickerson 1994, 50). In Highest Clarity, they appear as jade maidens with powers over the weather who regularly participate in celestial banquets. The *Baopuzi* associates them with talismans and registers, used to control supernatural forces (Inoue 1992, 20). The Six Jia as messengers of Lord Lao reappear variously, as for example in the *Laojun liujia fu* (Lord Lao's Talisman of the Six Jia), listed as part of *Daode jing* ordination in the *Fengdao kejie* (Rules and Precepts for Worshiping the Dao, DZ 1125, 4.7a), and in talismanic texts of the Song and Yuan.

[17] There are two "Yellow Court Scriptures," an inner (*nei*) and an outer (*wai*), the relative dates of which are disputed among scholars (Robinet 1993, 55–56). I follow the argument of Mugitani (1982, 35) and Schipper (1975a, pref.), seeing the "outer" text as the older, especially since the revelatory agent is Laozi, whereas the "inner" text is spoken by the Lord of Jade Morning Light, a Highest Clarity deity of later provenance. The edition and commentary used are contained in ch. 58 of the *Xiuzhen shishu* (Ten Books on the Cultivation of Perfection, DZ 263). The text is also found in DZ 403 and *YJQQ* 12. For partial translations and studies, see Kohn 1993, 181–88; Miyazawa 1994a; Kroll 1996; Saso 1995.

heaven and earth, yin and yang. In the spleen, Laozi is moreover flanked by the gods of the lungs and the liver called Baiyuan and Wuying. On occasion, he is also described as dividing into three energies—the primordial, mysterious, and beginning—representing the early stage of cosmic development.[18] In order to visualize the god properly, adepts must protect themselves by visualizing the four heraldic animals as defenders of the four quadrants. Once these are in place, the god appears in their midst (see Fig. 5) and activates his power to ensure immortality for the practitioner.

Playing a similar role but visualized somewhat differently, Laozi also appears in the *Laozi zhongjing* (Central Scripture of Laozi, DZ 1168), another early visualization scripture.[19] Called Yellow Lord Lao of the Central Ultimate (Huanglao zhongji jun), he is identified as the central god among the stars, the Dipper, and as the resident of the Yellow Court in the abdomen. His female aspect, or queen, is a jade maiden called Mysterious Radiance of Great Yin (Taiyin xuanguang yunü). Wearing robes of yellow cloudy energy, they join to give birth to the immortal embryo (18.7a).

To activate the pair, adepts visualize a sun and moon in their chests underneath their nipples, from which a yellow essence and a red energy radiate. These vapors then rise up to enter the Scarlet Palace in the heart and sink down to the Yellow Court in the abdomen. Filling these internal halls, the energies mingle and coagulate to form the immortal embryo, which grows gradually and becomes visible as an infant facing south, in the position of the ruler. As he is nurtured on the yellow essence and red energy still oozing from the adept's internal sun and moon, all illnesses are driven out and the myriad disasters are allayed (18.7ab).

While Lord Lao in these early visualization scriptures appears as the key agent of revelation and the central deity of the universe, a stellar god who is also present in the human body, in Highest Clarity Daoism he is not accorded a central or even high position. He is called Yellow Lord Lao or Yellow Venerable Lord (Huanglao jun)[20] and functions as the main member of a triad residing in the central cavity of the head, called

---

[18] For more on Laozi in the *Huangting jing*, see Robinet 1993, 57, 75; Homann 1971.

[19] The text is also found in YJQQ 18–19. For a study, see Schipper 1979.

[20] By the time this god became central in visualization practice, the title "Laojun" had acquired a certain generic nature, being read generally as "Venerable Lord," not unlike "Imperial Lord" (Dijun) or "Primal Lord" (Yuanjun). See Yamada 1989a, 27.

千乘萬騎仙童玉女擁之其形如左

Fig. 5. Lord Lao with the four heraldic animals and the celestial army.
Source: Cunsi tujue 21b–22b

Niwan Palace or Dongfang (Grotto Chamber).[21] Notably described in the *Ciyi wulao baojing* (Precious Scripture of the Five Elders of the Female One, DZ 1313), this palace is cosmically identical with Mount Kunlun, the central axis of the world and paradise of the immortals. As one of the Nine Palaces in the head, it is located three inches in from the mid-point between the eyebrows, the "Hall of Light" (*mingtang*)—one of Laozi's locations in the *Huangting jing*.

He resides there with Wuying and Baiyuan, the old gods of the lungs and the liver, to his left and right. He rules the nine heavens, wanders about Mount Kunlun, and has control over all existence, including the human body. To visualize him, adepts purify themselves and recite the *Ciyi jing* three times, then close their eyes and hold their breath first to visualize the Hall of Light, then to move further into the head and see the Cavern Chamber, where the triad resides "dressed in flowery purple caps, dragon skirts, and phoenix robes" (26a).[22]

In the visualization texts of the fourth century—part of the southern alchemical tradition and precursors of Highest Clarity practice—Lord Lao thus appears in the double role of revealer of instructions and object of meditation. As the central god of the universe and representative of the power of the cosmos, he governs and directs all, has unfathomable powers, and partakes in eternal life. He bestows some of these powers on devout adepts by providing them with relevant instructions for their own perfection and also by becoming one with them in formal visualization practice. Through Lord Lao adepts learn from the Dao and become one with it, worshiping the god both through recitation of the sacred texts and by creating a perfect, magical vision of him within themselves.

Tang Visualization

No further visualization texts associated with Lord Lao have come down to us from either the early Six Dynasties or the early Tang. Only when his name is linked with the practice of observation and the

---

[21] For a discussion of the various palaces and gods in the body, see Homann 1971; Schipper 1978; Maspero 1981, 350; Mugitani 1982; Kohn 1991a. A certain amount of debate surrounds the nature of Huanglao jun, who is either identified as a continuation of the god of the Great Peace movement (Maspero 1981, 392) or as a new god with the generic "Venerable Lord" (Yamada 1989a, 27).

[22] For discussions of the practice, see Andersen 1980; Maspero 1981, 371; Robinet 1984, 1:129; Yamada 1989a, 30.

spiritual cultivation of the mind ("purity and tranquility") does the god reappear as a teacher of visualization and textual recitation. This development also coincides with a renewed interest in the *Huangting jing*, commented on by Liangqiuzi (fl. 722) and developed into a technical medical supplement.[23] One Lord Lao text closely associated with the *Huangting jing* is the *Haoyuan jing* (Scripture of the Vast Prime, DZ 659), a short work composed in seven-character verse that merges the observation tradition with visualization practice by outlining the attainment of mental tranquility with the help of visualizing the gods. It also stresses the physical aspect of Daoist practice, noting the need to maintain health and renew vigor (see Ren and Zhong 1991, 469–70).

In addition, two texts in the canon emphasize *Daode jing* recitation in conjunction with visualization: the *Zhenzhong jing* (Pillowbook Scripture, DZ 1422), also reprinted under the title *Zhenzhong shenzhou jing* (Divine Spells of the Pillowbook, DZ 872), and the *Cunsi tujue* (Illustrated Visualization Instruction, DZ 875), all revealed by Lord Lao.[24] The former begins with a definition of the Dao and an admonition to adepts that they should purify the three karmic factors (body, speech, and mind) and eliminate desires. Reciting the *Daode jing* ten thousand times will heal diseases and prevent evil; a mere three times in the morning and at night will do wonders for one's clarity of vision and hearing, and make the body feel vigorous and light (1b). In addition, one should develop awareness of the 36,000 gods in the body, including the 1,200 celestial officers and 12,000 divine lights, and visualize their most important representatives as they illuminate and vitalize one's inner organs (1b).

Next, the text describes how to visualize Lord Lao as an infant seated in the center of the body, surrounded by gods of the sun, moon, thunder, wind, and rain, and guarded by the four heraldic animals (2a). These instructions closely echo earlier visualization practices but are

---

[23] The commentary is contained in *YJQQ* 11–12 and in *Xiuzhen shishu* 55–60 (Ten Books on the Cultivation of Perfection, DZ 263). The medical supplement is the *Huangting neijing wuzang liufu tu* (Diagrams of the Five Organs and Six Viscera According to the *Huangting jing*, DZ 432; DZ 263, ch. 54), which is dated to 848 and was compiled by the lady Daoist Hu An, also known as Jiansuzi. See Despeux 1995, 147. For further notes, see Boltz 1987, 338n 676; Li 1991, 1819–20; Zhu 1992, 106–7.

[24] The first text should not be confused with the *Zhenzhong ji* (Pillowbook Record, DZ 837), a technical collection of longevity practices by the seventh-century physician Sun Simiao; nor with the *Zhenzhong shu* (Pillowbook Text, *Baibu congshu* [Collection in a Hundred Sections]), a Highest Clarity description of the Daoist pantheon associated (vaguely) with Ge Hong. A "pillowbook" is a scroll held so dear that it was kept inside one's pillow, not a cushion but a hollow neck support made from bamboo, wood, porcelain, or jade.

more specific and integrated into the daily Daoist schedule. Before going to bed, says the text, the practitioner should raise the four heraldic animals from his body's organs, forming them visually from the energies residing there (2b). Once all demonic influences have been eliminated, the animals can be returned to their organs. Once they are gone, a red energy should issue from the mouth and be made to fill every corner of the room; it should then protect the adept in his sleep so that his dreams may take him to the heavens and the gods (3a).

Whereas the *Zhenzhong jing* limits itself to giving recitation instructions and teachings about the visualization of gods in preparation for sleep, the *Cunsi tujue* formulates Lord Lao's visualization methods for every circumstance in the Daoist's life. Divided into eighteen sections, each focusing on a specific situation, the text is lengthy and quite detailed. It has survived in two editions that complement each other. The complete text, without illustrations, survives in the *Yunji qiqian* (*YJQQ* 43.3a–17b), while its latter half (secs. 9–18) is found in the *Daozang* (DZ 875) and includes illustrations.[25]

The work first emphasizes the need to see the celestials as if they were real and imagine them as clearly as if looking at their pictures. Only then can one reach the purity and tranquility of mind necessary for the elimination of evil and attainment of the Dao. It is clear here that visualization is viewed as a another variant of observation, one that has a more concrete content but ultimately leads to the same goal. The text then details visualizations in four sections: during ordination (1–5), in daily activities (6–9), in heavenly audiences (10–13), and in advanced celestial interaction (14–18).

The first, visualization at ordination, begins when adepts take formal refuge in the Three Treasures—Dao, scriptures, and teachers—surrendering themselves to the Dao (Benn 1991, 66). The oath goes together with a mental actualization of the Three Treasures, beginning with the Dao:

> See the Highest Lord sit on the high throne, with Lord Lao on his left and the Primal Lord on his right, . . . while the ten heavens illuminate the scene and numerous guards stand at attention (no. 1, *YJQQ* 43.4b).

---

[25] On this text, see Ren and Zhong 1991, 637; Li 1991, 1877. Citations of an earlier work of the same title indicate that such visualizations associated with Lord Lao were present throughout the middle ages. See Rao 1991, 119; Sakade 1994a, 271.

Similarly, the scriptures are visualized to the Lord's west, placed on a jade table, and hidden behind precious awnings (no. 2, 4b–5a). The preceptors, including the ordinand's own teacher, are then seen to the Lord's east, sitting on velvet seats under flowery canopies. Attaining this image makes the mind tranquil, and only a tranquil mind can attain enlightenment (no. 3, 5a).

Next, ordinands bow to the ten directions while visualizing the Ten Heavenly Worthies (no. 4). They then receive the *Daode jing*. They

> clap their teeth thirty-six times and in their minds visualize the three palaces of the Niwan [in the head], the Scarlet Palace [in the heart], and the Cinnabar Field [in the abdomen]. See the Three Ones come forth, accompanied by a thousand chariots and ten thousand horsemen as guards of the text (no. 5, 6ab).

Here the visualization of Lord Lao in Highest Clarity Daoism, as the Yellow Venerable Lord in the Niwan Palace and as part of the Three Ones, is integrated into formal Daoist ordination and linked specifically with the transmission of the *Daode jing*, the second stage between the registers of the Celestial Masters and the arcana of Numinous Treasure and Highest Clarity (Benn 1991, 82).

The other parts of the text show the same integrative pattern. In their daily activities, as they leave and enter their chambers in the morning and evening, Daoists are to visualize four celestial guards (two jade maidens, two jade lads; nos. 6, 7). They should prepare for entering the sacred halls by picturing the preceptors in their minds (no. 8, 7b–8a) and place themselves in an active cosmic context by linking their five inner organs with the five sacred mountains, the five planets, and the five rulers of the five directions (no. 9, DZ 875, 8a–9b; *YJQQ* 43.8a–10b).

The third part of the text, on visualizations in heavenly audiences, begins with meditation instructions focusing on moral self-examination and aims at obliterating mental obstructions and attachment to delusions (no. 10, DZ 875, 10b). Adepts are encouraged to examine themselves in light of nine behavioral rules based on the *Daode jing* and first formulated by the early Celestial Masters and ten precepts that curb the karmic activity of body, speech, and mind (11a–12a). This practice can also be undertaken in a reclining posture, preferably "not lying straight back as if one were a corpse" (12a) but positioned on one's side (no. 11). The next two items specify the active visualization of celestial attendants as one presents oneself for audience above (nos. 12, 13; 13a–14b).

Finally, advanced interaction with the celestials includes regular practice of the Dao at the six daily periods of worship, in each case extrapolating one particular body energy to form the numinous animal suitable for the hour (see Table 4). Like massive clouds, the starry beasts gather around the adept, protecting him with their demon-dispelling powers (no. 14, 14b–18a).

Table 4
Visualization of numinous animals

Hour	Color	Animal	Guarding
morning	green	dragon, lion	front and back
noon	red	bird, phoenix	right and left
sunset	yellow	dragon, unicorn	four directions
evening	white	tiger, unicorn	inside and out
midnight	black	turtle, snake	above and below
dawn	purple	*bixie*, lion	body apparent and hidden

Source: *Cunsi tujue* 14b–16b

Next, focusing on the three energies in the body, one visualizes the Three Ones (no. 15) to then ecstatically encounter the Three Pure Ones (no. 16) and rise to heavenly dimensions, once again guarded by the four heraldic animals (no. 17, 21ab). The final stage is reached when the adept is formally received into the celestial realm by a cloudy dragon chariot. This culmination coincides with the successful completion of ten thousand *Daode jing* recitations (no. 18, 23ab). A concluding note to the text schedules this event at three years after ordination, provided one does not slacken but performs all rites as prescribed, visualizes regularly, and recites the text ten times daily. Then the Three Clarity heavens stand open to one's perusal and one is, for all intents and purposes, a perfected immortal.

In these several visualization scriptures, Lord Lao again appears as the practical teacher, the divine Daoist master working within a worldly setting to guide adepts to higher attainments of the Dao. Besides their emphasis on his teaching role, they show the strong continuity of the tradition as it joins earlier meditation and visualization practices associated with Lord Lao and the recitation of the *Daode jing* with the Daoists' more formalized ritual activities.

Longevity Techniques

Linked first with the physical methods of long life such as breathing and gymnastics in the *Liexian zhuan* of the former Han, Laozi in Ge Hong's *Shenxian zhuan* is credited with guiding energy through the body as well as with techniques of alchemy and dietetics. Few other remaining medieval texts on these practices claim Lord Lao as their master or originator; most physical techniques are associated with specific immortals of old, such as the herb-lord Master Redpine (Chisongzi) and the sexual master Perfect Face (Yongchengzi).[26] However, one passage in the *Laojun bianhua wuji jing* of the fourth century has Lord Lao teach his followers the sexual methods of the "three, five, seven, and nine, the union between the inner and the outer" (DZ 1195, 3b, 5a).[27] The anti-Daoist polemic *Bianzheng lun* of the early Tang cites an otherwise lost text, the *Zhenren neili daojia neishi lü* (Esoteric Rites of the Perfected and Rules for Daoists in Attendance in the Inner Chamber), which describes the god as a master of sexual immortality practices and sponsor of the infamous "harmonizing of energies" (*heqi*), a form of ritual intercourse practiced among the early Celestial Masters.[28] This text reads:

> Laozi says: "My teacher taught me the *Jindan jing* [Scripture of Gold and Cinnabar]. He made me concentrate my mind and nourish my jade stalk [penis], return the yin essence in the [creation] rhythm of three, five, seven, and nine. He taught me to regulate my breathing and guide my jade-pond fluid [saliva] into my mysterious darkness [abdomen]. Thus, I practiced the Dao of mutual guarding and ascended to Great Clarity." (52.545c; Kohn 1995, 148 n. 7)

Before the Tang then, Lord Lao was seen as a master of different physical practices, but information on his role in them is scarce. In the early Tang, his hagiography by Yin Wencao, the *Hunyuan zhenlu*, links him with a large number of physical, alchemical, and meditational practices, and has him give detailed instructions on them to Yin Xi. In the late Tang, he himself is described as a student of various practices in Du Guangting's *Yongcheng jixian lu*.[29]

---

[26] Laozi's biography in the *Liexian zhuan* makes him a master of breathing and energy practices (Kaltenmark 1953, 61), while the *Shenxian zhuan* credits him with the revelation of many different methods (Kohn 1996, 59). For more on the immortals named and their roles as master practitioners, see Yamada 1989 and Sakade 1985.

[27] On the practices described here, see Baldrian-Hussein 1990, 175; Kobayashi 1992.

[28] The *Bianzheng lun* is found in the Buddhist canon (T. 2110). On Daoist sexual practices, see Kobayashi 1992, 27–31; Wile 1992.

[29] On the *Hunyuan zhenlu*, see Kusuyama 1977; 1979; Baldrian-Hussein 1990, 173. On the *Yongcheng jixian lu*, see Cahill 1986; 1993, 121–22. According to this, Laozi receives instructions from the Mother Goddess in ten sections (trans. in Kohn 1989c): (1) the basic constituents of the body (2b); (2) the retribution of good and bad deeds (3b); (3) summary of retribution theory (5a); (4) types of personality,

Texts other than hagiographies that describe practices as revealed or modeled by Lord Lao remain only from the late Tang. There are notably two sources, the *Yangsheng jue* (Instructions on Nourishing Life, DZ 821) and the *Zhiyan zong* (Comprehensive Perfect Words, DZ 1033).[30]

First, the *Yangsheng jue* gives instructions in four physical practices: (1) The Five Animals; (2) Breathing the Six Qi; (3) Nourishing Life; and (4) Breathing Exercises.

The "Five Animals" are a set of gymnastic exercises designed by the third-century physician Hua Tuo in imitation of the movements of tigers, bears, deer, monkeys, and birds, stretching and bending different parts of the body in the mode of the beasts. Through them "the hundred diseases will be completely expelled" (2a). Next, the "Six Qi" are better known as the "Six Sounds" (*liuzi jue*). They designate various noises made as one exhales breath, each of which has a healing effect on a particular organ, such as *si* on the lungs, *ke* on the heart, and *hu* on the spleen (2ab).[31]

Third, the section on "Nourishing Life" has a summary of the structure of the human body, seen as parallel to that of the state, with the stomach as the imperial palace, the limbs as the provincial governments, the bones as the hundred officials, the arteries as major thoroughfares, and *qi*-energy as the people (3a). Cultivating the body as they would govern the state, adepts place primary emphasis on the smooth circulation of energy in addition to expelling the six harm-bringers: fame and gain, sights and sounds, wealth and possessions, smell and taste, deceit and falsehood, jealousy and envy (3b). Reciting the scriptures, they attain moderation in emotions and stability of mind (3b), also taking care not to strain the body: no long sitting, walking, looking, listening; no eating to excess, no waiting to eat until famished (4a). Together with

---

body, and spirit (5b); (5) overview of Taoist methods (6a); (6) talismans, drugs, and breathing (6b); (7) details of practice (7a); (8) texts and methods of alchemy (7a); (9) karmic conditions for elixirs (7b); (10) the role of the Tao in the world (8a).

[30] On the former, see Li Yuanguo 1991, 1816; Ren and Zhong 1991, 587. The latter is also partially contained in *YJQQ* 35. See Li 1991, 1881; Ren and Zhong 1991, 777. On its textual history and date (including its relation to the *Zhaijie lu* [Record of Purifications and Precepts]), see Yoshioka 1967. Another late Tang source that has Lord Lao give instructions on physical methods and the concoction of an immortality drug is the *Lingfei sanfang chuanxin lu* (Transmitted Register of the Numinous Flying Powder Method, *YJQQ* 74), a short text describing a drug concocted with mica and various plant substances that was frequently used among late-Tang aristocrats. See Yoshikawa 1997.

[31] For a discussion of these techniques, see Miura 1989; Despeux 1995.

getting up early, retiring in good time, and never overdoing anything, this will give one's life a sedate rhythm that makes the mind tranquil and the body healthy.[32]

Fourth and finally, the *Yangsheng jue* describes breathing exercises, repeating instructions on the Six Sounds on the basis of the various organs (6ab). Finding cosmic energy in human breath, it describes the ocean of energy in the body as collecting cosmic power "just as mountains gather clouds and the earth gathers marshes" (5a). Adepts should exercise both in the morning and at night, breathing deeply and consciously and repeating the exercise ten times. The section ends with a renewed emphasis on the human body as constituted by spirit and energy and the need to cultivate both in order to attain the Dao. In tone and outlook it is not unlike the seventh-century *Cunshen lianqi ming* (Inscription on Visualization of Spirit and Refinement of Energy, DZ 834, *YJQQ* 33; Kohn 1987, 119).

A similar series of physical exercises is also described in chapter two of Fan Xiuran's *Zhiyan zong* of the ninth century, which in addition outlines rites of purification and moderation (ch. 1), taboos against demons and the invocation of the Dipper (ch. 3), specific methods of circulating energy (ch. 4), and massages and gymnastics associated with Lord Lao (ch. 5). Running the full gamut of Daoist physical practices, this text actively links the god with the various longevity techniques of the religion, building on earlier models, such as the *Yangxing yanming lu* (On Nurturing Inner Nature and Extending Life, DZ 838), associated with Tao Hongjing (see Mugitani 1987), but never losing sight of the overall aim of purity and tranquility reached through the elimination of desires and the observation of body and mind. The immortality training associated with Lord Lao in the late Tang thus actively joins physical practices with visualizations and insight meditation, casting the god in the role of the one deity responsible for the practical instruction of humanity.

Inner Alchemy

Inner alchemy (*neidan*) has been the leading form of Daoist practice since the Song, when it was formulated by the so-called Southern School (Nanzong). Represented by the masters Liu Cao (fl. 1031) and Zhang

---

[32] This is also similar to instructions in the *Tianyinzi*, which emphasizes the need to moderate one's behavior and control one's physical activities (Kohn 1987a, 10–11).

Boduan (d. 1082), the Southern School continued the tradition of operative alchemy, adding to it interior forms of meditation and the Tang practice of observation. Inner alchemy in Daoist practice creates an immortal embryo in a process described in terms of external alchemy and the dynamics of the *Yijing*. The embryo then becomes the carrier of the adept's eternal life and undertakes excursions into the heavens.[33] Not many texts of inner alchemy bear any relation to Lord Lao, who is linked with operative alchemy only in hagiographies and rather late ones at that (Baldrian-Hussein 1990, 172–75). Like the alchemical techniques of old, the new inner alchemical practices tend to be associated with more practically oriented immortals or more accessible sages such as the famous Lü Dongbin. However, the few texts that do mention Lord Lao as their source clearly join the new alchemical practices with the tradition of purity and tranquility.

Two texts stand out in this context:[34] the *Nei riyong miaojing* (Wondrous Scripture of Inner Daily Practice, DZ 645; Li 1991, 1821) and the *Wai riyong miaojing* (Wondrous Scripture of Outer Daily Practice, DZ 646). They provide a set of instructions divided according to "inner" and "outer," indicating the division between meditational and ethical practices.

First, the text on inner practice begins with instructions for the attainment of deep mental concentration:

> Keep the lips close to each other
> And the teeth lightly touching.
> Your eyes don't see a single thing,
> Your ears don't hear a single sound. (1a)

---

[33] For studies on inner alchemy, see Needham et al. 1983; Baldrian-Hussein 1984; Robinet 1995. An anthology is found in Cleary 1991.

[34] In addition, there are also two less important texts associated with the god, the *Neidan jing* (Scripture on Inner Alchemy, DZ 643; Li 1991, 1815) and its offshoot, the *Neidan shouyi jing* (Scripture of Guarding the One in Inner Alchemy, DZ 644; Ren and Zhong 1991, 631). Both provide a philosophical description of the inner-alchemical process and frequently use phrases typical for Tang observation texts. While the *Neidan jing* is placed clearly in the mouth of Lord Lao, the *Neidan shouyi jing*, although containing the same instructions, is spoken by the Highest Emperor of Primordial Beginning and his assistant, the Lord of the Dao, showing the close relation and interaction of the three highest Daoist gods. The dates of the texts are not clear, and they are not identical to *Laozi neidan jing* (Laozi's Scripture on Inner Alchemy) cited by Yang Gu under Emperor Zhenzong. See Loon 1984, 135; Baldrian-Hussein 1990, 177.

With the mind thus unified and firmly focused on within, the breathing is made regular and allowed to grow subtle, "almost as if it weren't there at all." As a result of this, the inner alchemical energies begin to rotate:

> Then naturally the fire of your heart
> Will sink down to the water of your kidneys
> And rise up to the cavern of your mouth,
> Where sweet saliva will arise of itself. (1a)

Once this stage of natural energy rotation is reached, it has to be maintained, preserving purity and tranquility at all times. This in turn leads to the spirit being at peace and vital energy growing in density and quality. Eventually energy becomes pure and moves through the body "like wind blowing and rumbling like booming thunder" (1b).

In a next step, this heavenly energy and the pure spirit join forces to create the immortal embryo, which in turn is transmuted:

> Next, refine the combination in nine transmutations
> And you will produce the great cinnabar elixir.
> Spirit will leave and enter freely,
> And your years will match those of heaven and of earth.
> The sun and moon will join to shine on you,
> And you will be liberated from all life and death. (1b)

This wonderful goal, however, can only be reached if adepts take the practice very seriously and never slacken in their efforts but work on it continuously like "a chicken hatching an egg" (1b). If they persevere, their entire bodies will be transformed into the seven treasures, with their bones, brain, organs, and body fluids all as lasting as precious stones and minerals (1b–2a).

While this represents an inner-alchemical development of the Tang vision of purity and tranquility, it is also linked with a set of moral rules, reflecting a growing concern with ethical standards and behavioral models in the Song. Forty-five such moral maxims are contained in the second text of the pair, on "outer daily practice." They range from basic obedience to one's parents through encouragements to be modest and do good to demands for active compassion toward the poor. For example,

> To your superiors be honest and withdrawing,
> To your inferiors be harmonious and kind.
> All good things do, all bad things eschew.
> From perfect people learn,
> Debauched people avoid. (1a)
> ...

Think of the poor and orphaned,
Give aid to the homeless and indigent.
Save those in danger and trouble,
Accumulate hidden merit.
Always practice compassion
And never kill any beings. (1b)

Following these rules and undertaking the alchemical effort described in the "inner practice," one will "ascend to the beyond," become one with the Dao, and join the heavenly realm. Practitioners are thus inspired to follow the god's instructions and eventually become like him, venerating Lord Lao as seeker and teacher. Nevertheless, although the god appears in these materials, they are only two among a vast number of inner alchemical texts in which he plays no role at all, reflecting a lessening of his importance under the Song.[35]

Modern Qi Exercises

Inner alchemy is still the leading Daoist practice, but today it is reinterpreted and reorganized around the practice of *qigong* or "*qi* exercises*," a collection of physical and meditational practices that include breathing, gymnastics, meditations, massages, laying-on of hands, and martial arts. Making use of ancient Daoist longevity techniques and inner alchemy, *qigong* denudes these practices of their religious dimension and redefines them as physical therapies, making them both scientifically acceptable to Western medicine and politically free of associations with shamanism, feudalism, and superstition.[36]

Lord Lao in contemporary works on *qigong* appears in two distinct roles: as an inspired teacher of meditation and a revealer of key texts, such as the *Daode jing*, the *Qingjing jing*, and the *Neiguan jing*. He is also portrayed as an active practitioner of breathing exercises and gymnastics, methods that have proved invaluable in securing a long and healthy life.[37]

---

[35] I am indebted to Catherine Despeux for reconfirming the rarity of Lord Lao's involvement in Song inner alchemical works as well as his absence in Ming and Qing work of this type.

[36] For discussions of *qigong* in China today and its use of modern science, see Li Yuanguo 1988; Miura 1989; Kohn 1993a.

[37] I am indebted to Detlef Kohn for making various works on modern *qigong* accessible to me and pointing out the roles Lord Lao played in them.

In his first role, the god is lauded as an ancient progenitor of *qigong*, whose notions of "returning to the root" and "preserving the One," as formulated first in the *Daode jing*, constitute the basis of *qigong* thought. More than that, in Lord Lao's teachings transmitted to Yin Xi and in the physical methods described in the *Yangsheng jue*, he gave the tradition a master-disciple model and outlined basic structures of contemporary health practices, even specifying that the realization of perfection should take about one thousand days. In addition, he also inspired modern practitioners in various other works, including the *Neiguan jing* on inner observation, the *Huangting jing* on visualizing the gods, the *Qingjing jing* on purity and tranquility, and the talismanic *Huming jing* on creating an atmosphere of power and protection.[38]

Furthermore, a specific message by the god on the practice of *qigong* was discovered at Louguan in a fourteen-character inscription interpreted as instructions given by Lord Lao in celestial writing. All fourteen words are unusual combinations of characters and can be found in the "Kangxi dictionary" but not elsewhere (Ren 1983, 3). They are read by dividing them into their constituent parts. So deciphered, the text reads:

> There is a treasure in the body,
> An elixir in the body.
> Produced through inner fire
> Refined in the rhythm of the five phases,
> It grows with the intention to extend life
> To years uncountable—
> And it is all there, present right in oneself!
>
> The proper cultivation of purity
> Is through the Dao that resides in people's hearts.
> Applying the teachings that transform inner nature
> One arrives at completeness.
> The heavenly well filled to overflowing
> With humanity's inner essence,
> One reaches perfection in nine cycles.
> (Ren 1983, 2–16)

The message of this rather cryptic inscription is that the Dao is an undiscovered treasure in everyone's body. It takes the form of various energies that can be refined in the rhythm of the five phases with the help of fire and water. This inner cultivation, if undertaken in accordance

---

[38] This role of Lord Lao is described in Li Yuanguo 1987, 46, 166, 191–92; 1988, 107; Yan 1989, 262. The *Huming jing* is discussed in ch. 5 below.

with the right teachings, will eventually lead to unlimited life and, in nine cycles, make the body overflow with health and vitality.

Lord Lao is not only an inspiration through his spiritual revelations, but also serves modern *qigong* as a successful practitioner (see Fig. 6). According to the movement's doctrine, he employed the methods of harmonizing and nourishing energy and gained his particular longevity through them. One set of methods especially associated with Lord Lao is called "Great Clarity" after his divine heaven; another more popular set is named "Complete Perfection." The latter has been transmitted secretly through the ages and was publicly unveiled at a meeting of the Shenyang Qigong Association in 1984. It is a technique of deep abdominal breathing and gymnastics that gives the practitioner inner peace and longevity.[39]

Divided into four parts, the Complete Perfection exercises begin with preparatory breathing, massages of the abdomen, neck stretches, and shoulder and hip rolls. Then adepts move on to relaxation through meditation with closed eyes while sitting cross-legged on a chair, or while standing up. Next, they undertake a series of arm and leg movements "to drive out heteropathies" (*quxie gong*) and eventually reach the arts of "renewal breathing and gymnastics" (*tu'na daoyin shu*). Here, too, with the body in different positions, the hands and legs are moved, the mind is calm and concentrated and moves along with the flow of energy to ensure maximum effect. Breathing continues to be deep and focused on the cinnabar field in the abdomen as the body's yin and yang energies are harmonized.[40]

Lord Lao thus plays a minor role as the revealer of inner alchemical techniques and survives as a modern master of *qigong*, although here too only as a lesser figure among many successful *qigong* masters, both ancient and contemporary. His appearance shows that he remains active as immortality master but it also documents his lessened importance in a tradition that has changed significantly and in its present form has broken to a large extent with its religious forebears, using ancient spirituality in a new, more medical, mold.

* * * * *

---

[39] On the Great Clarity methods, see Yu 1991, 161. On the Shenyang unveiling, see Liu Lizhen 1988, 2. A description of this technique is found in Wang and Du 1991, 168.

[40] The description follows Wang and Du 1991, 170–79; Liu Lizhen 1988, 2–3.

Fig. 6. Lord Lao as hoary practitioner of *qigong*.
Source: Shisizi yangsheng jue

Lord Lao as the source of wisdom scriptures and meditative and physical practices has been important in Daoism from the Han to the present day. Extant materials can be dated to specific periods—Han, the fifth century, and late Tang for wisdom scriptures, the fourth century and late Tang for early meditation texts, Song for inner alchemy, and the present for *qigong*. We can assume that his influence has been continuous through the ages, even though relatively few original texts have survived and we have only summaries of teachings, such as the *Zhiyan zong* or the *Cunsi tujue*, supplementing our knowledge.

Similarly sporadic is the identification of those who received the teachings in visions and/or compiled the texts. Whereas the *Daode jing* had a fairly clear group of Han dynasty adherents among aristocrats at court, unemployed literati, and followers of Huang-Lao, the *Taisu jing* stands utterly alone and is only vaguely dated to the Later Han, with no personality or group claiming responsibility for it. The *Xisheng jing* is clearly linked with the Louguan group, but the *Qingjing jing* and similar texts on purity and tranquility do not have specific compilers or communities at their back, and can only be linked by inference to the mystical observation culture associated with the Highest Clarity patriarch Sima Chengzhen. The same holds true for the materials on visualization and long life. The earliest association of Lord Lao with longevity and meditative practices goes back to the magical practitioners of the Han and comes to the fore among the southern alchemists in the milieu of Ge Hong and the forerunners of the Highest Clarity school. Their late Tang counterparts, on the other hand, remain largely in obscurity and we do not know who or where or what they were, but only that they, too, were concerned with purity and tranquility and thus with the observation culture of the time.

Still, from the contents of these texts, with their emphasis on personal realization of the Dao and long life, one can assume that their compilers were largely individual seekers of immortality and reclusive ascetics who saw Lord Lao as the master of their particular way of salvation and so attributed both the practice and the teaching of their methods to him. Such individual practitioners, then, seem to have been instrumental in his continued veneration as master of wisdom and spiritual practices. While many of them remained anonymous and unattached to specific sects or schools, at least some of them can be linked with certain organized groups, such as the Daoists at Louguan in the fifth century, the mystical fellowship around Sima Chengzhen, and the Southern School of inner alchemy in the Song. Furthermore, the same kind of individual seeker still seems to be active today, though now engaged in a new mode of Daoist practice transformed by modern medical methods and interpretations. That seeker still seems to find in the old figure of Lord Lao at least one source for his or her techniques. There are, therefore, strong indications of the god's continuity in this role; he has never ceased to serve as the source of individual practices—however much those practices and their rationale have changed over the centuries.

This continuity is also carried in the concrete contents of the texts: the shared *Daode jing* phrasing and terminology of the wisdom texts, the emphasis on purity and tranquility that has dominated ideas associated with Lord Lao since the late Tang, and the god's strong association with the four heraldic animals, key protectors in visualizations and long life and regular attendants of the god. In addition, the god's role as seeker of wisdom and immortality is part of his hagiography. It is first described in Du Guangting's *Yongcheng jixian lu*, then reiterated in later hagiographies of Lord Lao's divine mother. Represented as a sagely person of strong will and perseverance who wanders along the same paths as his followers, Lord Lao in these texts is a man among men, a companion and guide on a difficult road who serves his like-minded disciples with all the flexibility of the Dao itself.

4

Rules and Rituals
Lord Lao as the Object of Communal Worship

R eligious communities commonly depend on rules and rituals that enhance their coherence and keep their followers together in a harmonious life and integrated spiritual purpose. Such rules and rituals range from moral guidelines and prohibitions through prescriptions for ordinary behavior that regulate the details of everyday activities—rising and retiring, washing and bathing, eating and resting—to highly formalized rites of worship and service to their god or gods. Both the contents of the rules and the exact procedures of the daily formalities and rituals are believed to issue directly from the wishes and instructions of the deity and often in their textual descriptions are either linked with revelation stories or with outlines of his heavenly activities, of which the earthly counterparts are either an imitation or a match.

In accordance with these general observations, the rules and rituals associated with Lord Lao in traditional China are all part of specific religious communities and recognized Daoist schools. Many of them, indeed, have tales of revelation and/or celestial activities of the god attached to them, linking them immediately with the physical presence of the deity and his personal wishes and instructions. None have survived from the early period; those extant and associated with Lord Lao begin only in the fifth century, but they continue actively throughout the late Tang and Song and into the present (see Table 5).

The first of these were revealed to the fifth century Celestial Masters, in both north and south China. Next, a set of spells and talismans linked with the constellation of the Dipper emerged in the late Tang. It was, however, mythically placed in the second century and associated with the revelation of the Dao to Zhang Daoling. The Song school of the Heavenly Heart (Tianxin) introduced both a visualization of the celestial Laozi and a revelation of talismans and spells from the god; its community on Mao-

Table 5
Texts on Lord Lao's rules and rituals

Text	English title, Source
Community Rules	
Laojun yinsong jiejing	Scripture of Recited Precepts of Lord Lao, DZ 785
Laojun shuo yibai bashi jie	180 Precepts Revealed by Lord Lao, DZ 768, YJQQ 39
Laojun jiejing	Scripture of Precepts of Lord Lao, DZ 784
Chuanshou jingjie yi zhujue	Annotated Explanation of the Transmission Formalities of Scriptures and Precepts, DZ 1238
The Dipper	
Beidou changsheng jing	Scripture of Attaining Longevity with the Help of the Northern Dipper, DZ 623
Beidou yansheng jing	Scripture of Extending Life with the Help of the Northern Dipper, DZ 622
Dongdou huming jing	Scripture of Protecting Life with the Help of the Eastern Dipper, DZ 625
Nandou duren jing	Scripture of Salvation with the Help of the Southern Dipper, DZ 624
Xidou hushen jing	Scripture of Protecting the Body with the Help of the Western Dipper, DZ 626
Zhongdou baoming jing	Scripture of Maintaining Life with the Help of the Central Dipper, DZ 627
Yisuan shenfu miaojing	Wondrous Scripture of Divine Talismans to Extend the Reckoning, DZ 672
Wudou shousheng jing	Scripture of the Five Dippers Granting Long Life, DZ 653
Heavenly Heart	
Yutang dafa	Great Methods of the Jade Hall, DZ 220
Changsheng yisuan miaojing	Wondrous Scripture of Extending the Reckoning and [Reaching] Eternal Life, DZ 650
Jiusheng jing	Scripture on Saving Living Beings, DZ 630
Protection of Life	
Huming jing	Scripture on Protecting Life, DZ 632
Yinfan jing	Scripture of Esoteric Brahma [Spells], DZ 633
Taishang laojun shuo xiaozai jing	Scripture for Dispelling Disasters, Revealed by Lord Lao, DZ 631

shan received from Lord Lao and presented to the court the eleventh-century *Huming jing*, a short but powerful text of incantations that was highly efficacious in the healing of diseases. In addition, the god was venerated by the two major schools, the Celestial Masters and Complete Perfection, a veneration that continues to the present day. He is still lauded as the root of their teachings and worshiped in various rituals.

Revelation stories associated with rules and rituals typically tell how the deity floated down from the sky, often accompanied by several attendants if not an extensive entourage, to reveal precepts and forms of ritual practice to his newly chosen representatives, who in turn become the central movers of new Daoist communities and lineages. The revelations typically follow the pattern established in the first revelation to Zhang Daoling. They are also consistent with visions of the god under the Tang, and in some cases they parallel ordination procedures in Daoist communities. These stories appear predominantly in texts on rules and rituals; they may also reflect visualization practices since Lord Lao appears in them not only as the revealer of methods but also as the object of the technique. They are different from texts on wisdom and longevity, which usually do not contain revelation stories, but only state "Laozi said" without specifying the context or vision of the deity.[1] Moreover, while wisdom texts often remain vague in their attribution and tend to focus more on the individual realization of the Dao, rules and rituals are closely connected with known communities and specific lineages.

Community Rules

Lord Lao became the giver of community rules only in the fifth century when he appeared to the Celestial Masters. At that time, he provided three sets of rules and ritual instruction, which still survive in the Daoist canon.[2]

He appeared first to the "new Celestial Master" Kou Qianzhi in 415 and 423, in an elaborate vision described in detail in the *Weishu* (History of the Northern Wei, ch. 114). Accompanied by celestial guards and assistants, he presented to Kou the so-called New Code, part of which is extant in the *Laojun yinsong jiejing* (Scripture of Recited Precepts of Lord Lao, DZ 785).[3] This text consists of thirty-six rules, each introduced with

---

[1] Exceptions are the *Daode jing* itself and the *Xisheng jing*, which are both set at the god's encounter with Yin Xi on the pass.

[2] Preceding these, rules associated with, if not revealed by, Lord Lao also appear in connection with the *Xianger* commentary to the *Daode jing*. See Bokenkamp 1997, 49–50.

[3] Kou Qianzhi (365–448) was born into a Celestial Masters family and became a visionary on Mount Sung. After a second revelation, he went to court, where he found the support of prime minister Cui Hao and became head of the Daoist theocracy that set up Daoist organizations and instituted rituals to bring stability to the northern (Toba) Wei empire. The high point of his career was reached in 440, when the emperor himself accepted Daoist initiation and changed the reign to True Lord of Great Peace. Successful for some time, the theocracy declined with Kou's death in 448 and ended with Cui's execution in 451. For details see Ware 1933; Yang 1956; Tang and Tang 1961; Tsukamoto 1961, 321; Ōzaki, 1979;

"Lord Lao said" and concluding with the admonition to "honor and follow this rule with awareness and care, in accordance with the statutes and ordinances!"[4]

The first six rules serve as an introduction, describing the text's revelation in terms similar to those in the *Weishu*. Thereafter, they appear in no particular order, presenting general guidelines, specific behavioral rules, and detailed ritual instructions. The general guidelines include an outline of the various offices and duties of Daoist followers and a survey of banquet meetings and communal rites (e.g., nos. 7–9). Specific behavioral rules describe the role of Daoists in relation to the civil administration, patterns of public conduct, and measures to be taken in case of sickness (e.g., no. 21). Detailed ritual instructions, finally, deal with the holding of communal banquets, the proper format of prayers and petitions to the Dao, ancestral offerings, funeral services, and immortality practices (e.g., no. 12). Lord Lao in the early fifth century is thus linked with the establishment and initiation of organized Daoist practice, guiding his followers in their communities to proper ritual worship and public conduct.

Lord Lao is also the source of the southern Celestial Masters' *Laojun shuo yibai bashi jie* (180 Precepts Revealed by Lord Lao, DZ 768, *YJQQ* 39), which scholars date to the fourth century and link with certain Buddhist *vinaya* rules (Penny 1996). The text reflects a continuation of early Celestial Masters rules, based largely on the *Daode jing*, and represents one step toward the overall reorganization of the southern community under the Liu-Song dynasty of the fifth century.[5]

Mather 1979; Tang 1981; Seidel 1983, 353–55; Zhu 1992, 65; Yamada 1995, 72; Robinet 1997, 74–76.

[4] This formula is a variant of the standard admonition used among the early Celestial Masters, "Swiftly, swiftly, in accordance with the statutes and ordinances!" Among extant texts, this occurs most commonly in the *Nüqing guilü* (Nüqing's Statutes Against Demons, DZ 790) of the fourth century. In addition, it appears in tomb texts of the Han dynasty (see Seidel 1987) and in the Japanese Shugendō ritual (see R. Maeda 1989; Miyake 1993; Miyazawa 1994).

[5] This text has not survived independently but is contained in various collections: *YJQQ* 39.1a–14b; *Laojun jinglü* (Scriptural Rules of Lord Lao, DZ 768); *Yaoxiu keyi* (Essential Rules and Observances, DZ 463) 5.14a–19a. In addition, it is found in two Dunhuang manuscripts (P. 4731, P. 4562), reprinted in Ōfuchi 1979, 685. A recent translation of the text is found in Hendrischke and Penny 1996; for a study and dating, see Penny 1996. See also Schmidt 1985. On other precepts of the Celestial Masters, see Bokenkamp 1993; Schipper 1994a, 67. For Lu Xiujing's reorganization of the school under the Liu-Song, see Bell 1987; 1988; Nickerson 1994; 1996. A general account and detailed study of all the texts is, moreover, found in Kobayashi 1990.

Its rules place a great emphasis on personal honesty and propriety in community life and strongly prohibit theft, adultery, killing, abortion, intoxication, the destruction of natural resources, and wasting food. They also prescribe proper behavior toward community members and outsiders, prohibiting fraternization with brigands and soldiers, punishing cruelty to slaves and animals, and insisting on polite distance when encountering outsiders and officials. In addition, many details of daily life are regulated, discouraging pettiness and rudeness as much as the accumulation of personal wealth. Members must not put down the merit of others, pick nice lodgings for themselves, or curse others as doing evil.

In addition, the preface of the text, a composite work that was edited in the sixth century, contains Lord Lao's words in praise of these precepts and his instructions on how to receive them.[6] According to this, the god said:

Even if human beings live as long as ten thousand years, without receiving the precepts how are they different from ancient trees or rocks? Much better to receive the precepts today and die as a man of the Dao and its virtue after living a life without evil. . . .

Before receiving the precepts, adepts must bathe and abstain from eating rich foods containing the five tastes and the five pungent vegetables. Next they change into formal robes, then pay formal respects to their instructors. Only after this may they prostrate themselves on the ground to hear and repeat the precepts. They also receive a written version of them, which they will copy at least once and recite daily (Maeda 1985, 84).

This text, then, links the deity not only with the concrete daily behavior of communal Daoists but also with formal ordination procedures, which here are prescribed directly by him. Lord Lao serves as the source of both organization and salvation in the Daoist community; he exerts a civilizing, morally uplifting, and overall stabilizing influence among the faithful, leading them to the Dao not only in doctrine but also in daily practice.

The third set of precepts associated with Lord Lao in the fifth century is contained in the incomplete *Laojun jiejing* (Scripture of Precepts of Lord Lao, DZ 784; trans. Kohn 1994). It consists of a group of five rules that follow the five precepts of Buddhism—no killing, stealing, lying, sexual misconduct, or intoxication—and are presented with heavy

---

[6] The preface has three parts, only the third of which goes back to the fifth century. The other two were added later to establish a link between the precepts and the *Taiping jing* (Scripture of Great Peace). See Maeda 1985.

reference to Daoist cosmology. Set at the meeting of Laozi and Yin Xi at Louguan, this text was compiled by Louguan Daoists toward the end of the fifth century and established basic community rules. It imitates Kou Qianzhi's "New Code" in that it begins with a description placing the god and human beings in the same location and introduces each section with "Lord Lao said." Beyond that, it also draws on the popular Buddhist *Tiwei boli jing* (Sūtra of [the Lay Followers] Trapusa and Bhallika), written around 450 by the monk Tanjing, a follower of Tanyao who developed the saṅgha-household system for the northern rulers.[7]

In content, it includes eight sections: an introductory description of Lord Lao's emigration, a song of praise in three stanzas, and answers to the six questions of Yin Xi:

1. What are the exact words of the precepts?
2. Why are there five?
3. What if one loses them?
4. What is their deepest root?
5. How does one receive them?
6. What violations are there in worshiping the scriptures?

In the answers to these questions, the god provides a detailed description, cosmological rationale, and explanation of the karmic relevance of all five precepts, ending with an account of Daoist ordination rites similar to that in the "180 Precepts" but under Buddhist influence. The text spells out the benefits and advantages of following the Dao, but does not hesitate to threaten hell and bad rebirths for nonbelievers. It ends inconclusively, however, since it has not survived in its entirety. Like its two earlier counterparts, it is concerned with the organization of a true society of the Dao, addressing community followers and postulants for higher office and showing Lord Lao as the giver of detailed rules and rituals for conducting a pious Daoist life on earth.

Another Louguan text that supplements the basic rules and ordination procedures is the *Chuanshou jingjie yi zhujue* (Annotated Explanation of the Transmission Formalities of Scriptures and Precepts, DZ 1238), a sixth-century technical manual on ordination. It consists of an introduction that describes Lord Lao as the highest sage of Great Mystery and teacher of the Dao, as well as thirteen sections that

---

[7] On this text, see Lai 1987, 13. On the saṅgha-households, see Sargent 1957. A further possible source of the text, from the southern school of Numinous Treasure, is the *Ziran wucheng jing* (The Five Spontaneous Correspondences, DZ 671), which also speaks of rules and five-phases cosmology in sections introduced with "Lord Lao said." See Kobayashi 1990, 197; Bokenkamp 1997, 63.

specify ordination procedures. These begin with a list of scriptures to be received, then move on to the masters and supporters necessary, the proper time schedule, the correct ways of copying the scriptures and memorials, and the required material pledges; they also provide exact formulations of the divine petitions to be filed with the gods (Ren and Zhong 1991, 979).

In accordance with Louguan doctrine, Lord Lao is at the center of worship, the highest lord who represents the pure ground of existence: "High without compare, he is called great; present but invisible, he is the mystery" (1a). Despite his formless heavenly stature, he arose among humanity, was born under the plum tree, and took the personal name Er. He served as an archivist under the Zhou and revealed the *Daode jing* to Yin Xi (1b–2a). The *Daode jing*, then, stands at the head of the altogether ten key scriptures, representing the first two, the *Daojing* and the *Dejing*. The remainder include the Heshang gong and *Xianger* commentaries (two texts each), a visualization chart centering on Lord Lao (possibly a precursor of the *Cunsi tujue*), a list of precepts, ordinances for worship, and instructions for communal purification ceremonies (4b–5a). The texts reappear later in the integrated ordination system as the scriptures transmitted in *Daode jing* ordination, which grants the rank of Preceptor of Lofty Mystery (Gaoxuan fashi). The ritual, too, is similar to later standardized procedures described in the *Fengdao kejie* (Rules and Precepts for Worshiping the Dao, DZ 1125) of the seventh century and detailed again by Zhang Wanfu in the eighth.[8]

Lord Lao among the medieval Celestial Masters is thus the giver of rules and ritual instructions, a celestial creator god who nonetheless appears among humanity, a figure both divine and human. He is divine as the personification of the ineffable Dao, the deepest power behind all salvational teachings and human as the teacher of Yin Xi and active guide of followers, both lay and ordained. He is a powerful communal god, a savior who accommodates human needs and responds to the demands of the time.

The Dipper

In a very similar role Lord Lao appears again in the late Tang to Song periods, when various Daoist groups that remain shrouded in mystery received revelations from him regarding the proper performance

---

[8] On Tang ordination, see Schipper 1985a; Benn 1991.

of Daoist rites and the activation of spells and talismans. Several sets of texts present Lord Lao in this function at this time. The first of them is a set of six texts that contain talismans and invocations of the Dippers of the five directions. These are divided according to geographical direction into materials concerning the Northern (DZ 622, 623), Southern (DZ 624), Eastern (DZ 625), Western (DZ 626), and Central Dippers (DZ 627; see Table 5 above). They present sacred spells associated with the constellation Ursa Major, providing talismans for summoning its gods and describing the benefits of the repeated recitation of the spells. Linked explicitly with Lord Lao, they purport to record a second major revelation to Zhang Daoling in 155 C.E., after he had already received the Covenant of Highest Unity in 142. The preface to the "Southern Dipper Scripture" (DZ 624), in particular, details the circumstances of the revelations and summarizes the standard biography of the first Celestial Master.

In content, these texts outline devotional measures of protection involving scriptural recitation and formal rites for the Dippers, preferably undertaken on one's birthday, on the new moon, or on generally auspicious days. For example:

> To recite this scripture, you must first develop the utmost sincerity and purify your mind. Then, facing east, clap your teeth and pay reverence in your heart. Kneeling, close your eyes and visualize the gods [of the Eastern Dipper] as if you physically saw the limitless realm of the east. Mysterious numinous forces, imperial lords, the realized perfected, and great sages—a countless host lines up before you. Looking at them will help you overcome days of disaster. (DZ 625, 2b)

In addition, the texts provide talismans for a petition to summon the six officers of the Dipper to protect life and help in difficulties.

> The True Lords of the Six Stars, the Divine Lads of the Six Stars, the Generals of Fire Bell—whenever you recite this text with utmost sincerity and pray to them with a pure heart, they will respond immediately. As long as you are diligent in worship and in the petition's presentation, the perfected sages will descend to protect you from all harm and extend your years. You will live as long as the Dao itself. (DZ 624, 5a)

The talismans are used in the presentation of the petition and contain the power to make the gods respond. The latter then hasten to assist the practitioner speedily and efficiently; they are utterly reliable and immediately available to rescue those in need.[9] Daoist practice, when supported by this powerful divine help, becomes smooth and harmonious, efficacious and successful.

The actual date of the Dipper texts' composition is not clear. Ren and Zhong date them to the Tang–Song transition (1991, 451), while Xu Daoling, a Yuan dynasty commentator on the "Northern Dipper Scripture" (DZ 750), links them with Du Guangting of the late Tang (Boltz 1987, 247). They were available in the Song[10] and later associated with the Heavenly Heart school, but this does not mean that they go back as far as the Tang. They show neither the strong concern for observation and mental purification typical of late Tang texts associated with Lord Lao, nor the technical nature and concern with numerology and *Yijing* hexagrams frequently found in Song materials on inner alchemy. On the other hand, they all agree that the revelation took place in Sichuan, locating it in the capital city. In some cases (DZ 622, 1a), they refer to Lord Lao's throne as the "Jade Seat" (*yuju*), the name of a monastery in Chengdu (Li 1985, 78), where according to Du Guangting Lord Lao made a miraculous appearance. This information might suggest that a local Sichuan Daoist of the Five Dynasties was the compiler of the Dipper texts.

Although these texts became part of the Heavenly Heart tradition under the Song, the Sichuan center continued to be fruitful, as is documented in a Yuan dynasty compilation. The *Yisuan shenfu miaojing* (Wondrous Scripture of Divine Talismans to Extend the Reckoning, DZ 672), another collection of spells and talismans linked with the Dipper, relates how Lord Lao and the Celestial Master wander to the celestial country of Chanli and observe how humanity suffers. Upon the request of the Celestial Master, Lord Lao explains how people can be liberated by pursuing purity through fasting, rituals, and the wearing of Dipper talismans. Then he accompanies the Celestial Master to Chengdu and there, on the seventh day of the first month in 155 C.E., sets up a jade

---

[9] This reputation for reliability has remained to the present day, when the Dipper gods are invoked regularly during so-called Dipper Festivals (*lidou fahui*) at popular temples in Taipei. The invocation usually lasts three to five days and involves the recitation of various of the Dipper scriptures discussed here. See Matsumoto 1997.

[10] Chao Gongwu mentions the Northern and Southern Dipper texts in his *Junzhai dushu zhi* (Record of Charts and Books in My Study) of the year 1151 (Loon 1984, 109, 116). See also Franke 1990, 98–100.

throne from which to teach him the divine law and dispense wondrous talismans.[11]

In addition, these later Dipper texts contributed to the creation of the Buddhist *Beidou jing* (Scripture of the Northern Dipper), which survives in Chinese, Uighur, Mongolian, and Tibetan versions, and several other sūtras on "rites and recitations for the Northern Dipper" that are associated with the eighth-century Tantric masters Vajrabodhi and Amoghavajra.[12] Although claiming to date back to the Tang, these texts were probably compiled under the Yuan when the 1281 proscription of Daoist materials encouraged the increased production of popular talismans and spells among Buddhists. In later years transmitted to Japan, they exerted a significant influence on the doctrines and practices of Yoshida Shintō.[13] This revelatory and communal aspect of the Daoist god was therefore not limited to China and Daoism but spread both into Buddhism and Japanese Shintō, infusing Dipper spells and talismans into various traditions of East Asia.

The School of the Heavenly Heart

Another organized group that made use of Lord Lao and his association with spells and talismans is the Heavenly Heart school, which had its roots in the Tang–Song transition but was officially founded only after the find of wondrous texts on Mount Huagai in 994. The school's texts and talismans were formally codified by Yuan Miaozong (fl. 1086–1116) in 1116 and popularized in later compendia.[14] It was one among several new lineages created by Daoist masters who, after the far-reaching changes in Daoist organization at the end of the

---

[11] Another Yuan dynasty text that continues the Dipper tradition is the *Wudou shousheng jing* (Scripture of the Five Dippers Granting Long Life, DZ 653), which also describes Lord Lao talismans for a variety of life situations. Ren and Zhong 1991, 466. Yet another related text of the Song is the *Beidi yansheng bijue* (Secret Instructions of the Northern Emperor on the Extension of Life, DZ 1265; YJQQ 25, 1a–10b). See Andersen 1991, 71.

[12] The *Beidou jing* is found in T. 1307; 21.25b–26b and discussed in Franke 1990. Other Buddhist texts concerning the Dipper are contained in T. 1305 and 1306, 21.423c–25a. The two Tantric masters' Chinese names are Jingangzhi (617–741) and Bukong jingang (705–775).

[13] On the linkage of the Buddhist texts with the Daoist persecution, see Franke 1990, 107. For a discussion of Dipper worship in Shintō, see Sakade and Masuo 1991.

[14] On this school and its texts, see Boltz 1987, 33–38; Andersen 1991; Drexler 1994; Skar 1997, 170.

Tang, lived as recluses while concocting their own teachings, which they devised as they traveled through the country and learned from other isolated figures. Many of them established new lines of doctrine and practice.[15] The therapeutic and protective methods of the Heavenly Heart focused specifically on the Dipper and Pole Star (the "heart of heaven"), but the school also favored visualizations in the Highest Clarity style.

Masters of the Heavenly Heart, like other (often itinerant) ritual practitioners of the time, offered treatments for diseases and social problems to the wider populace in performances that mixed therapeutics and theatrics. Among their most important methods were the so-called thunder rites (*leifa*) that established a link between the practicing Daoist and the powers of heaven, and often used lightning-struck wood in the production of efficacious talismans.[16] Instead of being mere earthly representatives of certain celestial deities, practitioners of this type "metamorphosed themselves" into the gods, taking charge of the world from a supernatural position and creating an ambience for their rituals that closely imitated celestial fittings (Boltz 1987, 25). They thus joined traditional visualization with formal rituals and the writing of talismans.

In one of the Heavenly Heart visualizations, Lord Lao appears in Lu Shizhong's *Yutang dafa* (Great Methods of the Jade Hall, DZ 220), dated to 1158 (see Andersen 1991, 97–101; Davis 1996, 115). According to this text, which claims to represent essential methods of Zhang Daoling revealed in a vision of his disciple Zhao Sheng to Lu Shizhong, the god is envisioned both in his celestial palace and in the head of the practitioner (see Fig. 7). The text runs:

Greeting the Primordial Energy During a Jade Hall Audience

The Master said: Those who pursue perfection to attend a formal audience [above] should enter the [meditation] chamber and sit upright, then visualize themselves enveloped by a perfected energy which radiates as brightly as the moon. In the middle of this radiance they then see the golden towers on the mountain of Mystery Metropolis [Xuandu], among which is a hall of white jade where Lord Lao resides. [Seeing him], they can ascend to the hall and meet him in formal audience.
 Now chant:

---

[15] An example for such a master is Wang Qixia, a Highest Clarity patriarch who sought to reestablish an orthodox line of transmission. See Sakauchi 1988. On the Song lineages, see Skar 1997, 176–77.

[16] See Boltz 1987, 24; Skar 1997, 161.

Fig. 7. Lord Lao visualized in the Jade Hall.
Source: Yutang dafa 3.2b-3a

Heaven is pure, the earth is flat,
The sun and moon issue bright radiance.
I stride on primordial energy
And ascend to greet the Lord of Heaven.
May the Lord of Heaven come to me
And make my body radiate with brightness!
May the mysterious, primordial, and beginning energies
Protect me forever and grant me long life!

Note: After chanting this incantation visualize Lord Lao between your eyebrows. His radiance divides into a sun and a moon, which shine within you. Breathing in, you inhale them and they illuminate your entire body. (3.2ab)

The god here is the ruler of heaven who resides in Mystery Metropolis and brings forth the three basic energies of the universe. The correct visualization of him combined with the proper spell allows adepts to rise up and greet him in his hall, then entice the deity to merge with them and shine through them with his celestial purity.

A more talismanic vision of the god is found in another text of the same affiliation, the *Changsheng yisuan miaojing* (Wondrous Scripture of Extending the Reckoning and [Reaching] Eternal Life, DZ 650). Here Lord Lao, again in a revelation scenario, orders the True Lord of Long Life of the Eastern Ultimate (Dongji changsheng zhenjun) to take the gods of the Six Jia and travel to all countries to give people talismans and registers and help them extend their lives. He encourages his followers to observe the rites and venerate the gods of the Dao, so that they can gradually free themselves from suffering. The deities mentioned in this text are astral constellations in the center of the sky and important gods of the Heavenly Heart tradition: the nine stars of the Dipper, the Three Terraces, and the five planets. Talismans include magical means to "open the heart," "extend the reckoning," "protect life," counter baleful energies, and dispel ghosts and demons. Practitioners obtain the talismans and venerate the starry deities to improve their lives and attain good fortune.[17]

The same pattern is further present in the *Jiusheng jing* (Scripture on Saving Living Beings, DZ 630), according to which Lord Lao resides in the heaven of Purple Tenuity (also in the center of the sky) and exhorts a host of 8,000 followers to observe the rites and recite his

---

[17] On this text, see Ren and Zhong 1991, 464–65. For the deities and talismans, see Drexler 1994, 85–99.

scriptures. Here, too, his main activity is the distribution of efficacious talismans and the sending out of his official agents, the Six Jia.[18]

The Protection of Life

Another important ritual text associated with Lord Lao in the Song was linked with the old Highest Clarity center on Maoshan. The *Huming jing* is a short incantation scripture of 400 characters and twenty-four talismans that appears in three editions in the Daoist canon (DZ 632, 633, 762) and has a preface by Emperor Zhenzong, dated to 1014.[19] The emperor lauds the text for its perfected words whose power inevitably elicits a divine response. He describes the scripture as the "secret declaration of Great Clarity, the precious talisman of [Lord] Goldtower" (16a), and praises its efficacy against evil. In addition, the *Yunji qiqian* recounts a miracle tale about the scripture, set in the year 892 (16b–18a). At that time Li Wanshou of Yizhou (Sichuan), having lost his family in the civil war leaves his ravaged hometown in search of distant relatives. Walking through the wilderness, he suddenly feels the sun darkening as if night were falling, and seeks shelter at a dilapidated hut.

His knock is answered by a woman who refuses to let him stay because her husband is a "sickness-causing demon king." Deciding that he might as well die at the hands of a demon as on the road, Li insists on being let in and she hides him in a large earthenware jar, where he recites the *Huming jing* to calm his terror. Eventually the demon returns, having fled from a terrible defeat that scattered his entourage, and reports that his house is surrounded by *vajras* (diamond bodhisattvas, *jingang*) and *vīras* (demi-gods, *lishi*) and enveloped in a purple haze, in which an immortal hovers on a white crane.[20] He and his group had encountered an old man (presumably Lord Lao) with four eyes and accompanied by over 300,000 troops who attacked them. The demon

---

[18] On the text see Ren and Zhong 1991, 153–54. For a discussion of the Six Jia gods, see chapter 3, note 16.

[19] The most frequently used version of the text (DZ 632) is also contained, with minor variants, in Hong Mai's (1123–1202) *Yijian zhi* (New Marvels from Yijian), 1784–85 (Beijing: Zhonghua, 1980). See Hervouet 1978, 344. For a discussion of the text and its history, see Skar 1997, 166–67, 173. The preface is also found in *Hunyuan shengji* 9.39b–40a.

[20] Such Tantric gods as summoned by Lord Lao in protection of the faithful also occur in the *Taishang laojun shuo xiaozai jing* (Scripture for Dispelling Disasters, Revealed by Lord Lao, DZ 631), a text of uncertain date set in a conversion setting. See Ren and Zhong 1991, 454.

barely managed to escape and was now looking for the civilian with magical powers who had caused all the trouble.

The woman denies her guest's existence, and the demon runs off again to be completely destroyed by the divine soldiers. Impressed by the powers of the scripture, his widow then begs Li to teach her its recitation. Together they leave the hut to find the darkness and bad miasma of the place changed to a divine light with wonderful fragrance. They return to her hometown where she is happily reunited with her natal family, while Li becomes a Daoist at a local monastery, chanting and transmitting the *Huming jing* with great success.

Although this story is certainly apocryphal, it gives a vivid impression of the powers associated with the scripture and its recitation. Not only credited with personal rescues, in a postface by Fu Xiao (DZ 632)[21] the text is also linked with the success of dynasties and put on par with Lord Lao's manifestation at the beginning of the Tang (3b–4a) and the Heavenly Treasure find of 741 (4b). Moreover, in 1109, in another revelation story associated with the scripture, it was presented by Lord Lao himself to the Maoshan Daoist Liang Wuzhen and proved efficacious in the curing of diseases (5ab).[22] The sequence of miracles and editions shows that the text enjoyed considerable standing among Daoists in general while also serving to increase the fame of the Highest Clarity center at Maoshan.

Among the several versions of the text, Fu Xiao's edition of 1144 (DZ 632) is used most commonly in connection with Lord Lao, even among modern *qigong* practitioners (see Li 1987, 191–92). This version is identical with the one used by Hou Shanyuan, who wrote a commentary on it in 1192 (DZ 762). It is not the oldest text, however, but seems to have been edited from an earlier, more Tantric version entitled *Yinfan jing* (Scripture of Esoteric Brahma [Spells], DZ 633), which goes back at least to the reign of Song Zhenzong. It has the same basic incantations as the later *Huming jing* but combines them with Tantric spells in Sanskrit and with the invocation of Song guardian deities and powerful gods of the thunder rites.[23]

---

[21] On Fu Xiao, a classical scholar, calligrapher, and Maoshan Daoist, see Boltz 1987, 134 nn. 263, 329; Strickmann 1981, 46–47.

[22] According to a variant, the events occurred in 1112. The Daoist was named Liang Guanzying, and the scripture cured him of leprosy. See *Hunyuan shengji* 9.46a.

[23] On the text's history and editions, see Ren and Zhong 1991, 455; Li 1991, 1824–25; Skar 1997, 167n 6, 168.

In content, the *Huming jing* leads the practitioner from ordinary life through several levels of divine help to harmony with the higher cosmic forces, and eventually guides him to the heart of the Dao. It begins, not unlike earlier meditations associated with Lord Lao, by setting up an active cosmic context:

> Sovereign heaven raises me,
> Sovereign earth supports me,
> Sun and moon glow for me,
> Stars and planets shine on me,
>
> All immortals assist me,
> The Ruler of Fates champions me,
> The Great Unity joins me,
> The Jade Star summons me,
>
> The Three Bureaus protect me,
> The Five Emperors guard me. (DZ 632, 1a)

Continuing along these lines, the text next summons jade maidens and the Six Jia gods, then invokes the four heraldic animals and other starry constellations:

> Before me is the vermilion bird,
> Behind me the dark warrior,
> To my left, the blue dragon,
> To my right, the white tiger.
>
> Above me hangs the flowery canopy,
> Below I step on the Kui star of the Dipper.
> The divine Dao illuminates all,
> Its majesty banning evil in the ten directions. (1b)

Established in this position of power, all the practitioner desires will be granted, and everything he attempts will succeed. Furthermore, with the help of thousands of celestial supporters, "swiftly, swiftly, in accordance with the statutes and ordinances," he can shape his environment to his will:

> All who love me shall live in peace!
> All who hate me shall meet with disaster!
> All who plot against me shall die!
> All who detest me shall perish!

Numinous lads and spirit maidens–
Destroy all evil with your diamond bolts!
All three thousand six hundred of you,
Always remain by my side!

Chanting these powerful lines while holding on to the twenty-four talismans, adepts place themselves in the center of the cosmos and concentrate its demon-quelling and healing powers on themselves to ensure their safety and bring beneficent energy to the world. Used in the performance of thunder rites, this scripture of Lord Lao was acknowledged by Song practitioners as a very important work, on equal footing with earlier texts of high rank and a major revelation of the deity (Skar 1997, 173). Lord Lao as the instructor of Daoist ritual was thus a force to be reckoned with, not only among the medieval Celestial Masters but also under the late Tang and Song.

The Object of Worship

Lord Lao as the revealer of rules and rituals was also continuously revered as a central high god by both the dominant schools of late imperial Daoism, Complete Perfection and the Celestial Masters.[24] While Complete Perfection Daoists were especially prominent under the Jin and Yuan, wrote variously about Lord Lao, and left behind artistic representations of the god, little is known about the activities of the Celestial Masters in the Song since they only reentered the national arena after the Yuan conquest of southern China in 1275.

Helping the Mongols to establish an administrative presence, they were rewarded with the official school name "Profound Teaching" (Xuanjiao), and their representatives, learned gentlemen like Yu Ji who combined Daoist and Confucian ideas with art and literature, were given high honors at court, leading to the appointment of the Celestial Master as an imperial official under the Ming.[25] At this time, the forty-third Master Zhang Yuchu (1361–1410) named Lord Lao as the originator of all Daoist teachings in his *Daomen shigui* (Ten Statutes for Daoist Followers, DZ 1232; Boltz 1987, 241) and attributed to him not only the ancient

---

[24] Among the Celestial Masters, he appears regularly as the high deity to whom petitions were addressed. An example, dated from the late Tang, is translated in Nickerson 1997.

[25] On the role of Daoists at court at this time, see Sun 1981; Ten Broeck and Yiu 1950. A general survey of the Celestial Masters under the Ming is found in Zhuang 1986, 53.

doctrines of the philosophers but also those of Huang-Lao Daoism and all religious revelations (3b–4a).[26]

Lord Lao as a senior god of Daoism, preceded by the Three Sovereigns and followed by the Dark Warrior, also appears in Zhu Quan's (1378–1448) *Tianhuang zhidao taiqing yuce* (Jade Fascicles of Great Clarity on the Perfect Dao of the Celestial Sovereign, DZ 1438). Dated to 1444, it gives an outline of the history and organization of Daoist teachings and contains a brief summary of the god's appearances from creation to Song Huizong (1.25b–30b).[27] Still, the Celestial Masters revered Lord Lao throughout the Song, a fact documented more in art than in texts. A Southern Song painting, for example, has a Daoist, quite possibly Zhang Daoling, bowing in veneration before the god, shown seated on a formal throne and surrounded by a celestial entourage (see Fig. 2 above). Similarly, there are numerous statues and paintings from later dynasties that show Lord Lao in a Celestial Masters devotional context.[28]

Complete Perfection Daoists, too, saw in Lord Lao a senior deity, naming him as the original source of their teachings in the *Jinlian xiangzhuan* of 1327 and the *Minghe yuyin* (Lingering Overtones of the Calling Crane, DZ 1100, 18a) of 1347. This, however, was a secondary development. In their *Jinlian zhenzong ji* (Record of the True Lineage of the Golden Lotus, DZ 173) of the year 1241, Lord Lao is mentioned only vaguely while the Imperial Lord of Eastern Florescence (Donghua dijun), a local Daoist hero of the Zhongnan mountains, takes center stage (1.2a).[29] The increase in Lord Lao's importance in the pantheon may be related to the power struggle under the Yuan and may show, as Yao suggests, an effort "to legitimate Quanzhen [Complete Perfection] as an orthodox sect and to enhance its prestige" (1980, 66). This again indicates the continued prestige and power of the ancient god who remained important in the religious world of traditional China.

The importance of Lord Lao for the Complete Perfection school is also evident from artistic representations of him. Among these, the murals in the Yongle gong, a temple compound dedicated to Lü Dongbin in Ruichang

---

[26] A similar statement of Zhang's is also found in his *Xianquan ji* (Anthology of the Alpine Spring, DZ 1311). See Boltz 1987, 193; Reiter 1988, 19.

[27] See Boltz 1987, 237 on this text. I am indebted to Catherine Despeux for this reference.

[28] I am indebted to Stephen Little of the Art Institute of Chicago for bringing these art works to my attention. Many objects showing Lord Lao will be presented in his exhibition of Daoist art in Chicago in the year 2000.

[29] On these various texts, see Boltz 1987, 189 and 64. On Donghua dijun, see Reiter 1985.

(Shanxi), are of outstanding quality.[30] The god is also depicted in a late twelfth-century mural recovered from the Longmen si (Dragon Gate Temple), a Complete Perfection institution in Shanxi. Now housed in the Royal Ontario Museum of Archaeology, the mural shows Lord Lao as follows:

> He wears a white under-tunic, a light yellow robe edged with blue and lined with green, and a red apron frontal, over which hangs a cream panel decorated with green and red, while narrow blue streamers flow from the belt at front. His mantle is green with a decorative border, and on each shoulder is a sun and moon respectively, floating in clouds, while on the sides of the mantle are mountains also set in clouds, which may be symbolic of the Daoist "isles of the blessed." (White 1940, 214)

This colorful and highly symbolic depiction shows Lord Lao as an imposing celestial divinity, rising above the clouds and controlling even the sun and the moon.

A similar representation is found in a Song marble statue of the god which, at least in the 1940s, resided in the Baiyun guan (White Cloud Monastery), the Complete Perfection school's headquarters in Beijing. Seventy-seven centimeters in height, it shows an old man,

> sitting erect and looking straight ahead. He has pulled his feet up on the seat of the chair; his left leg lies flat along the front edge of the seat, the right knee is drawn up. Both hands rest on the knees, fingers hanging down. His costume consists of a loose, long-sleeved garment, crossed in front and fastened over the chest with a narrow belt tied in a bow. (Erdberg 1942, 235)

The figure bears no inscription, but art historical comparison with Buddhist statues dates it to the late twelfth or early thirteenth century (Erdberg 1942, 239). It is yet another piece of evidence pointing to the high cultic standing the god enjoyed at that time.

Ritually, too, Lord Lao was actively present in Complete Perfection ceremonies, many of which included the invocation of his powers for assistance in the human plight. On occasion the god even showed himself in person. A prominent example is the performance of a Yellow Register (*huanglu*) rite by Wang Chuyi (1141–1217), one of the founder's disciples. As described in the *Tixuan zhenren xianyi lu* (Record of Manifest Wonders

---

[30] See chapter 2 above. On the murals and their accompanying inscriptions, see White 1940; Jing 1994, 289–306; Katz 1993; 1994; 1997.

by the Perfected Who Embodies Mystery, DZ 594),[31] he was sending off a "pure poem" prayer to Lord Lao in the holy fire when the crowd let out a collective gasp. "The Highest Lord Lao was clearly before them, riding on a five-colored luminous haze above the altar" (15b). Wang bowed in recognition of the vision and continued with the burning.

> Then the crowd saw the figure of a boy, little more than a foot high, of strange countenance and marvelous attire, rise from Wang's incense burner and greet the Highest Lord as if he were responding to a summons. When the burning of the poem was complete, there was no trace of Wang. (15b)

This shows not only the deity's divine powers of transformation but also the wonderful reward for active devotion in the form of a physical ascent to the heavens.

Lord Lao was also invoked on a regular basis during the birthday celebrations of the patriarchs Zhongli Quan and Lü Dongbin (on the fourteenth and fifteenth of the fourth month), as described in Chen Zhixu's (fl. 1329–1336) *Shangyangzi jindao dayao xianpai* (The Immortal Lineage of the Main Essentials of the Golden Elixir by the Master of Highest Yang, DZ 1070). The text lists the gods in order of importance before outlining the formal invitation for their descent and describing them with their wondrous retinues.[32] Lord Lao here is followed by a throng of ancient Louguan masters and Han dynasty immortals, but as Judith Boltz points out, the *Daozang jiyao* (Essential Collection from the Daoist Canon) version of the text gives him a longer retinue, including some Buddhist figures (1987, 186). It begins with Lord Lao, whom it distinguishes in two roles, one primordial and one patriarchal: Laozi of the Great Ultimate Before Heaven (Taiji xiantian Laozi) before his birth in human form, and Highest Lord Laozi, Latter Sage of Mystery Prime (Housheng xuanyuan taishang Laozi; 1ab) after his mundane manifestation. While the patriarchal figure is only mentioned briefly, the primordial god, in a recounting of his classical hagiography, is described as rising in the early stages of the universe to create heaven and earth, then transforming himself to develop culture, and eventually being born in human form (1ab; Reiter 1988a, 93).

This position of Lord Lao among the two dominant schools still continues to the present day. Not only worshiped as a member of the trinity, and honored commonly in Daoist temples, the god also has a hall

---

[31] On this text, see Boltz 1987, 66; Reiter 1988a, 83.

[32] On the text, see Boltz 1987, 186. For more on Chen Zhixu and his works, see Reiter 1988a.

of his own in several of their institutions as, for example, in the Baiyun guan in Beijing and the Changchun guan (Temple to Patriarch Qiu) in Wuchang. In addition, his sanctuaries at Bozhou, Louguan, and Chengdu, after suffering in the Cultural Revolution, are again flourishing centers of worship and tourism.[33]

Within Complete Perfection, moreover, Lord Lao still retains an active ritual role. His five precepts are formally bestowed upon adepts at the first stage of ordination, and his *Qingjing jing* is recited in daily services.[34] For both the Complete Perfection and Celestial Masters, his birthday on the fifteenth of the second month is one of the holiest days of the lunar year, dedicated to celebrating the continued presence of this "highest god of the Daoist religion, the Heavenly Worthy of the Dao and Its Virtue" in the world of grime and strife (Li 1993a, 46). Finally, the Celestial Masters place great value on his revelation to Zhang Daoling on the first day of the fifth month and celebrate it with formal rituals—not only in China but also in other parts of the world, as an account in *Frost Bell: The Newsletter of Orthodox Daoism in America* shows:

> [Sunday, May 28, 1995.] A usual observance would be to abstain from eating the five grains (starches) for three days and then on Saturday evening ritually purifying your home altar. On Sunday, upon rising, one would ritually bathe, perhaps consult the *I Ching* and spend the day in quiet study, alchemical meditation (Golden Elixir) or non-conceptual meditation (Tso Wang). In the evening your family and friends would prepare a special meal (still without grain) and after offering the dishes at your home altar share them in a modest celebratory mood. (Spring 1995, 7)

* * * * *

From the fifth century to the present, Lord Lao has been the object of communal worship and the source of revealed rules, rituals, and

---

[33] On Lord Lao in the two first institutions, see Yoshioka 1979, 251; Li 1993a, 28. On the last three, see Mugitani 1989; Porter 1993, 48; Li 1993a, 31–32; Yūsa 1986. For a general review of the situation of Daoism in China today, see Lagerwey 1997. In Louguan, Lord Lao is specially venerated as the patriarch of the Youlong pai ("Likes of Dragons"), founded in the 19th century by Li Xiyue after a planchette revelation from the early Ming immortal Zhang Sanfeng. See Seidel 1970, 511; Akioka 1994, 14. In addition, Lord Lao has several lesser places of honor, such as a temple on Mount Li, a boulder image in Quanzhou, and a grotto in Zhongqing. See Li 1993a, 40.

[34] See Min 1990. On the use of the precepts earlier in this century, see Hackmann 1920; 1931.

protective talismans that structure his followers' lives through behavioral instructions, daily formalities, and regular rites of worship. There is a shift over the centuries in the emphasis of extant texts, beginning with detailed moral prescriptions and behavioral guidelines, moving on to instructions for talismanic use and incantation, then focusing more on formal services to be offered to the god on specific days of the year—the most recent, and Western, example even including alchemical and other forms of meditation.

Still, the basic patterns remain highly similar. Adepts are instructed to lead a moral and upright life, to live in proper harmony with their families and communities, and to purify themselves with the help of abstentions, baths, and special diets for the daily services and regular rituals of the Dao. Although we have records only of the more pronounced and specialized forms of Lord Lao's worship and instructions, we may assume that there has been a fair amount of continuity in the veneration of the god and the communal practices associated with him. These probably go back to the very beginning when the early Celestial Masters, who worshiped Lord Lao by reciting the *Daode jing*, adopted a set of moral rules based on scripture, effected healings with divine means, and celebrated regular festivals that involved purifications and invocations like those associated with Lord Lao in later ages.[35] These forms of worship are still practiced today, both in China and in the West, attesting to the staying power and continued influence of the god.

---

[35] For the practices of the early Celestial Masters, see Maspero 1981; Ōfuchi 1985; 1985a; Kobayashi 1992; Cedzich 1987.

5

Sacred Tales
Lord Lao as the Model for Other Gods

Gods, however high, never stand alone. Even the god of the monotheistic Western religions has a plethora of angels, demons, and natural forces at his disposal, through which he can reward, punish, and communicate, and who share his powers and some of his characteristics. Most traditional and popular religions, moreover, have a whole pantheon of deities who are ranked according to power and celestial standing and interact with each other in a variety of ways, sometimes joining their might and merging into combined figures, sometimes dividing their tasks and growing into separate entities.

Daoism, too, has known large numbers of deities, and from the beginning Lord Lao was only one among them.[1] As the representative of central harmony, he was joined by the divine emperors of the cardinal directions; as a god in the human body, he was one of 36,000 divinities; in Highest Clarity Daoism, he was one of a triad; later he served as a member of the integrated trinity. His diverse functions and areas of efficacy made him a multifaceted deity, whose hagiography and image were influenced by those of other gods and supernatural forces. Outside influences on Lord Lao's image included, as noted earlier, traditional visions of cosmic harmony, legends surrounding the birth and activities of the Buddha, ethnic Chinese ideas of superiority vis-à-vis the barbarians, and notions of the ideal immortal and master of magic. At the same time Lord Lao had a certain influence on the deities around him as well. Certain features of his image spread to other figures and some of his functions split off to become the domain of others.

---

[1] On the pantheon of medieval Daoism, see Ishii 1983; Kubo 1986; Jing 1994; Robinet 1997, 196–97.

In the early middle ages, Lord Lao first exerted a hagiographic influence on the Buddha, who was seen as a foreign version of the Chinese sage and was cast in the image of Lord Lao, so that the two central gods mutually enhanced each other's position and myth. Next, with the revelation of new heavens and gods in the schools of Highest Clarity and Numinous Treasure, certain aspects of Lord Lao were adopted to various ends and a separate messiah figure took on his savior aspect. When the Daoist schools integrated in the fifth and sixth centuries, moreover, Lord Lao was demoted from central high god to the third god of a trinity, yet his characteristics and key functions, including that of creator and revealer of scriptures, survived in the figures of the other members of the group. In the Song period, downgraded from his role as imperial ancestor, Lord Lao's place in the Daoist pantheon changed once more. His central political position was taken over by the Dark Warrior and he increasingly became a sponsor for various up-and-coming popular deities, including the Dipper Mother (Doumu), Mazu, and the city god Chenghuang. Many of the gods thus related to Lord Lao took on certain aspects of his persona and hagiography, so that his image continued to exert a wide influence on the evolution and form of the Chinese pantheon (see Table 6).

Table 6
Texts on Lord Lao and other gods

Text	English title, Source
The Buddha	
A'nan tongxue jing	Sūtra of the Disciple Ānanda; T. 149, 2.874–75
Xiuxing benqi jing	Sūtra of the [Buddha's] Origin and Deeds, Cultivation and Practice; T. 184, 3.461–72
Mouzi lihuo lun	Mouzi's Correction of Errors; T. 2102, 52.1b–7a
Li Hong and Lord Goldtower	
Gaoshi zhuan	Biographies of Eminent Men
Laojun bianhua wuji jing	Scripture of Lord Lao's Infinite Transformations, DZ 1195
Shenzhou jing	Scripture of Divine Incantations, DZ 335
Taiping jingchao	Documents from the Scripture of Great Peace, DZ 1101
Housheng daojun lieji	Annals of the Latter Sage, Lord of the Dao, DZ 442
Zhenling weiye tu	Chart of the Ranks and Duties of the Numinous Perfected, DZ 167
The Gods of the Trinity	
Duren jing	Scripture of Universal Salvation, DZ 1
Duren benxing jing	Scripture of the Original Endeavor of Universal Salvation, P. 3022
Zhihui zuigen pin	The Roots of Wisdom and Sin, DZ 457

Table 6—*continued*

Text	English title, Source
Zhen'gao	Declarations of the Perfected, DZ 1016
Jiuzhen zhongjing	Central Scripture of Ninefold Perfection, DZ 1376
Merging the Gods	
Lingbao Laozi huahu miaojing	Wondrous Numinous Treasure Scripture of Laozi Converting the Barbarians, S. 2081
Shengxuan jing, ch. 4	Scripture of Ascension to the Mystery, P. 2474
Jiuhu jing	Scripture on Salvation and Protection, DZ 636
Yinyuan jing	Scripture of Karmic Retribution, DZ 336
Laozi xiangming jing	Laozi's Scripture on Images and Names, DZ 661
Bao fumu enzhong jing	Scripture on Repaying Parents' Kindness, DZ 662
Lunzhuan wudao jing	Scripture of Rebirth in the Five Realms, DZ 647
The Dark Warrior	
Xuantian shangdi qisheng lu	Revelation Record of the Emperor of Dark Heaven, DZ 958
Xuantian shangdi lingyi lu	Record of Marvels of the Emperor of Dark Heaven, DZ 961
Xuantian ruiying tulu	Illustrated Record of Auspicious Omens of Dark Heaven, DZ 960
Huguo xiaomo jing	Scripture of Protecting the Country and Dissolving Evil, DZ 655
Beiyou ji	Journey to the North
Popular Gods	
Tianfei jiuku lingyan jing	Scripture of the Celestial Consort's Miraculous Salvation from Suffering, DZ 649
Doumu jing	Scripture of the Dipper Mother, DZ 621
Doumu bensheng jing	Elementary Life of the Dipper Mother, DZ 45
Xiantian doumu zougao xuanke	Mysterious Observances to Petition to the Mother of Dipper, Born Before Heaven, DZ 1452
Beidou ershiba zhangjing	Scripture of Twenty-eight Stanzas of the Dipper, DZ 629
Chenghuang xiaozai jifu jing	Scripture of the Dispelling of Disasters and Accumulation of Happiness Through the City God, DZ 1447
Bixia yuanjun huguo baosheng jing	Scripture on the Guarding of Life and Protection of the Country Through the Goddess of the Morning Clouds, DZ 1445

The Buddha in Laozi's Image

Buddhism, as is generally known, was first officially introduced to China in the first century C.E., when it was understood to be a variant of Daoism.[2] At that time, the divinity of the Buddha was also described in terms of the deified Laozi, as a god who underwent transformations, reappeared in different periods of history, had multiple bodies, and was one with the cosmic power of the Dao. Laozi, the cultic deity of late Han movements, thus became the model on which the early Chinese under-

---

[2] On the beginnings of Buddhism in China, see Zürcher 1959, 26; Tsukamoto and Hurvitz 1985, 41.

standing of the Buddha was based, as may be seen in several passages found among early translations and commentaries on Buddhist texts.[3]

For example, the *A'nan tongxue jing* (Sūtra of the Disciple Ānanda; T. 149, 2.874–75), a text translated by An Shigao of the mid-second century, says:

> The Buddha can rise up into the air and undergo many transformations. . . .
> He may turn into stone and iron, or appear as gold and diamonds; he may show himself on the wall of a house or a city, or again appear on the sheer cliff of a high mountain. Lacking solidity, he passes through all, he emerges from and dives deep into the earth. He is like flowing water, unstable and without firm shape. . . .
>
> Transforming his body, he reaches the Brahma heavens, sitting, lying, and walking freely through empty air, or again appearing as flames and smoke. (2.874c–75a)

This description not only uses the term "transformation" commonly applied to Laozi but also shows the Buddha as a deity without definite form, who can appear and disappear at will and pass through earth and stone. Resembling the Dao, he is like flowing water; like Daoist immortals, he can walk on air, is invulnerable to fire and water, and controls the elements of the world.

A similar note, emphasizing the powers of the Buddha over the natural world and his own body, is found in Kang Mengxiang's commentary to the *Xiuxing benqi jing* (Sūtra of the [Buddha's] Origin and Deeds, Cultivation and Practice; T. 184, 3.461–72), which is the second Chinese translation of the Buddha's biography.[4] Kang writes:

> The Buddha had mastered the laws of change and transformation and could become whatever he wanted. Without any special practice, he could fly, be one person or turn into a hundred, a thousand, a million, countless bodies, then merge back again into a single form. He could enter deep into the earth and penetrate even the thickest stone wall. He could appear in a

---

[3] These passages have been collected and examined by Yoshioka (1959, 33–34).

[4] While the Buddha's birth is first described in a collection of Jātaka stories in the Pāli canon, its Mahāyāna version appears in the *Mahāvastu*, "a compilation of facts and tales, undertaken by the Mahāsamgika" (Paul 1979, 71), which was never translated into Chinese. Instead, the earliest Chinese hagiography of the Buddha is the *Zhong benqi jing* (Central Sūtra of the [Buddha's] Origin and Deeds; T. 196, 4.147), translated around 197 C.E. by the Indians Tanguo and Zhu Dali and the Sodgian Kang Mengxiang (Zürcher 1959, 36), author of the commentary cited here.

single spot, vanish in one moment and reappear in the next like waves of water.

The Buddha could freely enter water and fire, walk on rivers and tread on air. His body would never sink, and he could sit or float easily in empty air like a soaring bird. Standing up, he would reach to heaven, his hands taking hold of the sun and the moon. (3.471b; Yoshioka 1959, 34)

This characterizes the Buddha as having multiple bodies and great powers of physical transformation. He has control over the elements, can fly in the air and enter into the earth, and appear and disappear at will. He can sit under water and reach the sky when on earth, his hands holding the planets. His description closely echoes the understanding of the Dao as unlimited and eternally transforming as well as the traditional vision of the immortals who have conquered the Dao and can use its powers to their own ends, invulnerable to and unimpeded by the physical realities of the world.[5]

Even more obvious in its adaptation of Daoist terminology and imagery is the description of the Buddha given in the *Mouzi lihuo lun* (Mouzi's Correction of Errors; T. 2102, 52.1b–7a), a text of uncertain date that may be as early as the first and as late as the fifth century.[6] It relates that

Buddha is an honorary title, like that of the deities known as the Three Sovereigns and the sages known as the Five Emperors. The Buddha is the primordial ancestor of the Dao and its virtue, the ultimate origin of all gods and spirits. The word "buddha" means enlightenment.

Vague and obscure, he transforms continuously, multiplying his body and dividing his physical form. He sometimes is, then again he is not. He can be small or big, round or square, old or young, hidden or apparent.

Stepping on fire, he does not burn; walking over knives, he is not hurt; submerged in water, he does not get wet; encountering disasters, he is unaffected. He walks as if flying and sits issuing a bright radiance. Such is the Buddha. (52.2a)

This, as Yoshioka points out, clearly echoes the *Laozi bianhua jing* of the second century, an impression intensified by another *Mouzi* passage that describes the Buddha as the teacher of dynasties, arguing that however much the rulers of old may have learned from different teachers, each of those sages must himself have been inspired by the one and only

---

[5] A comprehensive description of these powers and features of immortals is found in Robinet 1986.

[6] On the date of and doubts about this text, see Zürcher 1959, 13.

true master of all (Buddha) and thus appeared as his representative on earth. "Yao, Shun, the Duke of Zhou, and Confucius all studied with him, as the Buddha's body with its signs and auspicious marks transformed and changed in unfathomable spirituality" (T. 2102, 52.2c; Yoshioka 1959, 35). The body of the Buddha, his powers and appearances, were thus seen by the Chinese as another variant of the transformations of Laozi, an Indian manifestation of the powers of the Dao and the immortals. Conversely, this shows how widespread and influential the originally political and sectarian vision of Lord Lao as high god of the Dao had already become in the third century, and the degree to which he typified divine power in early medieval China. It demonstrates just how much he contributed, from the very beginning, to shaping the Chinese vision of divinity.

Li Hong and Lord Goldtower

Another figure whose hagiography and religious role Lord Lao influenced and who took on certain activities of the god was the messiah of medieval Daoism. He was first identified with a Han dynasty sage by the name of Li Hong and later with a deity of Highest Clarity Daoism known as Lord Goldtower, the Latter Sage (Housheng). Li Hong is mentioned first in Huangfu Mi's *Gaoshi zhuan* (Biographies of Eminent Men) of the mid-third century, where he is a well-known man of wisdom and high virtue who refused both official position and unwarranted leniency for the crimes of his son.[7] By the fourth century his name was linked not only with a series of people named Li who, inspired by the *Taiping jing* (Scripture of Great Peace) and the *Laozi bianhua jing*, rose in rebellion because they saw themselves as chosen leaders of a new realm of Great Peace, but with Lord Lao himself. The messiah was identified as one of the numerous transformations of Lord Lao that appeared in Sichuan.[8]

In the fifth century, Li Hong further grew to be the central figure of a southern branch of the Celestial Masters whose only surviving text is the *Shenzhou jing* (Scripture of Divine Incantations, DZ 335). It relates that

> When the Perfect Lord [Li Hong] comes forth into the world, he will reign by nonaction. There will be no more suffering from armed violence, from punishment or prison. Under the reign of this sage king, people will have

---

[7] *Gaoshi zhuan* 2.17b; also in *Huayang guozhi* (Gazetteer of Huayang County) 10.1b. See Seidel 1969a, 236.

[8] So described in the *Laojun bianhua wuji jing* (2a). See Seidel 1969a, 237.

abundance and joy. . . . They will act only in accordance with Daoist doctrine, and the Daoist priests will be ministers. . . . One sowing will yield nine crops, and people will live up to 3,000 years. (1.10b)[9]

Around the same time, this messiah figure was also adopted in Highest Clarity Daoism, where he was identified as Lord Goldtower. Lord Goldtower was prophesied to come forth in a year with the cyclical signs *renchen* from Mount Qingcheng in Sichuan to establish a new universe peopled only with the chosen or "seed people" (*zhongmin*) of the Dao.[10] This figure is described at length in a Highest Clarity text placed in Jiangnan and dating from the late fourth century. It is called *Housheng daojun lieji* (Annals of the Latter Sage, Lord of the Dao, DZ 442) and contains a biography of Li Hong as Lord Goldtower while predicting an age of decadence and destruction before the complete renewal of the world. The same biography also appears, in slightly abbreviated fashion, in the *Taiping jingchao* (Documents from the Scripture of Great Peace, DZ 1101), which was compiled in the sixth century on the basis of lost *Taiping jing* passages.[11]

According to this text, Lord Goldtower in many respects resembled the divine Laozi and can even be called his "avatar" (Bokenkamp 1997, 340) or his "manifestation" (Davis 1996, 151). Not only did he have the family name Li and stand heir to the Highest Lord, but he was also the son of the Lord of Emptiness and Nonbeing, an epithet of the Dao. In addition, like Lord Lao, Lord Goldtower himself made the decision to be born among humanity, actively assembled his cosmic energy, completed his basic form, and "when virtue and punishment were evenly matched and all the stars were properly aligned," descended to be born in the mythical country of the north (1b). Like Laozi's Mother Li, his mother waited in the valley of the plum trees (*li*) that had been created from the mysterious emptiness of the realm above. There she was dreaming of the

---

[9] The passage is also cited in Seidel 1969a, 239; 1984a, 169. For a detailed study of the *Shenzhou jing*, see Mollier 1990. An index of the text is found in Yamada and Yūsa 1984.

[10] See Seidel 1969a, 236, 243. A more detailed analysis of the Highest Clarity messiah is found in Strickmann 1981. For a discussion of the term "seed people," see Bokenkamp 1994.

[11] Lord Goldtower's biography from the Highest Clarity text (1a–2b) is translated in Strickmann 1981, 209–11; Bokenkamp 1997, 339–42. Its *Taiping jingchao* version (1.1b–3a) is found in Wong 1997, 52–55. The original of the latter is also found in Wang Ming 1960, 2–3. On the history and compilation of the *Taiping jing*, see Kandel 1979. For a general discussion of Highest Clarity eschatology, see Kobayashi 1990, 430–54.

god's divinity approaching her "with the radiance of the sun and the moon, his spirit moving like lightning" (1b). After his smooth and painless emergence into the world, Lord Goldtower was honored by three suns rising in the east and, again like Lord Lao, nine dragons coming to sprinkle water over him. He grew up to be bright and beautiful, with a hearty curiosity about the movements of the planets and with various supernatural signs on his body. Inspired by the transience of the world, he began to practice immortality techniques.

> He took care to control his spirit soul and harmonize his material soul; he guarded his inner center [womb] and treasured his spirit; he gathered his essence and kept his blood replenished; he invigorated his body fluids and strengthened his muscles.
>
> At age seven, moreover, he learned to swallow light, nourish on mist, and chew the tendrils of the sun. At twice seven [twenty], he was of a golden beauty and had a jade complexion. Leaving the ordinary world, distancing himself from all desires, he pledged to transform and save the world. He therefore placed his essence under the impact of the Grand Immaculate, took instruction from the Three Primes, practiced according to the Three Caverns, and worked hard in all the nine directions. (*Taiping jingchao* 1.2a)

More like a seeker of immortality than an all-powerful god, Lord Goldtower here has traces of the Laozi of the magical practitioners, but otherwise represents more the ideal of the successful disciple, reminiscent of Yin Xi and his attainment of the Dao. Like the latter, he eventually attains full realization and gains access to the heavenly realms, winning power over mortals and immortals, heaven and earth, and—once more following Lord Lao's example—turning into "the sole ruler of the nine levels of heaven and ten ramparts of the earth" (1.2a). In due course he compiles his expertise and talismans in several sacred scriptures, which he reveals to suitable representatives on earth, thus allowing the chosen people to establish the perfect realm of the Dao.

The messiah figure of medieval Daoism, Li Hong or Lord Goldtower, is thus described in Lord Lao's image as a special functionary and divine helper of the world. Like the god, he time and again descends to save suffering humanity and is even born on earth to work for the ideal state of the pure Dao. To this end, the messiah, even more so than the old god, does not hesitate to take on any number of hardships and turns himself into a full-fledged immortal. Yet once he has reached this goal, he takes on again the role of the god and becomes a key revealing agent of salvific scriptures and instructions for the ideal sacred community. A lesser and more hands-on version of Lord Lao, this medieval savior represents a tangible and practical form of the high god, which takes on his salvific role and thus helps him be a more interactive member of the pantheon.[12]

The Heavenly Worthy and the Lord of the Dao

The four major Daoist schools of the middle ages, Celestial Masters, Three Sovereigns, Numinous Treasure, and Highest Clarity, in the fifth and sixth centuries joined to form an integrated teaching and organizational structure, which remained dominant throughout the Tang. Its first traces go back to the fifth-century division of Daoist texts into the Three Caverns.[13] The process of this integration is not well understood and has not yet been sufficiently studied, but a few general remarks can be made about it.

For one, it was a direct religious response to the political move toward unification that issued most strongly from the Northern Wei who desired to be rulers of all China, but also from the Han Chinese in the south who hoped to see their country reunited. For another, there were several competing models proposed for the joining of Daoist teachings, one of which was the Louguan vision of Lord Lao as the one and only major god of a unified teaching in a unified country. Another model was the Highest Clarity pantheon proposed in the integrationist *Zhenling weiye tu* (Chart of the Ranks and Duties of the Numinous Perfected, DZ 167), commonly associated with Tao Hongjing.[14]

---

[12] A popular text revealed by Lord Goldtower to Zhang Daoling appears prominently in the Song but is ascribed to the Tang astrologer Li Chunfeng (602–670). The *Jinsuo liuzhu yin* (Guide to the Flowing Pearls of the Golden Lock, DZ 1015) contains a description of immortality methods, mainly visualizations and ecstatic travels among the stars. See Davis 1994, 150–53.

[13] On the Three Caverns, which imitated the Buddhist division of the Three Vehicles, see Ōfuchi 1979a, 261; Kobayashi 1995, 30; Ōzaki 1995, 49. As the basic organizational pattern of the Daoist canon, see Liu 1973; Thompson 1985. They first occur in the *Jiutian shengshen zhangjing* (Verses to Bring Forth the Gods of the Nine Heavens, DZ 318), originally a Numinous Treasure scripture that was later adapted by the southern Celestial Masters (Kobayashi 1990, 236; Gauchet 1949, 328–29). On the mystical meaning of the number three in Daoism, see Gauchet 1949, 337–48; Robinet 1994, 97.

[14] On the text see Ishii 1983; Zhu 1992, 64–65; Noguchi et al. 1994, 128. Yamada thinks it was originally a commentary to a series of pictures (1995a, 18). Another early Highest Clarity text describing the same pantheon is the *Zhenzhong shu*, commonly associated with Ge Hong but definitely of later and Highest Clarity provenance. For a discussion of its mythology, see Jing 1994, 103–8. The classical

This text has a fourfold division of teachings and proposes the following schema:

No.	Realm	Central God	Period
1.	Jade Clarity	Heavenly Worthy	past
2.	Highest Clarity	Lord of Jade Dawn	present
3.	Great Ultimate	Lord Goldtower	future
4.	Great Clarity	Lord Lao	

According to this, Jade Clarity under the guidance of the Heavenly Worthy of Numinous Treasure ruled in the past, while the present is governed by the powers of Highest Clarity. The future is given over to the savior Lord Goldtower; gods and immortals in his realm are of Numinous Treasure provenance, but also include the Yellow Venerable Lord (8b) and the Confucian sage rulers (9b). Lord Lao, the representative of the Celestial Masters, appears only in a secondary function as the god of the fourth realm, which has no specific period assigned to it.[15]

Regardless, Daoism was finally unified through the southern model of the Three Caverns, developed by the schools of the Celestial Masters and Numinous Treasure, and the pantheon was reorganized to be headed by the trinity, a set of three gods known as the Three Pure Ones (Sanqing), who represented the major teachings. The Heavenly Worthy of Primordial Beginning stood for Highest Clarity, the Lord of the Dao (Taishang daojun) for Numinous Treasure, and Lord Lao for the Three Sovereigns and Celestial Masters (see Fig. 8). Although three and different, the gods were still understood to be ultimately one in their symbolization of the Dao, which is what makes them a trinity and not a mere triad of gods.[16]

---

hierarchy of Highest Clarity gods is found in the *Dadong zhenjing* (Perfect Scripture of Great Pervasion, DZ 6). See Robinet 1983.

[15] Jing sees this model as dominant at the time of integration and thinks that a compromise with the Louguan school under the leadership of Yin Wencao was responsible for the final establishment of the trinity (1994, 154–67).

[16] The idea of three-in-one goes back far in Daoism but is also rooted in the three bodies of the Buddha. See Fukunaga 1987; Robinet 1997, 199. Traditional Chinese thinkers were well aware of the connection between the various models. As Zhu Xi remarks, the "Daoist trinity originated from the Buddhist doctrine of the three bodies" (*Zhuzi yulei* [Collected Works of Zhu Xi] 125.17). See Liu 1962, 133.

Fig. 8. The Daoist trinity.
Source: Statue ("Triad dated 642") owned by the Freer Gallery, Washington, D.C.
Used with the kind permission of the owner.

The first among them, the Heavenly Worthy of Primordial Beginning, represents the cosmic and creative aspect of the trinity. He appears with his full title first around the year 480 in Yan Dong's commentary to the *Duren jing* (Scripture of Universal Salvation, DZ 1), one of the key scriptures of the Numinous Treasure school.[17] Before that he is called only Primordial Beginning (Yuanshi), a term for cosmic origination that first appears in the *Huainanzi* (ch. 1), thus perpetuating the veneration of primordiality found in ancient Daoist and Profound Learning (*xuanxue*) philosophy. Immortality practitioners were the first to add a heavenly title to Primordial Beginning; they named the ruler and creator of the world "Heavenly King of Primordial Beginning" (Yuanshi tianwang), a title duly adopted by the school of Highest Clarity. The latter styled him as the creator of the cosmos who produced sacred scriptures and talismans and had them carved in sacred script in the caverns of heaven, from which he would make them accessible to humanity.

Numinous Treasure Daoists, in turn, followed this but changed "Heavenly King" to "Heavenly Worthy," taking over a commonly used title of the Buddha, who later, in contrast to the Daoist deity, became generally known as the "Worldly Worthy" or "World-Honored One" (Shizun; Fukunaga 1987, 129). Later associated primarily with Highest Clarity doctrines, the Heavenly Worthy took on the role of the creator and underlying power of the universe. He represented the Dao at the root of all and its creation of the earliest and most powerful layer of scriptures, just as Lord Lao had among the earlier Daoist schools. Accordingly, his career, most especially his creation of the world and his continued reappearances in various kalpas, is reminiscent of Laozi's transformations.[18]

The second god of the trinity is the Lord of the Dao. Also known as the Highest Lord (Taishang) and often called simply "the Dao," he functions as the mouthpiece of the creative deity in the center and is the revealer of sacred scriptures after the Highest Worthy. He appears most prominently, and with an extensive biography, in the scriptures of the Numinous Treasure school, where he is characterized as the disciple and

---

[17] On this text, see Gauchet 1941; Sunayama 1984; Noguchi et al. 1994, 128l. A translation is found in Bokenkamp 1997, 373–438.

[18] See Fukunaga 1987, 140–41; Wang 1989, 67–68; Noguchi et al. 1994, 128; Robinet 1997, 198. He has a full biography in *YJQQ* 101.1a–2a, which describes him very much in terms of the deified Lord Lao. The Heavenly Worthy is also mentioned variously in the *Wushang biyao*, mainly as a revealer of scriptures and as the divine respondent to sagely questions. See Lagerwey 1981, 98, 101, 105, 111, 113, 119, 127.

messenger of the Heavenly Worthy. The relationship between the two deities is patterned on Mahāyāna Buddhism, with the Heavenly Worthy residing in celestial splendor above the known universe and the Lord of the Dao, his disciple and follower, begging for instruction that will help suffering humanity.

The Lord of the Dao's exploits are described variously, for example in the *Zhihui zuigen pin* (The Roots of Wisdom and Sin, DZ 457), a Numinous Treasure text of the fifth century.[19] It begins with a Mahāyāna-style description of the setting.

> The Highest Lord of the Dao at this time was in Southern Cinnabar, in the Cypress Mound Chamber of the Upper Hall of Pervading Yang. He knocked his head to the ground and with proper ceremony addressed the Heavenly Worthy of Primordial Beginning. (1.1a)

In his address, the Lord of the Dao then outlines his own progress, describing how he "for a hundred million kalpas has transformed along with the world" and "received instruction in the divine scriptures of the Three Treasures, was given the great precepts and told the sacred spells of the divine" (1.1a). Now he has again come before the deity to learn what he has not heard before, so that he can further aid humanity, helping "even souls already suffering for long kalpas to find salvation through me and be reborn in the halls of happiness" (1.1b).

The Heavenly Worthy decides to give further precepts to his senior disciple, a decision that creates a great stir of delight in heaven and on earth (1.2a). Next, the Heavenly Worthy tells how he himself came to earth repeatedly over several kalpas to set humanity on the right course but could not prevent a gradual decline, which now has to be set right by the Lord of the Dao, who has emerged as the prime agent of universal salvation. To make his task easier, the Heavenly Worthy then presents him with the scriptures and precepts. The Lord of the Dao as savior of humanity thus steps into and continues Lord Lao's role as the revealer of scriptures and precepts and takes on appropriate parts of his hagiography. Like Lord Lao, he is the Dao, and the Dao in both Celestial

---

[19] The god also has a hagiography in *YJQQ* 101.2a–3a, which characterizes him as the major revealer of scriptures and messenger of the Heavenly Worthy. The *Wushang biyao* mentions him both as a revealer and as a deity invoked in prayer. See Lagerwey 1981, 98, 111, 113, 127, 145, 153, 160, 162, and 180. It also cites the *Zhihui zuigen pin* (Lagerwey 1981, 148).

Masters and Numinous Treasure scriptures has a life story that goes back to the tale of Lord Lao's exploits.[20]

Finally, Lord Lao himself is integrated into the structure as the disciple of the Lord of the Dao, with whose help he becomes a perfected of lower celestial rank. Thus the *Zhen'gao* (Declarations of the Perfected, DZ 1016), Tao Hongjing's (456–536) annotated collection of Highest Clarity works, says:

> Lord Lao is a disciple of the Lord of the Dao. Even at age seven, he already knew the essentials of long life. Thus he became a Perfected of the Great Ultimate.
>
> There are four Perfected of the Great Ultimate, and Lord Lao is the one on the left. From his belt hang the talisman of the divine tiger and the bell of flowing gold. He holds a baton with purple feathers in his hand and wears the kerchief of golden essence on his head. As he walks, he is covered by a canopy of fluorescent morning light and strides high on clouds of the three simplicities. (5.1b–2a; Yoshioka 1959, 75).

Lord Lao here is a powerful figure whose duties involve reporting back to the celestial hierarchy on the behavior of humans on certain days of the month when he is specially worshiped.[21] With him in this role, the trinity is complete, a set of powerful gods, clearly divided yet intimately linked, who actively represent the Dao in its original, revelatory, and phenomenal appearance, seeing to both the creation and salvation of all beings.

The first scriptural description of the trinity is found in the *Fengdao kejie* of the early Tang. It lists the gods with their formal titles: "Law-King Above All, Heavenly Worthy of Primordial Beginning"; "Highest Sovereign of Emptiness, the Great Dao of Jade Dawn"; "Senior Lord, Lord Lao, the Heavenly Worthy of the Great One" (2.1a).[22] Before that, however, there are several stelae depicting three deities described as the "Three Worthies" (Sanzun), the first of which dates from 508 and was found at

---

[20] A description of the deeds of the Dao imitating Lord Lao's life story is found in the *Dadao jialing jie* (DZ 789) a history of the Celestial Masters (see Kobayashi 1995, 24). Another Numinous Treasure retelling of the life of the Lord of the Dao is also found in the *Duren benxing jing* (Scripture of the Original Endeavor of Universal Salvation), fragments of which remain in Dunhuang (P. 3022, Ōfuchi 1979, 54–55), *Wushang biyao* 47, and *YJQQ* 101.

[21] See also *Zhen'gao* 18.6a; Yoshioka 1959, 76. A similar description is also found in the *Jiuzhen zhongjing* (Central Scripture of Ninefold Perfection, DZ 1376, 1a–2a). See Robinet 1979a.

[22] On this text and its pantheon, see Akizuki 1965, 453; Yamada 1995, 27; Reiter 1988.

the Shihong Monastery in Fuzhou, with further works dated to 515, 521, 567, and 572, and many more that were produced under the Tang.[23] This suggests an active effort at Daoist integration throughout the sixth century, which eventually resulted in the establishment of the standard trinity of three gods who are ultimately one.

The Ultimate Oneness of the Gods

The ultimate unity of the three gods is made clear not only because they share similar attributes, many of which go back to Lord Lao, but also because they often appear in the same role in the same text and are explicitly or implicitly identified as one. An example is the Numinous Treasure version of the *Huahu jing*, which clearly names Laozi as the converting agent in its title,[24] then consistently refers to the Heavenly Worthy as the main protagonist of the story. While this might just be an abbreviation of Lord Lao's trinity title "Heavenly Worthy of the Great One," its deeper relevance is revealed toward the end of the text: "This scripture has [a protagonist with] three names: The first is Great Sage of Primordial Beginning; the second is Laozi; and the third is the Heavenly Worthy" (Seidel 1984, 349). The mention of "primordial beginning" here points to an intended identity of Lord Lao with the Heavenly Worthy, raising the stature of the converting agent to the creator and first god of the trinity.

Another example for the same conscious merging of gods is found in the *Shengxuan jing* (Scripture of Ascension to the Mystery), a sixth-century text that shows a clear effort toward the integration of various teachings.[25] Here Highest Clarity doctrines are revealed to the first Celestial Master, Zhang Daoling, by the bodhisattva-messenger of Numinous Treasure doctrine, the Lord of the Dao. The text explicitly merges the gods of the trinity into one:

> The Dao said, "I took the five energies and wandered around the eight ultimate ends of the universe. I was called Primordial Beginning or Lord

---

[23] For a description, see Kamitsuka 1993, 230; Pontynen 1983, 80.

[24] The full title is *Lingbao Laozi huahu miaojing* (Wondrous Numinous Treasure Scripture of Laozi Converting the Barbarians). A Dunhuang manuscript (S. 2081; Ōfuchi 1979, 681–84), the text is reprinted in Yoshioka 1959, 493–96, and translated in Seidel 1984.

[25] Originally in ten scrolls, the text survived in Dunhuang fragments, edited in Yamada 1992. Scroll 7 is also extant in the Daoist canon (DZ 1122).

Lao or Highest Lord or Tathāgata. Sometimes I was the teacher of the world; sometimes I was the ancestor of the mystery." (ch. 4, P. 2474; Ōfuchi 1979, 264)

Another expression of the ultimate unity of the three gods is their appearance in the same role in different versions of the same text. A case in point is the *Jiuhu jing* (Scripture on Salvation and Protection, DZ 636), in which Lord Lao is the creating agent of the Dao and as such encourages believers to take refuge in a group known as the Ten Heavenly Worthies or the Saviors from Suffering of the Ten Directions (Shifang jiuku tian-zun; 1a). His identity with the Heavenly Worthy is evident when the same text, in a slightly different version, appears in the *Yinyuan jing* (Scripture of Karmic Retribution, DZ 336) of the late sixth century, where the Heavenly Worthy is called creator instead of Lord Lao (6.4ab).[26]

Other cases include the *Laozi xiangming jing* (Laozi's Scripture on Images and Names, DZ 661), a Dunhuang manuscript of the early Tang in which Lord Lao takes the place of the Heavenly Worthy; and the *Bao fumu enzhong jing* (Scripture on Repaying Parents' Kindness, DZ 662), a Daoist adaptation of a Buddhist text of the same title, revealed by the Buddha. In the Daoist version, the Lord of the Dao appears in the Buddha's role.[27]

A striking integration of the roles of all three deities is further evident in the *Lunzhuan wudao jing* (Scripture of Rebirth in the Five Realms, DZ 647), a *Yinyuan jing* offshoot of eight pages, which begins with a description of Lord Lao sitting in celestial splendor, then has the Perfected of the Left Mystery ask questions of the Heavenly Worthy, and finally, has them answered by the Lord of the Dao ("the Dao").

To a certain extent, these variations in divine speakers may be due to the editing process during integration or to a shifting of transmission responsibilities away from the central god and toward Lord Lao. On the other hand, this does not explain the reverse process, which makes the Heavenly Worthy appear in one of Lord Lao's traditional roles, for example, as the converter of the barbarians. Also, the open identification of the various deities and the insistence that there is only one god who represents the Dao but appears in various forms and has different titles,

---

[26] On the Ten Worthies, see Yūsa 1989; for more on the *Yinyuan jing*, see Akizuki 1964; Nakajima 1984; Kohn 1998c.

[27] The *Laozi xiangming jing* is found in S. 1513, P. 3344; Ōfuchi 1979, 647–55. The Buddhist version of the *Bao fumu enzhong jing* appears in T. 684, 16.778–79. It has been studied in Ch'en 1973; Akizuki 1966; Xie 1984. A later Daoist version of the same text, with the same title and the same content (DZ 663), is revealed by the Dark Warrior, showing how Lord Lao's role was continued by that deity.

is a clear indication that the gods of the trinity, however different their names, roles, and hagiographies may be, were doctrinally conceived as one. This oneness, then, is the elemental oneness of the Dao, which in its earliest divinized form was represented by Lord Lao whose multiple functions and varied hagiographic features continued to be realized in the three gods of the trinity.

The Dark Warrior

While the trinity remained the central group of deities in the Daoist pantheon, several other, often new gods gained increased popularity in later ages. Some of them also took on features of Lord Lao, as for example the Dark Warrior, who replaced him as protector of the state and central deity of the world under the Song.

Originally a constellation in the northern sky, the Dark Warrior appears first in the Han dynasty as the mythical animal of the north. He is at that point depicted as an intertwined turtle and snake—replacing the more mundane symbol of the horse or camel of earlier periods.[28] Both the turtle and the snake are yin animals and thus represent the north. They are water animals, cold blooded, lurking in the dark, and hibernating in winter. The name "Dark Warrior," too, is an expression of the chthonic nature of the symbol: "Dark" indicates the mystery and obscurity of deep valleys and the ineffable northern darkness, while "warrior" means "hostile" or "in combat" and refers to the interlocking of the two animals, which may well be less aggressive than sexual in nature.[29] In addition, the turtle is an ancient symbol of the Chinese universe and image of the sky dome, while the snake is an emblem of earth that, as it winds around the turtle, shows the intertwining of heaven and earth in the process of continuous creation. Taken together, the Dark Warrior and its representation show yin at its maximum strength, indicating the continuous creation taking place at the hibernating, latent stage of the universe.

The Dark Warrior stands at the dark depth of cosmic creation, under-lying the first stirrings of order as the Dao develops.[30] In this position, he

---

[28] On the constellation, see Staal 1984. On his early role, see Major 1986, 68.

[29] So described in Major 1986, 74–75. For more on the turtle and its cosmic symbolism, see Allan 1991.

[30] In his role as the protector of the north, Xuanwu is also closely linked with the Emperor of the North, ruler of darkness and the underworld in medieval Daoism and the center of an important exorcistic tradition. See Mollier 1997.

is found behind Lord Lao in the visualization texts, which instruct the practitioner to see the deity—and at some point himself—in the center of the universe and surrounded by the four heraldic animals. A close link is thus established from an early time between Lord Lao in the center of the universe and the Dark Warrior at his back, symbolizing the power of the center and the strength behind it.

This symbolism was reinterpreted under the Song dynasty, when Lord Lao could no longer serve as the ancestor of the ruling house and lost some of his powerful standing. Rather than seeing the Dark Warrior merely as a guardian of the central deity, the Song found in him the force behind the moving energy of the universe and accordingly elevated him to replace Lord Lao as the prime protector of the state. Already under Emperor Taizu (r. 960–76), his cult was raised to national status, inspired by a manifestation of a martial deity who claimed to be an assistant of the Dark Warrior and appeared specifically to protect the dynasty. Recorded first in the *Xinjian taiping gong beiming* (Inscription on the Reconstruction of the Great Peace Temple), this event was later elaborated in a record by the official Yang Yi (974–1020), a co-editor of the *Cefu yuangui* (Magic Mirror in the Palace of Books). This god is identified as Black Killer (Heisha) who, under Tantric influence, is described as having "a human form, with fierce eyes and disheveled hair, riding a dragon and holding a sword."[31]

The imperial standing of the Dark Warrior was greatly enhanced under Emperor Zhenzong (r. 998–1022), when a turtle and snake made a miraculous appearance in a Kaifeng temple in 1017, and a healing spring bubbled up nearby in the following year. In 1019, a Hall to the Dark Warrior was first added to Lord Lao's Taiwei gong in Luoyang, expressing the close relation between the deities. In addition, in 1012, the Dark Warrior was renamed Perfect Warrior (Zhenwu) to avoid the taboo name of the first ancestor of the Song imperial family, and was given his first official title, with others following in 1202, 1257, and 1304.[32]

---

[31] Citation from Jing 1994, 215. The inscription is found in Chen et al. 1988, 217–18; for more on the *Cefu yuangui*, see Hervouet 1978, 320. On Tantrism in China, see Orzech 1989.

[32] These events in the Dark Warrior's evolution are described in Lagerwey 1992, 295. On his hall at Lord Lao's temple, see Ding 1979, 292. In addition, three texts by Wang Qinruo, leading compiler of the Song Daoist canon, describe the god in this period. First, the *Yisheng baode zhuan* (Biography of [the Perfected Lord] Assisting Sanctity and Protecting Virtue, DZ 1285, YJQQ 103) of the year 1016 is a comprehensive account of revelations made by Dark Warrior as the dynasty's protector in the beginning of the Song (Andersen 1991, 125–26). Next, the *Dajiao ke* (Rules for the Great Offerings, DZ 477–79), compiled in 1015 and presented in

The Dark Warrior saw a further elevation under Emperor Renzong (r. 1023–1063), who, in 1055, had a series of 104 frescoes painted that showed the god's protection of the state in five distinct areas: political administration, military success, climate control, healing of diseases, and prevention of disasters. The emperor also ordered a first collection of Dark Warrior mirabilia, which was later edited in the *Xuantian shangdi qisheng lu* (Revelation Record of the Emperor of Dark Heaven, DZ 958).[33] In this work, the Dark Warrior is styled along lines similar to those of Lord Lao and is, in fact, described as his eighty-second transformation (1.1b). In addition, the god, like Lord Lao, is an "embodiment of the Great Ultimate, representing the beginning energy prior to heaven"; again like Lord Lao, he descends during the reigns of all great mythical emperors. The text says:

> Under the Highest Sovereign, he descended and became the Perfected of the Great Beginning. Under the Middle Sovereign, he descended and became the Perfected of the Great Initiation. Under the Lower Sovereign, he descended and became the Perfected of the Great Simplicity.
>
> Under the Yellow Emperor, he descended and in a true match of the essence of great yang took refuge in the womb of Queen Goodness Victorious [Shansheng], wife of the king of the Country of Pure Happiness [Jingle guo]. Remaining in the womb for fourteen months, he appeared as the eighty-second transformation of the Highest Lord.
>
> At this time it was the beginning of the kalpa Highest Sovereign . . . and the Dark Emperor was born by emerging from his mother's left armpit. At that moment auspicious clouds covered the land and celestial flowers spread far and wide. A wondrous fragrance wafted sweetly, and his body shone forth brilliantly, filling the entire kingdom and transforming the earth. (1.1b–2a)

Similar to the deified Lord Lao and sharing major hagiographic events with him, the Dark Warrior is then described as growing into a mighty divinity who, powerful and intelligent, becomes a demon queller of the first order. Traveling throughout the world, he obtains a magical sword that contains the essence of the cosmos (1.3b) and perfects himself through personal cultivation (1.6a). Later he performs numerous miracles, often but not always ordered to do so by Lord Lao (e.g., 1.32b, 2.1a).

1024, contains daily rites as revealed by Dark Warrior, protector of the Song (Andersen 1991, 117–18). Third, the *Dajiao yi* (Observances of the Great Offerings, DZ 480), compiled around the same time, describes a ritual similar to that in *Dajiao ke* (Andersen 1991, 119). See also Nikaidō 1998.

[33] On the murals, see Boltz 1987, 88. The text is described in Lagerwey 1992, 326n 3.

On one occasion, he even appeared to Emperor Huizong, "his face stern and striking, his hair unbound, . . . wearing a breastplate of gold and a belt set with jewels. His hand brandished a sword, his feet were bare, and round his head there shone a halo of light, while the ends of his sash floated in the breeze" (White 1940, 170). This vision of the god is inspired by that of Vaiśravana, Tantric god of the north and another great demon queller. His worship was highly popular among Complete Perfection Daoists of the thirteenth century, and he was identified with the Dark Warrior. He, too, is a generalissimo who commands twenty-eight Yakśa generals and large numbers of divine troops. A similar image of the Dark Warrior is also found among temple frescoes recovered from a local temple in Shanxi, today housed in the Royal Ontario Museum of Archaeology.[34] Here, too, the god appears as a mighty warrior who easily outshines the older Lord Lao—especially since his martial prowess was in great demand against the invading North Asians (Lagerwey 1992, 295).

Despite his activity, however, the Song suffered military defeat. Nevertheless, the influence of the Dark Warrior did not wane but continued to grow, as Yuan and Ming collections of his deeds attest.[35] Under the latter in particular, the Dark Warrior was linked with the dynasty's coming to power and raised to an ever higher status, standing as a beneficent protector above all (see Fig. 9). The Ming set up regular sacrifices for him and between 1405 and 1418 greatly expanded his center on Mount Wudang in Hubei. The god's popularity was not only supported by both leading Daoist schools, Complete Perfection and Celestial Masters, it was also greatly bolstered by this imperial patronage. He duly appeared in popular literature and became the subject of a late Ming novel, the *Beiyou ji* (Journey to the North).[36] Recounting his

---

[34] See White 1940, Fig. 45. On Vaiśravana, see Getty 1988, 156.

[35] See the *Xuantian shangdi lingyi lu* (Record of Marvels of the Emperor of Dark Heaven, DZ 961), which collects praises of the god from 1270–1325, and the *Xuantian ruiying tulu* (Illustrated Record of Auspicious Omens of Dark Heaven, DZ 960; Boltz 1987, 88). In addition, the Yuan text *Huguo xiaomo jing* (Scripture of Protecting the Country and Dissolving Evil, DZ 655), in a discussion of the six palaces of Fengdu, has Lord Lao order two constellations to become the true warrior god and subdue demons there, reformulating the basic myth of the Dark Warrior (Boltz 1987, 88).

[36] This history of Xuanwu under the Ming is outlined in White 1940, 169; Lagerwey 1992, 299. On his role in popular literature, see Liu 1962, 152. The *Beiyou ji* was first studied in Grootaers 1952; a complete translation and analysis is contained in Seaman 1987. For a discussion of the god's progress in the novel in relation to Mount Wudang's peaks and sanctuaries, see Lagerwey 1992, 315–21.

Fig. 9. The Dark Warrior as protector above the clouds.
Source: Xuantian ruiying tulu 24a

adventures during several reincarnations, it shows his progress from human crown prince to divine emperor. Even at this late stage, however, the Dark Warrior's link with Lord Lao is not severed, and his birth as the crown prince of the Country of Pure Happiness again follows the model of the earlier god's hagiography (Seaman 1987, 88). Thus the new god continues to have much in common with the deified Lord Lao and still accepts orders from him, reconfirming both his own standing in the Daoist pantheon and the older god's continued, if increasingly secondary, importance.[37]

Popular Gods

In a different vein, Lord Lao exerted influence on the Daoist pantheon of the Ming and Qing dynasties by becoming the sponsor of popular deities. He thereby rose in general veneration, becoming a popular god himself, while also asserting the standing of other gods in the organized Daoist pantheon. There are several stories about popular gods that describe how Lord Lao, in an act of revelation and enfeoffment, bestowed specific powers upon them, charging them with missions of protection and salvation and imbuing them with unique powers of the Dao. The tales establish and confirm the popular gods' standing in the Daoist pantheon, while retaining Lord Lao's ultimate authority.

The most popular among the deities so sponsored is the goddess Celestial Consort (Tianfei) or Mazu, the divine protectress of seafarers in coastal China. Historically she developed from a popular to an increasingly national goddess, but in Daoist doctrine she receives her mission from Lord Lao. This is documented in the *Tianfei jiuku lingyan jing* (Scripture of the Celestial Consort's Miraculous Salvation from Suffering, DZ 649) of the year 1409.[38]

A ritual text, it begins with the astral origins of the goddess as a power that "sustains the Dipper" and offers "instant relief to those in distress" (Boltz 1986, 217). It then moves on to a hagiographic summary of her life, an invocation of her divinity, and a description of her heavenly nature. After this, in a section Judith Boltz calls the "sermon," Mazu receives her official mandate from Lord Lao. Residing in his heavenly residence, he observes the multiple sins and sufferings of humanity,

---

[37] After the end of the Ming, the worship of Dark Warrior declined on the mainland but remained active in Taiwan, where he is still popular today. See K. Ishida 1995.

[38] A historical study of the development of Mazu is found in Wädow 1992. The Daoist text about her is translated and studied in Boltz 1986.

especially those caused by "bogies and goblins, specters and phantoms," and various forms of taxation. In response, he commands "the Jade Maiden of Wondrous Deeds to descend and be incarnated in the mortal realm so that she might rescue humankind from the hardships suffered" (Boltz 1986, 223). He duly elevates the goddess with an official title and accepts her formal pledge—in close imitation of her Buddhist counterpart Guanyin—that "should anyone but reveal reverence and respect in his/her heart and call my name, then I will offer immediate and trustworthy response and cause him/her to attain whatever it is they wish" (Boltz 1986, 224). In what follows she is further empowered to command celestial troops and provide talismans. In response, she vows to rescue all seafarers and merchants, protect family and state, and do away with thieves and malevolent forces. This pledge moves Lord Lao to bestow on her still another celestial title, more wondrous garments, and a more extensive fighting guard. The text concludes with the dedication of the "Numinous Talisman of the Celestial Consort for Relieving Distress," including an empowering incantation and instructions for its use (Boltz 1986, 229).

A similar case is Doumu, the mother of the gods of the Dipper who controls the stars. Doumu is a Chinese adaptation of the Hindu goddess Marīci, the personification of light and an offspring of Brahma. Marīci resides in the Great Brahma Heaven and functions as a ruler of fates. Depicted with eight arms, holding the sun and the moon, she is the mother of the Buddha and a guardian of all nations who can see in all directions and has two arms to help each, thus saving people with great speed and efficiency.[39]

The Dipper Mother is also a goddess of radiance and power, independent and sovereign, a protectress against violence and peril. Her classical scripture, the *Doumu jing* (Scripture of the Dipper Mother, DZ 621), consists of three pages and is revealed by Lord Lao.[40] He begins by emphasizing the high sage energy of the Dipper Mother, her powers to bring rain and sunshine, regulate the seasons, and protect people from disasters and disease. Next he orders her to descend to earth to provide medicines, heal sicknesses, and dispel demonic influences with an eight-

---

[39] For a description of Marīci, see Getty 1988, 132–34; for Doumu, see Noguchi et al. 1994, 471.

[40] A longer version of this text has survived in a manuscript dated to 1439 and discovered in Hamburg, Germany. For a discussion, see Franke 1972; 1977, 214. I am indebted to Ute Engelhardt for procuring a microfilm copy from Munich library. Another description of the goddess is also found in the *Doumu bensheng jing* (Elementary Life of the Dipper Mother, DZ 45).

character seal. He gives her the power to control the stars of the Dipper, those powerful regulators of destiny also worshiped under Lord Lao's auspices. Finally he admonishes everyone to practice the Dao of highest mystery and achieve ascension to the Jade Capital in purity and tranquility, thus linking the worship of the Dipper Mother with a practice of mental purification specifically associated with Lord Lao.[41]

Yet another divine figure sponsored by Lord Lao as a member of the Daoist pantheon is Chenghuang, the city god, who is a generic deity, a divine officer localized to a specific place and serving a particular function. The institution of Chenghuang, a development of the ancient earth god (*she*) under the influence of increased urbanization from the late Tang, thus includes a whole group a gods who "share a label, not an identity."[42] In Ming China, these gods played a key role in popular worship, a role that was too important for the Daoist establishment to either ignore or combat. The latter responded by adopting the city god into the Daoist pantheon, and creating a celestial archetype in the process. This super city god resides with Lord Lao and the celestials, receives his powers from the Dao, and sponsors the various specific city gods on earth.

The Daoist role of the city god is documented in the *Chenghuang xiaozai jifu jing* (Scripture of the Dispelling of Disasters and Accumulation of Happiness Through the City God, DZ 1447, trans. Kohn 1997a), dated after 1376. In five pages, the text describes how Lord Lao, seated in a jeweled hall before a great assembly in the Grand Veil Heaven (*daluo tian*), answers the questions of the perfected Vast Wisdom (Guanghui) about humankind's chances for salvation. He explains that the best venue is through the various city gods and their divine administrators, who will come to aid people whenever they recite this scripture. As a

---

[41] Two further texts deal with Doumu in the Daoist canon, the *Xiantian doumu zougao xuanke* (Mysterious Observances to Petition to the Dipper Mother, Born Before Heaven, DZ 1452), which contains her hagiography together with a ritual dedicated to her; and the *Beidou ershiba zhangjing* (Scripture of Twenty-eight Stanzas of the Dipper, DZ 629). The latter has a story about Emperor Ming of the Later Han, who is commonly associated with the official introduction of Buddhism, meeting a woman on the road. She turns out to be the Dipper Mother and, in a story that closely resembles the revelation of Heshang gong to Emperor Wen, gives him startling and powerful revelations on how to prolong life and protect the country. Emphasizing that she is not simply one but seven-in-one, the true representative of all Dipper stars, she provides him with chants for each—contained in the 28 stanzas of the text.

[42] So characterized in Johnson 1985, 388. For more on the city god, see also Hansen 1990, 181; Zito 1996, 72.

result, the assembled host pays its respects to the city god and his powers of the Dao.

A related example is the Daoist enfeoffment of Goddess of the Morning Clouds (Bixia yuanjun) through the Heavenly Worthy of Primordial Beginning. A popular goddess whose cult began with the discovery of a statue on Mount Tai, she became known under the Ming as the mountain god's daughter and merciful helper of the dead that pass under his judgment.[43] As documented in the *Bixia yuanjun huguo baosheng jing* (Scripture on the Guarding of Life and Protection of the Country Through the Goddess of the Morning Clouds, DZ 1445), she was officially integrated into the Daoist pantheon through formal empowerment by the Heavenly Worthy, using formulas and ceremonies similar to those described above. Her case illustrates the wide reach of continuing Daoist expansion and also documents that Lord Lao, in his role as sponsor of popular gods, was on equal footing with the Heavenly Worthy. Thus he recovered a high cultic standing and at the same time became removed from more immediate interaction with living people.[44]

* * * * *

From his first full hagiography in the second century until well into the Ming dynasty, Lord Lao has served as an inspiration, model, and sponsor of other deities, Daoist, Buddhist, and popular. His tale, classic because it is the key hagiography of the Dao, combines a number of features necessary for proper divinity, including the god's emergence from the pure energies of the Dao, his repeated appearances over long periods of time, his supernatural birth among humanity, his training in the methods of immortality, and his salvific efforts on behalf of all beings. Lord Lao being the Dao, the Dao being only one, and all gods being part of the Dao, it is not surprising that some of his hagiographic and personal characteristics should be attributed to high-ranking deities or that certain separate gods should take on some of his functions.

Two general patterns emerge regarding the various gods with whom Lord Lao can be linked. Deities are characterized as being in the image of Lord Lao and are seen as direct representatives of the Dao; and certain aspects or specific functions of Lord Lao split off and are under-

---

[43] A description of the goddess and her origins is found in Naquin 1992, 334–45.

[44] The role of Lord Lao as sponsoring and supporting high god continues also today; he is the deity who gives orders to demon quellers and other divine emissaries that help people. See Dean 1993, 129–30.

stood as being fulfilled by separate gods. The first pattern is manifested in the casting of the Buddha in Lord Lao's image and applying a number of typical characteristics of the Dao to the foreign god, while emphasizing that there can be only one Dao and thus only one central god. All other sages or teachers of dynasties are then mere manifestations of it. This line of thinking is supported by both the Buddhist demand for the unity of all teachings and by the Daoist claim that Lord Lao and the Buddha are ultimately one. This pattern appears again with the identification of the Dark Warrior as Lord Lao's eighty-second transformation and with his hagiographic imitation of the earlier god, which lends strength to the Dark Warrior's standing at the center of heaven and his personification of the Dao.

The second pattern applies to other gods such as the messiah, the creator, and the revealer of scriptures in medieval Daoism, who all represent special functions of the Dao and assume certain aspects of Lord Lao's divine career. It also applies to the various popular gods of the Ming, who fulfill highly specialized functions in their roles as city god, mother of the Dipper, or protectress of seafarers, and provide their devotees with the protective and beneficent power of the Dao without, however, being the Dao themselves. In either case, these adaptations of the Lord Lao tradition were perpetuated by organized groups and educated believers, Buddhists, and members of the Highest Clarity and Numinous Treasure schools in the middle ages, and imperial officials and the Daoist establishments in later dynasties. They all make use of Lord Lao and the tales surrounding him to express their various concerns and understanding of the world. Whether they raise a messiah figure to high veneration, express Daoist integration through the trinity, designate a new celestial god as protector of the state, or define the status and powers of new popular gods, Lord Lao remains influential behind the scene. He functions as a legitimating force that can integrate even the most startling new developments into the hallowed currents of tradition.

6

Art, Literature, and Talismans
Lord Lao as Popular Protector

To judge the popularity of a deity, one looks at the number and social distribution of worshipers. Simply stated, the more people worship a deity, and the more temples, sanctuaries, offerings, and celebrations are dedicated to him or her, the more popular the god. Or again, the wider the social spectrum of devotees, the broader the variety of classes, trades, and professions of worshipers, the greater the god's popularity. To judge the standing of any given divinity in this respect is easiest in the present age, since one can go and find out how he or she is worshiped, in what numbers, and by which people.

Now, by any of these standards Lord Lao in China today is not a popular deity at all, having been left far behind by the gods he sponsored in the Ming, such as Mazu and the city god. Still, he continues to have an active presence in organized Daoist schools and has been the object of renewed general interest and a touchstone for touristic developments. Active worship of the god is practiced mainly by adherents of the organized schools and not by the larger populace, for whom Lord Lao is still first and foremost Laozi, the ancient philosopher of Daoist thought and author of the *Daode jing*. As such he has been popularized through this book, which is universally read and widely translated, has been adapted into comics and song, and even appears in a feline-themed version.[1] In addition, Laozi as the representative of classical Daoism appears in pictures and murals of popular temples that show him either riding his ox or standing with Confucius and the Buddha to represent the "harmony of the three teachings" (see Li 1993a, 36).

---

[1] Laozi in comics is found in Tsai et al. 1989. A version of his text, sung in a country-blues style, was created by the "Tao Alchemical Company" (see Dudley 1990), while the prime feline rendition of the text goes back to Waldo Japussy (1990).

To judge popularity historically is much more difficult, since information on the frequency of temple construction and the number and social class of visitors is scarce and irregular, the more so the farther one goes back in history. One way of appreciating the popularity of a traditional Chinese cult is to look at the titles bestowed upon its deity by the imperial government, often after a lengthy process of petition by the local community where it first appeared (see Hansen 1990). This, however, does not apply to Lord Lao who received his many and increasingly lengthy titles upon imperial orders as part of a centralized religious policy and not on popular demand. Still, there are a few sources that provide glimpses of Lord Lao as a popular god in Chinese history, although they are sporadic at best and not consistent in either their format or the type of information they provide.

There are first several stele inscriptions of the Northern Wei, in the late fifth and sixth centuries, in which Lord Lao is invoked for blessings and good fortune for people of lay and non-elite status. The information they provide is further supplemented by several fifth-century tomb contracts from south China, in which Lord Lao grants benefits to the deceased. Next, there is a report by Du Guangting on miracles wrought by the god in the Tang, both at temples dedicated to him and to ordinary people who prayed to him ardently. Third, there are a number of texts of late Tang and Song origin in the canon that present spells and talismans associated with Lord Lao for such mundane activities as running a business, building a house, planting a crop, and having a baby. Around the same time, with the shift of Daoist practice to itinerant ritual masters and thunder rites, two further groups of texts of a semi-popular nature appear. One focuses on attaining a long and healthy life with the help of talismans centered on the Dipper; the other, transmitted by the school of the Heavenly Heart, has the same aim, but relies on visualizations and incantations. In the Southern Song, moreover, the popular *Taishang ganying pian* (better known as the *Ganying pian*, The Highest Lord's Tract on Action and Response, DZ 1167) appeared. This is a morality treatise on divine rewards and punishments that initiated the widespread practice of keeping ledgers of merit and demerit (*gongguo ge*) and is linked loosely with Lord Lao. And finally, in the late Ming Lord Lao appears in two popular novels: in one as the master instructor of the Eight Immortals, in the other as a martial hero fighting demon armies at the end of the Shang (see Table 7).

Table 7
Popular inscriptions, protective talismans, and Ming novels

Text	English title, Date/Source
Popular Inscriptions	
Fodao bei	Buddho-Daoist Stele [of Wei Wenlang], dat. 424
Huang laojun bei	Stele of Sovereign Lord Lao [of Yao Boduo], dat. 496
Yang Lenghei bei	Stele of Yang Lenghei, dat. 500
Feng Shenyu bei	Stele of Feng Shenyu, dat. 505
Taishang bei	Highest Venerable [of Mr. Cai], dat. 548
Laojun bei	Venerable Lord [of Jiang Cuan], dat. 565
Laojun bei	Venerable Lord [of Du Chong—], dat. 568
Tianzun bei	Heavenly Worthy [of Li Yuanhai], dat. 572
Personal Miracles	
Daojiao lingyan ji	Record of Daoist Miracles, DZ 590
Spells and Talismans	
Anzhai bayang jing	Scripture on Building a Safe Home [Without Offending] the Eight Yang Energies, DZ 634
Buxie bayang jing	Scripture on Compensating the Eight Yang Energies, DZ 635
Hunyuan sanbu fu	Mystery Prime's Talismans of the Three Divisions, DZ 673
Popular Morality	
Taishang ganying pian	The Highest Lord's Tract on Action and Response, DZ 1167
Ming Novels	
Dongyou ji	Journey to the East, dat. 1566
Fengshen yanyi	Investiture of the Gods, c. 1580

Popular Inscriptions

Only a few traces of early Daoist art remain. There are tomb paintings and mirrors of the Later Han showing Daoist gods and immortals, such as the Queen Mother of the West. There are also talismans and pictures of gods as aids to visualization that survive in texts and a number of stelae under the Northern Wei that show Daoist figures and bear inscriptions of prayers to Daoist gods.[2] Among the latter, of which only about fifty objects have been found (as opposed to thousands of Buddhist works), most are dedicated to Lord Lao either alone or in conjunction with other figures occasionally identified as Buddhist. The earliest example is the Buddho-Daoist stele of Wei Wenlang of the year

---

[2] On Daoist art in the Han, see Wu 1986; Kominami 1991; 1997. On art in visualization, see Yamada 1995a. For details on Daoist statues and stelae, see Matsubara 1961; Kamitsuka 1993; 1998; Pontynen 1980; 1980a; 1983; James 1986; Abe 1997; Bokenkamp 1997a.

424, which shows a Daoist figure on one face and has Buddhist text and images on the other three. The stele with the longest and most detailed inscription is the "Sovereign Lord Lao" of Yao Boduo, dated to 496. Further objects include the stelae of Yang Lenghei (dat. 500), Feng Shenyu (dat. 505), Mr. Cai (dat. 548), Jiang Cuan (dat. 565), Du Chong— (dat. 568), and Li Yuanhai (dat. 572).[3]

Buddhist and Daoist images are often hard to distinguish. They share the dominant characteristics of Buddhist sculpture, including

> one or two dragons arched across the top; the lotus blossom pedestal; the flame-shaped mandorla, sometimes including the flame pattern on its surface; two attendants; celestial figures above the niche; lions to guard the throne; and patrons in lieu of attendants. (James 1986, 72)

They also use the same standard formula for their inscriptions, containing the date and donor of the object together with a prayer explaining its purpose. Daoist images moreover show a rectangular headdress, official-style robes, a beard, and a fly whisk, but often only the inscription makes the identity of the deity clear.[4]

Practically all known examples of Daoist sculpture before the unification in 589 show the deified Lord Lao in one form or another, referring to him as Highest Lord, Lord Lao, or Sovereign Lord Lao. For example, the second oldest stele, dated to 496, is called the "Sovereign Lord Lao" and depicts the god on its main face, sketchy in figure but accompanied by two attendants and wearing both a distinctive head-dress and a triangular beard. The accompanying inscription lauds the mystery and creative power of the Dao, then names Lord Lao, here called Li Er, as its foremost representative. It implores his salvific powers to support the creation of peace and political stability on earth, the speedy salvation of the Yao family ancestors, and the lasting good fortune of living relatives. The latter, in particular, are hoped to attain immortality in the future:

> May we soar freely through the great void,
> Where sounds of Brahma resonate,
> Be friends with the immortals,
> And pause to look at the great Jade Capital!
> (Kamitsuka 1993, 256; see also Bokenkamp 1997a, 59–60)

---

[3] The two earliest of these objects are discussed in Abe 1997; Bokenkamp 1997a; Kamitsuka 1998. On Yang Manhei's and Feng Shenyu's stelae, see Abe 1997, 76–79. On the latter four, see Kamitsuka 1993, 259–75.

[4] On the iconographic distinctions, see James 1986, 72; Abe 1997, 71.

Here, as in other parts of this inscription and in inscriptions of various other stelae, a thorough mixture of Buddhist and Daoist worldview is obvious, as is the lay and non-elite background of the donors (Abe 1997, 78). In the wake of the Daoist theocracy in the early part of the fifth century, the practice of Daoist rituals and the worship of Lord Lao for the sake of personal happiness and political stability had become part of the popular practice of religion. Daoist practices were increasingly mixed with Buddhist notions such as karma and retribution, rebirth and hell, and the coming of the savior Maitreya—all alluded to in the inscriptions.

In terms of Daoist doctrine, influence from the southern schools, where Lord Lao was increasingly worshiped as a popular god, can be detected.[5] From the south we have further archaeological evidence, in religious ordinances found in tombs. These so-called tomb contracts, first discovered in Later Han sites, served two purposes: to secure the land occupied by the deceased against this- and otherworldly claims and to ensure safe conduct and proper guidance for him on his journey to the underworld (see Seidel 1985; 1987; Nickerson 1996, 191–92). Five such tomb contracts, excavated from Hunan, are dated to between 433 and 520 and were published in Chinese archaeological journals (Nickerson 1996, 184 n. 9). They all "are written as edicts from the deified Laozi, the Most High," often called "Lord Lao newly arisen" (Nickerson 1996, 194). The god here grants the deceased the rights to his or her tomb plot and promises a smooth transition to the otherworld; he serves as a popular deity who provides support to suffering humanity, just as he does in inscriptions from the north. A mediator between heaven, earth, and the underworld, Lord Lao was present both in statues on mountainsides and in tomb edicts, providing an active connection with the divine. Praised as the savior of humanity and model sage, his powers could raise people from their earthly plight to the heavenly spheres or grant them a welcoming reception in the realm below.[6]

Personal Miracles

Lord Lao's wondrous powers used for the benefit of ordinary people are also documented in a number of miracles bestowed by the god or

---

[5] For an examination of specifically Numinous Treasure concepts in the Yao Boduo inscription, see Bokenkamp 1997a.

[6] This image of the god may go back to Mahāyāna Buddhist influence, notably ideas found in the *Vimalakīrti nideśa* and the Lotus Sūtra. See Pontynen 1980, 196–97; 1983, 31.

one of his representations (statues or images). Du Guangting of the late Tang records twenty-one such miraculous events in his *Daojiao lingyan ji* (see Table 8), presenting the events as responses of the numinous (*lingying*) or evidence for the numinous (*lingyan*), i.e., visible aspects of the universal law of impulse and response (*ganying*), according to which all good and bad deeds have their effect in heavenly signs and are part of the invisible yet pervasive activity of the cosmos. Lord Lao's deeds in this context are evidence for the continued close relationship of the deity with the people, and are thus, as Verellen has it, "evidential miracles in response to an act of devotion" (1992, 228).

The miracles can be divided into four groups: wondrous events in connection with a statue or painting (8 cases); appearances of the god in emergencies (8 cases); prophecies come true (2 cases); and rewards for meticulous worship (3 cases).

Table 8
Miraculous manifestations of Lord Lao in the *Daojiao lingyan ji*

No.	Page	Event and location
1	6.1a	In a wall painting in Sichuan (Ziji gong)
2	1b	With a black moustache in a painting in the Guangtian guan of Chang'an
3	2b	As a jade statue on Mount Zhongnan (Louguan)
4	3b	As a jade statue in the Yuju guan (Sichuan)
5	4a	In spontaneous patterns on a stone cliff in Langzhou (Sichuan)
6	4b	As an iron statue in Sichuan (Ziji gong)
7	5b	In Heishui in Sanquan (Shanxi)
8	6b	As an iron statue at the Lingji guan in Changming (Sichuan)
9	7a	In an encounter with Luo Quansi (Chang'an)
10	8b	In an encounter with Cui Qizhi (near Luoyang)
11	10a	In the prophecy of Recluse Lai (Jianghu, Taihu)
12	7.1a	In response to the worship of Jia Xiang (Chang'an)
13	2a	On Mount Longhe (Meizhou, Sichuan)
14	2b	At the Longrui guan
15	4a	In response to the worship of Xu Shu (Huzhou, Taihu)
16	5a	In response to the worship of Shen Ying (Zhejiang)
17	6b	As a stone statue at the Baihe guan on Mount Xiao (Zhejiang)
18	7b	At Tiantai guan (Zhejiang, Mount Tiantai)
19	8b	In the dream of Yang Nao'er (Chengdu, Sichuan)
20	9a	As the golden statue of Gou Daorong
21	9a	As a gift of gold to Yang Wenjian (Mianzhu, Sichuan)

To describe the first, wondrous events in connection with a divine representation include both the manifestation of unusual radiances indicative of the presence of a wondrous object that is duly recovered and the miraculous activity of an already existing image that supports the good and punishes the wicked. The most famous example of finding such a wondrous object is the Heavenly Treasure case of 741, after which Xuanzong renamed his reign (Table 8, no. 3; see also chapter 14). A similar occurrence is also recorded for the Yuju guan (Jade Office Monastery) in Chengdu, a major Daoist institution (Li 1985, 77), where a strange, high-reaching radiance was discovered emanating from the river in front of the monastery. It was red on top and white below and upon closer inspection looked just like Lord Lao. Emperor Xuanzong, after fleeing to Sichuan in 755, dreamed of just such an image. A matching statue was duly found in the river and set out in Lord Lao's local Taiqing gong (no. 4).

Another case occurred at the Baihe guan (White Crane Monastery) in Zhejiang. There, in 873, a strange glow was observed in the back of the main hall, rising nine feet from the floor. The Daoist Lü Jiansu paid his respects to the glow, which in response coagulated into a clear image of Lord Lao. Digging at the spot, the Daoists discovered a stone statue of the god, 4–5 feet in height. Lü had it washed and properly installed and worshiped it regularly, as a result of which he gained powers of healing and rainmaking (no. 17).[7]

Two cases involving statues are not records of wondrous finds but describe the miraculous survival of the object even through times of destruction or crime. In the Ziji gong (Purple Culmen Monastery) of Chengdu, for instance, an iron image of Lord Lao, five feet high and very ancient, withstood the destruction of its hall several times without coming to harm. Once recovered and set up with proper honors, it gave forth a vigorous radiance and brought good omens to the city (no. 6). Similarly, the image of Lord Lao in the Lingji guan (Monastery of the Numinous Assembly) in Changming, Sichuan, defended itself success-fully against theft. While the images of its two attendants were snatched by a father-son team and melted down for gain, it managed to abscond in time and take itself to the neighboring Anqi guan (Master Anqi Monastery), about five miles away. Here the resident monks discovered it sitting in front of the main gate. They installed it properly and in due course learned of its original whereabouts (no. 8).

Two numinous paintings of Lord Lao give further evidence of his miraculous powers. One, in the Ziji gong, actively defended itself against

---

[7] Another similar case is the find of a jade tablet on Mount Tiantai in Zhejiang. It carried the inscription: "Even when the water of the ocean is exhausted and Mount Tiantai crumbles, the imperial house will be honored and my blessings will continue without fail." The find is followed in 872 by the discovery of an image of Lord Lao nearby (Table 8, no. 18).

mockery when a man idly shot at the gold piece that signified Lord Lao's bench. The arrow ricocheted back and pinned him to a tree. "The blood running from his body would not stop," Du notes (no. 1). In the other case, a depiction of the deity in the Guangtian guan (Radiant Heaven Monastery) of Chang'an, showing him in full formal gear and surrounded by celestials, turned out to be identical in every detail to a vision of Emperor Daizong's (r. 763–780) who dreamed he was invited to join Lord Lao in a cosmic journey and got to see the gods for himself (no. 2). In all these cases, a representation of the god is either discovered on the appearance of celestial signs or found highly efficacious in its powers.

A second group of miracles concerns Lord Lao's support of people in emergencies. Here we have the case of Jia Xiang, a commoner living in Chang'an, who was rescued with his family from certain death at the hand of Huang Chao and his rebels because he never tired of worshiping the image of the god (no. 12).[8] Similarly saved from rebels were the official Luo Quansi and the commoner Shen Ying (nos. 9, 16). The peasant Xu Shu was pulled from poverty after a flood (no. 15), and the officials Gao Yuanyu and Wang Zongbian were saved from failure to procure rain after a drought (nos. 5, 14). In addition, when the Lord Lao temple in Sanquan (Shanxi) was threatened with destruction by a band of robbers, the god appeared in the form of a huge white snake and threatened them so vigorously that they fled (no. 7). He also appeared as a purple cloud to save a group of people who had taken refuge from marauding rebels in his sanctuary on Mount Longhe in Sichuan (no. 13).

A third group of miracles involves the appearance of Lord Lao either to fulfill a prophecy or transmit one. One case occurred in 873. The commoner Cui Qizhi was on his way to Luoyang when he saw an old man by the roadside. Like Zhang Liang in his encounter with the Master of the Yellow Stone (Huangshi gong; see Bauer 1956), the old man requested a drink; Cui complied and was rewarded with both a prophecy of great future unrest and the assurance that the deity would stand by to help. Once he had spoken, the old man vanished, confirming the supernatural nature of the encounter (no. 10). In another case, Recluse Lai from the Taihu area served as the retainer of Lord Yang and predicted correctly, with Lord Lao's help, the professional competence and success of two of his aides (no. 11).

The fourth category of Lord Lao's miraculous manifestations, as documented by Du Guangting, contains cases of special rewards for

---

[8] See Verellen 1989, 78–79. For more on late Tang rebellions, see Miyakawa 1964; 1974.

piety. In one, the family of the adolescent Yang Nao'er was exceedingly pious; he and his parents prayed regularly before a Lord Lao statue. When the boy was drafted into the army and got lost in a skirmish, the god appeared to his parents in a dream and they succeeded in getting him home safely (no. 19). Then again, there was Gou Daorong, a sculptor who wished nothing more than to fashion a gold image of Lord Lao but lacked the means. Lo and behold, while praying to the god, a wind arose and some wondrous pollen drifted onto the ground before him then changed into the precious metal (no. 20). Finally, there is the story of Yang Wenjian, a poverty-stricken peasant who worshiped Lord Lao without fail. During a heavy downpour, an old woman came to seek shelter with him and left him a bundle she claimed came from an old man. The bundle was full of gold. The old woman vanished, the old man was identified as Lord Lao, and Yang lived happily ever after (no. 21).

More than a third of these stories are set in Sichuan, Du Guang-ting's place of residence; five are located in the capital Chang'an or other central places (Louguan, Luoyang), three are set in Zhejiang, and two in the Taihu area. About half are not dated, with the remainder equally distributed between the mid-eighth and late ninth centuries. The record is thus spread both in time and space, showing the variety and steadiness of the deity's response to the faithful. As in the inscriptions surviving from the Northern Wei, in this record of miracles Lord Lao is an approachable and helpful god who will suffer no mockery but stands by his followers with infallible support. He bestows prophecies, grants visions, and leads followers to wondrous finds. He does so not only for people of lofty status but is equally supportive of commoners and peasants. He is very much a popular god, a deity worshiped widely by ordinary people.

Spells and Talismans

In a rather different line of popular support, there is evidence of Lord Lao providing spells and talismans for the protection of people in their ordinary activities. This also dates from the Tang and Song, when talismanic and exorcistic practices appear more prominently in the literature.[9] It appears in two sources: a pair of texts on rites and incantations

---

[9] On the use of talismans and seals in healing during these periods, see Strickmann 1993; Davis 1994, 216. For Song exorcistic rites and related Tantric and Daoist practices, such as the pursuit of demons by entire armies of divine forces, see Davis 1994, 223–38

to be undertaken during the planning and building of houses, and a collection of talismans for a wide variety of practical purposes.[10]

The spells on house building are found in the *Anzhai bayang jing* (Scripture on Building a Safe Home [Without Offending] the Eight Yang Energies, DZ 634) and the *Buxie bayang jing* (Scripture on Compensating the Eight Yang Energies, DZ 635). Both are short documents of two pages, presented as a celestial dialogue discussing protection against divine wrath when building a home. Typical of rites and meditations associated with Lord Lao, the four heraldic animals stand again in the center, joined by the gods of the sun and moon, the year star and celestial dragons, as well as the deities of the Six Jia and those of the twelve hours (DZ 634, 1b; DZ 635, 1ab).

The key passage of the texts, moreover, is almost identical with a section of the *Foshuo anzhai shenzhou jing* (Sūtra of Sacred Spells to Build a Safe Home, Preached by the Buddha, T. 1394, 21.211a–12b) and also appears in the *Foshuo tiandi bayang shenzhou jing* (Sūtra of Sacred Spells for the Eight Yang Energies of Heaven and Earth, Preached by the Buddha, T. 2897, 85.1422b–24a). The latter is a Chinese apocryphon associated with popular Buddhism of the seventh century, a copy of which was recovered from Dunhuang (S. 5373). It appears in Japanese bibliographies as early as 761 and has survived there in several editions.[11]

All these texts begin by warning practitioners that whatever building they erect, "an eastern corridor, a western hallway, a southern chamber, or a northern hall" (T. 21.912a), or even a well, a carriage house, or a stable for their livestock (DZ 634, 1a), they are bound to offend the gods of earth and sky. To protect themselves against the gods' revenge, they must recite the scripture with its powerful spells to offer apologies to the spirits and make the demons "hide in darkness, scatter to far corners of the four directions,

---

[10] An earlier link between Lord Lao and talismans, albeit in an alchemical and not popular setting, is found in the *Baopuzi*, which mentions a set of five Laozi talismans for entering the mountains (*Laozi rushan wufu*) and a Lord Lao talisman for transforming the body (*Laojun huashen fu*). See *Baopuzi* 11.3a, 8.13a. The same connection comes up again in the *Hunyuan zhenlu*, according to which the god transmits a scripture of eight talismans (*Taiqing bafu jing*) to Yin Xi (7b; see Kusuyama 1977; Baldrian-Hussein 1990, 173). Although part of popular practice, it is quite conceivable that the god's spells and talismans for ordinary purposes were also used by the Celestial Masters and thus played a role also in the organized religion. However, materials on institutional usage have not survived, and because this aspect of the god is more visible in the dynastic sources, it comes to be classified as part of popular worship.

[11] On this Buddhist text and its Japanese editions, see Masuo 1994, 392–405; 1998.

and never dare to do any harm."[12] One's estate, including even granaries, cattle pens, chicken coops, stables, and gardens (DZ 634, 1b), will not only be free from disaster, it will be blessed with good fortune, yin and yang rising in harmony and the dragon deities of the earth well contented (2a). This state, in turn, will create blessings for one's descendants, community, and the country at large (DZ 635, 1b).

A similar concern with daily activities and the well-being of people in their ordinary lives is found in a large collection of Lord Lao talismans contained in the *Hunyuan sanbu fu* (Mystery Prime's Talismans of the Three Divisions, DZ 673), a Song dynasty work in three scrolls (Ren and Zhong 1991, 481). The text contains hundreds of talismans, each with brief instructions for application on all kinds of occasions. They serve to ensure home security, grant protection during moves and travel, help in planting and sowing, support the prolonging of life and the pacification of restless souls, ensure safe pregnancies and deliveries, and give success in office and help advance rank (see Fig. 10). They are also useful against nightmares and bad tempers, sicknesses and fevers; they help dispel dangers and disasters, ghosts and demons, and tame the "hundred sprites." The latter seem to have been especially noxious, being able to take up residence in rats, snakes, foxes, chickens, birds, horses, pigs, and other apparently commonplace creatures. Further, special talismans are provided for protection during different hours of the day and for special months and seasons of the year. There is even a group of ten useful devices that help people consume large quantities of liquor without getting drunk (*Sanbu fu* 3.31b–32a).

Lord Lao in these talismanic scriptures again appears as a broadly popular god whose prime concern is the day-to-day well-being and happiness of the common people. Here, too, he protects the faithful from harm and demons and provides special support for all sorts of occasions and situations.

Morality and Fiction

In a completely different vein, Lord Lao is associated with a popular morality treatise that originated in the Southern Song. The *Ganying pian* is a short text of 1,280 characters that has been edited and commented on numerous times in China and translated variously into

---

[12] This passage appears both in the Daoist and Buddhist texts. See DZ 634, 1b; T. 85.1422c–23a; Masuo 1994, 395.

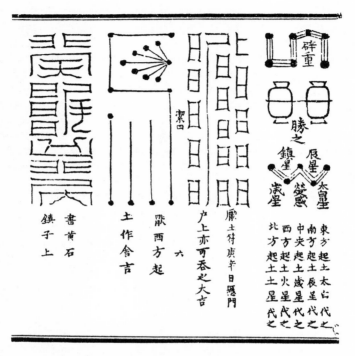

Fig. 10. Protective talismans dispensed by Lord Lao.
Source: Hunyuan sanbu fu 1.7b

English.[13] It was first published around 1164 in the southern part of the country in an edition by Li Zhiji (d. 1182), an official from Sichuan who was broadly educated but seems to have had little contact with organized religions. A Neo-Confucian moralistic tendency is clearly present in the work.

The *Ganying pian* is divided into four sections. The first is an introduction that outlines the blessings and punishments of heaven meted out by the celestial administration. The second section exhorts people to be socially conscious and do good, specifying the rewards of benevolence and saintliness. The third and longest part details the nature and eventual punishment of evildoers, while the fourth and last section reverts again to more general admonitions and encouragement to do good.[14]

The connection of this work to Lord Lao is both spurious and well established. It is spurious because the text itself only mentions the Highest Lord (Taishang) as its speaker, and aside from one preface by Chen Huan in the year 1233 (DZ 1167, 4b), the commentators do not mention Lord Lao or even trouble to identify the Highest Lord. Yet the connection is also well established since authors, both ancient and contemporary, take it for granted that only one deity could possibly be the "Highest Lord." Thus Carus and Suzuki in their translation *Treatise on Response and Retribution* say this text is "by Lao Tze" (1973), and even Brokaw has no doubt that "Taishang" is "the title given the philosopher Lord Lao in his status as a god" (1991, 36).

Following Chen Huan's lead and joining the general consensus, I will assume that Lord Lao has been considered responsible for the *Ganying pian* at least since Yuan times. This reveals yet another popular dimension of the god, one that in a different way recovers his role as the revealer of moral rules among the medieval Celestial Masters. However, the Lord Lao of the Song was also a popular deity, and his morality addressed less the ordained practitioners of the Dao than a large lay population. This is in line with the fact that the text's compiler, Li Zhiji, was not a Daoist hermit who encountered a divine vision, but a Confucian official who perceived an acute need to educate the masses. Similarly, these moral rules do not form the foundation of new Daoist groups or sectarian organizations but stand at the beginning of a merit-counting craze, formulated in its practical details in the *Taiwei xianjun*

---

[13] English translations of the text are found in Carus and Suzuki 1973; Coyle 1981. For its history in China, see Bell 1992. On its author, see Brokaw 1991, 42.

[14] See Carus and Suzuki 1973, 51–66; Brokaw 1991, 38.

gongguo ge (Ledger of Merit and Demerit of the Immortal of Great Tenuity, DZ 186), that engulfed the country in later centuries.[15]

A completely different image of the god appears in popular fiction of the Ming dynasty, where he is featured in the vernacular *Dongyou ji* (Journey to the East) and *Fengshen yanyi* (Investiture of the Gods).[16] The *Dongyou ji*, written by Wu Yuantai (fl. 1566) in the mid-sixteenth century, is a story about the Eight Immortals and their adventures as they travel east toward realization of the Dao. It features Lord Lao in its second and third sections, after describing Li Tieguai's initial cultivation of perfection (1a–2b). The god is introduced first with a lengthy retelling of his hagiography (2b–9b), then is shown on Mount Hua as an immortality teacher joined by a fellow immortal (9b–11a).

The retelling of Lord Lao's hagiography relies heavily on accounts of Yin Xi's life and makes much use of the *Xisheng jing*. It first states that Laozi and Lord Lao are one and the same, a deity who has undergone regular transformations since the creation of the world. Next, it details the god's life: his birth under the Shang, the origins of Yin Xi, the encounter between the two sages, the testing of Xu Jia, the transmission of the *Daode jing*, Yin Xi's practice and authorship of Daoist texts, the second meeting in Sichuan, the celestial recognition of Yin Xi and liberation of his ancestors. Skipping over the conversion of the barbarians, the text next describes Lord Lao's appearances in Chinese history, from his meeting with Confucius through his revelation of the Dao to Gan Ji and Zhang Daoling to his helpful manifestations under the Tang. In each case, the most pertinent event is depicted in an illustration (see Table 9), while the narrative as a whole culminates in praise of Lord Lao as eternal and unchanging in his essence, unfathomable in his vagueness, endless in his changes, and beneficent savior of people in the heavenly realms. Two short citations from historical and literary sources conclude the hagiography.

Supplementing this information, Lord Lao's colleague is introduced, the immortal Wanqiu, an obscure figure otherwise described only in the *Dongxian zhuan* (Pervasive Immortals' Biographies). A man of the Shang dynasty, Wanqiu lived for well over a millennium and served as the teacher of Pengzu the long-lived, who was identified with Lord Lao during the Han. According to the *Dongyou ji*, Daoist teaching in all its forms emerged through the cooperation of these two, Lord Lao standing for its

---

[15] On the latter text and the activity of merit counting, see Brokaw 1991, 36.

[16] I am indebted to Patrick Hanan for pointing out the appearance of Lord Lao in the *Dongyou ji*.

salvific and cosmological dimensions, and Wanqiu representing its technical and administrative side.

This retelling of the hagiography and repositioning of Lord Lao reflects the rewriting of his career after the debates under the Yuan. Leaving out his early transformations, emphasizing Yin Xi and the *Xisheng jing*, and bypassing the entire conversion complex, it shows that the god was acceptable as a representative of the Dao, as the teacher of Yin Xi, and as a source of revelations; but he had no place transforming into an advisor of rulers, claiming identity with the Buddha, or converting the barbarians.

Table 9

Events in Lord Lao's life illustrated in the *Dongyou ji*

Page	Caption
3a	The Jade Maiden gives birth to Laozi under the plum tree
3b	Yin Xi studies the celestial signs
4a	Laozi rides an ox to leave through the Hangu Pass
4b	Yin Xi beseeches Laozi to stay and speak about the Dao
5a	Lord Lao transforms [into a woman] to test Xu Jia
5b	Yin Xi begs Lord Lao to transmit the Dao
6a	Lord Lao strides onto a cloud and ascends to heaven
6b	Yin Xi arrives in Sichuan in search of the black sheep shop
7a	Yin Xi once again meets Lord Lao
7b	Lord Lao summons the host of immortals
8a	Emperor Wen sends an envoy to ask about the Dao
8b	Lord Lao descends during several generations
9a	Ji Shanxing meets an immortal on Mount Yangjiao
9b	Lord Lao and Wanqiu speak about the Dao on Mount Hua
10a	Li Tiekuai arrives on Mount Hua in pursuit of the Dao
10b	Lord Lao transmits the Dao to Li Tieguai
11a	Li Tiekuai makes his apologies and leaves Lord Lao

Lord Lao's role is reduced to a strictly religious function, leaving the political aside—except for his support of the Tang house, which claimed him as an ancestor. In addition, paired with the immortal Wanqiu, his teaching is limited to the salvific and theoretical, while the latter is responsible for Daoism's more practical aspects. Not surprisingly, in this role he appears soft and pliant:

> Lord Lao was seated on a throne, bathed in a bright radiance, and surrounded by damask stars and auspicious clouds. His flesh and body were soft and modest, as if he were a young girl in the women's quarters. His essence and spirit were ample and full, as if he were a babe in swaddling cloths (10a).

Whereas Lord Lao is here a soft and feminine representation of the original Dao, Wanqiu is said to have "boyish looks and crane-white hair, bright blue pupils and noble eyebrows"; he is also the more outgoing and active of the pair (10ab).

Lord Lao's teaching, too, is one of softness, silence, and harmony. Instructing Li Tiekuai, he says:

> Let me tell you: The essence of the Dao is obscure and vague; its ultimate is dark and silent. There is no [tangible] Dao, nothing to be heard. Just embrace spirit and be tranquil; then your body will naturally find its rest. You must be pure, you must be tranquil! Never exert your body, never stir your essence, never activate your thoughts! Always be steady, and you can find eternal life. (10b–11a)

This abstract and rather general instruction is then supplemented by Wanqiu with the assurance that Li's name is already inscribed in the immortal registers. He inspires Li to practice solitary meditation and become the leader of the Eight Immortals.

Lord Lao in this novel is part of a pair of immortals, an active teacher of individual aspirants in the purity and tranquility of the Dao. Visually he is presented as the pure origin of the Dao, a personification of universal creation who advises seekers to calm their minds so they can feel the vague obscurity of the Dao within. He is a nonpolitical god whose main activity is the advising and guiding of devout adepts, a potent yet accessible instructor in the Dao.

A rather different picture emerges in the roughly contemporaneous novel *Fengshen yanyi*, attributed to either Xu Zhonglin (d. 1566) or Lu Xixing (ca. 1520–1601; see Liu 1962, 118), which describes in mythological fashion the fight of the rising Zhou against the last tyrant of the Shang. In each case, developments on earth are paralleled by activities in the heavens, and Lord Lao appears repeatedly to support the fight of the righteous Daoist group, the Promulgating Sect (Shanjiao), against the opposing Intercepting Sect (Jiejiao), led by the Grand Master of Heaven. This latter group lays various traps for the advancing Zhou army, and time and again Lord Lao is asked to give advice and support, provide weapons and help, mastermind battle plans, or seek truce and adjudication.[17]

Called upon to help spring a particularly nasty trap, he even joins the battle, becoming manifest as "a saint on a blue fairy ox" (Gu 1992,

---

[17] On the two competing sects, see Liu 1962, 132. Laozi appears in chs. 44, 66, 83, and 84.

258) and taking an active hand in the fighting (see Fig. 11). Supported by the third powerful god of Daoism, the Heavenly Primogenitor, he begins by trying to parley with the enemy; then, still on his faithful ox, he enters the trap to engage his divine opponent in one-on-one combat. Auspicious lights flash forth, white mists rise up, magical charts turn into bridges, walking sticks become wondrous weapons, and swords glitter with numinous brilliance. Then, in the middle of the battle

> Laozi suddenly pulled in his rein and jumped out of the combat circle. He pushed his fishtail coronet to one side, and three columns of gas released from his head transformed into three immortals, called the 'clarities.'[18]

The three immortals identify themselves as representatives of the Three Clarity heavens, and together with Laozi proceed to attack his opponent from all sides. Not being real, they cannot harm him, but distract him sufficiently so that the god can hit him with his divine stick. Eventually the two fighters break up and retire to reassemble their forces. Next, Lord Lao and the Heavenly Primogenitor decide they need two extra immortals to break the trap and invite two buddhas from the western Pure Land to join them. Protected by auspicious clouds, flowers, jade necklaces, and precious pearls, they proceed to attack with Buddhist relics and lotus blossoms, and successfully enter the trap. Lord Lao promptly sends "a crash of lightning across the field," making a yellow fog spring up. Thus protected, the heroes force the nasty rebel to his knees, and make him flee for his life, scattering his followers in all directions. This supernatural defeat at the same time opens the road for the Zhou army to advance.[19]

No longer the calm and composed representative of the Dao, female and childlike, Lord Lao here emerges as a sword-swinging master of magic, a martial hero who masterminds a vigorous campaign to stamp out evil and impediments to rightful cultural progress. He is a fighter and trickster, a conjurer and wizard, who knows right and wrong and never hesitates to fight actively for his goals. Lord Lao throws talismans and bolts of lightning, brings forth gases and obscuring mists; he is a marvelous heavenly combatant on the side of all that is good and just. The active figure of Lord Lao in this work, so unlike the contemplative representative of the Dao in the contemporaneous *Dongyou ji*, reflects the

---

[18] This story appears in ch. 77. See Gu 1992, 2:258–60; Wang Deyou 1991, 27.
[19] This part of the tale is found in ch. 78. See Gu 1992, 263–67.

Fig. 11. Lord Lao as a martial hero, fighting for the good.
Source: Fengshen yanyi

popular imagination of the time that saw gods as martial heroes and warrior magicians. Coming alive with unheard-of vibrancy, this version of the deity is still the master immortal Laozi, the bringer of miracles, giver of talismans, and helper of the people.

* * * * *

Evidence from the Northern Wei in the fifth and sixth centuries well into the Ming dynasty suggests a lively tradition of popular worship of and lore about Lord Lao. It consists of inscriptions compiled by non-elite followers to pray for health and good fortune, miracle tales in which commoners are saved from a variety of disasters because of their proper devotion to the deity, scriptures containing spells and talismans that protect people from harm during everyday activities, as well as moral instructions for daily living and tales found in vernacular literature. The evidence is sporadic and gives only a glimpse of the most important and influential roles the god played in the popular mind, but even so one can deduce the existence of a widespread popular cult that persisted for centuries.

To characterize it in general terms on the basis of the material available, this cult included prayers to the deity for personal health, happiness, and success, as well as for the safety of one's family members, both living and ancestral, and for peace and stability of the state. Often the deity's special help was sought for the undertaking of major ventures, such as starting a business, building a home, or bearing a child, but more commonplace daily activities such as clearing one's home of nasty sprites or getting drunk in the tavern, were also placed under his special protection. In addition, the popular cult of Lord Lao was commonly based on material objects, be they stelae with pictures and inscriptions, statues of the deity, or various types of images and written talismans. These material objects, seen as mediators between this world and the heavens, were thought to be imbued with the god's energy and thus could protect followers from harm and rescue them from disaster. Both their proper use and their amazing efficacy are described in the texts, some revealed, others told by humans. Morality also entered in, in the sense that the right forms of behavior and ritual practice were believed to carry their proper rewards while misdemeanors toward people and the gods would be punished through retribution or by other-worldly agents. Lord Lao, always on the side of the good, did not stand by idly as his devotees were wronged or endangered but would always help, sometimes subtly, sometimes mightily—swinging his sword like a hero-warrior. Lord Lao as a popular god never failed to respond to the prayers and invocations of the faithful, and so has played an active role in the lives of his devotees over the centuries.

Conclusion to Part One

Lord Lao, an important god in traditional China and the Daoist religion, appears in many different guises and plays a variety of roles in Chinese society and religion. Examining the highly complex materials concerning him, four major roles stand out. First, Lord Lao is the central god of organized Daoist communities, notably of the Celestial Masters and Complete Perfection, but to a lesser degree also of the Heavenly Heart and the cult of the Dipper. Second, he is the symbol of political stability and cosmic harmony, venerated by the imperial court and, under foreign rulers, used to further the regime's ends through organized Daoism. Third, Lord Lao is also the teacher and model practitioner of wisdom, longevity, and immortality techniques, followed by numerous adepts of various teachings, many of whom were not part of an organized setting and remain vague if not actually unknown. And fourth, Lord Lao is the protector and helper of ordinary people in their daily lives, whose help was sought through prayers, inscriptions, and talismans by larger segments of the population and told about in miracle tales and novels. In addition, the deity had an important standing in the Chinese pantheon, which included Daoist as well as officially sanctioned, popular, and Buddhist deities; he exerted a considerable influence on the hagiographies of some of these deities and on their positions as well. It can be said that Lord Lao meant different things to different people and was both worshiped and characterized variously in accordance with their respective needs and perspectives.

To establish a ranking among these different forms of the deity in terms of their historical origins, the role of teacher of wisdom and longevity methods stands at the root of the tradition, followed by his standing as the symbol of political stability. This role culminated in Lord Lao's becoming the central god of organized communities and finally a deity of popular veneration. From a different perspective—that regarding the continuity of the god's power and influence—the ranking is somewhat different. In this case, the communal god is the most consistent and persistent figure of Lord Lao over the ages. It is followed by his roles as teacher of wisdom and longevity and as popular protector, about which materials are less common, but which also demonstrate a high degree of continuity and show his widespread influence among different segments of the population. The political cult of Lord Lao would then be ranked last because it changed most severely, figuring only in conjunction with certain dynastic developments, and having its heyday under the Tang and its most polemical manifestations under the foreign dynasties.

These evaluations of the various roles of the god are modern and based on a critical scholarly perspective. In contrast, the tradition itself has also established a set of priorities, which can be seen from the ranking of texts associated with Lord Lao in the Spirit Cavern of the Ming edition of the canon. Texts here date from the Six Dynasties to the Ming and are arranged according to the overall organizational scheme of the canon, which divides materials into several categories: fundamental texts (revealed scriptures), talismans, hagiographies, moral rules, practical methods, local records, and various supplements (see Table 10). First, then, the Spirit Cavern section on revealed scriptures contains the largest number of texts and clearly ranks them according to priority. Highest among them are philosophical and meditative works on purity and tranquility, visualization, and inner alchemy—reflecting the worldview and techniques most important to active practitioners in the Ming. Second, this section contains ritual works, including texts on the Dipper, talismans, protective measures, and the *Huming jing*, again focusing predominantly on practices actively pursued at the time of the canon's compilation. A third group of texts includes works on popular gods within the Daoist pantheon whom Lord Lao sponsored, materials on the conversion of the barbarians, and works of the Three Sovereigns school, reflecting a lesser interest in these topics.

Beyond the class of revealed scriptures, there are numerous commentaries to the *Daode jing* and other philosophical texts associated with Lord Lao (not listed in Table 10). In the section following these are two works on divine talismans, which provide a collection of popular protective devices and a number of hagiographic works on Lord Lao. They date mainly from the Song and are closely associated with Xie Shouhao. After these come medieval works on precepts, various practical works on physical cultivation, and collections of inscriptions placed at major Lord Lao temples, each in their own section. Finally, some of the most influential popular works (e.g., the *Ganying pian*) and the earliest visualization materials (e.g., the *Mingjian jing* and the *Laozi zhongjing*), are located in the supplements and

Table 10
Texts associated with Lord Lao in the Daoist canon

DZ no.	Title	Date	Category
	Spirit Cavern[a]		
	Fundamental Texts		
620	Qingjing jing	Tang	purity and tranquility
621	Doumu jing	Ming	sponsor of gods
622	Beidou yansheng jing	5 Dyn	Dipper
623	Beidou changsheng jing	5 Dyn	Dipper
624	Nandou duren jing	5 Dyn	Dipper
625	Dongdou huming jing	5 Dyn	Dipper
626	Xidou hushen jing	5 Dyn	Dipper
627	Zhongdou baoming jing	5 Dyn	Dipper
628	Zhongdou shenzhou jing	Yuan	Dipper
629*[b]	Beidou ershiba zhangjing	Yuan	Dipper
630	Jiusheng jing	Song	protection
631	Xiaozai jing	Tang	conversion
632	Huming jing	Song	talismans
633	Yinfan jing	Yuan	talismans (Xuanwu)
634	Anzhai bayang jing	Tang	protection
635	Buxie bayang jing	Tang	protection
636	Jiuhu jing	Tang	karma and retribution
637*	Feibu wuxing jing	6 Dyn	Three Sovereigns tradition
638*	Feibu nandou jing	6 Dyn	Three Sovereigns tradition
639*	Lingshu ziwen	6 Dyn	Highest Clarity tradition
640*	Badi jing	6 Dyn	Three Sovereigns tradition
641	Neiguan jing	Tang	purity and tranquility
642	Liaoxin jing	Tang	purity and tranquility
643	Neidan jing	Song	inner alchemy
644	Shouyi zhending jing	Song	inner alchemy
645	Nei riyong miaojing	Song	inner alchemy
646	Wai riyong miaojing	Song	inner alchemy
647	Lunzhuan wudao jing	Tang	karma and retribution
648	Dushi jing	5 Dyn	purity and tranquility
649	Tianfei jiuku lingyan jing	Ming	sponsor of gods
650	Changsheng yisuan miaojing	Song	protection
651	Sanyuan fushou jing	Yuan	protection
652	Jieshi zhouzu jing	Yuan	conversion/protection
653	Wudou shousheng jing	Yuan	Dipper
654	Xiaomo huguo jing	Yuan	conversion/protection
655	Huguo xiaomo jing	Yuan	sponsor of gods
656*	Riyue hunyuan jing	Song	inner alchemy
657*	Riyue hunchang jing	Yuan	Dipper
658	Miaoshi jing	Tang	conversion
659	Haoyuan jing	Tang	visualization
660*	Hunyuan bajing jing	Song	inner alchemy

[a] The list does not include commentaries (nos. 676–762).

[b] Items marked with an asterisk are texts not directly related to Lord Lao.

Table 10—*continued*

DZ no.	Title	Date	Category
661	*Laozi xiangming jing*	Tang	karma and retribution
662	*Bao fumu enzhong jing*	Tang	karma and retribution
663	*Bao fumu enzhong jing*	Song	karma (Xuanwu)
664	*Daode jing*	Zhou	philosophy
665	*Daode jing*	Zhou	philosophy
763	*Wuchu jing*	Tang	purity and tranquility
	Divine Talismans		
672	*Yisuan shenfu miaojing*	Yuan	Dipper
673	*Hunyuan sanbu fu*	Song	talismans
	Genealogical Registers		
770	*Hunyuan shengji*	Song	hagiography
771	*Laojun nianpu yaolüe*	Song	hagiography
772	*Jinshu neixu*	Song	hagiography
773	*Laozi shilüe*	Song	hagiography
774	*Youlong zhuan*	Song	hagiography
	Precepts and Regulations		
784	*Laojun jiejing*	6 Dyn.	precepts
785	*Laojun yinsong jiejing*	6 Dyn.	precepts
786	*Laojun jinglü*	6 Dyn.	precepts
787	*Taishang jingjie*	6 Dyn.	precepts
	Practical Methods		
821	*Yangsheng jue*	Tang	longevity
862	*Xuanmiao yunü zichuan xiandao*	Song	longevity
872	*Zhenzhong shenzhou jing*	Tang	visualization
875	*Cunsi tujue*	Tang	visualization
	Records and Biographies		
954	*Hunyuan zhenlu*	Tang	hagiography
956	*Zhongnan shan lidai beiji*	Yuan	inscriptions
957	*Gu Louguan ziyun yanqing ji*	Yuan	inscriptions
964	*Qingyang gong beiming*	Tang	inscriptions
968	*Longjiao shanji*	Yuan	inscriptions
	Hymns of Praise		
974	*Qingjing jing song*		purity and tranquility
975	*Beidou zhang*		Dipper
977	*Daode zhangsong*		Daode jing
978	*Daode jing song*		Daode jing
	Great Clarity Supplement		
1167	*Ganying pian*	Song	karma and retribution
1168	*Laozi zhongjing*	6 Dyn	visualization
1169	*Qingjing xinjing*	Tang	purity and tranquility
1170	*Jifu jing*	?	Dipper
	Orthodox Unity Supplement		
1207	*Mingjian jing*	6 Dyn	visualization
1238	*Chuanshou jingjie yi zhujue*	6 Dyn	ordination

Table 10—*continued*

DZ no.	Title	Date	Category
	Canon Supplement (Xu Daozang)		
1422	*Zhenzhong jing*	Tang	visualization
1424	*Taisu jing*	6 Dyn	philosophy
1438	*Xuwu benqi jing*	Tang	purity and tranquility
1445	*Bixia yuanjun huguo baosheng jing*	Ming	sponsor (Tianzun)
1447	*Chenghuang ganying jing*	Ming	sponsor of gods

not in the Spirit Cavern proper. The compilers of the Ming canon therefore saw Lord Lao predominantly as a representative of the thought and practice of purity and tranquility as well as a revealer of talismans and protective scriptures, a god invoked in ritual, cultivation, and popular worship. Materials on the political role of the god and on his early veneration in Daoist communities are secondary; practical instructions and inscriptions are ranked lowest.

Leaving the problem of ranking behind and changing the mode of examination, we can also look at the roles of the god chronologically and describe his evolution in six distinct stages:

1. philosopher and author of the *Daode jing* (500–100 B.C.E.);
2. immortal, representative of cosmic harmony, popular savior (100 B.C.E.–320 C.E);
3. central god of the Celestial Masters, secondary figure in other Daoist schools (320–500);
4. third god of the trinity, protector of the state, and ancestor of the imperial house of Tang (500–900);
5. protector of the faithful, god of new schools, dispenser of talismans (960–1300);
6. main god of Daoist schools, sponsor of popular gods and morality teachings, wondrous immortal and martial hero (1300–present).

These six stages of the god's development, with their specific characteristics and historical relevance, can in turn be matched with certain periods defined for the development of the Daoist religion. Recent Japanese scholarship, for example, divides the history of Daoism into three periods: ancient, medieval, and modern. The first includes ancient philosophies and immortality practices of the Zhou and Han dynasties. The second, lasting from the Han through the Tang, includes various revelations, the establishment of schools, and the integrative organization of the religion. The third, lasting from the Song to the present, includes the establishment of various new schools and the increased popular impact of Daoism.[1]

Conjoining this model with the ancient division of philosophical and religious Daoism, Russell Kirkland (1997) distinguishes two major phases, classical Daoism and later Daoism, with the dividing line in the Han dynasty. He then subdivides the latter into an early and a later phase (traditional Daoism and new Daoism), with the twelfth century as a cut-off point. Traditional Daoism, moreover, is further divided into two kinds: incipient organized and organized. This division is pegged to the late fifth century, when the various schools, already established separately, begin to integrate. In other words, he has four periods:

1. classical (through the Han)
2. traditional: incipient organized (through the 5th c.)
3. traditional: organized (through the Song)
4. new (to the present)

To make the system more detailed and improve its fit with the realities of the religion, I would propose to integrate the phases of Lord Lao's changing roles and create a six-stage model of periodization. While retaining Kirkland's basic scheme, I suggest two adjustments: (1) that a transitional period be inserted between classical and incipient organized Daoism to highlight the cataclysmic changes of the Han dynasty, such as the rise of immortality practitioners, the installation of Daoist politics through Huang-Lao Daoism, the increased imperial worship of the Dao, and the first messianic movements; and (2) that the new Daoism be subdivided into (a) a structuring stage during the Song and Yuan, when many new schools emerged and the practices of both thunder rites and inner alchemy were formalized, and (b) a stage of increasing popularization, lasting from the Ming to today. The latter is characterized by the standardization of practice under the Celestial Masters and Complete Perfection schools and the increased interaction of Daoism and popular religion.

---

[1] These three periods are called *daojia*, *daojiao*, and *xin daojiao*, and interpreted to indicate the classical, organized ("church"), and popular forms of Daoism that were prevalent in their respective periods but always existed side by side. See Sakade 1994, 12–13; Noguchi et al. 1994, 441; Kohn 1995a, 159. The model revises the traditional distinction between philosophical and religious Daoism, long criticized as a hindrance to fruitful scholarship (see Seidel 1990; Fukui 1995) and superseded by studies showing the continuity between the two (see Robinet 1983a; Kohn 1991; Schipper 1994) and the meditational tendencies of the ancients (see Roth 1995; 1996).

To avoid the traditional dichotomy of "philosophical" and "religious" as well as evolutionary or sociological expressions that might be considered evaluative, I propose a set of descriptive terms that highlight the characteristic movements or tendencies of Daoism in each respective period. They are as follows:

1. The seminal stage (400–100 B.C.E.): Ancient philosophical texts set the basic theoretical framework of Daoist thought, hinting at budding religious practices but in the absence of religious organization.
2. The gestative stage (100 B.C.E.–300 C.E.): Magical practitioners develop immortality techniques, the court worships the Dao as cosmic harmony, and new cults spring up, expecting the coming of a new age of the Dao.
3. The formative stage (300–500): New revelations of the Dao lead to the establishment of five major Daoist schools: Highest Clarity, Numinous Treasure, the Three Sovereigns, and the northern and southern Celestial Masters, each with its own scriptures, precepts, rituals, and ordination system.
4. The integrative stage (500–900): The schools join together as one religion and develop an integrated ordination structure, system of beliefs, and formal pantheon, which is favored by the Tang rulers.
5. The restructive stage (900–1400): Daoist organization and teachings change, new schools and systems of practice develop, and the religion broadens its influence on larger segments of the population.
6. The expansive stage (1400–present): Daoism expands to include popular gods and myths; it also integrates the worldview of Confucianism and Buddhism as part of a "harmonization of the three teachings."

This division not only matches the temporal division into ancient, medieval, and modern, but can also be seen as a subdivision of the Japanese model into classical, organized, and popular Daoism. In addition it has the advantage of acknowledging the major watersheds in Chinese religious history, a fact that is documented by its correspondence to the fourfold division of the development of Chinese Buddhism as described by Arthur Wright (1959). He distinguishes:

1. The period of preparation (ca. 65–317 C.E.): From its first official mention in the Later Han to the end of the Western Jin, this is a time of initial translation and first active contact.
2. The period of domestication (ca. 317–589): Through the Eastern Jin and the Six Dynasties, Buddhism continues to grow, increasing its translated materials, developing its own terminology, establishing its organization firmly on Chinese ground, and coming to terms with both indigenous society and beliefs.
3. The period of independent growth (ca. 589–900): During the Sui and Tang dynasties, Chinese Buddhism flourishes as a philosophical system and active religion in its own right, seeing the beginnings of important schools such as Chan and developing the particular Chinese brand of the Buddhist vision.
4. The period of appropriation (ca. 900–1900): With the revival of Confucianism under the Song, Buddhism is further appropriated by indigenous traditions and becomes part of Chinese lay religions and popular sects. The high philosophy of the earlier schools gives way to devotional practices, as much as the number of schools grows less and their distinctions are weakened. Buddhism becomes firmly Chinese.[2]

This fourfold scheme matches the stages of Daoism closely and shares with it some major dividing lines: first, the break between the Western and Eastern Jin, a major upheaval in Chinese society that sparked an increased interest in otherworldly realms and practices of transcendence (see Strickmann 1978); second, in the sixth century, the end of the period of disunity and reunification under the Sui, which saw rapid growth in religion and the formulation of integrated systems (see Kobayashi 1995); and third, the Tang–Song transition, which again brought a major social revolution and change in outlook among the Chinese people (see Ebrey and Gregory 1993).

Within this scheme of stages and distinctive periods, then, sociological distinctions between the political, communal, individual, and popular can be made. They are suggested by the study of the different roles of Lord Lao outlined earlier and may apply to the religion as a whole. Lord Lao, a central god of the Dao, far from being an object of

---

[2] Arthur Wright's basic system was linked with Western schemes of religious periodization by Whalen Lai (1980), who specifically cites Robert Bellah (1970). Like Gustav Mensching (1976, 267–73), Bellah proposes a generic evolutionary scheme for Western religions that is divided into five stages: primitive (mystic unity), archaic (cults), historic (transcendence), early modern (reformation), and modern (decline toward popularism). These stages could possibly be made to fit the Daoist pattern, with a sixth stage added between the historic and the early modern to account for the heyday and integration of the religion under the Tang.

interest only to students of hagiography and the pantheon, can serve as a model for Daoist practice in China historically and for *qigong* practices today. Moreover, he inspires further exploration of the different dimensions of the Daoist religion, in particular, Daoist mythology and visions of history, which will be the focus of Part Two.

Part Two: Myth

Introduction to Part Two

I n the following passage from Sima Qian's *Shiji* (ch. 63), which summarizes a longer tale found in the *Zhuangzi* (ch. 14), Laozi first receives the epithet "like unto a dragon" (*youlong*):

> Confucius once traveled to Zhou because he wished to ask Laozi about the rites. Laozi said: "The sages you speak about have long withered along with their bones. Also, when a gentleman attains proper timeliness, he rides in a carriage; when his time has not come, he wanders about with the wind. I have heard that a good merchant fills his storehouses but appears to have nothing; a true gentleman is overflowing with virtue but looks as if he were a fool. Give up your prideful airs and your manifold desires, get rid of your stiff deportment and your lascivious thoughts. All these do you no good at all. I have nothing else to tell you."
>
> Confucius left and later told his disciples, "Birds, I know, can fly; fish, I know, can swim; animals, I know, can run. For the running one can make a net; for the swimming one can make a line; for the flying one can make an arrow. But when it comes to the dragon, I have no means of knowing how it rides the wind and the clouds and ascends into heaven. Today I have seen Laozi and he really is like unto a dragon."

This term was applied to Laozi over the ages and eventually appeared in the title of one of the most extensive and certainly the best integrated hagiography of the god, the *Youlong zhuan* (DZ 774). Written by Jia Shanxiang, a Daoist serving at the Taiqing gong (Great Clarity Temple) in Laozi's birthplace, Bozhou (Boltz 1987, 131), the text describes the exploits of the deity in six scrolls and thirty sections. It gives a complete account of his supernatural abilities and actions: how Lord Lao existed prior to all, created the world, descended as the teacher of dynasties, was born supernaturally and served as an archivist under the Zhou, transmitted the *Daode jing* to Yin Xi and made him his partner, emigrated west to convert the barbarians, and returned to give revelations of the Dao and work miracles in China (see Table 11).

The preface of the *Youlong zhuan* is dated to the year 1086, the same year as Sima Guang's *Zizhi tongjian* (Hervouet, 1978, 69–70). This simultaneity is not entirely coincidental, since both texts respond, within their own traditions, to the historiographic concerns of the Song. In that period Chinese literati sought to reassert their heritage and place themselves within the overall unfolding of their culture, so the writing of "universal" histories became an important issue.[1] Therefore, the *Youlong zhuan*, while presenting an extensive hagiography of Lord Lao, also functions as a universal account of the Dao, proposing a Daoist view of how and why the world came into being and history unfolded as it did. While at base a religious document, this work is not so much a history of the Daoist religion as an extensive exercise in Daoist mythology, a chronological account of the divine presence and relevance of the Dao in Chinese history and culture.

The *Youlong zhuan*, of course, does not stand alone but relies on numerous earlier accounts of the deity and his exploits. Especially close to it are the two other systematic hagiographies of the late Tang and the Song, Du Guangting's *Daode zhenjing guangsheng yi* (DZ 725) of the year 901, and Xie Shouhao's *Hunyuan shengji* (DZ 770), dated to 1191. All three texts, though they divide the material into different numbers of items, share the same basic outline of the deity's exploits, which can be divided into eight major mythical episodes (see Table 12).

Looking at each episode in turn, the following study presents the basic story of Lord Lao found in these three major hagiographies then proceeds with a discussion of the material on three levels. First, it relates the basic story to versions found in other religious Daoist texts; second, it offers a comparison with similar materials in other Chinese traditions, including the mainstream myths of Confucianism, the imported stories and motifs of Buddhism, and the tales of ancient Daoism. Third, it presents similar or comparable tales and motifs from non-Chinese and Western religions.

Through this expanding circle of mythical analysis, the nature of not only the Laozi story but also Daoism as a religion gradually becomes clearer. By finding variants within Daoism, we gain a fuller picture of the mythical content of individual episodes and motifs and a more complete view of the Laozi myth than would be possible through consideration of

---

[1] For a discussion of this cultural phenomenon in the Song and its manifestation in the Buddhist work *Fozu tongji* of the year 1250, see Schmidt-Glintzer 1986.

Table 11
Section headings/page numbers for Laozi myth motifs in the *Youlong zhuan*

No.	Page	Section heading
1	1.1a	Arising from the Nonbeginning
2	1.2a	Endowed with Spontaneity
3	1.3b	Manifesting the True Body
4	1.6a	Revelations as Teacher
5	1.7b	Passing Through the Kalpas
6	2.1a	Creating Heaven and Earth
7	2.6b	Setting up the Ranking System
8	2.8a	Ordering the Numinous Documents
9	2.10b	Selecting Immortals' Charts
10	2.12b	Transmitting the Scriptures
11	2.13b	Serving as the Teacher of Emperors
12	3.1a	Descending to Be Born in the World
13	3.5b	Explaining His Noble Ancestry
14	3.8b	Seventy-two Marks and Eighty-one Characteristics
15	3.10a	Becoming a Historian
16	3.11a	Leaving the Zhou
17	3.12a	Testing Xu Jia
18	3.13a	Going Beyond the Pass and Testing Yin Xi
19	3.16b	Transmitting the *Daode jing*
20	4.1a	Meeting Through a Black Sheep
21	4.5a	Converting the Barbarians Across the Desert
22	4.9b	Explaining the Rites to Confucius
23	4.16a	Appearing as the Master on the River
24	4.17b	Giving the *Taiping jing* to Gan Ji
25	5.1a	Delivering the Celestial Masters under the Han
26	5.7a	Revealing Rites to Ge Xuan
27	5.9a	Bestowing a Daoist Title on the Wei Emperor
28	5.11a	Sage Ancestor of the Great Tang (I)
29	6.1a	Sage Ancestor of the Great Tang (II)
30	6.10a	Veneration by Emperor Zhenzong of the Song

Table 12
Subject division/sections in the three later hagiographies

Episode	*Guangsheng yi*	*Youlong zhuan*	*Hunyuan shengji*
creation	sect. 1–7	sect. 1–6	2.1a–9b
ordering	sect. 8	sect. 7–10	2.9b–25b
transformations	sect. 9–24	sect. 11	2.25b–33b
birth	sect. 25–28 (incl. 17 items)	sect. 12–14	2.33b–45b
transmission	—	sect. 15–20	ch. 3
conversion	—	sect. 21	chs. 4–5
revelations	—	sect. 22–27	chs. 6–7
miracles	sect. 20–30	sect. 28–30	chs. 8–9

only a single instance. At the same time, the historical changes in and development of the religion become clearer. Looking at comparable tales in other Chinese traditions, the sources of certain symbols and motifs become obvious; the Daoist tales are clearly deeply embedded in the broader Chinese tradition. Moreover, the comparison clarifies the nature of Daoism as a religion. Then again, by looking at similar stories and motifs in Western and other mythologies and examining the studies made of them, a wider comparative religious dimension is added to the material. This not only helps to place the Laozi myths in a broader intercultural context but also allows a glimpse of what possible general interpretations might attach to them. In addition, it raises awareness of the deeper mythological significance of specific formulations, episodes, or motifs. This third step of the analysis is the most speculative and may at times seem far-fetched. It is geared less toward a historical and religious interpretation of Daoism than toward an understanding of the basic nature of religious Daoist thinking, opening potential new ways of comparative examination.[2]

In terms of recent mythological scholarship, the material on Lord Lao can be described as a "mythological corpus," which consists of an integrated network of stories that all work together rather than a single tale in its unfolding variants. To be more p ecise, a "mythological corpus" is defined as

> a usually complex network of myths that are culturally important imaginal stories, conveying by means of metaphoric and symbolic diction, graphic imagery, and emotional conviction and participation, the primal, foundational accounts of aspects of the real, experienced world and humankind's roles and relative statuses within it. (Doty 1986, 11)

This definition is valuable in that it presents three different aspects of the stories that are integrated in the texts but have to be looked at separately. First, there are the "myths" proper, which form the basic "network." They are what I call "mythical episodes," the basic tales, the fundamental narratives that make up the larger picture. In the case of Lord Lao there are eight, which exist separately and can be told independently but make more sense and become more religiously relevant when looked at as a complete set.

---

[2] The comparative approach in this respect is basically phenomenological and follows the study of religion as undertaken by Mircea Eliade, examining traditional myths as expressions of the different modalities of human consciousness. See Eliade 1957.

Second, there is the "metaphoric and symbolic diction" together with the "graphic imagery" employed in the stories, a phenomenon typical to all mythical literature, which I refer to as "symbols and motifs." These include special characteristics of protagonists, settings, or other features: for example, the names of the deity, his appearance, the tree under which he is born, his animal helpers, and so on. All these symbols and motifs can occur many times and in various forms; they can play different roles in the larger narrative, and by being employed in different ways they can change the overall thrust and importance of the story. Often the symbols and motifs are shared by several traditions; the tree under which the deity or hero is born, for example, occurs throughout the world. Certain typical symbols, moreover, are linked with certain ideas and visions universally, allowing a wide comparative perspective that aids the understanding of specific applications in unique traditions.

While the episodes or basic narratives are the backbone of a myth, the symbols and motifs give it depth and emotional intensity. This leads to the third element of the "mythological corpus," the emotional conviction and response it elicits from the listener, and the representation it gives of the believer's participation and position in "the real, experienced world." Myths are not mere stories or assemblages of wondrous motifs. They fulfill an important function in human culture and have in fact been linked with the cognitive problems that arose among primitive humans when they first tried to join the "conflicting perception of both brain hemispheres" (d'Aquili and Laughlin 1979, 172)—the analytic left with its polar opposites and the simultaneous right with its unified experience—into an organized whole.

Myths can therefore be described bio-anthropologically as a means to satisfy "the cognitive imperative" of human existence; they are "the instruments by which we continually struggle to make our experience intelligible to ourselves."[3] They are moreover said to provide a "translation of experiences from other dimensions into the imagery of this world" (Thompson 1981, 39), and are thus considered culturally important inventions of meaning that are fictionalized onto the world in an active creation of experiential truth (Doty 1986, 15). Myths are relevant in social and cultural life because they produce order out of chaos, meaning out of senselessness, purpose out of vagueness, and

---

[3] The bio-anthropological approach to myth and ritual is presented in d'Aquili and Laughlin 1979, esp. 172–75. The description of myth as a "continuous struggle" goes back to Murray 1968, 355.

formulate an inherent sense of goodness and of truth in the world. As the philosopher Alfred North Whitehead has it:

> The order of the world is no accident. There is nothing actual which could be actual without some measure of order. The religious insight is the grasping of this truth: That the order of the world, the depth of reality of the world, the value of the world in its whole and in its parts, the beauty of the world, the zest of life, the peace of life, and the mastery of evil, are all bound together—not accidentally but by reason of this truth: That the universe exhibits a creativity with infinite freedom. (1927, 105–6)

The study of myths not only provides greater historical knowledge of the development of a religion or the way its symbols and motifs were adopted from or into various other traditions; it also opens up an understanding of the unique way believers make sense of their world and bring order to chaos in their culture.

Defined as "sacred narrative," as "traditional tale," or simply as "story," myths in all cases are and remain a phenomenon of language.[4] For this reason, however complex, simultaneous, and multilayered their intended meaning may be, they are always linear and sequential in their basic expression. They may appear as short explanatory notes, as apparently fragmentary episodes, or as long, involved tales; but whichever form they take, they are myths not so much because they deal with gods or creation, or because of their placement in the remote past,[5] but first of all because of their practical use—as Walter Burkert puts it, their "secondary, partial reference to something of collective importance" (1979, 23). The ability of the myth to "delineate the *macrocosmic* dimension of the perceived social and natural world in symbolic terms that enable individuals to situate themselves *microcosmically* within them" (Doty 1986, 31) is precisely what makes a myth a myth rather than some other kind of story.

Myths are therefore, as Malinowski has it, "a statement of a primeval, greater, and more relevant reality, by which the present life, facts, and activities of mankind are determined" (1926, 39). Yet they are also always inextricably linked with actual life, a link found commonly in the names of places and people mentioned in them that connect their stories with actually existing "families, tribes, cities, places, rituals, [and] festivals" (Burkert 1979, 25). This connection with actual places and people gives a sense of reality to the myth, makes its content real and believable,

---

[4] So defined in Dundes 1984, 2; Burkert 1979, 2; Doty 1986, 16.

[5] For myths defined by these characteristics, see Kirk 1970, 261; Eliade 1963, 18.

however abstruse or strange its basic tale may be. This power of the myth to engage continuously with varying historical realities is known as its "crystallization." More specifically, crystallization denotes the continued embellishment of myths with new motifs and their expansion into new dimensions in the course of their historical transmission. This transformation of sacred narrative is at the same time the life pulse of the religious reality it describes, the "appropriate story generated in each stage of the evolution of consciousness" (Thompson 1981, 251). While the mythical narrative gives expression to a higher and often ineffable truth, its interaction with historical reality, the structural changes it undergoes, the development of its symbols and motifs, and its varying links with real places and people, make it a relevant document in the history of religions. Myth is thus a useful object of academic study and an invaluable window onto the inner realities of any given tradition.

7

The Creation of Heaven and Earth

The *Youlong zhuan* begins its account of Lord Lao's divine career by describing him as emerging directly from the Dao and placing him firmly at the origin of all.[1] Its first section, "Arising in the Nonbeginning," thus has:

> Before chaos divided and before any numinosity arose, there was the deep root of obscure wonder, the Dao. What we mean by Dao is something so deep one cannot plumb its root, so vast one cannot fathom its shores. Then there was a great sage endowed with it, who rose in its midst. Thus we speak of him as in the Nonbeginning. He is the Highest Lord. (1.1a)

Next, the text defines this primordial entity with a series of negatives: It is beginningless, causeless, formless, soundless, and the prime source of all beings. This primordial One then undergoes a series of changes, dividing into three energies which in turn give rise to various further sets of three energies. Each of these is identified with one aspect of the deity: the all-highest, the perfect elder, the highest, the venerable lord, so that after four transformations the complete deity, the first personification of the Dao, has arisen. This, in turn, brings forth the Jade Maiden of Mystery and Wonder, who becomes pregnant by swallowing the three energies combined into a small pill and, after a pregnancy of eighty-one years, gives birth through her left armpit to a white-haired baby whom she calls Laozi or "Old Child." He is the true creator, the first god to shape and order the universe. The text continues:

---

[1] Its first six sections on creation closely follow Du Guangting's *Guangsheng yi* (2.1a–7b), even to headings and numbering. The *Hunyuan shengji* presents the same material but in a different order, beginning with Lord Lao in the void (2.1a), moving on to the ordering of heaven, earth, and immortals (2.2a–5a), and only then speaking of his true body and multiple manifestations (2.5b–8b).

Laozi is Lord Lao. He is the body of the Dao, the first ancestor of primordial energy, the deepest root of heaven and earth. The Great Dao, Mystery and Wonder, sprang forth from spontaneity, was born in the unborn, lived before there was any before. Raised in emptiness and pervasion, educated by [the cosmic trigrams] *qian* and *kun*, he is called All-Highest. He is the Dao of order and perfection. His spirit sojourns in the subtle and the remote. He cannot be named. He says of himself:

I was born prior to the shapeless and
Arose before the Grand Antecedence.
I grew on the verge of the Grand Initiation and
Wandered in the prime of the Grand Simplicity.
I floated freely through the Dark Void,
Moved in and out of the hidden and mysterious.
I contemplated chaos as yet undifferentiated
Viewed the clear and turbid in union.

The three luminants did not yet shine,
The myriad beings did not yet have shape.
Only I can sojourn in the garden of the blurred and vague,
Wander through the fields of open vastness!
Lofty, I stand alone!
Great, I am without equal!
I see the invisible.
I hear the inaudible.
I touch the unattainable.
Thus I am called Chaos Primordial—
And from here take my beginning.
(1.1b–2a)

Lord Lao in the Void

In its presentation here, the *Youlong zhuan* follows the established Daoist tradition of the creation through Laozi as the Dao and presents an integrated vision that grew first in the early middle ages. Three stages of this development can be distinguished within the history of the religion. First, Laozi as completely identical with the Dao is described in the documents of the Later Han. Thus the *Laozi ming*, sponsored by Emperor Huan in 165 C.E., says: "Laozi is unified with the energy of primordial chaos, within it yet separate. He lives as long as the three luminants [sun, moon, stars]" (Seidel 1969, 123). A similar description is found in the first section of the *Daode zhenjing xujue*. It says:

Laozi embodies spontaneity and just is. Born prior to Great Nonbeing, he arises without cause and passes freely through heaven and earth. His beginning and end cannot be estimated. He ends with the never-ending, penetrates the impenetrable, reaches the nonultimate. Thus he is himself without ultimate end. (S. 75; Ōfuchi 1979, 509)]

As in the god's speech in the *Youlong zhuan*, so Laozi here is described in the same terms as the Dao in the *Daode jing*—merged with the spontaneous *ziran* (so-being) of the cosmos (ch. 25), at the root of all being and nothingness (ch. 1), easily merging with all that is, invisible, inaudible, and subtle (ch. 14). He is vague and obscure, yet also sparkling and imposing, the power at the root of heaven and earth, the sun and the moon, and the most basic patterns of male and female, the trigrams *qian* (heaven) and *kun* (earth). Like the Dao of old, he does not favor any but cherishes all (ch. 16).

A second stage of development of the myth is already discernible in the Later Han. At this time, two texts describe Laozi not only as the personification of the Dao, the seed of a creation that ultimately unfolds spontaneously and without external guidance, but a deity within the Dao, who has consciousness and knowledge, views the Dao as if from a distance, and takes active steps in guiding it. This view is first presented in the *Shengmu bei* of 153 C.E. It says:

Laozi, the Dao:
Born prior to the shapeless,
Grown before the Grand Initiation,
Living in the prime of Grand Simplicity,
Floating freely through the Six Voids.
He passes in and out of darkness and confusion,
Contemplating chaos as yet undifferentiated,
And viewing the clear and turbid in union.
(Kusuyama 1979, 317)

This echoes immediately the words spoken by Lord Lao in the *Youlong zhuan*,[2] which describe the god as an active mover of creation and a deity with a will of his own.

This same characterization is also found in the *Laozi bianhua jing* of the late second century, according to which "Laozi established the Great Beginning and circulated in the Great Origin; he contemplated chaos before its differentiation and knew the clear and turbid in union" (S. 2295;

---

[2] There is one additional source between these two works, which contains an expansion of the verse: the *Hunyuan huangdi shengji*, cited in *YJQQ* 102.2ab.

Seidel 1969, 60). In this crystallization of the myth, Laozi is like the Dao in that he rests in the void, yet he is also different in that he is a conscious person, an active deity, a transcendent entity, who is separate from chaos and the Dao and exerts control over them. As an individuated cosmic force in human shape, he acts consciously and with a will. Where the Dao, and even Laozi as the Dao, was a mere seed of order that emerged from chaos and became manifest in cosmic rhythms, now it has become a god who imposes his will. The seed of order stands up and actively begins to shape and arrange things. Laozi grows to be Lord Lao; he "establishes" and "knows." Creation in religious Daoism thus shifts from the vision of spontaneous emergence from chaos to an active creation out of chaos, or to use the terminological distinction of C. F. von Weizsäcker—cosmogony, the explanation of the world as process, is for the first time transformed into creation proper, the act of a god (1964, 24).[3]

A third stage of the creation myth, also featured in the *Youlong zhuan*, is documented first in the fifth century, in the *Santian neijie jing* (DZ 1205) of the southern Celestial Masters. This text actively integrates the cosmogony through energy, described earlier in classical works such as the *Huainanzi* (DZ 1184), with the creation of the world through Lord Lao as the Dao. Cosmic energy (*qi*) in ancient thought is the material aspect of the Dao, which is concretely manifest in the air and water of the atmosphere and the breath and blood of human beings, and serves as a bridge between primordiality and creation.[4] The Dao, then, is pure and unified energy in the beginning, the cosmic One that transforms and divides. In the ancient *Daode jing*, it moves from one to two to three; in the religious texts, it moves from one to three to nine.[5] As the *Santian neijie jing* says, "In the midst of emptiness and pervasion, Great Nonbeing was born. Great Nonbeing transformed and changed into the three energies: primordial, mysterious, and beginning" (1.2b). These in turn bring forth Lord Lao, the heavens, and the scriptures. The god at the root of creation thus grows out of a series of energy transformations and is a creator figure developed from a cosmogonic unfolding of energies.

---

[3] For more details on the concept of cosmogony and its impact on culture, see also Lovin and Reynolds 1985.

[4] This concept is ubiquitous in Chinese thought, religion, and medicine. For studies, see Onozawa 1978; Ishida 1987a; 1989; Porkert 1974; Engelhardt 1987; and Sivin 1988.

[5] The classical passage for the ancient cosmogony is *Daode jing* 42. It has been discussed variously, e.g., Kaltenmark 1980, 4–8; Yu 1981; Girardot 1976; 1983, 56; Le Blanc 1987, 118; Robinet 1994a; Major 1993, 62.

A slightly different way of integrating cosmogonic unfolding in the creation through Lord Lao is found in the *Kaitian jing* of the sixth century. Here the god is described as the Dao, the seed of order in the midst of chaos, who with the help of sacred scriptures guides the universe through various stages of evolution to eventually create heaven and earth. The world undergoes a number of precreation stages, named Vast Prime (*hongyuan*), Grand Antecedence (*taichu*), Grand Initiation (*taishi*), and Grand Simplicity (*taisu*; 1b), which reflect an ancient system described in the *Xici* (Great Commentary) supplement to the *Yijing*, the *Bohu tong* (Discussions at the White Tiger Hall) of the Later Han, and the *Liezi* (Book of Master Lie).[6]

In both medieval sources, then, creation is integrated with cosmogony, and Lord Lao is at the root of the Dao yet grows out of its transformations; he is identical with the Dao yet consciously acts vis-à-vis it; part of the Nonbeginning that precedes the universe, he is also manifest in all that exists. He is the key transitional factor between chaos and the created world, occupying a position between primordiality and the world.[7] The *Youlong zhuan* then pulls together the complexities of the myth as it evolved in the middle ages, presenting the basic paradox of creation as the transition from something that is not to something that is; the contradiction between the presence of formless, numinous divinity and the existence of the world of form.

Spontaneity and the Invisible Form

Having established Lord Lao's cosmic existence, the text in its second section entitled "Endowed with Spontaneity," proceeds to endow the god's image with a higher sophistication by specifying his relationship to *ziran*, the natural so-being or self-so state of the Dao—that which is and just is as it is. *Ziran*, naturalness or spontaneity, is a prime characteristic of the Dao already in the classical texts and is considered one of

---

[6] These stages are found, with some variation in *Xici* 1.11 (Sung 1971); *Bohu tong* 4 (Mathieu 1992, 73); and *Liezi* 1 (Graham 1960, 18). For a discussion in a Daoist context, see Robinet 1990; in Neo-Confucianism, see Chan 1963, 463.

[7] The increased emphasis on the layer between chaos and creation in religious Daoism also reflects changes in the ritual system, which saw the establishment of a priestly hierarchy between the pure Dao and the crowds of the faithful. On the ritual changes, see Bell 1988.

its major values in philosophical interpretations today.[8] Philosophically it is used to describe the ineffable, to convey that nothing further can be said. As such, it indicates a different approach to the nature of existence: Rather than carried by a deep source that can be traced back to the Nonbeginning, existence is just as it is and cannot be traced back to anything else. As the classic passage in Guo Xiang's commentary to the *Zhuangzi* says:

> What came into existence before there were beings? If I say that yin and yang came first, then since yin and yang are themselves entities, what came before them? Suppose I say *ziran* came first. But *ziran* is only things being themselves. Suppose I say perfect Dao came first. But perfect Dao is perfect nonbeing. Since it is nonbeing, how can it come before anything else? Then, what came before it? There must be another thing, and so on *ad infinitum*. We must understand that things are what they are spontaneously, and not caused by anything else. (ch. 22; Chan 1963, 335; Knaul 1985, 19)

The *Youlong zhuan*, adding this dimension to the god, develops the ancient philosophical point with ample mythological imagery, showing how Lord Lao is utterly beyond human imagination. As a result, the presentation is an exercise in superlatives. For example:

> Striding on the earth as his carriage,
> Holding up heaven as his canopy,
> Galloping through the vastness,
> Soaring to the eight ultimate points—
> All this does not suffice to express his greatness. (1.2b)

The text goes on to describe him as extremely swift—faster than rays of light, gusts of wind and thunder, and sharply shot arrows; highly stable—more solid than all the roots of the nine layers of earth or all the rocks of the eight seas taken together; full of spirit power—unfathomable as yin and yang, changing without constancy, dancing through the myriad beings; and extremely perspicacious—penetrating all without obstacle, seeing the source even of mysterious yang. He is so small that he can enter even the darkest and deepest subtlety; his voice is so complex that it is more powerful than all eight tones played together; and his radiance is more glittering than all five colors shining forth together (1.2a–3b).

---

[8] For a discussion of spontaneity in ancient thought, see Graham 1989, 186; in the *Zhuangzi*, see Graham 1981, 6–8; on naturalness as a Daoist value today, see Liu 1998.

With this new and extensive characterization of the *ziran* quality of the god, the *Youlong zhuan* presents a concrete image of the Dao, showing in colorful terms how Lord Lao—and through him all existence pervaded by the Dao—is just as he is and yet remains unfathomable. Part of emptiness and nonbeing, mystery and wonder, he is and yet he cannot be truly grasped. He is not chaos, but he participates in it; he is inherent order, but also represents the power over all. He is creation in the center of uncreatedness, being in a mass of nonbeing, a willful potential of growth and transformation, which cannot be described, imagined, or fathomed in any way, yet which is *ziran*, just as it is, and thus a continued presence in the real, existing universe.

The same thrust continues in the next section, on "Manifesting the True Body" (see Fig. 12). Lord Lao's true body, the *Youlong zhuan* says, is formed from "combined energies and coagulated perfection" (1.3b); it is "utterly complete and entirely still, never arising, never passing" (1.5a). Although completely still, it transforms continuously; although ultimately invisible, it appears in different forms and shapes. For example:

> Sometimes he rests above the cloudy canopy, his body a golden color, his face radiating with fivefold brilliance arising spontaneously. Spirit kings and mighty warriors, green dragons and white beasts, unicorns and lions are standing guard before him. (1.3b)

Lord Lao can appear in a thousand-petaled lotus blossom, riding in the jade carriage of the Eight Luminants, or sitting on a golden throne behind jeweled awnings. Although originally one with the Dao and formless—"the Dao cannot be seen; if you see it, it is not the Dao" (1.4b)—the deity has a true body that can be visualized, imagined, and represented in art. Statues of the god are thus more than mere images, they are visual manifestations of the Dao and guides to its emptiness and nonbeing.

Adepts, therefore, should pray before a statue as if they were facing the god's true body, striving to "observe with proper penetration." Soon they find that "his body is no longer a proper body" (1.5a), that the image has coincided with the void, has revealed its inherent mystery and shown them the emptiness of the Nonbeginning. Although ultimately invisible, the deity manifests himself in a concrete form that can be visualized in meditation and captured in statues and images. All religious icons are thus the visible aspect of the Dao, a manifestation that is different from, but actively points back to, its pure origin. Just as Lord

Fig. 12. Lord Lao manifest as the true body of the Dao before the universe is created. *Source*: *Laojun bashiyi hua tushuo*, no. 2

Lao never leaves the void, so his statues are always part of the primordial, a trace of perfection that guides adepts back to the Nonbeginning. Lord Lao as the Dao is always both—the primordial and the created, the formless and the visible—and so are his representations.

While the characterization of Lord Lao as spontaneity draws on ancient philosophy, the problem of his true body and its representation in art is entirely of medieval origin. Visualizations of the god are first described in works of the fourth century, such as Ge Hong's *Baopuzi* (DZ 1185), and certain early works of the Highest Clarity school, such as the *Laozi zhongjing* (DZ 1168) and the *Ciyi jing* (DZ 1313).[9] The first statues mentioned in the literature were fashioned in the fifth century, but actual works of art survive mainly from the sixth. In one of the best preserved objects, the "Lord Lao of Du Chong——" (dated 568), the god is depicted clad in a thick robe with a formal square headdress and a straight triangular beard, a fly-whisk and tablet in his hands. He is flanked by two attendants, and the entire group is placed on a lotus-type platform, guarded on the right and left by lions, with an incense burner in front of the platform.[10]

Inspired by Buddhist models, these images conflict with the basic doctrine that the Dao is invisible and are thus interpreted as pointers to the utterly other, not unlike the texts of scriptures, which are primarily indicators of the ineffable and translations of celestial originals. The basic paradox of the Dao as nonbeing that still forms the root of all existence, and of Lord Lao as an utterly other yet omnipresent deity, is thus expressed visually in meditation and art. The focusing of undivided attention upon a work of art, moreover, aids the perception of the invisible because, as studies by Mike and Nancy Samuels have shown, "if a person's gaze becomes absolutely fixed while looking at an object, the image of the object will extinguish within seconds" (1975, 59). Therefore, when the *Youlong zhuan* says that Lord Lao's body soon appears "no longer as a proper body" when viewed in fixed concentration, and that his image coincides with the void, it speaks from the meditator's perspective, relating adepts' actual practice to the mythical nonbeing of the deity and thereby embedding the myth in real life experience.

---

[9] In the *Baopuzi*, especially ch. 15; see Ware 1966, 256–57; Yamada 1995, 23. In the *Laozi zhongjing*, especially YJQQ 18.7a; on the text, see Schipper 1979. In the *Ciyi jing*, p. 26a; see Maspero 1981, 371; Robinet 1984, 1:129; Yamada 1989a, 20.

[10] For a discussion of Lord Lao in Daoist statues and iconography, see chapter 6 above.

Scriptures, Kalpas, and Multiple Heavens

The next two sections of the *Youlong zhuan* describe the ultimate, cosmic nature of the deity before he finally reaches the point of "Creating Heaven and Earth."

First, "Initiating Teachers and Materials" (sect. 4) details the pre-creation transmission of the Daoist teaching, coeternal with the Dao and thus existing prior to the world. Lord Lao as the Dao represents this teaching, which is formless and ineffable: "nothing to be understood, nothing to be cultivated" (1.6a). But he also documents and initiates it, causing it to be present in scriptures and talismans and as such able to be handed down through a lineage of teachers. While the entire conception of Laozi as teacher goes back to the notion of the Dao as teacher, already described in the *Zhuangzi* (ch. 6) and cited from there in the *Youlong zhuan* (1.7a), in the latter Lord Lao as a specific divinity appears to be the third transmitter and not the first. In close accordance with the medieval trinity of the Dao, he appears as the disciple of the Lord of the Dao, who in turn is the student of the Heavenly Worthy of Primordial Beginning (1.6b).

These two deities, originally of Numinous Treasure and Highest Clarity origin, are the two senior gods of the Daoist trinity as it developed with the integration of Daoist schools in the sixth century. Together with Lord Lao they represent the three main schools of the Daoist teaching. They also revealed the key scriptures of their respective schools, appearing in a succession of precreation kalpas, known as Dragon Country (*longhan*), Red Radiance (*chiming*), and Opening Sovereign (*kaihuang*), each of which underwent the complete cycle of cosmic creation, flourishing, decline, and destruction. The present world, then, is part of the created universe and is characterized by the birth of Lord Lao in human form. It is in the fourth kalpa, known as Highest Sovereign (*shanghuang*).[11]

This temporal aspect of the precreation is also described in the fifth section of the *Youlong zhuan*, "Passing Through the Kalpas." Outlining a sequence of five rather than four kalpas, by adding Extended Health (*yankang*) after Red Radiance (1.8a), the text aligns the kalpas with the five phases—in their productive cycle of wood, fire, earth, metal, and water—and insists on a regular pattern of arising and declining. Lord Lao as the underlying Dao, however, does not participate in these cycles

---

[11] On Daoist gods and their ranking in the middle ages, see Ishii 1983; Kubo 1986. For details on the kalpas and the cycle of creation and destruction, see Kobayashi 1990.

but "survives eternally" (1.7b). The text here links cosmic pre-existence with the cycles of history on earth, integrating them with the vision of political cosmology developed in the late Zhou, according to which each dynasty rules under a specific phase that determines its main color, standard number, and placement in the cycle. The Qin dynasty, which unified China in 221 B.C.E., for example, ruled under the phase water, garbing its officials in black and standardizing all measurements to the number five; it was soon succeeded by the Han, which identified with the phase earth.[12]

Both the teachings and the kalpa transformations give yet another expression to the elementary paradox of the Dao, showing it not only as nonbeginning yet existent, formless yet visible, but also as ineffable yet manifest in words, and as eternal yet moving in continuous cycles. Through these variations of the same basic theme, the text makes the original tension between the absolute and its creation tangible and describes Daoist teaching as part of the original cosmic nature of the Dao. Not only are statues and scriptures sanctioned as ultimately uncreated, but the salvific qualities and powers of the gods are embedded firmly in the beginning of all, as much a part of the universe as the air we breathe. Like Lord Lao, Daoist teaching may have manifold expressions in statues, scriptures, teachers, and the cycles of time, yet it ultimately lies at the root of all and remains continuously part of the unshaped void. Separation from the Dao or its teaching is an illusion, however many stages it may pass through and however many forms it may take.

Only after the elementary structures of the Dao's teaching have been established does the god finally move on to "Create Heaven and Earth" (sect. 6). Allowing the energies to unfold and multiply, he establishes the sky and the earth, the cyclical revolutions of the sun and the moon, the alternation of the four seasons, and the productivity of the five phases (2.1ab). Then, to give order to the heavens, he sets up the Three Clarities (sanqing), each of which multiplies by three so that nine heavens come into existence. They bear strongly Buddhist-inspired names like, for example, "Poluo nimi buqiao letian" (2.2a), which goes back to the Sanskrit expression paranirmita-vaśavartin, "obedient to the will of those who are transformed by others."[13]

---

[12] For details on the doctrine of the five phases and its political application, see Eberhard 1933; Fung and Bodde 1952; Bauer 1956; Graham 1986.

[13] For this translation of the expression, see Soothill and Hudous 1937, 266. Similar names and their provenance are discussed in Mochizuki 1936, 4:3467a.

Each of these nine heavens then produces three sub-heavens of its own, making a total of thirty-six, i.e., nine original and twenty-seven subsequent heavens. They are divided into four groups: the twenty-eight at the bottom encompass the Three Worlds of Desire (6), Form (18), and Formlessness (4); next come the four Brahma Heavens for true believers; then there are the Three Clarities; and, at the very top, the Grand Veil Heaven. All thirty-six heavens have names, for example, "Vast Yellow," "Emptiness and Nonbeing," and "Seven Stars" (1.2ab). In terms of their nature, only the lower twenty-eight heavens of the Three Worlds are subject to kalpa disasters and cyclical renewal. The four Brahma Heavens contain no sun or moon but are irradiated by the shining light of their inhabitants' bodies. In them, there is no more birth or death, but beings attain an unlimited life span and even the greatest kalpa clashes have no effect on them. The Three Clarities heavens are similar, only more splendid, while the huge original blocks of the sacred scriptures are stored in the Grand Veil Heaven. The entire complex of the upper heavens consists of pure yang energy and exists forever without change (2.3b).

This structure of the heavens closely matches the cosmology of medieval Daoism as it was systematized and integrated in the sixth century. It is more complex than the ancient vision of the nine heavens or nine layers of the world, which it transforms under Buddhist influence.[14] The same also holds true for the matching structure of the earth, which, according to the *Youlong zhuan*, first arises when Lord Lao creates nine clods or ramparts (*lei*) named poetically "Great Wind Marsh," "Water-controlled Land," "Glossy-looking Earth," and the like (2.3b). Each of them is layered threefold: with earth, water, and wind, so that they too make a total of thirty-six, consisting of the nine basic clods plus their twenty-seven layers. Under the earth, moreover, is an intricate network of deep channels, empty, mysterious, and unfathomable (2.4a), while on the earth there are ten greater and thirty-six lesser grotto-heavens. Both sets of openings lead to a network that runs within the earth and to the heavens. They were opened especially for the salvation of the universe by Lord Lao (2.6a).[15]

The creation of heaven and earth in the *Youlong zhuan* thus is a cosmic undertaking of major proportions that happens only after the

---

[14] For a description of the Daoist heavens, see Kobayashi 1990; Kohn 1993, 65–71; Kohn 1995, 123–26. On the ancient system of nine heavens, see Maspero 1924.

[15] For the early division of the earth into nine quadrants, see Wheatley 1971; Major 1984. On grotto-heavens, see Miura 1983; Kaltenmark 1980, 47–50; Verellen 1995.

lengthy, precreation unfolding of Lord Lao as the Dao, and of images, scriptures, gods, and the cycles of the Daoist teaching. Although perpetuated ultimately and forever by the Dao, the creation is not a direct product of it but a conscious act that follows only *after* the key features of the religion have been produced. This vision places not only the Dao but also its various expressions prior to the concrete existence of heaven and earth and thus makes them more essential. Moreover, since heaven and earth are both created in thirty-six layers, with various channels of communication between them, it is by the will of the deity that their connection is never ruptured. In this vision they are the active product of a conscious creator; neither primary nor central, they represent the last stage of a long and varied creative effort.

The Mainstream Vision

Unlike the Daoist religion, the ancient mainstream traditions of China, including Confucianism, Yin-Yang cosmology, and ancient Daoism, do not propose a conscious, active creator at the beginning of things but rely on cosmogony rather than creation, emphasizing the interaction and unfolding of cosmic forces. Within this framework two distinct visions of the world's beginning can be distinguished: The first entails emergence through the destruction of chaos; the second, and more dominant vision, entails the spontaneous emergence of the world from chaos. The first is found in the *Zhuangzi*, in the myth of Hundun, the emperor of the center who is "bored to death" by his friends, the emperors of the north and the south.[16] Described as a shapeless lump of flesh, without any sense openings or other signs of order and culture, he is likened in folklore to a leather sack, a calabash, or a dumpling. The image of chaos he represents is, as Girardot points out, that of a watery, embryonic state; a dark, void abyss; a harmonious, womb-like enclosure (1983, 24). He stands for the world before creation, with its egg-like lack of internal structure, its utter potentiality and powerful nothingness.

Hundun—later linked with the cosmic giant Pangu, the Chinese version of Puruśa, who breaks open the original egg and transforms himself into the world—is sacrificed so that the world can come into existence. Sensory openings are bored into him one by one, until "on the seventh day, Hundun dies." Chaos, so demolished, is irretrievably lost. The

---

[16] This myth is found in the *Zhuangzi*, ch. 7; see also Watson 1968, 97. It is discussed in detail in Girardot 1983. The description of Hundun here relies on Girardot 1985, 69.

world can proceed but its mighty, unspecified potential is destroyed. Creation has succeeded, but the price is high—the return to the origin, the recovery of spontaneous chaos must remain forever out of reach.[17]

While this vision played an important role in early China to explain how the world lost its original dimension, some texts, notably Daoist documents such as the *Daode jing* and the *Huainanzi* as well as the mainstream work *Tianwen* (Questions of Heaven; Birrell 1993, 27), focus more on the gradual emergence of the world from chaos. Chaos here is transformed through the growth of the Dao within it, a seed of order in the midst of nothingness that is not chaos but still close to it, sharing many of its characteristics. As the classic passage in the *Daode jing* says:

> There is a being, in chaos yet complete;
> It preceded even heaven and earth.
> Silent it is, and solitary;
> Standing alone, it never changes; . . .
> To call it something, I speak of Dao.
> (ch. 25; Chan 1963, 152)

Similarly, the *Huainanzi* has:

> Heaven and Earth were still shapeless,
> And all was ascending, flying, diving, delving.
> This was Great Brightness.
> Then the Dao began in obscure void,
> which first produced the cosmos.
> (ch. 3; see Major 1993, 62)

The shapeless or obscure void in these documents is the womb of the Dao. It is unformed, uncreated, vague, and obscure—the egg from which everything grows. Yet it is not sacrificed or destroyed; though empty and dark, it is called "great" and "bright." In the midst of this radiant primordiality then, for no specific reason, is the Dao—silent, alone, eternal, moving, the mother of the universe-to-be. The Dao gives rise to the world not by sacrifice, as with Hundun, but by emergence, creating One, then Two, then Three, then the myriad beings (*Daode jing* 42).

The One here is the Dao in its first move toward creation, at the root of the universe *in statu nascendi*, a phase that in later documents is

---

[17] On Pangu as Puruśa, see Lincoln 1975. On Pangu in mainstream Chinese myth, see Liu Chenghuai 1988; Yuan 1985; 1986; 1988. For Hundun's death and its evaluation, see Girardot 1983, 81, 97.

expressed as the Great Ultimate (*taiji*) or the moment of first movement. The One relates to the Dao as the Dao relates to the void: It is the tiny seed of order, of creation, in the midst of the unformed and uncreated. Later, when the Dao was personified in the divinized Laozi, the One also became an important deity located in both the stars and the body; it could be activated in worship and meditation.[18]

A more detailed version of creation through the Dao is found in the *Huainanzi*, which describes the Dao as the power that embraces heaven and supports earth, contains the shapeless potential of all and causes all things to be what they are.[19] But the process of creation is smooth and continuous, the world never breaks with the primordial state. The Dao, the first trace of order in the depth of cosmic nothingness, is chaos and yet is not chaos, is primordial and yet exists in creation. Primordial, it is blurred and indistinct, beyond all sensory perception and language, and shares the power and characteristics of chaos. Existing, it is systematic and ordered, evident in the rhythmic transformations of the world, and definable in temporal and spatial terms.

Early Chinese texts therefore do not yet describe a creation from nothingness by the conscious will of a transcendent creator but focus on the Dao as the mediator between chaos and creation. Seen this way, the Dao here can be interpreted as the Chinese expression of the widespread ancient world model that sees everything originating from the One as opposed to the Zero. Representing the ultimate unity of all beings in their origin and existence, the One is that "from which all things come," the first "scream of individuation" (Colavito 1992, 21, 42). The One resides at the root of all, there is nothing outside it and all created beings must by necessity be its offshoot and in their entirety partake of it. Producing the multiplicity of beings from itself, the Dao as the One is thus the bridge between chaos and the created world. It is also the raft that can take humanity back to its origins, the umbilical cord to life's most basic power that may be twisted and blocked but is never cut.

This vision, so central in early China and ancient Daoism, remains fundamental also in the later Daoist religion, but is modified to accommodate the Daoist belief in immortality. This necessitated a certain measure of control over the natural emergence of the Dao—to allow practitioners to overcome the natural course of decay—and the existence of a pure heavenly realm or paradise where successful immortals can

---

[18] For a discussion of these concepts, see Robinet 1990; 1994a; Kohn 1989a.

[19] Especially in its first chapter. See Morgan 1934, 2; Larre et al. 1993, 41. For a discussion of the myth, see also Mathieu 1992.

enjoy eternal life. In the Laozi myth, this finds expression in two ways: First, the Dao, personified in Lord Lao, emerges as an active creator god above and beyond the natural evolution of the Dao; second, before the actual creation of the world, cosmic energies bring forth gods, heavens, and scriptures in a precreated heavenly realm of pure immortality. Therefore, just as the Dao in the earlier vision stood between chaos and the created world, so now Lord Lao stands between the Dao and its natural creation, and in addition, a celestial refuge is established. The religion thus proposes an entirely new realm between chaos and the created world, a sort of buffer between primordiality and lived existence, a realm that is transcendent and beyond the world but still remains part of the greater universe of the One.

The Meaning of Creation Myths

The basic paradoxes of the Dao and Lord Lao are typical expressions of creation myths in general, which in their narratives and images explain not only why the world is but also how it came to be so.[20] To describe the beginning, every culture has to go back to something or someone that existed before that beginning. The not-yet-beginning has to be determined and visualized. Since this state by definition cannot have begun, it must be absolute and totally other—it must be unlimited, nameless, and all-encompassing, in contrast to the world with its limits, names, and divisions.

Creation myths deal with precisely this problem. As Barbara Sproul puts it:

> Creation myths attempt to reveal the absolute dimension of the relative world. They proclaim the Holy as the ground of being and, taking into account the human experience of alienation from this ground, proclaim it also as the goal of all being. They encourage people to understand themselves, physically, mentally, and spiritually, in the context of the cyclic flow of being and not-being and ultimately in the absolute union of these two. (1979, 29)

Sproul goes on to define the absolute as something that cannot possibly be a thing or a being "because all things and beings are dependent on it for their existence" (1979, 6). Any absolute must be eternal, self-created, independent, creative, unchanging, as well as omnipresent, omniscient,

---

[20] This evaluation of creation myths follows Eliade 1958, xi; Leeming 1990, 16.

and omnipotent. Although utterly different, the absolute is relevant in the created world not only because it was there at the beginning of time but because it is eternal, a "power or force which centers and gives definiteness to the life of a human community" (Sproul 1979, 29). It is in fact the central constituent factor in the basic definition of human life, eternity in the midst of infinity.[21]

For this reason, creation myths continue to be relevant even as cultures change; they are frequently reenacted in cyclical rituals, retaining their essential validity because of their central concern with mediating the eternal presence of the absolute in the day-to-day lives of people.[22] At the same time, the absolute cannot be properly expressed in language, whether abstract as in philosophical discourse or concrete as in myth, because language is itself part of the created world.[23] Its expression can only approximate, symbolize, or give metaphors for what is forever unknowable and ineffable. Still, myth attempts to describe primordial reality, pointing to "chaos," an uncharted void, or open emptiness, in which the first One appears, a first sign that things have begun to solidify or diversify into definable parts. From there creation proceeds in an ongoing process of either production or division (Biallas 1986, 44).

Existence thus develops from chaos, yet is never separate from it. When the question is raised whether existence or chaos ultimately is the absolute, the answer is always "Both!" The difference between life and its primordial state is never one of fundamental quality but always one of gradation. The absolute in its concentrated form is in the center, at the beginning of creation; in its differentiated form, it is present in everything that exists—visible, knowable, and capable of being put into words. The transition between the two occurs either through evolution

---

[21] On the eternal presence of myths, see Eliade 1984, 146; for their role in "human community," see Long 1963, 23. Also, a discussion of the philosophical vision of eternity, the ground that extends vertically beneath life, as opposed to infinity, time that extends forever horizontally, is found in Parkes 1984. Isaac Asimov explores the same problem in his novel *The End of Eternity*. There eternity is a high-rise administrative building that connects, by way of elevators, the different phases of human history and culture.

[22] On the enactment of creation myths in rituals, see Eliade 1965; in daily life, see Long 1963, 18; in different forms of discourse, see Biallas 1986, 51.

[23] The problem of language, moreover, is also part of the perennial problem of mystics who have experienced the absolute but find it impossible to describe it. For a discussion, see Proudfoot 1985; Kohn 1992.

or disruption, either through the power of a transcendent creator or the interaction of natural elements.[24]

Described in philosophical and cosmological discourse as occurring in phases of cosmic diversification, it is expressed in myth with the help of various symbols and images. This leads to many different types of creation myths. Typical patterns include the three major modes found in Western culture: the creation from nothing by a transcendent creator as expressed in the "Genesis" chapter of the Bible; creation through the sexual union of primordial deities as found in Hesiod's *Theogony*; and the Indo-European creation through sacrifice.[25] There were also six types found in a worldwide study: the monotheistic creation from nothing, creation through world-parents, the sacrifice of the creator or destruction of chaos, the growth of the world from a cosmic egg, a process of natural emergence, and creation through the earth-diver who drops the first speck of dirt into the cosmic ocean.[26] Barbara Sproul, finding similar patterns, also sees the different types as meaningful metaphors that describe particular relationships of the world to its creator. She distinguishes four modes: creation through the word of a single creator, the creator as administrator, sexual procreation, and the sacrifice of the creator.[27]

Many aspects of these general discussions and worldwide comparisons of creation myths bear a direct relevance to the Chinese case. In their light, the Dao can be easily described as the absolute in both the mainstream Chinese and Daoist traditions regardless of what textual form it takes—be it more philosophical or more mythical. In addition, early mainstream myths are dominantly cosmogonic, showing a process of natural emergence; but some also indicate a vision of creative sacrifice in the destruction of chaos or Hundun. The later religious Daoist myths, on the other hand, acknowledge the existence of a powerful, active creator god and are in fact closer to the monotheistic creation from nothingness through a conscious god. The shift between these two, as

---

[24] See Sproul 1979, 10; James 1969, 118; Doria and Lenowitz 1976, xxiii; Biallas 1986, 44.

[25] For these different modes in the Western tradition, see O'Brien and Major 1982, 35, 50; Lincoln 1986.

[26] Outlined in Long 1987, 94. He describes these same types and a combined account of the creation through chaos and from the cosmic egg in his earlier work (Long 1963). A similar division is also found in Biallas 1986, 45. For a detailed analysis of the earth-diver myth, see Dundes 1984a.

[27] Sproul 1979, 19. Still another understanding of creation modes appears in von Franz (1972), where they are related to forms of human creativity and Jungian psychology.

documented in texts of the Later Han dynasty, occurred gradually and in stages. The creation myth was again modified in its medieval and later versions, which integrate a heavy dose of cosmogony by describing the unfolding and emergence of three or nine energies, or a series of stages, before the creation of heaven and earth.

The Daoist tradition, therefore, in light of its own development and through comparison with both mainstream Chinese myth and creation myths from around the world, can be described as a unique and powerful mixture of types. It is dominantly oriented toward creation from nothingness yet never completely denies cosmogony or the gradual unfolding of the world from chaos.[28] Lord Lao as the Dao stands at the center of this mythic vision, carrying all without fail, forever part of *ziran* and the absolute, yet unceasingly present in the world of change.

---

[28] To express the same idea in the terms of David Dilworth, the reality of religious Daoism would then be a mixture of existential and noumenal, again lying between established categories. See Dilworth 1989, 146–50.

8

The Order of the Universe

The creation of heaven and earth is the starting point for a long and involved cultural and salvific development of the world, which begins with the establishment of universal order. Order is created by the deity on three levels: in the heavens through the establishment of a formal celestial hierarchy and administration; on earth through revelations that give guidance to people of different eras; and in the overall structure of the universe through the introduction of cycles that, in a continuous rhythm of rising and declining, account for the world's different needs at different times.[1]

Before any order is established, of course, the universe is populated by a number of different creatures, including animals, divine beings, ghosts, and humans, who are created from energy upon Lord Lao's command. As the *Youlong zhuan* says:

Floating up, it [energy] becomes clouds.
Sinking down, it becomes mist.
Drumming, it becomes thunder.
Rousing, it becomes rumbling.
Light, it becomes snow.
Heavy, it becomes frost. . . .
Numinous, it becomes a spirit.
Essential, it becomes a man.

---

[1] The *Guangsheng yi* and *Hunyuan shengji* also present a similar sequence of events. The *Guangsheng yi* covers the initial order of the universe in items 8–12, from the "establishment of the immortal hierarchy" through the revelation of the scriptures of the Three Caverns under the reigns of the Three Sovereigns. The *Hunyuan shengji* also retells the events surrounding Lord Goldtower (9b–12b, 17a–18b) but interrupts them by describing Lord Lao's instruction of the Yellow Emperor (13b–16a) in an attempt to integrate the hagiography of the Queen Mother of the West into the narrative. This account tends to be more a collection of materials than an organized story, showing the bibliographic preferences of its author.

Resting, it becomes a ghost.
Squirming, it becomes a worm.
Adulterated, it becomes an animal.
Vile, it becomes a specter. (2.5b)

In addition to this multitude of earthly beings, there is a huge
celestial population, consisting of immortals, imperial lords, ministers,
and various heavenly officials, who are all organized and supervised by
Lord Lao. This hierarchy is specifically described in section 7, "Setting
Up the Ranking System." Here, the celestial administration looks like a
pyramid:

> three great immortals
> nine major emperors
> twenty-seven heavenly lords
> eighty-one senior ministers
> twelve hundred immortal officials
> twenty-four thousand numinous officers
> seventy thousand immortal lads and jade maidens
> five hundred billion celestial spirits and divine kings (2.7b)

Surrounding these basic ranks and officers, there are also fierce numinous guards, dragons and lions, pheasants and phoenixes, heavenly
horses and unicorns that complete the colorful array of the heavenly host.

Lord Lao not only creates this system and makes sure that all its
members have their proper rank; from his residence in "the Jade Hall,
Purple Tower, Cinnabar Terrace, Palace of the Great Ultimate in the
Great Clarity Heaven" (2.7b), he also takes up the double duty of ascending to the Heavenly Worthy to report on the activities of people and
immortals and of descending to give directives to the Jade Emperor,
head of the administration in the Nine Palaces, where the ledgers of life
and death are housed (2.7b).

Human beings on earth, moreover, are subject to evaluation and
punishment in this system but do not cause a basic disruption in the
universal flow. Rather, created from the essences of heaven and earth,
they are both in the beginning and throughout history an integral part of
the universe. Because the Dao is active in all aspects of creation, the
emergence of humanity does not presage a break between the primordial
and the mundane; there is no proper "fall" to speak of, only the cyclical
decline that is built into the system. Thus the god continues to "bring
forth, develop, support, and transform everything" (2.6a), providing a
proper place for humanity and concerning himself with its continued
salvation in the Dao.

Humans and Immortals

In both the description of the celestial hierarchy and the emergence of humanity, the *Youlong zhuan* closely follows its medieval predecessors, which also combine Daoist myths of a central divinity with ancient notions of multiple cosmogonic forces.

The hierarchical structure of celestial beings goes back to an ancient Chinese administrative ideal, formulated first in the *Liji* (Book of Rites; 5.10). Here the feudal ranking order consists of three dukes, nine ministers, twenty-seven high officials, and eighty-one secretaries, who are placed in concentric circles around one king residing in the very center of the nine provinces, 120 prefectures, and 1,200 districts. Just as the provinces and palaces focus on the spatial center of the king, so does his administration place him at the center of power. A similar structure was applied to the supernatural realm, which was, even in Shang times, thought of as a hierarchy of different ancestors with varied areas of concern. While there was a clear mutual relationship between the mundane and the supernatural administrations, it may well be that the religious one was prior.[2]

The religious administration of the supernatural, with a special Department of Destiny and a Ruler of Fates (Siming) who supervised the ledgers of life and death, is first clearly mentioned in a manuscript of the fourth century B.C.E. According to this work, a man named Dan was sent back to the living after three years upon the underworld authorities finding that he had died an untimely, unjustly death. While further glimpses of the netherworld administration are found in tomb texts of the Later Han, the supernatural hierarchy in Daoism first appears in the *Lingbao wufu xu* (Explanation of the Five Talismans of Numinous Treasure, DZ 388).[3] It closely imitates the *Liji* system but places the divine hierarchy entirely inside the human body:

---

[2] For the *Liji* passage, see Legge 1885. A recent group of studies on the supernatural hierarchy in Chinese religion is found in Shahar and Weller 1996. On the Shang system of ancestors, see Shahar and Weller 1996, 4. The suspicion that civil administrative systems were built upon religious models and not vice versa appears first in Seidel 1990, 256.

[3] This fourth-century manuscript is translated and studied in Harper 1994. For Han tomb contracts, see Seidel 1985; 1987. The *Lingbao wufu xu* goes back to the Han and was edited in its present form in the fourth and fifth centuries. See Ishii 1983; Kubo 1986; Kobayashi 1990; Kohn 1995, 216. The passage with annotation is translated in Kohn 1995, 87. The celestial ledgers of life and death kept in the otherworld have since the Song been imitated by ordinary people as ledgers of merit and demerit. See Brokaw 1991. Otherworld officials since that time, in

> The human body contains heaven and earth, the sun and the moon, the Northern Dipper, the Jade Sighting Tube, the Equalizer, the five sacred mountains. . . . Moreover, there are an emperor, three dukes, nine ministers, twenty-seven high officials, and eighty-one secretaries inside it. It also contains nine provinces, 120 prefectures, 1,200 districts, 18,000 counties, 36,000 communities, and 180,000 villages. (1.19b)

Later medieval works again place the hierarchy in the heavens, distinguishing twenty-seven ranks, nine each of sages, perfected, and immortals, as its core. These are surrounded by ministers, officials, guards, and numinous animals, also described in the *Youlong zhuan*.

Its description of the creation of human beings, too, follows the medieval system. According to the *Kaitian jing*, for example, it was during Grand Antecedence that Lord Lao "took the essence of heaven from above and the essence of earth from below, joined them in the middle and created a spiritual being called man" (2a). According to the *Santian neijie jing*, first "energy underwent transformations and changes, and heaven, earth, humanity, and all living beings arose" (1.2b), then "Lord Lao harmonized the three energies and formed the nine continents and on each placed nine people, three men and six women" (1.3a). In both cases, as in the later formulation of the myth, humanity came into being through the activity of the god and consisted of a mixture of the heavenly and the earthly, constituting a necessary and important component of the "three forces" (*sancai*).

This understanding of the creation of humanity is closely related to classical Daoist cosmogony and Han cosmology, according to which "pure energy rose up and became heaven, turbid energy sank down and became earth, and the conjoined energies in the middle became yin and yang [which formed humanity]."[4] Yet in its description of an active creator, the Daoist myth also integrates the mainstream story of the ancient creator goddess Nügua who, according to the *Fengsu tongyi* (General Account of Popular Customs),

> molded yellow earth and made human beings. Exerting herself in the great effort, she did not rest in her toils. Then she pulled a thread through variegated mud, making human beings from that, too. As a result, all those

---

addition, have become financial administrators of a celestial treasury. See Hou 1975.

[4] So described in *Huainanzi* 3. See Major 1993, 62.

wealthy and noble were originally made from yellow earth; while all those poor and humble were originally made from variegated mud.[5]

Here not only the existence of people in the world is explained but also their different social status. The story was widespread in traditional China and influenced the Daoist tradition variously, not only shaping the image of Lord Lao as creator of humanity, but in one version actually having him mold people from mud. Thus the *Shengxuan jing* of the sixth century relates:

> Emerging from the darkness and entering obscurity, the Dao [Lord Lao] moved along with all without bent. Thus, he created heaven and earth, brought forth the various gods, set up the five phases, the sun, the moon, and the three main constellations. He divided yin and yang and established the distinction between winter and spring. Concluding all, he set up continents and countries. Then he molded earth to form human beings, patterning them on heaven and earth and establishing rulers and vassals among them.[6]

Despite, or maybe because of, the ingrained existence of social differences from the very beginning, human beings created in this fashion lived for a considerable time in perfect harmony with their surroundings, being fed sweet dew from heaven and earth, enjoying a peaceful existence with few working hours, and living to hoary old age without sickness. There were no social restraints, everybody participated equally in the activities of the community, and there were no formal rituals. Rather, "upon death they would not bury the corpse, but abandoned it in a distant wilderness" (*Kaitian jing* 3a). While this may or may not reflect a distant racial memory of the paleolithic, when people were few, the land fertile, consciousness communal, and working hours only fifteen per week,[7] the Daoist vision of the golden age is placed significantly earlier and envisioned as freer from political and ritual structures than its Confucian counterpart. In the latter, the golden age occurs not before time and history but in the quasi-historical period of

---

[5] The text is found cited in *Taiping yulan* 78.5a. For other translations, see Biallas 1986, 47; Birrell 1993, 35.

[6] *Shengxuan jing*, ch. 8; P. 2474, Ōfuchi 1979, 264; Yamada 1992, 31. An earlier adaptation of the Nügua story in Daoist myth is also found in the *Santian zhengfa jing* (Scripture of the Proper Law of the Three Heavens, DZ 1203). Here the Yellow Emperor is the one to mold people from mud. See Kohn 1995, 66n 1.

[7] For a description of paleolithic ease, based on ancient myths and anthropological research, see Thompson 1981. An account in recent fiction is found in John Darton's novel *Neanderthal*.

the mythical sage rulers Yao, Shun, and Yu, whose benign government and exceptional sense of filial and social duty made the world a harmonious and delightful place in which to live.[8]

The creation of human beings and ordering of the celestial administration in the *Youlong zhuan*, therefore, draws ancient mainstream cosmogony and myth into close relation with the medieval Daoist vision, just as it joins the creation of heaven and earth through emerging energies to the act of creation by a deity. In the larger sequence of creative moves, human beings, while special because their bodies contain the entire universe, are still part of the overall unfolding of the world and do not disrupt the harmony of the universe. They are, at least in the early stages, free from consciousness, sickness, and social constraints, living a happy and long life in close communion with heaven and earth. Over time this state is restored to them by periodic revelations bestowed by the deity.

Lord Goldtower's Revelations

In the second phase of establishing order, Lord Lao appears as a revealing deity who gives guidance to the world. Although he descends under many different names in the course of history, at this early point in the myth he appears as the messiah Lord Goldtower, also known as the Latter Sage. Originally a deity of Highest Clarity Daoism, this figure was prophesied to come forth in a *renchen* year from Mount Qingcheng in Sichuan to establish a new world that would be peopled by the "chosen ones" or "seed people" (*zhongmin*). He is a continuation of the earlier messiah Li Hong, who was either a transformation of Lord Lao himself or his messenger. He was expected to descend at the end of a major world cycle to cleanse all with scourges and establish the reign of Great Peace (see chapter 5 above). Unlike this medieval figure who is an apocalyptic messiah, the *Youlong zhuan* introduces Lord Goldtower right at the beginning, and establishes through him a pattern of benevolent revelations that show the active, salvific concern of the deity for his creation.

Standing between the celestial gods of the Dao and the newly created humanity, this divine messenger is the recipient of various sacred materials that he then transmits to earth. The *Youlong zhuan* describes the different kinds of texts in its next three sections, in each case linking

---

[8] On the Confucian vision of early humanity, see Allan 1981; Birrell 1993, 81; Ching 1997, 56–58.

them to the activities of the main god, whom it clearly identifies as Lord Lao (2.9a). First, in section 8, "Ordering the Numinous Documents," it gives a general description of the divine writings, including numinous talismans and precious stanzas, the immediate representations of the hidden signs and names of creation. "Congealed from the flying, mysterious energy of spontaneity" (2.9a), they are part of a reality truer than the created world and show the signs of primordiality in their original form.

In section 9, "Selecting Immortals' Charts," it identifies the charts and registers, maps of sacred places, and lists of divine names, all of which "contain the secret words of the highest sages" (2.10b) and provide detailed knowledge of the otherworld. Although revealed in human language, they still contain images and sounds alien to the common world and carry a power higher than any on earth. Finally, in section 10, "Transmitting the Scriptures," the text discusses the scriptures proper, ranked in the Three Caverns and consisting of a total of thirty-six classes (twelve per Cavern), which match the cosmology of heaven and earth. Arisen as "cloudy seals at the beginning of the kalpas" (2.12b), their original language is not a mortal tongue but the speech of heaven, the "hidden language of Great Brahma" (2.12b), an adaptation of Sanskrit, unintelligible to humans but carrying the powers of the Dao. They appear in the world, revealed by Lord Goldtower in successive eons, in an approximate translation to make their instructions intelligible to limited human faculties.

This complex network of scriptures and sacred writings—all of which Lord Goldtower has access to and transmits for the benefit of humanity—goes back to the medieval Daoist worldview as first formulated in Highest Clarity doctrine. Here the scriptures were originally pure rays of light, a condensed form of the heavenly order that survives forever. "Heaven and earth may be destroyed, they may rise and fall ten thousand times, yet the true writings will shine forth for eternity," the *Wushang biyao* says (DZ 1138, 21.1a).[9] Just as human beings can receive the manifold sacred writings from the gods of the Dao, so the divine messenger himself must receive them in revelation from the higher gods. The myth accordingly tells of his revelatory encounter with the Heavenly King of Primordial Beginning, which establishes the pattern for all later

---

[9] For more on sacred texts in Highest Clarity Daoism, see Robinet 1997, 128; 1993, 21; 1997, 115; Bumbacher 1995. On the sacrality of the written word in ancient China in general, see Chaves 1977; in Daoist revelations, see Ledderose 1984. On the *Wushang biyao*, see Lagerwey 1981.

revelations of texts both in heaven and on earth. It begins with a description of the setting:

> On the tenth day of the ninth month of the first year of Highest Sovereign, Lord Goldtower was wandering west of the river and passing a monastery, when he unexpectedly encountered the Heavenly King of Primordial Beginning.
> The deity approached from heaven riding in a jade carriage of the Eight Luminants, drawn by mysterious dragons of the Nine Colors, and supported by floating clouds of the Three Simplicities. Followed by a host of immortals who were waving flowery banners and surrounded by lions and snow-geese who were singing and whistling in great harmony, he floated closer, descending through the air to land west of the river. (2.10b)[10]

In the next few moments, Lord Goldtower kowtows, rendered "almost speechless with delight" at this unexpected encounter. Then he expresses his dedication to the Dao and explains that "although I obtained the twenty-four numinous charts, I have not yet penetrated their mystery; although I can roundly praise them, I have not yet found their right image" (2.11a). He concludes with a formal request for instruction. In gracious response, the Heavenly King "from his mouth emitted the jade talisman for inner observation of Cavern Prime and handed it to the Lord with instructions to purify himself for one thousand days" (2.11a). He assures his disciple that by this method the charts would soon come alive in intelligible patterns. Lord Goldtower, deeply moved, kowtows again and, after the celestial entourage vanishes into the haze, fulfills his end of the bargain by practicing assiduously and becoming a teacher of later generations himself (2.11a).

This story demonstrates the classic form of a revelatory encounter with the Dao. Usually set in the wilderness on a mountain or in a grotto, it involves the descent of the deity surrounded by a heavenly entourage and accompanied by wondrous music and often by fragrance. A clear request by the seeker to be taught is followed by graciously given instruction, the deity's vanishing, and the seeker's successful cultivation, usually over 1,000 days or three years—the period for both mourning and resurrection in ancient China (Harper 1994, 21). By placing the revelation in the central phase of early cosmic ordering, the *Youlong zhuan* in effect defines it as a model for all the revelations to follow. Revelation

---

[10] This account of the *Youlong zhuan* is an abbreviated version of the extensive revelation story contained in the *Housheng daojun lieji* (DZ 442) and also found in *Taiping jingchao* (DZ 1101). See Strickmann 1981, 213–24; Wong 1997, 52–55. See also chapter 5 above.

becomes the key means by which the Dao orders the world and maintains a divine presence as the mundane realm of humanity unfolds.

Decline Through Kalpa Cycles

Not every age can have access to all the scriptures, and certain materials are suited only for specific historical phases. Some scriptures have a higher rate of survival in cosmic clashes than others. As the medieval *Duming miaojing* describes it:

> When a great kalpa comes to an end, heaven tumbles and the earth is submerged. The four seas are merged in darkness, and even gold and jade begin to melt. The myriad aspects of the Dao cease to exist, and only this scripture survives, its teaching never ending.
>
> All writings on the various methods, on techniques of gymnastics and nourishing life, change with the kalpas and are scattered among ordinary folk. They are tied to the Six Heavens, the World of Desire. When a small kalpa ends, these methods perish along with everything else and vanish completely.
>
> The transformative talismans and charts of the Highest Clarity [school], the *Taiping jing*, the methods and techniques of the Dao proper, and the lesser sections of the scriptures continue to circulate up and down throughout the eighteen heavens of the World of Form. (14b–15a; Kohn 1995, 123–24)]

This presents a hierarchy of scriptures in relation to the thirty-six heavens, evaluating their survival rate at the end of a kalpa cycle. Lower materials, dealing with practical methods and techniques, perish with the lowest Six Heavens in the World of Desire; medium-type writings, such as Highest Clarity talismans and charts and the *Taiping jing*, remain in the World of Form but vanish as, and when, this part of the universe also collapses. Only the highest type of writings, such as the scriptures of the Highest Clarity and Numinous Treasure schools, including the work from which the above passage is taken, will survive at all times, being part of the highest heavens where cyclical decline and destruction never reach.

The cyclical pattern of kalpic revolutions is the third mode of order Lord Lao imposes on the world, according to the *Youlong zhuan*. It matches the early phases of universal history with the precreation pattern of energy revolutions. The myth thereby not only explains why certain texts are available only in certain ages, but also why social harmony, economic security, human lifespan, and religious purity vary from age to age and go into phases of decline.

Daoism, as pointed out earlier, has four key kalpas, which are first described in the early Numinous Treasure text, *Zhihui zuigen pin*.[11] They are:

1. Dragon Country (*longhan*): People were pure and free from evil and led a simple life. The Heavenly Worthy descended to help them live in perfect accordance with the rule of the Dao. There was no sin. At the end of this kalpa the world collapsed.
2. Red Radiance (*chiming*): There was a trace of impurity and evil among living beings; karma and retribution first began. The Heavenly Worthy saved as many as he could and established the first colonies of celestial beings above. Again, the kalpa ended with the complete destruction of everything.
3. Opening Sovereign (*kaihuang*): People were still living simply, but there were the beginnings of culture and civilization, as exemplified in the knotting of cords for reckoning. Since the minds of people were simple and still largely unconscious, their life spans were as long as 36,000 years. Again, the Heavenly Worthy supported the age.
4. Highest Sovereign (*shanghuang*): Culture developed fully and the world declined seriously. There were strife and jealousy, hatred and war, bringing about a dark age of humanity that still continues. To the present, the Heavenly Worthy has handed down precepts and rules to ensure the survival and salvation of at least a few (2a–3a).

These four kalpas—reminiscent also of Hesiod's four ages (gold, silver, bronze, and iron) of primordiality, timelessness, history, and decay (Colavito 1992, 88)—are a combination of the traditional Chinese stages of cultural cycles (five phases) and the Indian notion of declining ages or *yugas*. Here the perfect age, Krta Yuga, is followed by a time of slight decline in the Tretā Yuga, which proceeds to a time of shortened life-spans and advanced culture in the Dvāpara Yuga, and finally ends in a dark age of evil and corruption, the Kali Yuga (see Eliade 1957a). After the world has passed through an entire cycle of four phases (*mahāyuga*), it is completely destroyed and begins anew. The powers underlying all existence are present throughout and appear in set intervals.

---

[11] On the Numinous Treasure corpus, see Ōfuchi 1974; Bokenkamp 1983; Kobayashi 1990.

Daoists use a combination of the two schemes to express their own particular worldview. For them, every kalpa is a full world cycle and ends with the utter annihilation of all concrete existence. Complete cultural disintegration happens over several cycles, each one bringing greater corruption. Heavenly beings are in attendance but they can help only so much. The world is in decline and finds relief only in the form of precepts and proper rituals. However, despite this progressive movement toward destruction with each cycle and over several cycles, there remains a continuous and permanent level beyond created existence. This level, located in the highest heavens, consists of the key gods and their most powerful scriptures. Lord Lao as the Dao, although declining with the ongoing development of the kalpas in the created world, also remains with the highest gods, heavens, and scriptures. As each kalpa enters a state of destruction, the material manifestation of the world is destroyed, but the most sacred writings and the most faithful believers are saved in the higher heavens, immune to all disasters.

In the early phases of prehistory, then, Lord Lao descended under different names and arranged for the main texts of the Three Caverns to be revealed in the first three kalpas. In Dragon Country he appeared under the name of Preceptor of the Mysterious Center (Xuanzhong fashi) and revealed the Highest Clarity scriptures; in Red Radiance he was the Old Master (Gu xiansheng) and gave the world the Numinous Treasure writings; in Opening Sovereign he came as Lord Goldtower and brought the texts of the Spirit Cavern (2.13a). In each case, he assured perfect government in a perfect world that as yet showed signs of only incipient decline. The major phase of decline, however, arrived with the fourth kalpa, Highest Sovereign, of which our present age is a part. Ever since the inception of this kalpa, the activities of the deity have become manifold and his revelations highly complex, including not only general talismans and beneficent scriptures but also detailed ritual instructions and practical measures. This, then, is the salvific history of the Dao as it has manifested itself in all ages of Chinese cul ure and continues to lead people to heavenly purity however deeply they may be mired in worldly dust and grime.

"The Fall"

The Daoist attitude toward the decline of the world, or what other religions might call "the fall" is highly ambivalent. The Dao as Lord Lao and in its pure manifestation in heavens, gods, and scriptures is forever free from any sort of diminishment or impurity and remains at the calm center of all. Nevertheless human life, culture, and history undergo phases of rise and decline, are pure and highly developed at one time but show depravity and disintegration at others. Because the world was created by the Dao and continues to be fully part of it, it should by rights never leave the realm of purity and remain always in harmony and well-being. Any loss of this state cannot, therefore, signal a separation from the Dao, which is basically impossible, but must be a temporary aberration, a lessening of the Dao's active presence in the world. This presence, however, can be restored either with the help of the correct rituals here and now or through renewed revelations in the future.

The *Youlong zhuan*, following the Numinous Treasure model, accounts for the decline of the world with the theory of kalpa cycles. Other medieval texts use slightly different models. The *Santian neijie jing*, for example, sees the cause of the decline of human life in the loss of proper ritual practice and the abandonment of the inherent, natural order of the world that occurs when people turn to blood sacrifices and ecstatic cults. It says:

> Ever since Lower Antiquity, people have had reduced and distorted life-spans, have exposed their corpses and bones to the wolves, and have never lived out their full longevity.
>
> This was because in their cultivation they lost the true origins, in their marriages they did not stick to the proper ritual. They disturbed their energy, and it became disordered and turbid. They developed faith in the false and abandoned the true. With the original Dao so falsified, the masses became ignorant and utterly confused. None knew the source of their misfortunes.
>
> They slaughtered and cooked the six domestic animals as sacrifices to emptiness and nothingness. They sang songs and danced to the beat of drums, pursuing the Dao with offerings of wine and meat. They imagined they could by these means gain life and reject death. Yet this falseness soon made their heads ache and their feet itch. Human affairs were no longer harmonized, prayers and incantations were distorted and went awry. Thus it happened that people began to lose their lives in early death. (1.1b–2a)

This account links the loss of purity with the absence of proper religious guidance, the perversion of offerings and rituals, and the end of perfect longevity. It also focuses heavily on social customs and basic errors in consciousness that make people act in depraved ways. Contrasting the state of decline with the right practice of the pure Dao, the text provides an explanation for the unhappy state of the world, while also establishing compelling reasons why people should follow the Dao here and now.

However depraved the overall customs of society may be, the Dao is never far and can always be reached by turning back to the pure rites. The continued presence of the Dao in the world is guaranteed and can be invoked in the practice of the religion; it is never lost but only submerged under a complexity of culture and depravity of cult.

The *Kaitian jing* presents a similar vision of cultural devolution by linking the Daoist notion of culture-as-decline with the Confucian vision of the mythical sage rulers as positive sources of civilization. Doing so, it describes the continued presence of the Dao in Lord Lao's reappearances under every ruler of antiquity. First, during the four "grand" stages of prehistory, the god appears regularly to bring forth sacred scriptures and guide the cosmos toward creation. Next, he inspires Daoist cosmic rulers, including Chaos, the Nine Palaces, and the Three Sovereigns, to bring harmony to the world, yet he also allows consciousness, language, and a rudimentary form of imperial government to emerge (3b–4a).

Third, during the rule of the Confucian sage rulers Lord Lao guides the world with the help of various scriptures, promoting the establishment of culture as it manifests itself in writing and reckoning, names and appellations, fire and pottery, agriculture and markets, social ranks and political structures. The *Kaitian jing* ends its account (probably fragmentary) with the god's support of Tang, the righteous first ruler of the Shang (4a–5b). The Dao as Lord Lao in this version never leaves the world, yet he is not submerged in its depravity and disorder; he continues to keep a close watch on the evolution of culture, allowing it to come forth while still holding it to the purity and harmony of creation. The decline here, as in the *Youlong zhuan* version, is planned and steered directly by the deity; it is minimized and part of an educational experience, not a proper "fall" at all.

In this respect, the religious Daoist myth differs significantly from its ancient Daoist and mainstream Chinese counterparts, which like many other religions acknowledge a break between the present time and the golden age of the past. In ancient Daoism, such a break is described in the *Zhuangzi* as the four-stage development of discriminating consciousness. First there is the primordial state of "Chaos Complete," characterized, as Guo Xiang says in his commentary, as "the complete forgetfulness of heaven and earth," a mental state of utter unconsciousness, "boundless and free from fetters, going along with beings and fully according with all." Second, there is the stage of "Beings," which means that discrete entities are recognized but are not yet categorized. This happens in the third stage called "Distinctions," when things are clearly delimited into "this and that" but not yet critically evaluated. Critical evaluation represents the last and most declined state, called "Right and Wrong," and signals the "destruction of the Dao."[12]

Supplementary to this, the ancient Daoist understanding finds the key to the fall in the establishment of Confucian morality. As the *Daode jing* says:

> When the Great Dao declined,
> There were the ideas of benevolence and social responsibility.
> When knowledge and wisdom appeared,
> Great hypocrisy arose.
> When the six family relationships were no longer in harmony,
> Filial piety and the love for children were stressed. (ch. 18)

Along very similar lines, the *Zhuangzi* holds the reigns of the mythical sage emperors responsible for the decline, each one establishing further delimitations and "differentiating the hearts of the people by their sense of kinship" (ch. 14). According to this, increasing complexity of consciousness goes hand in hand with a more intricate social structure and more sophisticated levels of culture. As Girardot has shown, Daoists speak essentially about the "sociocultural development when men start to classify themselves into particular lineage groups, into a cosmological system of order that is formally reflected in an honorific language of respect, in systems of potlatching prestation designed to gain the return of social prestige, and in discriminating modes of thought" (1985, 84). Consciousness, therefore, is only one aspect of a general increase in the complexity of culture and society.

In contrast to this, the Confucian or mainstream Chinese understanding of the break from primordial harmony focuses more on social disruption than on consciousness. As described in a myth in the *Guoyu* (Discourses of the States), the key event is the severance of the link between heaven and earth. The story first describes the wholeness of primitive life in terms of an easy access between the spheres, with humans able to travel to the realms of the gods, and gods descending to earth. Then a period of decline set in and the cosmic powers were disrupted. "Gods and humans intermingled and became indistinguishable, and it became impossible to determine who were mortal creatures. Everyone performed sacrifices as if they were shaman officials, and they lost their essential sincerity of faith" (Birrell 1993, 94). As a result, the

---

[12] For further discussion, see Knaul 1985, 25. Aside from this classical version, the Hundun myth can also be read as an expression of the evolution of complex consciousness. See Girardot 1983, 97.

universe was out of joint and calamities were visited upon the people that could only be stopped by establishing rigid boundaries and ruthlessly cutting the ties between the realms. This vision, too, links strict social rules with the evolution of culture and sees social boundaries as a form of decline from the integrated and harmonious life of old. It presents the fall as a painful break, in this case even a physical and concrete break, and thus—like the classical Daoist vision—stands in contrast to the religious Daoist myth. The religious myth does not allow for a fundamental separation of Dao and world and therefore accounts for cultural complexity and religious misconduct as part of a planned evolution and salvific history.

The Daoist order established immediately after creation and its postulation of a continued underlying Dao-presence—despite the kalpic decline and even destruction presented in the *Youlong zhuan* and medieval crystallizations of the creation myth—is at odds with the ancient Chinese vision found in classical Daoism and mainstream Confucianism. The latter traditions closely match what in Western and other religions is termed "the fall," a painful transition of primordial humanity to its present state of strife, the change from timelessness to time and history. In mythical narrative generally, the fall accounts for the mutation of an entirely harmonious world into one of good and evil, and for the development of culture from the simple to the complex, which brings the beginning of disharmony and evil in the world (Weizsäcker 1964, 53). The gradual emergence of more intricate forms of living is experienced as the irreparable loss of a pristine golden age and often mythically described as a single traumatic event. Thus it can be

> the Fall of the One into the many, the emergence of the physical universe out of a transcendent God, the Fall of the soul into time, the entrapment of an angelic soul into the body of Australopithecus afrarensis, or the Fall of an unconditioned consciousness beyond subject and object into the syntax of thought pounded into form by each heartbeat. (Thompson 1981, 9–10)

However the Fall is described, be it the expulsion from the Garden of Eden, the betrayal of a brother, the battle between light and darkness, the loss of unified consciousness, or the derailing of enlightened government, it is always about cultural progress, the ongoing transformation of the world into more complex forms, the diversification of society into various segments, and the production of more intricate living conditions. All these are seen with a sense of great regret so that, as Douglas Adams puts it in his *Hitchhiker's Guide to the Galaxy*, people came to feel that "they'd all made a big mistake in coming down from the trees in the first place. And some said that even the trees had been a bad move, and that no one should have left the oceans."[13]

In a more psychological reading, the Fall is also often associated with the beginning and increasing complexity of consciousness through which, in the words of Edward Edinger, "man is separated and alienated from his original wholeness" (1972, 18). This then means that the Ego grows out of, and in opposition to, the Self and breaks the original identity between the two. This occurs in a series of steps toward individuation and is "experienced as a crime against the collective, because it challenges the individual's identification with some representative of the collective" (1972, 26). Jungians, therefore, like ancient Chinese and classical Daoists, link the development of consciousness, defined as the experience of conflict and the awareness of opposites, with the disruption of social harmony and community cohesion.

Religious Daoists, however, do not allow for this, claiming that all the developments of history and culture were intentionally instituted by the personified Dao for the greater benefit and ultimate salvation of humanity. The deity under manifold names and guises continues to guide the world through its various stages of development, never leaving it to its own devices and never separating from it. Although this vision seems to sharply contradict the older myths, a line of historical development can be detected. Compared to Confucian myth, classical Daoists place the fall earlier and into a more primordial stage of the universe. And compared to the ancient Daoists, religious Daoists in their turn move it even further from the created world and into the realm of the Dao. At first, as documented in the *Santian neijie jing*, they retain a notion of separation and loss, then abandon even this in favor of the continued presence of the Dao, and eventually, as described in the *Youlong zhuan*, locate many elements of active Daoist practice, such as statues, teachers, and scriptures, in the stages of precreation.

One expression of this historical development can be seen in the placement of mainstream and classical Daoist creator deities in the religious myth. Pangu and Hundun, for example, appear only after the stage of timelessness is over, at the beginning of the mundane world when history has commenced. This is clear in the *Kaitian jing*, where Hundun is the first ruler of Middle Antiquity, and in the *Yuanqi lun* (On Primordial Energy, *YJQQ* 56), where Pangu only appears after the energies have combined to create the heavens. Chaos is destroyed, the cosmos becomes

---

[13] Cited in Girardot 1985, 77. The varied concrete descriptions of the Fall are found in Mercatante 1978; for an early discussion, see Frazer 1984; on its characterization as diversification, see Sproul 1979, 24.

anthropomorphic, and creation is linked with sacrifice *only* when the mundane world is unfolding—the pure world of the Dao remains unaffected.

This pure world of the Dao, then, manifested in the supernatural hierarchy, the revelation of scriptures, and the kalpa cycles, is part of an increasingly large buffer between primordiality and the world; it is paralleled by the establishment of a priestly hierarchy in Daoist communal ritual (see Bell 1988). Placing key features of the religion in the realm of creation, importance is shifted away from the mundane and toward the primordial, which in turn is divided into two levels, a phase before creation or "precosmic primordiality" and a stage immediately after creation or "universal timelessness." This division is something Daoism again has in common with other religions; it is a phenomenon described by Mircea Eliade as the stages of original chaos and the proto-creation of the gods, which in turn produce two levels of religious striving: "The longing to reintegrate the primordial totality that existed before the creation; and the longing to recover the primordial epoch that began immediately after the creation" (1984, 151).

Matching this differentiation, practicing religious Daoists strive first for the position of Pangu as the single human being in the existing world then for that of Hundun as integrated consciousness—although neither is their final goal. Rather, for them these are starting points for their reintegration with primordial totality, for ascending to the heavens and attaining oneness with the Dao *before* creation. In their meditations, adepts accordingly place themselves firmly in the center of the universe and become one with the world at creation; from this position they can then establish communication with the primordial gods and come closer to the Dao. Higher levels of Daoist practice involve ecstatic travels to the stars and meetings with the celestials. Through these, Daoists overcome even precreation by going back to the absolute root of being, the Dao in its pure form at the very beginning. They transcend death by recovering the state before history, then attain oneness with the universe by going back to the ultimate root of all, becoming Lord Lao first as the central power of the created world, then as the Dao itself.[14]

---

[14] For Daoist practice as the recovery of Hundun or chaos, see Girardot 1983. On the levels of Daoist meditative attainment, see Kohn 1989b; Robinet 1993.

9

The Unfolding of Culture

Supported by the well-ordered realm of the Dao at the base of the created world, Lord Lao next proceeds to direct the unfolding of culture. He does so by descending to every major ruler of early history under a different sage name and issuing a scripture from his mouth, thereby teaching that ruler the steps culture needs to take. This sequence of appearances of the deity is known in the texts as "Serving as the Teacher of Emperors" (*dishi*), the title also found in the relevant section of the *Youlong zhuan* (sect. 11).[1] In Western studies it is known as "Laozi's Transformations" after the first scripture that describes them, the *Laozi bianhua jing* of the Later Han.

Most texts give just the basic list of the god's sage names and the emperors under which he appeared, a list that varied in the early middle ages but was standardized in the *Santian neijie jing* of the fifth century and has since appeared in all major Laozi hagiographies (see Table 13). The most extensive description of each "transformation" is found in the *Kaitian jing*.

The sequence of rulers, the Three Sovereigns (*sanhuang*),[2] the Five Emperors (*wudi*), and the Three Dynasties (*sandai*), closely follows Confucian myth as it was established under the Han dynasty, when the empire was unified and various local mythologies were integrated into one system (see Karlgren 1946).

---

[1] Matching materials are found in items 13–24 in the *Guangsheng yi* and in *Hunyuan shengji* 2.25b–33b.

[2] These are the Confucian or mainstream Three Sovereigns as distinct from the cosmic Three Sovereigns of Daoist myth who ruled in the early kalpas with the help of divine talismans and also gave the name to an early medieval Daoist school. For a general study, see Gu 1936; Kaltenmark 1980, 22–26. On the Daoist school and its texts, see Ōfuchi 1964, 277–343; Chen 1975, 71–78; Kobayashi 1990, 223–25; Kohn 1995, 207–8.

Table 13
Laozi's transformations

Three Sovereigns			
Text	Fu Xi	Shennong	Zhurong
Laozi bianhua jing	Wenshuangzi	Chunchengzi	Guangchengzi
Shenxian zhuan	Yuhuazi	Jiuling Laozi	Guangshouzi
Huahu jing	Jiushuangzi	Dachengzi	Fuyuzi
	Tianyezi	Guochengzi	Guangshouzi
Kaitian jing	Yuhuazi	Dachengzi	Guangshouzi
Miaomen youqi	Jiushuangzi	Dachengzi	Guangchengzi
Santian neijie jing	Yuhuazi	Dachengzi	Guangshouzi

Five Emperors					
Text	Huangdi	Zhuanxu	Di Ku	Yao	Shun
Bianhua	Tianlao	Chijingzi	Zhenzi	Maochengzi	Guoshuzi
Shenxian	Guangchengzi	Chijingzi	Lutuzi	Wuchengzi	Yinshouzi
Huahu	Guangchengzi	—	Lutuzi	Wuchengzi	Yinshouzi
Kaitian	Guangchengzi	Chijingzi	Suiyingzi	Wuchengzi	Junshouzi
Miaomen	Li Mu	Chijingzi	Heijingzi	Wuchengzi	Junshouzi
Santian	Guangchengzi	Chijingzi	Lutuzi	Wuchengzi	Yinshouzi

Three Dynasties			
Text	Yu/Xia	Tang/Shang	Wen/Zhou
Bianhua	Li Er	official	historian
Shenxian	Zhenxingzi	Xizezi	Wenyi xiansheng
Huahu	Li Zixu	Xizezi	Xieyizi
Kaitian	Zhenxingzi	—	Guoshuzi
Miaomen	Li Xuzi	Xishouzi	historian
Santian	Zhenxingzi	Xizezi	—

Editions: *Laozi bianhua jing*: S. 2295; *Shenxian zhuan*: *Daozang jinghua* 5.11; *Huahu jing*: *Sandong zhunang* 9.6b–7b; *Kaitian jing*: DZ 1437; *Miaomen youqi*: DZ 1125; *Santian neijie jing*: DZ 1205.
Note: The *Santian neijie jing* establishes the standard list, which later appears in: *Guangsheng yi* 2.8b–11a, *Youlong zhuan* 2.14a–18a, *Hunyuan shengji* 1.6b–19a and 2.13a–33a, *Laozi shilüe* (DZ 773), *Laojun nianpu yaolüe* (DZ 771), *Laojun bashiyi hua tushuo* (Reiter 1990). For comparative listings, see Yoshioka 1959, 89–90; Kusuyama 1979, 350.

In this myth, the Three Sovereigns, Fu Xi, Shennong, and Zhurong, are responsible for the basic attainments of civilization, such as a system of reckoning, agriculture, and the use of fire. The Five Emperors, who include the Yellow Emperor as well as Yao and Shun, brought forth basic aspects of culture, such as ritual procedures, official ranks, proper garments, coffins for burials, houses instead of caves, boats and carriages for transportation, legal punishments and prisons, regular markets, communal assemblies, and so on. The Three Dynasties, finally, saw not only the control of the flood under Yu of Xia but also the beginning of the Chinese empire under Tang of Shang and the establishment of the Zhou dynasty under King Wen.[3] The Daoist myth, then, uses this basic system of Confucian mythical history to present its own vision of how Lord Lao continues to guide humanity in the Dao, providing for the unfolding of culture while still working toward universal salvation.

Culture and Salvation

In his first act as bringer of culture, Lord Lao descends during the rule of Fu Xi under the name Master of Luxuriant Florescence (Yuhuazi) to bring forth the *Yuanyang jing* (Scripture of Primordial Yang) from his mouth.[4] He thereby teaches Fu Xi the eight trigrams and basic writing systems, thus opening the way for the beginning of cultural organization (*Youlong zhuan* 2.14a). Next he appears under Shennong with the name Master of Great Perfection (Dachengzi) and issues the *Yuanjing jing* (Scripture of Primordial Essence) to guide the ruler in developing agriculture, animal husbandry, weaving, and pharmacology (2.14b). Under Zhurong, the third of the Confucian Three Sovereigns, Lord Lao assumes the name Master of Vast Longevity (Guangshouzi), brings forth the *Anmo tongjing jing* (Scripture of Massage and Pervasion of Essence), and teaches people to control fire and make pottery (2.14b; see Fig. 13). During this early period, the god in addition inspires the development of other aspects of culture, such as proper houses, carriages, markets, a legal system, and funerary rites. These cultural attainments are commonly associated with the Yellow Emperor, who in mainstream myth is the epitome of governmental organization and the hero of the first righteous war against the Wormy Rebel (Chiyou; see Lewis 1990).

---

[3] This Confucian vision of early Chinese history is described in the *Xici* commentary to the *Yijing* (2.2). See Sung 1971, 309–13; Haloun 1925, 245; Kaltenmark 1980, 26–34; Wu 1982, 55–101. A variant list of rulers appears in the *Hanshu* (History of the Former Han). See Haloun 1925, 250; Eberhard 1968, 158. In addition, Fu Xi and Nügua are depicted in art as half-human, half-animal figures. See Wen 1956, 18. The numbers of the various groups are symbolic of the totality of the cosmos, three standing for the vertical totality of the three forces and five for the horizontal one of the five phases.

[4] This *Yuanyang jing*, much like the other texts mentioned as revealed in the early phases of history, is probably not identical with a text of this title summarized in the *Shangqing jing* (Scriptures of the Realm of Highest Clarity, DZ 8, 1.4a–6a). The fact that the text issues from the mouth of the deity is reminiscent of the motif of the earth-diver, who picks up the first matter from an ocean of primordiality with his mouth and spits it forth to begin creation (Dundes 1984a, 278).

第十二化

置陶冶

太上老君在祝融
時為人食生冷以
天漢元年就廣
壽子說拔
摩通精經
祝融行之
乃鑽木出
火陶冶為
器

Fig. 13. Lord Lao oversees the production of the first pottery from his heavenly abode. *Source: Laojun bashiyi hua tushuo*, no. 12

In the religious Daoist vision, however, these attainments are located in an earlier period to open the path for a reinterpretation of the activities of the Five Emperors and Three Dynasties, who are no longer merely bringers of increased cultural complexity but divinely inspired practitioners of the Dao. First among them is the Yellow Emperor, who is now also the first to receive instruction in active Daoist cultivation, thus leading the world not to more culture but toward the salvation of the Dao. The earliest documentation of the Yellow Emperor's Daoist efforts, also cited at length in the *Youlong zhuan* (2.15a–16b) and the *Hunyuan shengji* (2.13b–15a), is contained in the *Zhuangzi*, which describes his humble search for truth in an encounter with the sage Master of Vast Perfection (Guangchengzi), who in the later myth becomes another of Laozi's transformations. According to this, after being refused the first time,

> the Yellow Emperor resigned, gave up the empire, erected himself a hermitage, and put a mat of bleached straw [on the floor]. There he spent three months in solitude, before he again went to visit the Master.
> He found the Master lying prone, his head towards the south. The Yellow Emperor went near him on his knees, his attitude all humility. He kowtowed repeatedly and said: "I have heard that you, my Master, have attained the perfect Dao. May I dare to ask you about the way to cultivate the body? What should I do so that I can attain true longevity?" (ch. 11; see also Watson 1968, 119)

No longer the creator of culture, even under the guidance of divine inspiration, this ruler is now the first to humble himself to receive the Dao and attain its cultivation. Guangchengzi instructs him in the basic rules of Daoist longevity techniques; the Yellow Emperor follows them and wanders through the country to learn from other masters. This basic story in the *Zhuangzi* is expanded in the Han dynasty to include the Yellow Emperor's casting of the Nine Tripods as symbols of his rule over the world and his ascension to heaven in broad daylight on the back of a dragon, which showed him to be a Daoist immortal.[5]

The complex Daoist myth uses both parts of the tale in conjunction with the patriarchal vision of the Louguan Daoists, which claims Daoist cultivation at Louguan ever since the dawn of history (Kohn 1997, 95–102). It adds that the Yellow Emperor received Laozi's *Daojie jing* (Scripture of Precepts of the Dao) and was a protégé of the Queen Mother

---

[5] See Yü 1964. In addition, studies on the Yellow Emperor are found in Tetsui 1970; 1972; 1990; Lewis 1990. On his role in mainstream Chinese myth, see also Liu Chenghuai 1988; Yuan 1985; 1986; 1988. The *Youlong zhuan* also recounts this (2.16b).

of the West. It was she who gave him divine talismans to subdue the Wormy Rebel as well as a jade image of the Heavenly Worthy, which he then set up in a building of its own, offering it incense and flowers and worshiping it every morning and evening.[6] In doing so, the Yellow Emperor created the first Daoist institution and set up the first active forms of Daoist ritual. More than that, he spread the practice throughout the country, opening Daoist monasteries (*guan*) on over 300 mountains, establishing a schedule of annual purification ceremonies and festivals, and helping numerous practitioners to ascend to the immortals (*Youlong zhuan* 2.17a; *Hunyuan shengji* 2.21a–24a).

In the Daoist myth, the Yellow Emperor is thus transformed from the creator of cultural sophistication to the first active seeker and worshiper of the Dao. Whereas earlier rulers had made human life more civilized and given it better organization, he sanctified it through religious Daoist activities and thus became the first king who not only learned from the Dao but himself attained it. The world, far from declining ever further through the development of cultural complexity, made use of the expanding culture and underwent a transformation toward religious salvation. It passed from an unconscious, inherent Dao through a period of timelessness and growing culture to a stage of proper Daoist worship.

All rulers after the Yellow Emperor, as the Daoist myth describes them, followed the same basic pattern. Instead of developing cultural features and political institutions, they articulated moral values and introduced various forms of Daoist worship or doctrine. Accordingly, Zhuanxu, who was taught by Lord Lao as Master of Red Essence (Chijingzi), gave the world the Dao of filial piety and obedience; Di Ku developed the Dao of purity and harmony; Yao propagated the Dao of modesty and respect; and Shun, the recipient of a celestial version of the *Daode jing*, developed the Dao of nonaction, purity, and tranquility (*Youlong zhuan* 2.17ab, *Hunyuan shengji* 2.25a–26a).

The same holds true for the founders of the Three Dynasties. Yu, the first ruler of the Xia, taught by Lord Lao under the name of Master of True Practice (Zhenxingzi), developed the Dao of diligence and frugality. Since he was faced with the particular difficulty of the flood, he also received five Numinous Treasure talismans, with whose help he summoned spirits and demons and thus managed to contain the waters and

---

[6] *Youlong zhuan* 2.17a, *Hunyuan shengji* 2.15b. For the role of Queen Mother of the West in this story, see Cahill 1993, 109.

chisel out new riverbeds (*Hunyuan shengji* 2.32a).[7] King Tang, the founder of the Shang, developed the Dao of reverence and love. In practicing it, he looked upon other beings as himself, his good grace extending even to worms and insects (*Youlong zhuan* 2.17b, *Hunyuan shengji* 2.33a). King Wen, finally, the first Zhou regent, also received tokens of goodwill from the deity but in a different form, since at this time Lord Lao descended to be born and serve the dynasty as an archivist.

This positive evaluation of the Confucian sage rulers and the acknowledgment of culture as a basis for Daoist cultivation stands in stark contrast to the ancient Daoist vision, which holds the unfolding of culture responsible for all evils in the world and does not accept anything positive about the Confucian sages. "'Culture,' the *Zhuangzi* says, "destroyed the substantial, and 'breadth' drowned the mind. After this the people began to be confused and disordered."[8] For the ancient Daoists, the worst culprits were the emperors most venerated by the Confucians—Yao, Shun, and Yu:

> They said they were governing the world but in fact the disorder they created has yet to find its match! The rule of the Three Sovereigns: above, it obscured the light of the sun and the moon; below, it estranged the essence of the mountains and rivers; and in the center, it ruined the regular cycles of the four seasons. (ch. 14; see Watson 1968, 165)

For the ancient thinkers, the increase in cultural complexity thus spelled the end of the pure Dao and the decline of the world into confusion and disorder. It was harmful and had to be revoked, abolished, undone.

The religious version, on the contrary, allows culture to unfold and accepts it as a divinely inspired and thus positive step toward the establishment of Daoist practice. It integrates the sequence of rulers from mainstream myth but reinterprets their virtues as directly inspired by Lord Lao and thus active manifestations of the Daoist teaching. Harmony in the social and political spheres is reached, not despite, but because of cultural complexity and Confucian ritual organization; not despite, but because of the rulers' power, used to serve the Dao and worship it in its proper setting. Cultural achievements become a vehicle for the extended practice of the religion through sacred images, monastic institutions, and regular rituals as the proper expressions of the under-

---

[7] This integrates the basic Numinous Treasure myth about the reception and development of its central five talismans. For the story, see Bokenkamp 1986; Kohn 1993, 43–48.

[8] Cited from ch. 16; Watson 1968, 173. For a discussion, see Allan 1981, 139.

lying perfection of the Dao. All these things, far from being degradations of the Dao, are seen as rooted in it even before creation. They are taught to rulers by Lord Lao himself in his various manifestations as an inspired sage.

The Myth of the Imperial Adviser

The notion of divine inspiration given to a ruler or a dynasty is not originally Daoist but goes back to the mainstream myth of the imperial adviser, which first developed when the Qin overthrew the Zhou. To justify the rule by a new dynasty that had no hereditary claim to the throne, thinkers at the time proposed the doctrines of the Mandate of Heaven (*tianming*) and of cyclical dynastic changes based on the five phases. Mythologically, they reinterpreted ancient history to accommodate the deposing of a rightful but depraved heir in favor of the politically powerless but virtuous sage. In a typical story, the old ruler, himself a virtuous person, realizes that his heir is useless and tries to offer the empire to the sage. The latter steadfastly refuses and another wise yet politically acceptable person is found who becomes first adviser, then regent, and finally the new ruler. The new dynasty in this system is thus a mediation between the conflicting ideals of the heir and the sage.[9]

This sort of dynastic transition was first attributed to the reigns of Yao and Shun, with Xu You and Shan Juan as the relevant sages and Shun and Yu as the able successors (Allan 1981, 41). The same theme was also adopted for later successions at the end of the Xia and Shang dynasties, when Tang of Shang and King Wu of Zhou took over the kingdom. The difference in these later cases, however, was that historical records showed that the transition had not been peaceful but had involved a period of disorder so that the throne was only won by force. As a result, in the mythological rewriting of these events, the depraved heir and the old ruler merged, creating the image of a tyrannical last king. The contrast, accordingly, shifted from between the heir and the sage to the old ruler and the sage, a contrast mediated by the new ruler. The old ruler, no longer virtuous, had become a tyrant; the sage, no longer steadfastly refusing to rule, had become an imperial adviser and founding saint. They differed both in their basic positions, the ruler being at the top, the sage at the bottom of the social scale, and in their fundamental attitudes, the

---

[9] On the Mandate of Heaven and other theories of the early Han, see Fung and Bodde 1952; Ching 1997. For a study of the mythical paradigm of the heir and the sage in ancient China, see Allan 1981.

ruler taking more from the people than they could give and the sage not accepting from the new ruler what was freely offered (Allan 1981, 44).

As a result, imperial advisers as founding saints have two distinct characteristics. They are in an initial position of poverty or obscurity, simple and ordinary folk who do menial labor; and they at first refuse the offer to rule and to enjoy a much more comfortable state. In the end, however, the new ruler mediates between the two, raising up the lowly sage and with his help lowering the depraved tyrant. The sage accepts what he did not originally want; the tyrant is forced to give up what he originally enjoyed. The new ruler thus reestablishes harmony and balance in society, further proving his humility and virtue by trying to abdicate to a hermit sage (Allan 1981, 45–46).

This type of adviser was envisioned for the beginning of the Shang dynasty, when Tang wrested the rule from the tyrant Jie, using the commoner Yi Yin as his counselor. In the middle of the dynasty, King Wuding turned to the sage Fu Yue in his restructuring of the government. The Zhou rulers, moreover, only succeeded in defeating the Shang with the help of Taigong Wang, also known as Lü Wang or Lü Shang. He was the first to support King Wen with the help of a sacred text, in this case a treatise on warfare known as *Taigong bingfa* (Military Methods of Taigong) and of a set of governmental instructions, the *Danshu* (Cinnabar Book).[10]

In the Han dynasty, the Confucian ideal of the imperial adviser underwent two major developments, which made it a ready model for the later myth of Laozi's transformations. On the one hand, advisers were styled as divine personages and formal lists were established that provided each ancient ruler with a divine teacher. On the other hand, the ideal of the adviser was merged with the vision of the Daoist immortal so that counselors like Taigong Wang gained magical powers and immortals were styled as founding saints.

The transition from the Confucian myth to Laozi's transformations is well documented. First instances of divine sage teachers for ancient rulers appear in the *Lüshi chunqiu*, which mentions Xu You, Yi Yin, and Taigong Wang, and in addition claims that Shennong learned from Fan Zhu, Huangdi from Da Yao, Zhuanxu from Bo Yi, and Di Ku from Bo Zhao (Yoshioka 1959, 36). While these are otherwise unknown figures, sages associated with Laozi appear as divine teachers in the Confucian

---

[10] On Yi Yin, see Wu 1982, 133; Allan 1981, 51; Chan 1968, 41. On Fu Yue, see Allan 1981, 46. For Taigong Wang, see Chan 1968, 41; Wu 1982, 254; Allan 1972; 1981, 109.

work *Hanshi waizhuan* (Han's Outer Tradition of the "Songs"). Here we have:

> Lord Ai asked Zixia: "Must one learn in order to pacify the country and protect the people?"
>
> "It has never happened that someone did so without learning."
>
> "If that is so, did the Five Emperors also have teachers?"
>
> "Indeed," Zixia answered, "I have heard that the Yellow Emperor learned from Dazhenzi, Zhuanxu learned from Lutuzi, Di Ku learned from Chisongzi, Yao learned from Wuchengzi, Shun learned from Yinshouzi, Yu learned from Xiwang guo, Tang learned from Huozi Xiang, King Wen learned from Xishouzi, King Wu learned from Taigong Wang, Confucius learned from Lao Dan.
>
> "None of these eleven sage-kings, if he had not met his teacher, could have spread his merit and power through all-under-heaven, nor would his name and fame have been transmitted to later generations."[11]

This passage clearly mentions many names later associated with Laozi's transformations (see Table 14), linking them with established imperial advisers, such as Taigong Wang, and expressly mentioning Lao Dan as the teacher of Confucius. In addition, several names also occur independently as advisers of mythical rulers in early texts: Guangchengzi as the teacher of the Yellow Emperor in the *Zhuangzi*; Wuchengzi as a master of cosmology and government in the bibliographic section of the *Hanshu* (History of the Former Han); Chijingzi as minister of Zhuanxu in the *Hanshu* (ch. 75); and Yuhuazi as Fu Xi's teacher and the preceptor of the immortal Wang Qiao in the *Baopuzi* (Kusuyama 1979, 352). All these teachers were well known in the Han dynasty as divinely inspired sages and were later associated with Daoist immortals who had attained eternal life and mastery over the world. Once the idea took hold in the Later Han that Laozi was Lord Lao and identical with the Dao, they were merged into one deity who appeared in different forms over the ages. This followed the pattern of Laozi's earlier identification with several grand astrologers of old, all of whom had given good advice to their rulers.[12]

---

[11] Cited from ch. 2. See Kusuyama 1979, 352–53. The passage is also found in Liu Xiang's *Xinxu* (New Explanations); see Yoshioka 1959, 36.

[12] For Laozi's identity with the grand astrologers Boyang and Dan, see Seidel 1969, 36. On the joining of the figures into one deity, see Kusuyama 1979, 354.

Table 14
Translation of Laozi's names

Chijingzi 赤精子	Master of Red Essence
Chuanyuzi 傳豫子	Master of Teaching and Foreknowledge
Chunchengzi 春成子	Master of Spring Perfected
Dachengzi 大成子	Master of Great Perfection
Guangchengzi 廣成子	Master of Vast Perfection
Guangshouzi 廣壽子	Master of Vast Longevity
Guochengzi 郭成子	Master of Regions Perfected
Guoshuzi 郭叔子	Master of Regions Adjusted
Heijingzi 黑精子	Master of Black Essence
Jiuling laozi 九靈老子	Old Master of Ninefold Numen
Jiushuangzi 究爽子	Master of Pervading Vigor
Junshouzi 君壽子	Master of Ruling Longevity
Laozi 老子	Old Master
Lutuzi 錄圖子	Master of Registers and Charts
Maochengzi 茂成子	Master of Exuberant Perfection
Suiyingzi 隨應子	Master of Following in Accordance
Tianlao 天老	Old Man of Heaven
Tianyezi 天野子	Master of Fields and Wilderness
Weichengzi 衛成子	Master of Guarding Perfection
Wenshuangzi 溫爽子	Master of Warm Vigor
Wuchengzi 務成子	Master of Perfected Duty
Xieyizi 燮邑子	Master of Adjusting the Towns
Xishouzi 錫壽子	Master of Granting Longevity
Xizezi 錫則子	Master of Granting Rules
Yinshouzi 尹壽子	Master of Ruling Longevity
Yuanyangzi 元陽子	Master of Primordial Yang
Yuchengzi 與成子	Master of Nurturing Perfection
Yuhuazi 鬱華子	Master of Luxuriant Florescence
Zhenxingzi 眞行子	Master of Perfect Practice
Zhenzi 眞子	Perfect Master

Lord Lao, as both the Dao and a divine immortal, was believed to be present not only at the root of creation but also in the continuous cyclical transformations of the world. He could appropriate human shape, appear and disappear at will, and live forever. As classical adviser and divine teacher he also paved the way for various Daoist immortals to serve as founding saints in later ages.[13]

---

[13] Later immortals who became founding saints include Wang Yuanzhi of the Tang (Schafer 1980, 45–56; Strickmann 1981, 32; Yoshikawa 1990); Chen Tuan of the Song (Knaul 1981; Kohn 1990); and Zhang Zhong of the Ming (Chan 1973; Seidel 1970, 488). In addition, early founding saints were also styled as Daoist immortals. They include Taigong Wang, Ma Dan, and Fan Li of the Zhou who appeared in the *Liexian zhuan* (Kaltenmark 1953, 72, 91, 102), as well as Zhang Liang, the founding saint of the Han (Bauer 1956; Kusuyama 1979, 358).

Chinese Sacred Government

The Daoist myth of Lord Lao as the teacher of dynasties is thus a continuation of an originally Confucian vision, both in its sequence of rulers and in the ideal of the divinely inspired adviser who sees that the king fulfills his tasks. The division of roles into an active executor of politics and a wise or even supernatural sage, moreover, is a development of the late Zhou, when philosophers attempted to restore social and political harmony by becoming advisers to local rulers. This is clearly expressed in ancient Daoist texts, which describe the Dao as the power behind the throne, the central guideline to follow, the teacher to obey, the mother to rely on, and the old home to return to.

The key expression of this is found in the *Zhuangzi*:

> Oh, my teacher! Oh, my teacher! He judges the myriad beings but does not consider himself righteous. His richness extends to a myriad generations but he does not consider himself humane. He has lived since before high antiquity but does not consider himself long-lived. He protects heaven and supports earth, sculpts and molds the multitude of shaped things, but he does not consider himself handy.[14]

Used to explain the role of the Dao as teacher and describe its responsibility in creating order in the world, this passage claims that the Dao is the one force that gave "spirituality to the spirits and gods, [and] birth to heaven and earth; it exists beyond the highest point, yet cannot be called lofty; it exists beneath the limit of the six directions, yet cannot be called deep" (Watson 1968, 81). The Dao is what made the various sage rulers and heavenly deities what they are; only when taught by the Dao can the king perform his duties properly. The same notion is also found in the *Daode jing*, which describes the Dao variously as the mother of the world (ch. 1), the model for heaven (ch. 25), and the creative power behind all beings (ch. 42). It likens the Dao to water, which flows naturally yet is the most powerful and most life-giving force of all, and it insists that the sage or ruler must learn from the Dao and be its mediator on earth. The purpose of this vision, like its later manifestation in Lord Lao as the teacher of dynasties, was to ensure the continued sacredness of government, the unbroken closeness of the supernatural or divine sphere to the activities of the king on earth.

---

[14] Ch. 6; see also Watson 1968, 90; cited also in *Zhuangzi* 13 and *Youlong zhuan* 2.13b.

This view stands in contrast to the understanding in Shang and early Zhou times when the king was already the center of cosmic activity and the sole guarantor of harmony on earth. He was father of the land and representative of Heaven, responsible for the fertility of the soil, harmonious interaction among his people, and ongoing communication with heaven and the ancestors (Granet 1930, 378–80). In the Shang, for example,

> all power emanated from the theocrat because he was the channel, "the one man," who could appeal for the ancestral blessings, or dissipate the ancestral curses, which affected the commonality. It was the king who made fruitful harvest and victories possible by the sacrifices he offered, the rituals he performed, and the divinations he made. (Keightley 1978, 213)

Standing vertically at the apex of human society and horizontally at the center of the world, the king was surrounded by servants and courtiers, received the best and most of everything, and had his retainers follow him even into death. His capital, wherever it was established, signified the center of the known world, the midpoint of the five directions, from which all power issued; the ritual activity of the king, in the act of divination, ensured the continued connection with the otherworld.[15]

In the Western Zhou, too, the ruler was at the center of the world, giving order to it temporally by performing regular seasonal sacrifices, setting up the calendar, and undertaking a series of formal activities in the course of the year.[16] Not only the key to temporal order, he also centered the world in space; his palace was located in the middle of the central city of the kingdom and consisted of several successive courtyards and two major halls arranged in squares. His regular inspection tours took him all around the four quarters of the world (Bilsky 1975, 35, 46, 65).

The Shang and Western Zhou rulers of ancient China thus played a central and highly active role in maintaining the basic order of the universe, a role that in the Warring States was lessened in favor of more

---

[15] On the ritual centrality of the Shang king, see Chang 1976, 51–52; 1980, 203; 1983, 45. For details of Shang cosmology and center symbolism, see Allan 1991. For a more general discussion, see also Granet 1930; Zito 1997, 132–34.

[16] On the ritual activities of the Western Zhou king, see Bilsky 1975, 39–42. A Han description of the sacrifices is found in Bodde 1975, 224. On the calendar, its importance and difficulties, see Bilsky 1975, 43; Bodde 1975, 226–27. The seasonal system was later formalized in the "Monthly Ordinances" (*yueling*), described in the *Liji* (Legge 1885), *Lüshi chunqiu* (Wilhelm 1971), and *Huainanzi* (Major 1993, 217–68). See also Soothill 1952, 22–51. A general study of kingship and its symbols in traditional China is found in Ching 1997.

passive political and ritual activity guided by an adviser or inspired sage. In the religious Daoist myth as it is retold in the *Youlong zhuan*, however, the old ideal is picked up again in the figure of the Yellow Emperor and other perfect monarchs who are not only inspired by the Dao but also actively practice and attain it. The ruler in the later Daoist vision again holds the central position and is an active provider of peace on earth, following the guidance of the Dao but also acting as its main propagator and active representative.

The Sacred King

The ideal Daoist ruler, much like the king in Shang and Zhou times, can be compared with what Western studies have described as the sacred king, typically characterized as a father figure, a hero warrior, and the key to the land's fertility. In his primary role as the father of society, the king is the central axis between heaven and earth, the ancestors and the living; he is the central institution that rewards and punishes the people, and the judge of good and evil. He is the apex of the civil administration, and the pivot of a complex bureaucracy designed to help him execute his functions of protecting and developing his country.[17]

Second, as hero warrior, the king is also a military leader who ensures the victory of order and goodness over the forces of darkness— outside peoples or "barbarians" who attack the borders of the country, or again demons who make the people's lives insecure from within. The forces of darkness, as documented especially in sources of the ancient Near East, also include the chthonic powers of chaos and the potentially destructive energies of creation in its untamed, unformed state. These are often associated with the female—the darkness of primordial creation and the sphere of death, from which all life comes and to which it returns. The female symbolizes turbulence and threat of destruction but is also the power of primordial creation and as such should be cultivated and made accessible. Again, the sacred king stands between two principles and, like the high god himself, serves as the mediator between light and darkness, heaven and earth; he is bound to suppress darkness and yet make use of its powers.[18]

---

[17] For discussions of the sacred king as father figure, see Allwohn 1959, 45; Hocart 1969, 56; Perry 1966, 19.

[18] For the sacred king as warrior and the contrast of male and female principles in this context, see Allwohn 1959, 43; Perry 1966, 27–28.

Third, as the guarantor of fertility, the sacred king has to perform certain seasonal rites that assure the productivity of the soil, the timeliness of rain and sunshine, and the harmony of the cosmic forces with the activities of humanity. In this he represents the creative powers of the earth, although at the same time he is often styled a descendant of the sun. Again, he is the mediator between the different principles and forces of the cosmos, the living central axis of the world.[19] The sacred king, therefore, in his three major functions acts as the ruler and governor of society, the upholder of the ordered world vis-à-vis the raw powers of primordiality—the mainstay of order in the face of chaos, and the savior of centrality and totality from the centrifugal movements of diversification and unbounded growth. He represents the original creation on earth yet also keeps it under tight control, ensuring its continued reappearance as fertility, while battling against it as anarchy and chaos.

The sacred king of the archaic world as he is known mainly from Near Eastern sources and some African cultures[20] was thus a symbolic expression of centrality and totality; installed spatially in the axis-mundi palace, he played a key temporal role in the rites of cyclical renewal. A living representative of the universe at large, he was the power of creation incarnate, expressing in his very person the "many-sided unity of the world."[21]

In terms of the overall unfolding of myth, the symbolism of the sacred king can moreover be placed, in an evolutionary sequence that leads from the creation of the world to the development of society and the installation of order. Alan Watts, in his foreword to *Lord of the Four Quarters*, describes it in graphic images: The world arises first from an undifferentiated matrix (the empty circle) to develop a seed of creation (a dot in the empty circle). Next, it polarizes into a pair of opposites (a vertical line in the circle), to finally flower into systems of complex organized polarities (a central cross in the circle; Perry 1966, vii). The geometrical pattern of a square cross in a perfect circle is thus distinctive

---

[19] See Allwohn 1959, 39; Perry 1966, 18.

[20] This phenomenon was first described by Sir James Frazer (1911–15), then developed in the myth-ritual theory of sacred kingship by Hocart (1969; 1970) and Hooke (1933; 1935). Criticized in the 1940s (Frankfort 1948), it was reformulated more carefully in the 1950s (Hooke 1958; Brandon 1958; Edsman 1959) and later taken up by political anthropologists focusing on Africa (Hadfield 1949; Feeley-Harnik 1985). Its methods of creating sociopolitical solidarity, moreover, can still be found in modern politics (Lincoln 1986, 50; Geertz 1977, 171).

[21] This characterization follows Perry 1966, 3; Grottanelli 1987, 313; Hooke 1933; and Hidding 1959, 56.

for the kind of thinking that lies at the root of sacred kingship—it is a key symbol for the centeredness of "archaic ontology," as Eliade calls this worldview. Striving to maintain a close link with the underlying power of creation, with primordiality, heavens, and gods, it is at the same time concerned with keeping the untamed force of creative chaos safely at bay.[22]

The vision of the sacred king as the mediator between opposing realms and principles who stands at the temporal and spatial center of the universe is a widespread pattern in archaic cultures, and is also present in the political system of Shang and early Zhou China. In later Zhou and Han thinking, this pattern is expanded to include the role of a power behind the throne, a divinely inspired adviser or sage. Even there, however, it does not lose its symbolism or power but simply shifts its focus. Instead of only one key figure at the center of the world, there are two: the king and the sage, the ruler and his adviser, the emperor and Laozi. Through this division of power into the spiritual and practical, the Daoist tradition integrates the untamed forces of creative chaos instead of suppressing them and allows a continuity of creation in the midst of the created world.

The Daoist Myth

Using both the ancient ideal of the sacred king and the notion of the imperial adviser, the basic story of Laozi's transformations and his appearances as the teacher of dynasties is first formulated in the Later Han. In the later Daoist myth, it is rewritten to fully recover the ideal of the sacred king. In figures like the Yellow Emperor who are inspired by the Dao and also become one with it, the sacred center of the universe is regained—if not by birth or position, then through divine inspiration and personal realization.

The myth of Lord Lao as the teacher of dynasties, then, stands as the political charter of the Daoist religion. It explains why the ruler governs in perfect harmony, justifies the necessity of active Daoist practice either by a sage adviser or (preferably) by the ruler himself, and rewrites ancient Chinese history to establish a reason for the existence of state-sponsored Daoist rites and monasteries. Mythologically it combines three different visions: the veneration of centrality and totality like that

---

[22] The latter observation is found in Perry 1966, 34; for more studies on the various symbols and expressions of centrality, see Gesick 1983.

in the system of sacred kingship; the mainstream Chinese effort to maintain harmony both within a given rule through the organization of space and time, and during the transition between rules through the mediation of the imperial adviser; and finally, the classical Daoist vision of the Dao behind the throne—the underlying power of the world that appears in regular intervals to guide and support good government.

In terms of its actualization in history, this basic understanding of Lord Lao was manifest among the early Celestial Masters, who saw themselves as leading advisers to the dynasty. In this they took a completely different position from the followers of the Great Peace movement who found the ideal ruler in their leader and rose in rebellion against the Han (Seidel 1984a, 168). In the middle ages, the rewritten myth of Lord Lao corresponded to the Celestial Masters' ideal of a Daoist theocracy. Accordingly, they strove to convert rulers to their creed and bestowed Daoist registers and divine talismans on them, thus creating a sacred king by the power of the Dao. Many medieval Chinese rulers, both of northern and southern dynasties, followed their lead, accepted formal ordination as religious Daoists, and sent out special Daoist envoys to "scout for auspicious omina" (Seidel 1983, 351). Some, such as Emperor Taiwu of the Northern Wei (r. 424–452), even installed Daoists as leading ministers and changed their reign titles to Daoist themes, creating a theocracy in practice. Daoist ministers also abounded during the Tang dynasty, especially under the reign of Xuanzong who saw himself as a living representative of the Dao, and members of the religion remained politically influential in the Song and Ming.[23]

On a more mythological note, the transformations of Laozi represent a necessary step between the creation of the world through the Dao and the individual's practice of its methods. They play a significant part in the establishment of a harmonious human community, in which only organized Daoist practices can be performed. The Dao here is no longer merely the underlying absolute order of the world, or an incarnate human manifestation committed to saving it. In its transformations and changes, it is both, continuing to sustain order and saving humanity. This introduces a phase between the eternal power of the Dao at creation and the soteriological activities of the Dao on a developed and culturally complex earth. Standing between heaven and earth, the Dao is like the sacred king in that it mediates the power of heaven and the social

---

[23] On the theocracy, see Mather 1979. For Xuanzong, see Benn 1987; Ding 1979. On the Ming, see Zhuang 1986.

realities of the realm; yet it is always also more than the king because it originally participates in the underlying absolute.

Transformation in Daoism thus takes on several meanings. Following traditional Chinese cosmology, it first indicates the cyclical rhythm of the days and seasons, the orderly procession of the world along its charted course, the movements of the planets, the growth and decay of plants, the continued coming and going of life and death (see Sivin 1991). Second, transformation means the appearance of Lord Lao in different ages under different names, revealing scriptures and giving instructions to the rulers. This is a mythologized form of the cosmic transformations in that Lord Lao represents the cosmos both in its essential creative power and in its cyclical return. It joins the vision of the continued activity of the Dao with the traditional myth of the imperial adviser and integrates both with an understanding of cultural unfolding that developed in the Han dynasty. At the same time, the transformations of Laozi support the Daoist claim of centrality and totality for both its deity and the ruler perfected in the Dao.

Third, transformation means metamorphosis, the changes immortals can undergo at will (see Robinet 1979). It means not only the natural way things change, or the way Lord Lao appears and disappears, but also the power an individual can attain through the Dao, using its movements and cycles to his own advantage. The transformations of the immortals are the magical powers of the Dao and the mythological expression of its wonder, its unpredictability. They are powers that come to bear both in Laozi's transformations and in the attainments of the sacred king who has realized the Dao.

10

The Birth of the God

Having guided the world through the attainment of culture and the establishment of the Daoist religion, Lord Lao next decides to appear in human form on earth. To do so, as the *Youlong zhuan* describes it,[1] he first changes into rays of sunlight that form a five-colored pearl, and in this form enters the mouth of the Jade Maiden of Mystery and Wonder, whom he has ordered to Bozhou to become a human woman. She carries him for eighty-one years, after which he splits open her left armpit and steps out, already able to walk. Blessed by the gods of the sun, moon, and stars, and bathed by nine dragons who spring up from the earth, he next takes nine steps. With each step a lotus blossom sprouts forth, announcing his superior stature in heaven and on earth. Growing rapidly and undergoing nine transformations, he has many different names and shows the wondrous bodily marks of a divine being. To begin his life's work he next asks his mother about the Daoist teaching and receives instructions on its many aspects, from moral cultivation through physical practices to alchemical elixirs and ecstatic excursions. Seeing her off to the heavens, he undertakes the practice of various arts, becoming a model seeker of Daoist cultivation in the world. Attaining this highest goal, he ascends back into heaven to be honored by emperors throughout history.

This integrated story, as told in the systematic hagiographies, is a conglomerate of different sets of information that appear in Daoist literature of the middle ages. Lord Lao's descent on his own decision, his conception via the form of a five-colored pearl, his supernatural birth,

---

[1] See section 12, "Descending to Be Born in the World" (3.1b–4a). The text divides the events into twenty-one items, seventeen of which are identical with those found in Du Guangting's *Guangsheng yi* (2.12b–15b). The same information, without the formal division into items, is also contained in *Hunyuan shengji* 2.33b–39b.

and his post-natal actions are first found in the *Santian neijie jing* and in the *Xuanmiao neipian* of the fifth century. His various names appear initially in the *Laozi bianhua jing* and the *Shenxian zhuan*, and are expanded in medieval texts such as the *Fuzhai jing* (On the Performance of Rites, DZ 532), an ancient Numinous Treasure work, and the *Huahu jing* of the sixth century. His marvelous physiognomic signs, too, are first described in the earlier texts, then developed in great detail in the medieval *Falun jing* and the *Lingbao sanbu bajing jing.*[2]

The second part of this birth story, the role of the god's mother in instructing him and her ascent back to heaven, is first described in Du Guangting's biography of the Holy Mother Goddess in his *Yongcheng jixian lu* (DZ 783), then repeated in various later collections.[3] Finally, the account of Lord Lao's role as Daoist adept is diffuse and appears in many different texts by various groups of practitioners, all claiming his divine guidance for their techniques. Pulling all these materials together, the major hagiographies present an integrated and systematized version of the birth story that contains both specifically Daoist aspects and elements taken originally from Buddhist sources, the latter often changed to suit Daoist symbolism and concerns. In addition, the story bears close resemblance to Western tales of virgin birth and the birth of the hero.

Place and Date

Both the place and date of Lord Lao's birth are determined almost entirely by the Daoist tradition and depend largely on its indigenous Chinese context. The birthplace, Bozhou, named after its Shang dynasty appellation, is today in the Luyi District of Henan Province, in a village called Taiqing zhen (Great Clarity Hamlet) after its Lord Lao sanctuary, the Taiqing gong. The village is located about two kilometers east of the district town and still has a temple to Lord Lao (in recent decades used variously as an elementary school, a village office, and a military committee headquarters), a hall to the Mother Goddess, and a Shengxian tai (Terrace of Ascension to Immortality), from which the god allegedly left the world to return to heaven. The latter is a round brick platform about ten meters high and twenty meters wide, with three small halls on top, which now serve as the county museum. In addition, there are

---

[2] These texts on the god's physiognomic signs are edited in *SDZN* 8.14a–15a and 8.10b–12b. For a translation and discussion, see Kohn 1996a.

[3] *Yongcheng jixian lu* 1.1a–9a. For later retellings, see chapter 1 above.

various stone stelae, an iron pillar erected for Lord Lao under the Tang, and two cypresses, claimed to be the ones that blossomed again when the Tang came to power.[4]

Bozhou has long been known as the god's birthplace from Laozi's biography in the *Shiji*; Sima Qian evidently thought it politic to locate him near the ancestral home of the Han ruling house (Graham 1990, 123). It has since served as a homestead for the god's cult and has been the location of many imperial honors, including Emperor Huan's *Laozi ming* of 165, the Sui inscription *Laoshi bei* of 586, and Tang Gaozong's worship in 666. Reaching its heyday under Emperor Xuanzong in the mid-eighth century, Bozhou had "two palaces and two monasteries, more than 1,000 old cypresses, over 700 rooms and halls, and 500 soldiers stationed there as guards."[5] Although less keen on Lord Lao than their predecessors, the Song and Yuan emperors still continued to hold regular sacrifices there, and the *Youlong zhuan* itself is the product of its fertile Daoist environment.

While the god's birthplace remained stable and unchanged in its basic location, his birthdate underwent some serious revisions, especially in the middle ages. At first characterized as a contemporary of Confucius in the *Zhuangzi* and the *Shiji*, the god's lifetime was moved back as Buddhism became more popular and the conversion myth flourished. Once identified not only as the founder of Buddhism but increasingly as the Buddha himself, Lord Lao by necessity had to be born earlier than 689 B.C.E., the birth date of the Buddha determined in accordance with marvelous signs observed on the western sky and recorded in the *Zuozhuan* (Mr. Zuo's Commentary to the Spring and Autumn Annals).[6]

For Lord Lao to travel by land to India, or to ascend to heaven and be reborn there by that time, he had to leave China in the eighth century B.C.E. The most traumatic event in Chinese history associated with this period was the relocation of the Zhou capital under King You, who fled east in 771 B.C.E. Lord Lao's emigration was consequently linked with King You's defeat, the most contemporaneous example of the "decline of the virtue of the Zhou," specified as the cause of his emigration in the

---

[4] A detailed description of modern Bozhou is found in Mugitani 1989, 73–75. A more recent account of major Daoist centers, which does not speak specifically of Bozhou, is found in Li 1993.

[5] This description follows Du Guangting's *Daojiao lingyan ji* (1.8b–9b; Reiter 1983, 371–73). A description of the Taiqing gong and its role in Tang imperial worship is found in Ding 1979, 294–95. For the various inscriptions in honor of the god, see chapter 2 above.

[6] This information as well as the following discussion is based on the detailed study in Kusuyama 1976, 12–30; 1979, 373–81.

Shiji. Several third-century texts accordingly state that Lord Lao was born at the end of the Shang to be the teacher of the Zhou, but later left when his beneficial efforts proved fruitless. The same dating was still current in the fifth century, when it appears in the *Santian neijie jing* (1.4a).[7]

The date changed once again, to reach its later standard, in 520 during a debate between Buddhists and Daoists held at the Northern Wei court. At this time the Buddhists, wishing to refute the Daoist claim that the Buddha was a follower of Lord Lao after the latter's emigration, placed the Buddha's birth in the year 1029 B.C.E. under King Zhao of Zhou. They bolstered their contention with passages from the *Mu Tianzi zhuan* (Record of King Mu of Zhou, DZ 291), which describe particularly auspicious signs in the western sky at that time. Daoists countered this by placing their god's emigration immediately prior to that, and his birth at 1311, the ninth year of Wuding, twenty-second king of the Shang—a ruler already known as the renewer of the dynasty who had been advised by the sage Fu Yue. Lord Lao's conception, dated eighty-one years earlier to allow for the long pregnancy, accordingly occurred in 1392, the seventeenth year of Yangjia, eighteenth king of Shang.[8]

The change in Lord Lao's birth date in medieval China reflects historically the increasing Daoist drive for religious dominance and the growing confrontation with Buddhism in an atmosphere charged with the political and intellectual push toward unification. Mythologically it shows the coming-of-age of the religion and the crystallization of Lord Lao into a more universal deity who could claim dominance over China and her neighboring countries. Once established in 520, the date remained in place, even though Buddhists won that round of the debates and had the *Kaitian jing* destroyed. Since then, the standard date has given a temporal stability to the god's human manifestation just as his birthplace has settled him firmly in space.

---

[7] Earlier texts include the *Liexian zhuan* (Kaltenmark 1953, 61) and the *Gaoshi zhuan* (Zürcher 1959, 292). For a discussion of the *Santian neijie jing* citation, see Kusuyama 1979, 379.

[8] These dates are standard in all versions of the myth. They are found in *Guangsheng yi* 2.12b; *Youlong zhuan* 3.3a; *Hunyuan shengji* 1.16ab. A record of the 520 debate is found in the *Guang hongming ji* (Expanded Record to Spread and Clarify [Buddhist Doctrine], T. 2103, 52.403a). For Western descriptions, see Zürcher 1982, 18; Lai 1986, 67; Kohn 1995, 24.

The Birth of the Buddha

Both the story of Lord Lao's planned celestial conception and the events surrounding his birth closely follow tales surrounding the Buddha, especially as contained in the *Taizi ruiying benqi jing*, translated by Zhi Qian in the early third century.[9] Here we have:

> The bodhisattva transformed himself and, riding a white elephant, descended like a ray of the sun. His mother took an afternoon nap during which he appeared to her in a dream and entered her through her right hip. (473b; see also Karetzky 1992, 9)

Here, as well as in other Buddhist accounts,[10] the Buddha arrives on a white elephant, a symbol of royalty and celestial favor common in Indian myth, descending like the radiant light of the sun and accompanied by a formal entourage. This shows the divine nature of the figure and links the Buddha to the powers of heaven and the purity of the sun.[11] In the Daoist version, the elephant appears only in early sources and in accounts of Lord Lao's birth as the Buddha in India. Thus the *Santian neijie jing* relates:

> When Queen Qingmiao (Māyā) was taking an afternoon nap, Laozi ordered Yin Xi to ride on a white elephant and change into a yellow sparrow. In this shape he flew into the mouth of the queen. To her he appeared as a shooting star coming down from heaven. (1.4ab)

The shooting star, a common motif in birth stories among Confucian mythical rulers, is the cause of Lord Lao's conception in the *Shenxian zhuan*. Later hagiographies, however, replace both elephant and star with nine dragons of pure light. In either case, the symbolism of light and sun, of the pure yang energy of the god, is central to the story. This was already noted by Du Guangting:

> Laozi rode on the essence of the sun and shaped it into a pearl of five colors. This fact illustrates his yang energy. The Dao then rode on a chariot

---

[9] This text is found in T. 185, 3.471–83. For more on Zhi Qian, see Zürcher 1959, 48–51. For a translation of the biography and a discussion of its representations in medieval art, see Karetzky 1992. For studies of the Indian traditions of the Buddha's birth, see Thomas 1927; Pye 1979; and Pyysiainen 1987.

[10] The most important of these is found in the *Xiuxing benqi jing* (T. 184; 3.461–72). See Karetzky 1992, 10.

[11] For the Indian symbolism involved in the Buddha's conception, see Wayman 1957, 245; Karetzky 1992, 11.

of nine dragons. Shrinking in size, they adopted the shape of five-colored light rays. As such they flowed down to earth and into the mouth of the Jade Maiden. This again shows his pure essence of yang.[12]

The sun-like quality of the embryo, moreover, has an immediate effect on the well-being and inner radiance of his mother, who never feels tired or ill and, protected by good spirits, radiates supernatural beauty and harmony. In addition, the child is conscious even in the womb—the Buddha observing all around him as if looking through a gauze curtain, Lord Lao reciting scriptures during his long sojourn in the womb.[13]

The events at the god's birth, too, closely follow the Buddhist model. To begin, his birthday—the fifteenth of the second month of the lunar calendar—is the day of the Buddha's parinirvāna, when the latter concluded his existence on earth and dissolved forever into nothingness. Lord Lao arising upon the Buddha's dissolution is a way of showing his power not only over life and death but also over permanent extinction and eternal life. In addition, both Lord Lao's emergence from the womb and his first deeds on earth are highly similar to those of the Indian founder. According to the Buddhist story,

> Queen Māyā was taking a stroll through the grove at Lumbini, where all flowers were wonderfully in blossom. The stars were all out. Then she grasped the branch of a tree, and the bodhisattva emerged from her right hip. (*Xiuxing benqi jing*, 3.363a; see also Karetzky 1992, 15)

Furthermore, after taking his first steps,

> heaven and earth were shaken by a great commotion, and the whole place was illuminated by a flash. Brahma, Indra, and the spirit kings descended, appearing in the sky to wait upon the bodhisattva. The four dragon kings erected a golden bench and bathed the prince with heavenly fragrant water. (*Taizi ruiying benqi jing*, 3.473c; see also Karetzky 1992, 18)

In distinction to the Buddhist myth, Lord Lao's mother does not hold on to the branch of a *sal* tree but is supported by a plum (*li*), symbolic of

---

[12] *Guangsheng yi* 2.12a; *Youlong zhuan* 3.1b. The same yang quality is again symbolized in the duration of the divine pregnancy, seventy-two (9 [yang] x 8 [yin]) years in the early sources, eighty-one (9 [yang] x 9 [yang]) from the middle ages onward. See *Guangsheng yi* 2.12a; *Youlong zhuan* 3.1a.

[13] For the Buddha, see Karetzky 1992, 12–13. The god's mother is described in *Guangsheng yi* 2.12a; *Youlong zhuan* 3.1b. The *Santian neijie jing* is the first to mention a text he recited before birth.

the god's human surname Li. Also, the Daoist god emerges from the left side of his mother's body, not the right, and from the armpit, not the hip. This, as described first in the *Shenxian zhuan* and the *Santian neijie jing* (1.2b), shows the Chinese preference for the left or yang side over the right or yin, and their higher esteem for the upper parts of the body. Lord Lao's more elevated form of birth thus implicitly symbolizes the higher status of the Daoist tradition vis-à-vis Buddhism. This is clear already in the *Santian neijie jing*:

> Lord Lao emphasized the transformation of life, whereas Śākyamuni focused on the transformation of death. This is why Laozi was born by splitting open the left armpit, for he favored the left, which is the side of yang energy, and thereby placed first emphasis on the records of life in the Blue Palace above. Śākyamuni, on the other hand, was born by splitting open the right hip. This is because he favors the right side, which represents yin energy, and thereby placed primary importance on the records of death in the Black Registers. (1.9b; see Zürcher 1980, 95–96).

Next, in both cases the divine child is honored by the presence of heavenly deities and given his first bath by divine dragons (see Fig. 14). The highest gods of heaven, in India represented by Brahma and Indra, are the sun and the moon in China; similarly the dragons descend from heaven in the Buddhist story but spring from the earth at Laozi's birth, again reflecting basic differences in Indian versus Chinese mythology. Not only are the highest gods different, but nāgas or dragon kings are celestial rulers in the Hindu pantheon while they are predominantly associated with water in China, ruling oceans, rivers, lakes, and springs on earth (see Schafer 1973). In addition, the dragons provide a clear physical link between the myth and the sanctuary, leaving behind nine wells at the Taiqing gong in Bozhou that could still be visited in the Tang and the Song (*Youlong zhuan* 3.2a).

Emerging as a divine child, the newborn god is already able to walk:

> He strode forward nine paces. With each step a lotus flower sprouted forth to support his foot. The sun and the moon bathed him in their brilliance and myriads of numinous beings came down to wait upon him.
>
> He pointed at the plum tree and said, "This will be my surname." Thus he came to be named Li. His contemporaries duly used "Mother Li" to refer to the Holy Mother Goddess.

After the nine steps, Lord Lao pointed at the sky with his left hand, and at the earth with his right. He exclaimed: "Chief am I above and below heaven. The world is nothing but suffering, what is there to enjoy?"[14]

Thus, the god knows immediately who he is and where he is and loses no time declaring his power and his mission to the world. The Buddha does exactly the same thing, taking seven steps, albeit without lotuses, then making the same famous pronouncement, if in a slightly different formulation. He says:

Among all divine beings, only I am Lord, most holy and victorious. The three worlds are nothing but misery. I have come here through immeasurable births and deaths for the benefit of men and gods. (*Xiuxing benqi jing*, 3.463c; see also Karetzky 1992, 16)

The same pattern of adaptation is found in the position of the two gods' hands. The Buddha points to the earth with his left and holds his right hand up to his face, while Lord Lao points to heaven with his left and to the earth with his right, adding a more pronounced heaven-earth symbolism (Zürcher 1959, 301).

Having given birth to the savior of the world, the mother in both cases is rendered secondary and soon removed. Thus, the Buddha's mother dies within a week of his birth, and the Mother Goddess returns to heaven after she has given Lord Lao instructions in Daoist practices. Buddhist doctrine at this point says that the divine child should not be raised by his mother, and she is reborn in a high heaven. The Daoist version draws on this but also takes into account the traditional Chinese notion that divine females serve as practical teachers for inspired sages, mythical rulers, and immortals. That tradition is exemplified in the story of the Yellow Emperor receiving sexual techniques from the Pure Woman (Sunü) and the Mystery Woman (Xuannü).[15]

---

[14] This account follows the *Yongcheng jixian lu* (1.1b–2a). An annotated translation of the passage is found in Kohn 1989c, 71–74. It also appears in *Guangsheng yi* 2.13a; *Youlong zhuan* 3.2b.

[15] The Daoist story is found in the *Yongcheng jixian lu* (Kohn 1989c, 103) as well as in the *Youlong zhuan* (3.3b). For the Buddhist tale, see Karetzky 1992, 29. For a more detailed examination of stories on the Buddha's mother, see Durt 1996. A general evaluation of divine mothers and their paradoxical role is found in Leeming 1973, 48.

第十八化　誕聖日

太上老君以殷十八
王陽甲庚申歲十八
玉女晝寢夢吞日精
化五色流珠因而有
孕八十一年至二十二
王武丁庚辰二月
十五日聖母因舉會
樹剖左腋而生又玄
中記所載李靈
飛得修真之道
不仕其妻尸氏
晝寢夢天開數
丈見太上來
日精篤九龍
而下化五
色流珠春
之有孕

Fig. 14. The birth of the divine Laozi and his first bath.
Source: Laojun bashiyi hua tushuo, no. 6

The Holy Family

The connection with the female continues to be the dominant theme in the discussion of the deity's earthly manifestations in the *Youlong zhuan*. Section 13, "Explaining His Noble Ancestry," which is closely based on Du Guangting's *Guangsheng yi* (Wide Sage Meaning [of the *Daode jing*]), outlines the extended family tree surrounding Lord Lao, reaching both back to his ancestors at the dawn of prehistory and forward to his descendants under the Tang. This part of the myth was developed for the most part in Tang times, when the imperial family claimed descent from Lord Lao; it is again entirely Daoist rather than Buddhist in origin and harks back to the ancient *Shiji* biography, which describes his immediate descendants:

> Laozi's son was called Zong. He served as military commander in the state of Wei and was enfeoffed in Duangan. His son had the name Zhu. He in turn had a son called Gong. The great-grandson of Gong was known as Jia. He served under Emperor Wen of the Han [179–156 B.C.E.]. His son was Jie, the tutor of Prince Jiaoxi. He lived in Qi. (ch. 63; see Fung and Bodde 1952, 1:171)

Here, as in later expansions of the genealogy, the deity is linked with real people, such as Duangan Zong and Li Jie, who had some historical significance in their own right but profited greatly from their connection with the ancient venerable. Following this pattern, in the Tang Lord Lao was made ancestor of the Li clan, and the birth of the sage was reinterpreted accordingly. One text, entitled *Lishi dazong pu* (Record of the Great Lineage of the Li Family), cited in Du Guangting's *Guangsheng yi*, describes his mother as a member of the Pei clan, descended from the Yellow Emperor. In this story, her pregnancy is caused by the ingestion of plums and gives her much grief. Ready to abort the child, her hand is stayed by divine intervention. Miss Pei gives birth holding on to a plum branch, then explains her predicament to the child, who receives the family name Li after the plums his mother ate. The story traces Lord Lao's lineage back to the Yellow Emperor yet still preserves his quasi-divine conception and birth. It holds on to the mysteries surrounding the emergence of the deity, yet makes him more accessible to living people (2.19a–20a).

Another text, the *Da Tang tianyan yutie* (Jade Leaves of the Celestial Records of the Great Tang), also cited by Du Guangting, traces Lord Lao's ancestry back to the sage-ruler Zhuanxu. Again, the family name is explained by the ingestion of plums, but this time a male member of the family does the eating, and the god has a proper father. Called Li Lingfei, both he and his own father, Li Qingbin, were active practitioners of immortality techniques and "ascended to heaven in broad daylight" (*Guangsheng yi* 2.17b–18a). The attainments of Lord Lao's father and grandfather are further described in the *Xuanzhong ji* (Record of the Mysterious Center). Here Li Lingfei witnesses his father's bodily ascension and decides to dedicate his life to the Dao. Nevertheless,

> he married the daughter of the Yin family of Tianshui and lived with her in Lai county [Bozhou]. Once Mrs. Li took an afternoon nap and dreamt that the sky opened wide and a host of immortals emerged toward her, holding up the sun. After a long time she saw the sun gradually shrink and come down to her from heaven. (*Guangsheng yi* 2.18b–19a; *Youlong zhuan* 3.7a)

In this account Lord Lao's birth follows the standard myth as it developed in the middle ages, but his mother is properly married and identified as a daughter of the Yins of Tianshui in the far west of China. This family in Tang times brought forth Yin Wencao (622–688), abbot of Louguan and senior hagiographer of the god, who greatly desired to promote his family into a position of personal relation with Lord Lao and thus with the Tang emperors (Kusuyama 1979, 404). The same story, with a further mythological twist is again told in the *Xuanmiao yunü yuanjun neizhuan* (Inner Biography of the Goddess Jade Maiden of Mystery and Wonder). Here Lord Lao "orders the Jade Maiden to descend to earth to become the daughter of the Yins of Tianshui and marry Li Lingfei" (*Guangsheng yi* 2.20b–21a; *Youlong zhuan* 3.7b). Once this is accomplished, the god duly rides on the essence of the sun and comes to take refuge in her womb.

This last account, like other expansions of the holy genealogy, serves the purpose of preserving the celestial nature of the events and enhancing the supernatural stature of the god. At the same time, it links him by blood-ties with the Yin family and makes him accessible to people living centuries later, thus establishing a vital and living presence of the god's divinity on earth and connecting the mythical events of the past with real people.

Divine Names and Bodily Marks

Other characteristics of the god closely associated with his birth are the names that describe the different aspects of his divinity and the bodily marks that show his remarkable nature even in infancy.[16] Even the

---

[16] The *Youlong zhuan* (sect. 13) has a list of nine names together with the mention of thirty-six titles and seventy-two appellations (3.7b–8a). It also gives a complete

name Laozi, translated as "Old Child," is full of symbolism, showing how the god was born already old (after eighty-one years in the womb), and how, unlike ordinary people who move toward old age and death, he proceeds toward youth and eternal life.[17] His personal names Er and Dan by which he is known in the *Shiji* and *Zhuangzi*, also take on symbolic interpretations.

Er means "ear" and has been explained as referring to Laozi's large ears. This characteristic is indicative of his wisdom, since keen hearing is the foremost mark of the sage (DeWoskin 1982, 37). *Dan* occurs in four variants, written with either the "ear" or the "tongue" radical, or again, with a character that goes back to the name of the Grand Historiographer of the Zhou with whom Laozi was identified under the Qin (Graham 1990, 119). The word has the basic meaning of "rimless," which in its "ear" variant indicates the long ears of the sage and the longevity of the immortal (Kaltenmark 1953, 64), and is thus another version of the name Er. In its "tongue" variant, it refers to the fact that the tongue is stronger than the teeth, which in turn indicates Laozi's philosophy that the weak overcomes the strong. This is elaborated in the *Huahu jing* account of Laozi's first meeting with Yin Xi, where we read:

> Yin Xi said, "May I please ask the venerable master's name and appellation?"
>
> Laozi stuck out his long tongue and showed it to him. "All the teeth in my mouth have already fallen out," he explained. "Only the tongue is left."
>
> Yin Xi understood. "Old Rimless [Lao Dan]! There are thirty-six teeth in the mouth, hard and strong like frost. Now all the teeth have fallen out and only the tongue is left all by itself. Thus I know that the soft can control the hard, and the weak can overcome the strong." (*SDZN* 9.16a)

In addition, the deity was blessed with nine complete sets of names, a personal name (*ming*) and an appellation (*zi*), given in two variants in the *Laozi bianhua jing* and the *Youlong zhuan* (see Table 15). They symbolize the nine changes he underwent in accordance with the sun and pure yang energy, and are activated in meditation with the help of a magical

---

account of the standard eighty-one bodily marks, following the medieval *Falun jing*. The latter is found in section 14, "The Seventy-two Marks and Eighty-one Characteristics" (3.8b–10a).

[17] Explanations of the name Laozi as "Old Child" are already found in the *Shenxian zhuan* and *Santian neijie jing*. An extensive scholastic interpretation is given in the *Guangsheng yi* (2.16a; see Kohn 1989c, 76–77; 1998e).

mirror.[18] Many of these names indicate his original and primordial nature, using words like "Center," "Prime," "Radiance," or "Virtue." Others again emphasize his power, such as "Summon," "Loyalty," and "Elegance," or his solidity and reliability as the Dao underlying all creation and at the root of salvation. For this sense we have words like "Stone," "Security," "Refuge," "Vow," and "Seriousness."

Table 15
Laozi's nine names and appellations

Bianhua jing Name	*Youlong zhuan* Name
Lao 老, Old	Er 耳, Ear
Dan 耽, Ear	Ya 雅, Elegance
Zhong 中, Center	Zhong 忠, Loyalty
Shi 石, Stone	Shi 石, Stone
Zhao 召, Summon	Zhong 重, Seriousness
Zhai 宅, Refuge	Ding 定, Security
Yuan 元, Prime	Yuan 元, Prime
Yuan 願, Vow	Xian 顯, Radiance
De 德, Virtue	De 德, Virtue

Bianhua jing Appellation	*Youlong zhuan* Appellation
Yuanyang 元陽, Prime Yang	Boyang 伯陽, Lord of Yang
Boyang 伯陽, Lord of Yang	Bozong 伯宗, Lord of Ancestors
Boguang 伯光, Lord of Light	Bolao 伯老, Lord of Old Age
Ziguang 子光, Master of Light	Menggong 孟公, Duke of Loyalty
Ziwen 子文, Master of Culture	Ziwen 子文, Master of Culture
Zichang 子長, Master of Longevity	Yuanyang 元陽, Primordial Yang
Zishi 子始, Master of Beginning	Boshi 伯始, Lord of the Beginning
Zisheng 子生, Master of Life	Yuansheng 元生, Primordial Life
Bowen 伯文, Lord of Culture	Bowen 伯文, Lord of Culture

His appellations, except for Primordial Yang and Primordial Life, which clearly refer to his original nature as the essence of the cosmos, typically consist of two characters, including the words *zi* (master) or *bo* (lord) together with a descriptive suffix. They can be read as "Master of" or "Lord of." Again the terms are similar to those used in his names, reinforcing his divine and primordial nature and linking him with the world of humanity.

---

[18] This practice, which is also mentioned in the *Baopuzi* and probably goes back to the third or fourth century, is described in detail—and under mention of Lord Lao's names—in the *Mingjian jing*. See chapter 3 above.

In addition, the god has ten divine titles (see Table 16), including his standard appellations together with more subtle names and certain Buddhist-inspired honorifics. The ten titles occur in two variants in late Six Dynasties scriptures and, while mythologically giving expression to the universal powers and high rank of the god, developed historically under the influence of Buddhism. The ten honorific titles of the Buddha were based in a cosmology of ten rather than eight or nine (i.e., the eight directions plus above and below) and are documented in the ancient Pāli sūtras. These titles, transmitted to China, were applied to his Daoist counterpart, the Heavenly Worthy of Primordial Beginning (see Table 17). From him, certain individual titles and the idea of a ten-item list were then applied to Lord Lao, the representative of the Dao on earth.

The various titles describe the celestial status of the deity, his foremost characteristics, and his power over heaven and earth, endowing him with the official recognition his supernatural status requires and placing him among the highest of the celestials in the lofty heavens of the Dao. Originally written in sacred Brahma language, Lord Lao's titles are described as kept in a secure chest in the highest heaven, indicating the god's position at the source of the Dao, his ultimate freedom from worldly connections, his persistence through uncountable kalpas, and his original radiance and illuminating power (*Shihao jing* [Scripture of the Ten Titles] 4ab). As defined by his titles, he is a model for immortals and the perfected, a teacher of worthies, and the eternal savior of humanity.

Another important aspect of Lord Lao's divinity is his physical appearance, systematically itemized in a list of seventy-two bodily marks and eighty-one (72 plus 9) physical characteristics that reveal him as the body of the Dao. The earliest source of this is entirely Daoist, the *Shenxian zhuan*, which bases its account on the *Laozi bianhua jing*.

> Laozi had a yellow-whitish complexion, beautiful eyebrows, and a broad forehead. He possessed long ears, big eyes, gap teeth, a square mouth, and thick lips. On his forehead he had the signs of the three [powers] and five [phases]. He had the sun horn and the moon crescent sticking out above his eyebrows. His nose was broad and straight and had four nostrils, while his ears had three openings. On the soles of his feet he had the signs of the two [forces, yin and yang] and the five [phases], on his palms the character for the number ten.[19]

---

[19] Cited from ch. 1, translated in Kohn 1996a, 59. See also Yoshioka 1959, 142.

Table 16
Lord Lao's ten titles

Fuzhai jing (DZ 532.3b)	Huahu jing (T. 2139; 54.1266b)
Highest Great Dao of Nonultimate 太上無極大道	Highest Venerable Lord 太上老君
Highest Great Lord of the Dao 太上大道君	Perfect Divine Wisdom 圓神智
Highest Venerable Lord 太上老君	All-Highest Worthy 無上尊
Highest Elder 太上丈夫	Teacher of Emperors and Kings 帝王師
All-Highest Old Man of Mystery 無上玄老	Great Officer 大丈夫
Great Dao of the Ten Directions 十方無極大道	Great Immortal Worthy 大仙尊
Heavenly Worthy of Dao and Virtue 道德衆聖天尊	Father of Gods and People 天人父
Great Emperor of Utmost Perfection 至眞大道	Highest One of Nonaction 無爲上人
Emperor of Heaven 天帝	Great Compassionate and Benevolent One 大悲仁者
Lord of the Celestial Master 天師君	Heavenly Worthy of Primordial Beginning 元始天尊

Table 17
The ten titles of the Buddha and the Heavenly Worthy

Samyuktāgama (T. 101, 2.441b)	Shihao jing (DZ 337.3b)
Thusgone 如來	All-Highest Dao 無上道
Worthy of Worship 應供	Primordial Beginning 元始
All-Knowing 正邊知	Great Ultimate 大極
Perfect in Conduct 明行足	Lofty Sovereign 高皇
Well-Departed 菩逝	Radiant Brightness 光明
Fully Liberated 世間解	Jade Emperor 玉王
Unsurpassed 上士	King of the Proper Law 正法王
Fully in Control 調御	Father of Great Compassion 大慈父
Teacher of Gods and People 天人師	Teacher of Immortals and Perfected 仙眞師
Buddha, the Worldly Worthy 佛世尊	Heavenly Worthy 天尊

Displaying the ancient characteristics of wisdom such as long ears and protruding bones above the eyebrows, Lord Lao is also described as an immortal who carries divine marks on his feet and forehead. In addition, his looks are reminiscent of the Confucian sage ruler Yu, who had three openings in his ears to indicate his unusual powers of perception. Later lists imitate the Buddhist example of thirty-two marks and eighty characteristics, and integrate additional signs of longevity and immortality, such as a golden complexion and radiant skin, a lightness and unusual hairiness of the body, a melodious voice, fragrant breath, and a noble posture. They also include more features of the ancient sage rulers, such as the square pupils of the filial ruler Shun that indicate his penetrating vision, and specifically Buddhist characteristics, such as purple hairs between the eyebrows, a high and straight nose, a well-rounded abdomen, and swastika signs on the soles of his feet.[20]

Both through his divine names and bodily signs, the newly born Daoist god exhibits his divinity; he is set apart from ordinary people while still sharing the basic human characteristics of having a name and a body. The god has become flesh and can be clearly named; he stands as a visible and tangible symbol of the Dao and brings salvation to humankind through his various deeds and activities.

The Birth of the Hero

The early events surrounding the conception and birth of Lord Lao, aside from representing an integration of mythical episodes and motifs from the mainstream, Buddhist, and Daoist traditions, also correspond closely to the birth of the hero and virgin birth myths known in many cultures and also in the West.[21] According to these traditions, heroes are not conceived through sexual intercourse but under unusual circumstances; they are commonly fathered by a natural force or an animal—a thunderstorm, a bull, a swan, a shower of gold. Their conception could also be brought about by the wind, thunder, a bird, or a round

---

[20] For the Confucian signs, see Yoshioka 1959, 37; Forke 1972, 304. A discussion is found in Kohn 1996, 202–5. For the Buddha's divine marks, see Wayman 1957; Kohn 1996, 205–7.

[21] Descriptions of the classical hero pattern, including typical birth stories, are found and interpreted with varying anthropological, ritual, and psychological theories, in Rank 1952; 1990 (orig. 1909); Raglan 1934, 1990 (orig. 1936); Campbell 1949; Jung 1949; 1960; Leeming 1973 (also 1990, 215–311); Dundes 1990; and, in reprint and summary, in Segal 1990.

object of various sorts, or again the sunlight, a blade of grass, a pebble, a magic apple, and the like.[22] Lord Lao follows this pattern just as Christ does in the classic Western birth story (Hartland 1971, 1:21). He is a powerful god of the Dao who enters the womb of the Mother Goddess, herself another constellation of pure Dao-energy, on his own initiative.

The birth of the hero is as supernatural as his conception. Heroes are not really born, they emerge from a mother who remains sexually pure. This shows that the hero is in the world but not of it, that he remains free from the fetters of the flesh. In more of a "depth-psychology" reading, such as that described by John Layard, the mother's pregnant-yet-untouched state also symbolizes her "virginity" in another sense, that of "the untrammeled law of pregnant though as yet chaotic nature" or "the pregnancy of nature, free and uncontrolled" (1972, 291). The word "virgin," as in its ancient Greek and Hebrew uses, does not refer to being sexually chaste but legally unmarried, a state of unbounded potential and uncontrolled fertility, such as that of a "virgin forest." Such a forest, like other manifestations of untapped potential, can be regarded in two ways—as something to be destroyed, uprooted, made accessible to civilization, or as the "supreme manifestation of pregnant nature" (1972, 290). Society commonly adopts the former approach, taming the sexual potential of virgins through marriage rites and formal ownership (Hartland 1910, 2:103). But the myth of the hero's birth clearly documents the latter, showing in mythical images the continuity of raw creative potential within the world and thus the possibility of every human being finding a close connection with it.

This understanding of the virgin birth is meaningful in light of the Daoist myth, which also keeps the Mother Goddess free of sexual taint and has Lord Lao step from her side unbloodied, aware, and able to walk. It shows the raw power of the Dao as it is manifested in the world and thereby becomes not only visible and tangible but also subject to interaction with and control through human agents. The Dao, the untrammeled potential of creation, makes itself accessible to humanity by being born in human shape yet also retains its inherent power and cannot, therefore, be born in the normal way.

Another common aspect of virgin birth is its occurrence in a natural environment, which actively links the birthing mother with Mother Nature. This, the great mother of all, the incarnate representation of the power of life, is often also venerated in female form, as the classic mother

---

[22] Different variants of the conception are discussed in Raglan 1990, 149; Jones 1951, 279; Biallas 1986, 116.

goddess of many religions, who creates and destroys, nurtures and devours (see Preston 1982). Accordingly, the setting of the hero's birth is characterized by womb-symbols, such as a grove of trees, a cave, stable, rock, or water pot (Leeming 1973, 48). Other key events in the hero's life are also linked with such natural features, for example the Buddha's birth, enlightenment, first sermon, and parinirvāna all occur under a tree.

The Buddha's mother, in close imitation of the Yakśi, "a female fertility spirit that personifies the spirit of a tree" (Karetzky 1992, 15), stands under the natural cover and holds on to a branch. Lord Lao, too, comes to earth and leaves it through a tree: the former when his mother, holding onto a plum branch, gives birth, and gives the child the surname Li; and the latter when the accomplished deity ascends back to heaven from the top of a cypress. Trees also give birth to other ancient Chinese culture heroes—Yi Yin, for example, emerges from a hollow mulberry (Birrell 1993, 128). They often provide the food of the immortals; famous masters such as Master Redpine and the Cinnamon Father (Danfu) live entirely on their fruit (Kaltenmark 1953, 35, 118). Trees, moreover, often image the cosmos at large and in many cultures play an important symbolic role. They stand at the center of universal development, represent the continued fruitfulness of the world, show the possibility of ascent to the otherworld, and symbolize the power of communication and growth (Cook 1974). Upright and reaching into the sky, trees symbolize the connection between the mundane and the heavenly. As such they are used as sky ladders in shamanic practice (Cook 1974, 15), while also appearing as the media of divine manifestation in Western religions, as for example, in the appearance of the Blessed Virgin Mary in Fatima, Portugal (Rogo 1982, 224).

Aside from the strong tree symbolism, the birth of the hero is placed squarely in a natural environment by the presence of animals. In the typical hero story, animals take care of the child after he has been abandoned by his natural parents and exposed in a river or on a mountain (Biallas 1986, 118). In the Asian stories of the great founders, too, nāgas and dragons appear as divine messengers from heaven and demonstrate the joy of the celestials by purifying the child and paying obeisance to him.

Lord Lao's conception, birth, physical characteristics, names, and family lineage can be described as based on the active integration of episodes and motifs from the mainstream, Buddhist, and Daoist traditions. While Lord Lao's birthplace, year of birth, and family genealogy are determined largely by considerations of the Daoist religion and its standing among the major traditions and ruling clans of China, his conception and birth are adapted from the Buddhist model. This mixture documents the close interaction of the two religions in the middle ages. Lord Lao's names and attributes, moreover, document the creative give-and-take of the indigenous Chinese and Buddhist traditions, putting the god at the center of a multilayered and complex interaction that gives rise to the unique Chinese vision of divinity.

Still, the story as a whole corresponds to widely recognized themes that appear in the myths of virgin birth and the birth of the hero. Seen in this way, the Daoist story expresses in its own particular way how the divine can manifest itself in the mundane, how a god can become flesh. Lord Lao as the divine child is another form of the mediator between the primordial state of instinctive oneness and the complex culture of the present age. Like other divine children and heroes, he stands for a new beginning, new hope, a new birth of goodness and purity in the world. The birth of the deity among humanity thus physically reveals the extraordinary activity and creative power of the absolute; it represents a renewed and more tangible form of cosmic creation, and is a manifestation of eternal potential in the world of imperfection and transience.

11

The Transmission of the Daode jing

Once he arrives in the world, the Lord Lao of the myth is associated with many activities, including a number of practices that lead to longevity and immortality, and he becomes a master of them all. Hagiographically, however, he is most commonly said to have become a government servant in the archives of the Zhou court from which, having found the virtue of the dynasty lacking, he decided to emigrate. Stopped on the western pass by the border guard Yin Xi, who recognized him as an important thinker, he was asked to leave his teachings behind and compiled the *Daode jing*, his first and most important revelation. Following this transmission, he continued his westward journey, either vanishing into the desert wilderness or reappearing as the teacher of Buddhism, depending on the account.

While this story in its original form in the *Shiji* contains only two major episodes—the emigration of a civil servant and the transmission of the *Daode jing*—over the centuries it grew into a complex narrative. The two basic tales were expanded both in depth, through additional motifs and symbols, and in structure, with new episodes built around them. While the main body of the later standard myth was already present in Louguan texts of the sixth century (*Wenshi neizhuan, Huahu jing*), the *Youlong zhuan* has still more variants and adds details that strengthen the narrative and heighten its celestial aspect.

The text devotes six complete sections to the earthly life of the god: "Becoming a Historian" (sect. 15, 3.10a); "Leaving the Zhou" (16, 3.11a); "Testing Xu Jia" (17, 3.12a); "Going Beyond the Pass and Testing Yin Xi" (18, 3.13a); "Transmitting the *Daode jing*" (19, 3.16b–18b); and "Meeting Through a Black Sheep" (20, 4.1a–5a).[1] The first two sections on Laozi's

---

[1] The *Guangsheng yi* retells this part of the deity's career not in its hagiographic explanations in ch. 2, but in a later section (3.14a–18b). The same materials are also found in the *Hunyuan shengji*, which devotes its entire third scroll to it.

career in the Zhou archives and his reasons for emigration are rather short and repeat the information given in the *Shiji*. They add only the explanation that the deity took on a lowly position in the government because all sages like to hide their traces and that he made the decision to emigrate because sages tend to withdraw and become reclusive in times of political turmoil. Thus actively linked with the mainstream Confucian vision of the sage, and actually compared with Confucius himself in his minor political role (3.10b), Lord Lao as the presence of the Dao on earth is made accessible and understandable in mainstream terms. At the same time, this account in effect ranks the numerous sages and recluses of the Confucian tradition as lesser manifestations of the Dao.

Unlike these first two sections of the *Youlong zhuan*, the remaining four go far beyond anything contained in the *Shiji* and expand the simple episodes of emigration and transmission into four major events, all of high complexity and subtle mythological impact. First, Lord Lao does not simply arrive on the pass and let himself be persuaded to transmit his teaching; Yin Xi actually has prior knowledge of his sagely nature and actively blocks the god's path. Lord Lao in turn does not accept him on sight but administers several tests before he agrees to teach him, hiding his true identity at first and making Yin Xi outline his astrological observations and efforts at self-cultivation.

Second, Lord Lao no longer travels alone but has a servant by the name of Xu Jia whom he agrees to pay upon the successful completion of their journey. Bewitched by a beautiful woman he meets on the pass—actually Lord Lao in disguise according to the *Youlong zhuan* (3.12b)—he greedily demands his pay and is reduced to a heap of bones when the god removes a life-giving talisman from him. Yin Xi, the devoted and selfless student, mediates between the two and has Xu restored to life and sent on his way.

Third, the transmission of the *Daode jing* is expanded to include a number of other, related texts, such as the Heshang gong and *Xianger* commentaries. Here Lord Lao also takes time to give oral instructions about the text's use to Yin Xi, who is described as having all the necessary talents for the study of the Dao (3.17ab), and teaches him a number of Daoist techniques.

Fourth and finally, Lord Lao agrees to Yin Xi's request that he take him along on his travels. He gives Yin Xi three years to perfect his Dao, after which the two are to meet again with the help of a black sheep in Chengdu. After the reunion, the god examines his disciple and finds that he has successfully mastered his methods. Together they set out on an ecstatic excursion to the far ends of the earth and through the nine heavens before proceeding on their journey west to convert the barbarians. This episode, like the Xu Jia story, is completely new in medieval versions of the myth, but while the former was already present in the *Shenxian zhuan* of the fourth century, the latter only appears, as do most new motifs, in the sixth century when Yin Xi's importance is raised in the teaching of the Louguan school. The entire sequence, moreover, can be interpreted as presenting the progress of the practicing devotee toward the Dao in an ideal, mythical format. It provides a template for the different requirements and stages of medieval Daoist ordination.

Encounter on the Pass

Daoist endeavors begin when the newly aspiring practitioner, having set his mind on the Dao, first meets an inspired master or sage and makes a formal request to be taught. Recasting the emigration of Lord Lao in this mode, the meeting of the god and Yin Xi is no longer accidental but becomes the preordained encounter of two heavenly beings, who are both born under supernatural auspices and plan their meeting carefully.[2] Lord Lao then leaves China because his key mission is to spread the Dao and raise Yin Xi as his major disciple. Thus, as the *Youlong zhuan* says, in a citation from the *Wenshi neizhuan*:

> In the fifth month on a *renwu* day in the twenty-fifth year of King Zhao (*guichou*), Lord Lao left the Zhou to live in seclusion. He wished to go west through the floating sands to convert all those of strange customs. Therefore he moved to the Hangu Pass, covered by a cloud of purple energy. (3.13b)

The pass, here named Hangu, was not clearly identified in the Han; neither the *Shiji* nor other texts mention it by name. Some sources, cited at length in the *Hunyuan shengji* (3.3a), mention a Sanguan, located north of the Huanghe-Wei confluence and marking the border to the ancient province of Long. Only in the Later Han, as documented in Li You's (c. 89–140 C.E.) *Hangu guan fu* (Rhapsody on the Hangu Pass), was the location firmly identified as the Hangu Pass in the eastern part of the Zhongnan mountains. Located in Taolin District, twelve Chinese miles south of the district town, it lies east of Mount Hua and south of the

---

[2] The divine nature of Yin Xi is first described in the *Wenshi neizhuan*, especially as cited in the *Yiwen leiju* (78.1330). For a study of his hagiography, see Zhang 1990; Kohn 1997.

Huanghe-Wei junction. It marks the border of Eastern Zhou and separates the flat river plains from the massive Zhongnan mountain range.[3]

Lord Lao, as he slowly approaches the pass sitting in a carriage drawn by a black ox—or, in many versions, riding on a black ox[4]—and guided by his servant Xu Jia, is revealed as a sage not only by the cloud of purple energy that hovers above him but also by a number of special constellations that appear in the sky to mark his emigration. This leads to his recognition as a sage and to his being retained on the pass. As the *Youlong zhuan* continues:

> A minister under King Zhao named Yin Xi was good at reading the heavenly signs and thus knew a sage would be crossing the pass. He applied for a position there and became the Guardian of the Pass. He fasted and purified himself and widened the road; he burned incense and swept and cleaned everything so he could properly receive the sage. (3.14a)

Historically, Yin Xi is first known as an ancient philosopher called Guanyinzi and associated with a text of this name that was reconstituted in the Yuan dynasty as the *Wenshi zhenjing*. Mentioned in the *Shiji* as the border guard who requested Laozi's *Daode jing*, he gradually grew into a sage and immortal in his own right, especially through the efforts of Yin Tong, a fifth-century descendant, who claimed that his family home was not only Yin Xi's old residence but also the actual place of the *Daode jing* transmission (see Kohn 1997). Known as Louguan or "Observation Tower" in keeping with Yin Xi's supposed astrological activities, it is located sixty kilometers southwest of Xi'an in the foothills of the Zhongnan Mountains. It became famous as the first known monastic institution of Daoism; from the Tang to the Yuan it was a major center of the religion and is still an active Complete Perfection monastery today.[5]

According to the myth, then, Yin Xi left his old home at the critical time and had himself stationed on the Hangu Pass, instructing the officer

---

[3] On the problems of identifying the pass, see Zhang 1990, 30. On the pass today, see Porter 1993, 39–41.

[4] The color of this ox—a glowing black or shimmering dark gray—is the same as that of the sheep in Sichuan. *Qing* is the color associated with spring and the east. The word is most commonly rendered "green" or "blue" and indicates the fresh color of vegetation in the spring (see Porkert 1961; Baxter 1983). It also refers to the gray-black coloring of very old yet vigorous animals or people and is thus a symbol of longevity and eternal youth.

[5] For more details on Louguan history, see Kohn 1997. On the institution as the first Daoist monastery, see Schipper 1984. A description of its present state is found in Porter 1993, 43–45.

on duty not to let any old or unusual customer pass without his approval. Then, on a *jiazi* day, the first day of the sixty-day cycle, the encounter occurred (see Fig. 15).

"There is an old man outside," the officer reported, "riding in a carriage drawn by a black ox. He is coming from the east and requests passage."

"Ah, the sage has come!" Yin Xi replied. "I shall go and see him immediately." Donning his formal garb, he went outside and received the old man with the rites proper for a disciple. "It is my wish," he said, "that you, oh venerable sage, stay here with me for a little while."

"I am just a poor humble old man," Lord Lao said apologetically. "My house is on the east side of the pass, but my fields are to the west. I merely wish to go across for a short time. Why should I stay? Please let me pass." (*Youlong zhuan* 3.14ab)

Yin Xi insists that the old man is in fact a sage and Lord Lao eventually admits his divine nature, then questions Yin Xi in detail about his astrological training and Daoist aspirations. Administering a total of three tests to his future disciple and companion, the god confirms the divinely intended nature of the encounter. In doing so he provides a model for Daoist aptitude tests applied before novices are admitted to the study of the Dao. The intimate connection of the story with actual ordination procedures, moreover, is clarified in the *Youlong zhuan*, which connects Yin Xi's three tests with the twenty-five conditions aspiring Daoists have to meet before they are allowed to train for ordination (3.21a).[6]

The most drastic version of Yin Xi's examination, however, is contained in a *Huahu jing* passage cited in the anti-Daoist polemic *Bianzheng lun* (T. 2110). Here Yin Xi has to cut off all social relations and worldly concerns before he can follow his master. The text has:

Yin Xi wished to follow Lao Dan, but the latter told him: "If you have completely made up your mind to follow me, then you must first cut off the heads of the seven members of your family—your father, mother, wife, and children. Only then can you go with me."

---

[6] The text does not specify what these conditions were. However, a section entitled "Conditions for Ordination" is contained in the *Fengdao kejie* of the early Tang (sect. 7, 2.7a–15a). It has several lists of twenty-five items, including one for the kinds of people that can be ordained (7b–8b) and one of behavioral guidelines for aspirants (12a–13a).

> Yin Xi made up his mind and went to behead the seven members of his family, including his father and mother. But when he brought the seven heads before Lao Dan, they had changed into the heads of seven pigs. (T. 52.526bc; Kohn 1995, 118n.1)

As the text further explains, Yin Xi's actions show that he had utterly overcome his attachments to family, position, and wealth, being thus ready to give his full loyalty to the Dao.

The first encounter of Lord Lao with Yin Xi in the myth therefore becomes a divinely preordained event that is the turning point not only in the god's and Yin Xi's lives—Lord Lao no longer a clerk but an active teacher of the Dao and Yin Xi no longer a customs officer but an inspired disciple. In paradigmatic form, it marks a turning point for Daoist teaching as a whole. This encounter, like all later preordination meetings, is the initial step toward the first Daoist revelation.

The importance of this event, moreover, stands in an intimate relationship with its setting, both spatially at the border pass and developmentally in Lord Lao's earthly progress. It is precisely because the god emigrates that the transmission of the *Daode jing* is made possible. Because he is between China and countries to the west, and between being a clerk and a divine savior, a new beginning can be made and the textual manifestation of Daoist teachings can arise. The setting of the *Daode jing*'s origin, emphasized from the first and embellished variously in the literature, is essential to the centrality of the book. The text would not have the same pivotal power without its being taken, in symbolic inversion, from the thinker against his express will; nor would it be the same set anywhere but on the pass, the threshold between plains and mountains, between China and countries to the west, between Laozi the philosopher and Lord Lao the god.

The Demands of Xu Jia

Having acknowledged his disciple's basic aptitude for the Dao and his unconditioned willingness to follow it, Lord Lao next commits Yin Xi to a particular form of religious service. This is described in the story about Xu Jia, the god's greedy retainer.

As related in the *Wenshi neizhuan*, Xu Jia had been hired by Lord Lao for one hundred cash a day with the understanding that he would be paid in full after their successful journey west. However,

Fig. 15. Lord Lao rides across the pass.
Source: Zengxiang liexian zhuan 1.1a

as Jia saw that Laozi was about to set off, he had second thoughts, since he had not received any pay yet. On the pass, at the same time, there was a beautiful, sensuous woman who heard that Jia would receive a lot of money. She secretly said to him: "Why don't you bring a legal case and demand your pay? I will become your wife!" (*SDZN* 9.9a)

Xu Jia complies and goes after Lord Lao for his money to find that he cannot furnish the necessary amount, seven million cash. Instead, the god calls in his debt, the "Long Life Talisman of Great Mystery," which had kept Xu Jia alive for the past two hundred years. As he summons the talisman,

all saw it fly out of Jia's mouth and return to Laozi. The writing was as clear as if it had been newly written. Jia, however, had collapsed into a heap of white bones. (9.9b)

At this point Yin Xi steps in and pleads for Xu Jia, promising to pay the debt on Laozi's behalf and begging the god to restore the man's life. Lord Lao, sympathizing, tells him:

"Xi, this has happened not because I am angry at Jia. It is that Jia has betrayed his earlier promise. Thus the Dao has left him." (9.9b)

Still, he proceeds to revive the servant by placing the talisman on the heap of bones. The story ends with the two sages sending the man off, repentant but in disgrace.

This story occurs in a number of variants and three major crystallizations. In early immortality literature, such as the *Shenxian zhuan*, it shows Laozi as a master of wondrous arts, controlling life and death with the magic of the immortals (Kohn 1996a, 62). In medieval ordination materials, it contrasts the dedicated, selfless Daoist (Yin Xi) with the greedy shaman (Xu Jia), emphasizing the priority of universal salvation over material gain. In modern Daoist ritual lore, finally, it establishes mythologically the existence of the two levels of Daoist priesthood—the classical and the popular, represented by the black-head and red-head Daoists of modern Taiwan (see Schipper 1985).

The medieval crystallization of the myth, moreover, has several variants. The *Hunyuan zhenlu*, for example, has the same narrative but adds that the entire episode was created as a further test for Yin Xi, to ascertain his sympathy for weaker beings and his ability to stand up in a crisis as a representative of the Dao (6ab). Du Guangting in his *Guangsheng yi* (3.14b–16a) adds that Lord Lao raised Xu Jia from the dead even before he became his servant, finding him as an exposed skeleton lying by the roadside (Schipper 1985, 42–43). Finally, in the Song hagiographies Lord Lao himself turns into the beautiful woman who seduces Jia as a test of both his servant and Yin Xi (*Youlong zhuan* 3.12a–13a; *Hunyuan shengji* 3.9b).

The key purpose of the medieval story is to contrast the vulgar shaman and the noble Daoist ordinand, clarifying the right route for future aspirants to take and documenting the need for clear dedication to the Dao. The contrast, moreover, is effective on all levels: Xu Jia is a servant and Yin Xi an official; Xu Jia is illiterate, while Yin Xi writes down the *Daode jing* and becomes the Master at the Beginning of the Scripture (Wenshi xiansheng). Xu Jia is greedy for worldly goods, but Yin Xi strives only for perfection and celestial joys; Xu Jia is easily led astray by seductive beauties, while Yin Xi stays steadily on the path to the Dao. Xu Jia fails his test, but Yin Xi passes his. Xu Jia, in a word, is the failure, the negative model, while Yin Xi is the success, the predestined attendant of the Dao (Schipper 1985, 44).

Unlike this radical contrast between two types of practitioners in the medieval myth, the modern crystallization reconciles the conflict to a certain degree and allots a certain value within Daoism even to the failed Xu Jia. A modern story collected by K. M. Schipper in Tainan in 1976, has Xu Jia begin as a dead skeleton that is revived by Lord Lao. The sage trains Xu in elementary Daoist methods but puts him to the test by placing him into the seductive company of a beautiful lady—a classic motif also common in stories of immortals and fox fairies.[7] Like the innocent Confucian scholar in the latter, Xu Jia weakens and spends a wonderful night with the woman only to wake up and find himself in a graveyard. Desperate, he recites whatever spells come to mind, without paying any attention to ritual purity and even while performing physical necessities. At this point, Lord Lao appears. He scolds Xu furiously and gives him two basic ritual implements, a buffalo horn and a bell, leaving him to follow the Dao in this primitive way (Schipper 1985, 38–39). Other oral versions emphasize Xu Jia's stupidity and vulgar nature, detailing his instructions from Lord Lao and his duties in the world (Schipper 1985, 40–41).

Xu Jia in Daoist ritual today is thus the first red-head Daoist, the disciple who was revived and taught some elementary methods despite his vulgar character. A skeleton on the roadside, he is a demon-ghost of the unknown dead, resurrected to serve humanity in a branch of the Dao

---

[7] Among immortals who successfully resist temptation, Lü Dongbin, who was tested in this way by his master Zhongli Quan, is especially noteworthy (see Yetts 1916). On fox fairies and their vampirizing of young Confucian scholars, see Giles 1916; Krappe 1944; Johnson 1974.

that may not be the highest, but is necessary and efficacious. By just blowing on the buffalo horn, Xu Jia becomes a lower-level immortal and gains the powers of the Dao; an illiterate, he does not use scriptures but relies on oral spells and incantations for his practice (Schipper 1985, 40; Davis 1996, 183).

The Xu Jia story in its medieval and modern modes therefore plays a key part in the process of Daoist ordination and, in its demand for firm dedication, represents a second level after the initial examination of aptitude. In its three crystallizations, moreover, it documents some of the major changes the Daoist religion underwent over the course of history. First a cult of immortality, centered on the attainment of eternal life and power over life and death, it grew into an organized religion with a formal ordination structure that distinguished it sharply from the common shamanic practitioners of the ordinary people. Only in its modern development did Daoism make peace with vulgar ritual and integrate it into its ranks as a necessary, if lowly and less efficacious, form of Daoist practice.

Transmitting the Daode jing

The third step Lord Lao takes in his interaction with Yin Xi is the actual transmission of scriptures and precepts, which is the central focus of both the ordination ritual and the Daoist myth. Having passed the necessary examinations and declared his firm dedication to the Dao, the ordinand, like Yin Xi, can now request the master's instruction. The most detailed version of this episode is found in Yin Wencao's *Hunyuan zhenlu* of the early Tang. That text relates:

> "Today I have realized," Yin Xi said, "that the utmost Dao was originally an abyss which, after existing for myriads of kalpas, has now been born anew in the world. I am therefore sincerely grateful that we were predestined to meet like this and would like to beg you, O Heavenly Worthy and Great Man, to compose a text for me that explains the meaning of the Great Dao. I will worship and cultivate it."
>
> "In order to do so," Laozi explained, "you should give up your work for the empire and wisely abandon ordinary life. You must commit yourself to the transmission of the vast Dao and act fully like a divine immortal."
>
> Yin Xi consequently retired from office, giving grounds of illness. On the twenty-fifth day of the twelfth month of that year, he then invited Laozi to return home with him. Three days later, on the twenty-eighth day, he received the *Daode jing* from Laozi in his old home [at Louguan]. (11b–12a)

Yin Xi thus formally asks to receive the teaching and is advised that he has to give up his official position, dedicating himself fully to the Dao. Doing so, he takes the god home with him to Louguan, 250 kilometers west of the Hangu Pass, where the two sages can go about their work at leisure.[8]

There, Yin Xi begins by swearing a formal pledge of allegiance to Lord Lao. To do this, he has to fast for a specific period, then give a certain amount of gold as a formal token of recognition, and finally swear an oath of fealty and secrecy, smearing himself with the blood of a white horse. The procedure is similar to the blood covenants in ancient China used to establish political ties among non-kinship groups and to the pledges practiced in Daoist alchemy.[9] Yin Xi, undergoing the necessary ceremony, is thus readied for ordination proper, the central act of which is the transmission of the *Daode jing*.

According to early sources, it took Lord Lao three days and three nights to recite the text to him, while Yin Xi wrote it down, thus concluding the transmission. From the fifth century onward, a more complex ordination rite is reported, during which several texts change hands. The *Santian neijie jing*, for example, says that Lord Lao gave Yin Xi three scrolls, two of the *Daode jing* and one *Shangxia zhongjing* (Central Scripture of Above and Below), otherwise known as the *Laozi zhongjing* (1.4a). The *Xisheng jing* in addition reports the detailed oral instructions Laozi gave to the Guardian of the Pass. The *Daode zhenjing xujue*, moreover, brings the legend of the Master on the River (Heshang gong) into the transmission, integrating an earlier commentary into the canonical sphere of the text.[10] The full list contains eleven texts (see Table 18) associated with the *Daode jing* and transmitted in the ordination to the rank of Disciple of Exalted Mystery (Gaoxuan dizi) or Highest Preceptor of Exalted Mystery (Taishang gaoxuan fashi). It is first mentioned in the *Hunyuan zhenlu* version of the myth, which also claims that Lord Lao

---

[8] This shift in location is immediately linked with the rise of Louguan as an important Daoist center in the fifth century. For details, see Zhang 1991; Kohn 1997.

[9] The description of the pledge for the *Daode jing* is found in the *Laozi jiejie* (Sectional Interpretation of the *Laozi* [*Daode jing*]), a lost commentary to the text, cited in *Bianzheng lun* 2 (T. 2110, 52.500b). See Kusuyama 1976a; 1979, 408. For the procedures in ancient China (usually involving sheep), see Lewis 1990, 46. On alchemical pledges, see Ware 1966, 75. Their use in the transmission of Highest Clarity scriptures is described in Smith 1994.

[10] On the *Xisheng jing* (DZ 726), see Kohn 1991, 42; the *Xujue* is a Dunhuang manuscript (S. 75, P. 2370; see Kohn 1995, 202–3). Both date from the fifth century. Heshang gong is the author of the earliest religious commentary to the *Daode jing*. For a study of this work, see Chan 1991.

taught Yin Xi how to practice Daoist alchemy, spells and talismans, grain avoidance, breath control, gymnastics, meditation, and the visualization of the Three Ones (Kusuyama 1977; 1979, 493).

Table 18
Texts transmitted with the *Daode jing* in formal ordination*

Title	English title	Source
Commentaries		
Heshang zhangju	Heshang gong commentary	DZ 682
Xianger zhu	Xianger commentary	Rao 1991
Laozi neijie	Inner Interpretation of *Daode jing*	lost
Laozi jiejie	Sectional Interpretation of *Daode jing*	see Kusuyama 1976a
Philosophical Interpretations		
Xisheng jing	Scripture of Western Ascension	DZ 726
Miaozhen jing	Scripture of Wondrous Perfection	see Maeda 1987
Meditations and Rituals		
Laozi zhongjing	Central Scripture of Laozi	DZ 1168
Wuqian wen chaoyi	Audience Rites for Daode jing	lost
Sanyi biaowen	Three-One Memorial	lost
Hagiographies		
Wenshi neizhuan	Essential Biography of Master Wenshi	SDZN
Laozi neizhuan	Essential Biography of Laozi	lost

*Note: See Benn 1991, 84–85.

The myth's account, moreover, like the actual ordination ceremony, proceeds in question-and-answer fashion, with Yin Xi requesting detailed instruction and explication of the teachings. In addition, a set of ten precepts is handed over, which were classically—and are to the twentieth century—associated with the *Daode jing*.[11] More than that, at ordination masters taught their adepts about the workings of the universe, and Laozi does the same for Yin Xi. According to the *Wenshi neizhuan*, he explains the shape of heaven and earth, the distance that separates them, the events that accompany their creation and kalpic destruction, and the nature and activities of the gods who rule them.[12]

---

[11] The ten precepts are found in the *Shijie jing* (The Ten Precepts, DZ 459) and consist of five prohibitive rules against killing, stealing, lying, sexual misconduct, and intoxication, as well as five prescriptive rules, adaptations of bodhisattva vows that demand maintaining harmony in the family, rejoicing in goodness, aiding the unfortunate, suffering illness with patience, and laboring for the salvation of all. Their use in twentieth-century Daoist institutions is described in Hackmann 1920.

[12] Passages of Laozi's teaching in the *Wenshi neizhuan* are cited in *Taiping yulan* (677.2b), *Chuxue ji* (1.13), and *Xiaodao lun*, sects. 9, 10, 16, 25, and 28.

In addition, certain methods were associated closely with the *Daode jing* rank of ordination. Foremost among them is the recitation of the text itself, a practice first taken up for its magical efficacy by the Celestial Masters of the Han and highly valued already in the *Laozi bianhua jing*. Even the *Baopuzi* emphasizes the beneficial properties of *Daode jing* recitation, but warns that it is not sufficient to guarantee ascension. Finally, the *Daode zhenjing xujue* gives detailed visualization instructions that will summon the gods prior to recitation of the *Daode jing*.[13] In addition, alchemical, physical, and visualization methods were associated with the *Daode jing* transmission as described in the *Hunyuan zhenlu*; they had been linked in a more general way with Laozi as early as the *Shenxian zhuan*.

Bolstered by precepts, scriptures, and methods, the *Daode jing* in medieval ordination is a formally ritualized document, the possession and recitation of which bestows magical powers and immortality. It is integrated with a set of Daoist teachings and techniques that change over time as the religion advances. Where early sources focus on the *Daode jing* itself and the instructions for its recitation, sixth-century materials link it with a set of precepts and with cosmological instructions. Only in the seventh century, with the rise of a greater interest in self-cultivation, are the text and its transmission associated with alchemical, physical, and meditative practices. Similarly, while Yin Xi in earlier sources attains the Dao fully upon merely receiving the text, later mythical accounts that reflect integrated ordination practices present the *Daode jing* as only the initial foothold on path to the Dao. Practitioners who have received it—including Yin Xi in the transmission story—have more to undergo as they continue their practice and move toward the advanced stages of formal ordination.

Black Sheep and Ecstatic Travels

Yin Xi, like the ideal medieval ordinand, is happy to have gained the *Daode jing* and its instructions but does not stop there. Seeing the great expanse of the divine universe looming above, he asks Lord Lao to take him along on his distant wanderings; but the deity refuses because Yin Xi's Dao is not yet complete. To attain perfection, he has to "recite the scripture ten thousand times," then, after one thousand days, "come and

---

[13] On the Celestial Masters, see Kobayashi 1992, 31; on the *Bianhua jing*, see Yoshioka 1959, 122; the *Baopuzi* passage is found in Ware 1966, 142. For more details on the practice, see Kohn 1998a.

look for me in a black sheep shop at the gate of Chengdu market"
(*Wenshi neizhuan*, SDZN 9.10ab). Yin Xi performs his recitations, then
travels to Sichuan to meet the god as arranged. There he hopes to be
accepted fully into the Dao, to become Lord Lao's partner, and to go on
distant journeys with him as an immortal. He succeeds in his endeavor,
but not without difficulty. Attaining the perfection of the Dao involves
yet another formal ordination procedure that includes tests, a renewal of
dedication, and a second transmission.

The test in this case is for Yin Xi to find the Dao (Lord Lao) again, to
locate him at a place cryptically identified through the sign of a "black
sheep." This expression may have indicated a strange formation of mica
(see Schafer 1955), but according to the tradition it meant a real sheep of
great age with a shining coat. That sheep is still represented in bronze at
the gate of the Qingyang gong in Chengdu.[14] The story of the meeting
occurs in three major crystallizations that again show changes in the
Daoist perception of the god and his activity on earth.

First, there is the *Wenshi neizhuan*, according to which

> Yin Xi's Dao was perfected. He duly went to look for a black sheep shop at
> the gate of Chengdu market, eagerly searching for Laozi. But although he
> kept looking for days, he could not find him. Day and night he was alert.
> Only after nine days did he encounter a man advancing toward him with a
> black sheep for sale. (*SDZN* 9.10b–11a)

Upon inquiry, the man admits that the sheep belongs to his master's
guest but refuses to take Yin Xi to him. Only after extensive pleading and
humiliation on Yin Xi's part is the disciple led into the presence of the
Dao (Kusuyama 1978; 1979, 426). Received in formal audience, he then
sees Lord Lao as the true representative of divine power, seated on the
lotus seat of spontaneity, firmly grasping his staff of nine knots.

In a second crystallization, the god ascends to heaven and is reborn
as the son of the local prefect in yet another virgin birth:

> Laozi emerged from his mother's chest. His hair and temples were white
> and he was sixteen feet tall. He wore the cap of heaven and held a staff of
> gold. (*Xiaodao lun* 1; Kohn 1995, 53)

---

[14] The alleged site of Lord Lao's meeting with Yin Xi, this has been a flourishing
Daoist center since the Tang. Today restored to some of its former glory, the
complex contains not only a number of Daoist halls (to the Three Pure Ones and
the Dipper Mother) and statues of the sheep at the entrance, but also a statue of
Lord Lao on his black ox, a hall dedicated to him, and a stone bedstead where the
god allegedly slept, which, if rested upon, will dispel nightmares. For
descriptions, see Yūsa 1986; Li 1993, 31–33.

Here the meeting between the two sages is raised from the reunion of teacher and disciple to a cosmic joining, the coming together of two divine forces, expressed powerfully in the heavenly signs that accompany Lord Lao's new descent. Still, Yin Xi has some difficulty locating the child; he has to be patient and persistent in his search for the Dao.

A third variant appears first in Yue Penggui's *Xichuan qingyang gong beiming* (DZ 964) of the year 884. Here even the sheep is a celestial agent, a dragon or attendant of the Green (*qing*) Emperor of the East, ordered by Lord Lao to descend to earth as the animal. The story has Yin Xi spot the promised sign at the market and ask about it. The servant answers:

> Recently a son was born in my master's family. He cries and cries and never stops. Even thrown into water and fire, he comes to no harm. A fortune teller says that the crying will only stop if we give him the milk of a black ewe. So here I am, buying one. (*Youlong zhuan* 4.1ab; *Hunyuan shengji* 3.25a)

Instead of selling the sheep, the family retainer is buying it; instead of residing quietly as a noble guest, Lord Lao is a newborn baby wailing endlessly and thus causing the family to reveal to Yin Xi the divine sign (Kusuyama 1979, 427). Whereas in earlier versions the Dao was hard to find and could be reached only after overcoming the servant's reluctance, here the Dao is actively—and loudly—crying out for the disciple to come. Following the sign, Yin Xi duly comes before the god, who reveals his true stature by growing to ten feet, emitting a radiance like that of the seven planets, wearing a nine-colored cloak, and formally announcing his divinity (*Youlong zhuan* 4.1b; *Hunyuan shengji* 3.25b).

The Dao in all three crystallizations is obviously supernatural and perceived by the disciple in its true celestial stature, whether as an infant on a lotus throne, in a miraculous birth, or as a baby transformed into a radiant vision of divinity. Unlike on the pass where it appeared as an innocuous old man, the Dao here is a truly celestial power, present in all its might but apparent only to its long-term practitioners and not to the ordinary people around them. In addition, the different crystallizations reveal changes in the understanding of the Dao on earth: It first seen as a powerful human master, then as a divine child silently hiding among humans, then again as an openly beckoning agent of divinity. The Dao becomes both more divine and more accessible in the course of the transmission story's development from the sixth to the tenth centuries, ending as a wondrous otherworldly force that cries out for people to recognize and follow it.

Yin Xi, seeing the Dao for what it is, passes his test. A renewal of his dedication is required next. After inquiring about Yin Xi's practice and learning that he "recited the scripture and gained eternal life and the state of no-death," Lord Lao asks him, "Do you still wish to follow me on my distant wanderings?" Yin Xi without hesitation replies that his wish still stands (*Wenshi neizhuan, SDZN* 9.11b). Thus having rededicated himself to the Dao, he receives another transmission, not of scriptures this time—although they played a role in actual medieval practice—but of celestial rank and title. Acknowledging Yin Xi as a full immortal, Lord Lao gives him a celestial appointment, stating that his "golden name is now listed in the perfected charts and jade ledgers." Immediately a celestial procession appears to bestow upon Yin Xi the proper immortal garb—a purple headdress, a flying feathery skirt, a robe with cinnabar sleeves, embroidered slippers, and other paraphernalia. Now a full celestial, he receives the formal title "Master at the Beginning of the Scripture" and the celestial rank of All-Highest Perfected (Wushang zhenren; *Youlong zhuan* 4.2a; *Hunyuan shengji* 3.26b).

The bestowal of formal robes and rank also plays an important part in medieval ordination. Ordinands take refuge in the Three Treasures (the Dao, teachers, and scriptures), then pay their respects to the three masters of ordination. As they kneel on the ground,

> first the Master Who Protects the Elevation presents them with the ritual skirt; next, the Master Who Supervises the Ordinands presents them with the cloudy sleeves; third, the Master of the Ordination presents them with the ritual robe. (*Fengdao kejie* 6.10a)

Then they are elevated to a new rank and given a new title commensurate with their higher powers and elevated standing.

Yin Xi, and with him any newly ordained Daoist, is thus a fully acknowledged immortal and promptly goes on an ecstatic journey to the far ends of the world and into the heavens above. Together with Lord Lao he visits the isles of the immortals and the Fusang tree of the sun in the east, travels to the Queen Mother and the Ruo wood in the west, passes through all nine heavens, where he exchanges formal greetings and teachings with celestial rulers, and eventually returns to earth to commence his mundane career of spreading the Dao far and wide.[15]

The celestial journey of the two sages is the mythological equivalent of the highest form of medieval Daoist practice, ecstatic excursions to the otherworld undertaken in the Highest Clarity tradition, and reached with the rank of Preceptor of the Three Caverns, Disciple of Highest

---

[15] This journey is first described in *Wenshi neizhuan* citations. The full range of the sages' ecstatic travels is described in *Youlong zhuan* 4.2b–4b; *Hunyuan shengji* 4.1ab.

Clarity.[16] As documented in the myth, attainment at this level makes the practicing Daoist a full member of the celestial hierarchy, an official of the otherworld who obeys the full set of 300 precepts found in the *Dajie wen* (The Great Precepts; DZ 1363). The last fifty of these specifically concern the practice of ecstatic excursions and describe the adept's endeavor to "wander to all the heavens to listen to celestial music," going beyond the ten directions, and paying respects to all the perfected (15a). Yin Xi, standing for the ideal adept of the Dao, thus attains the highest level of mastery and becomes a partner of the god.

Threshold and Transition

The entire sequence of four major episodes told about Lord Lao's emigration and the transmission of the *Daode jing* represents the ordination process of medieval Daoism in a mythical, narrative format. From the perspective of comparative mythology on the other hand, the story can also be linked with the quest of the hero, which typically includes the following significant episodes. The hero is born under unusual circumstances or virginally; he is exposed and abandoned but saved by local people or animals; he passes through a period of transition; and finally, he returns to his rightful kingdom where he overcomes all resistance and rules as king.

The key motif in the hero myth is discrepancy: his dislocation from home and rightful rank, the gap between his early life and later fulfillment, and the resistance that has to be overcome between the two stages of his life. The exposure of the child is not the main point, rather it is the attempted prevention of the hero's quest. This can be achieved either by separating him from his family or by closeting him within it. In either case, the hero is separated from his true home in the world. He may be first separated then violently reunited with it, or first united then violently torn away. In either case, the transition from one to the other, crossing the "threshold of adventure" between safe childhood and vigorous adulthood (Campbell 1949, 245), prepares him for full autonomy as king in the next stage of his career (Dundes 1990, 195).[17] This always

---

[16] For a survey of the medieval ordination system see Benn 1991, 72–98. See also Kusuyama 1992; Despeux 1986; 1990; Schipper 1985a.

[17] The same structure also applies to the Buddha's life story, in which he is kept strictly within the confines of his home and only leaves as an adult, and very much against his father's will, to seek out his true kingdom, the attainment of enlightenment. See Pye 1979; Pyysiainen 1987.

entails overcoming an obstacle, "a shadow presence that guards the passage"; it is often also characterized by a period of withdrawal, a "vision quest" of growing awareness of the impending task.[18]

The time of transition is usually characterized by temptations and the summons of fate, as well as by an initial refusal to do the required work and an attempt to remain in the realm of childhood. It is a stage between roles and positions and thus part of the phenomenon that in ritual has been described as liminality (see Gennep 1960, Turner 1969). It is signaled by the simultaneous presence of joy and suffering, unity and diversity, present and future, way and goal, shrine and home. In concrete terms, the same threshold phenomenon is often also evoked in pilgrimages, and the hero sets out to travel during this phase (Biallas 1986, 153). In symbolic terms, it appears as inversion, a turning upside-down of established order that creates "a *Spielraum*, a space in which to take chances with new roles and ideas" (Babcock 1978, 25). Overall, it is a period of transition, in which both danger to the old and high hopes for the new come together in a potentially explosive mixture.

In terms of Daoism, the entire process of ordination is literally a rite of passage, guiding the adept from humanity to immortality, from being a socially centered individual to a cosmic partner of the Dao. Many of the typical motifs associated with this transition or threshold situation thus appear equally in the myth of Lord Lao's interaction with Yin Xi and in the hero's quest for his kingdom. The heroes, Lord Lao and Yin Xi, both travel far from home, and encounter new and potentially threatening situations; they grow only by pursuing their quest with single-minded determination.

In addition, issues of separation from ordinary life and the inversion of common values are clearly present in religious aptitude tests, radical and often tortuous ordeals of symbolic inversion. Such tests are "acts of expressive behavior which inverts, contradicts, abrogates, or in some fashion presents an alternative to commonly held cultural codes, values, and norms" (Babcock, 1978, 14). They are administered not only to Yin Xi and the hero but also to classical Daoist immortals, followers of the Celestial Masters and Complete Perfection schools, as well as to aspiring trainees of Chan Buddhism.

Among immortals, tests are typically difficult situations engineered by a master for a prospective disciple. They may include the eating of excrement, resistance to a woman's seduction, killing or burying one's family members, and giving selfless help to ungrateful wretches. They

---

[18] See Campbell 1949, 245; Leeming 1973, 185; Biallas 1986, 141.

cover three major areas—detachment from mundane goods and relation-ships, the overcoming of desires and fears, and the development of com-passion for all beings—and make sure that the future immortal is completely free from the demands and lures of the ordinary world, can withstand the hardships of the training, and will not abuse whatever powers he may gain.[19] Among the early Celestial Masters, tests involved formalized ritual intercourse as a means of tying cult members closer to the Dao than to their own families. Fathers and brothers had to watch their daughters and sisters copulate with total strangers, and husbands had to stand quietly by as their wives were ravished and their sons thrown into wells (Stein 1963, 57).

These various types of tests, gruesome though they may be, aimed at reinforcing the follower's perception of himself and the world as part of the religious community and increasing his dedication to the teaching. They were actively applied throughout Daoist history and have played an important role in the school of Complete Perfection, which developed them in imitation of similar practices in Chan Buddhism. In the latter, the first and classic example is Huike who cut off his arm to be accepted as disciple by the first patriarch Bodhidharma. To the present day applicants have to suffer abuse and rejection for several days before being let in at the temple gates.[20] Not an isolated phenomenon, the various tests and stages Yin Xi has to undergo in the Daoist myth, as well as the hardships and rituals that accompany them, are part of a universal pattern of delimiting and controlling passage from one major social or religious state to another. They are expressions of both the difficulties and rewards of passing from a lower to a higher level of being. Just as Yin Xi ends his training by becoming a full-fledged immortal who makes ecstatic journeys around the universe, so the hero, after passing the threshold, is in a position to claim his kingdom. Similarly practitioners of various cults and religions, after successfully passing tests and initiatory ordeals, are accepted as full members of their communities. Ordination procedures, tests through hardship, and mythical narratives of heroes or adepts who win full acceptance are thus different expressions of the same basic religious phenomenon—the transition from humanity to divinity, from ordinary to cosmic life.

---

[19] Classical test stories are those of Gourd Master (Hugong) and Zhang Daoling in the *Shenxian zhuan* (see Güntsch 1988; Giles 1948) as well as of Lü Dongbin in the *Fengxiang liexian zhuan*. See Yetts 1916; 1922; Imbault-Huart 1884; DeWoskin 1983; Kohn 1993, 119–32.

[20] On tests in the Complete Perfection school, see Hawkes 1981; for Huike and Bodhidharma, see Dumoulin 1988, 92; on Zen monks today, see Morinaga 1988.

12

The Conversion of the Barbarians

Having successfully delivered Yin Xi to celestial rank, Lord Lao next takes him on a western journey with the goal of, as the *Youlong zhuan* has it, "Converting the Barbarians Across the Desert" (sect. 21).[1] To begin, they pass through the great desert, probably the Taklamakan, and settle on a lonely mountain, usually located in Kashmir, where the barbarian king finds them during a hunt. Intrigued by the strangers, he accepts their invitation to a banquet, which is a great success. The return invitation, however, runs into problems when Lord Lao brings the heavenly host along and, after forty days of continuous revelry, the king's treasury faces depletion. Afraid that his guests are in fact demons, he tries to kill the god and his companion in various hellish ways—by burning, drowning, boiling, and stabbing—but the Daoists survive the ordeals and emerge all the stronger. Appearing in full celestial splendor, Lord Lao awes the king into submission and installs the rules and regulations of Buddhism (shaved head, brown robes, celibacy, vegetarianism) throughout the kingdom. This done, he leaves the routine administration to Yin Xi and sets out to effect further conversions, eventually returning to heaven.

This part of Lord Lao's endeavors during his life on earth can be described as the fulfillment of his divine purpose, the winning of the whole world to his kingdom of the Dao. Unlike the narrative of his emigration and transmission of the *Daode jing*, which is almost exclusively Daoist in nature and shows only minimal Buddhist influence (as in the precepts, for example), the conversion is historically based on

---

[1] Du Guangting does not speak of the conversion at all, and the *Youlong zhuan* treats it rather briefly. The *Hunyuan shengji*, on the other hand, gives it extensive coverage and cites numerous different versions, devoting almost its entire fourth scroll and half of the fifth to it (4.4a–20a; 5.1a–6b). Its detailed account is mirrored in the Yuan dynasty *Laojun bashiyi hua tushuo* (Reiter 1990).

Buddhist models. The interaction of saṅgha and state, of enlightened being and worldly king, draws especially on stories surrounding King Aśoka, the ideal Buddhist ruler. In addition, this episode is part of the conversion literature that first developed after the introduction of Buddhism in the second century C.E. It was originally created as an explanation for the similarities between the two teachings and the appearance of Buddhism in countries to the west. The conversion story, however, was soon used polemically to document the superiority of Daoism over the intruding new religion. It became highly controversial, and its scripture, the *Huahu jing*, continued to both flourish and be proscribed over many centuries until the 1281 proscription of all Daoist texts under the Yuan.

Four versions of the *Huahu jing* are known today. Its earliest stratum goes back to about the year 300 C.E., but only a few fragments remain of this. A second version, expanded from the early text, appeared in the sixth century. It was created in the same Louguan milieu that produced the *Wenshi neizhuan* and matches it in both narrative style and increased emphasis on the activities of Yin Xi. A third edition consists of altogether ten scrolls, about one third of which (nos. 1, 2, 8, 10) survive in Dunhuang manuscripts. They retell not only Lord Lao's exploits both in third-person and first-person narrative but also contain many philosophical discussions between the deity and the barbarian king, as well as demonological and cosmological expositions. As documented in a Numinous Treasure version of the early Tang, the conversion had become as much an working part of Daoist myth as it was a form of anti-Buddhist polemic. A fourth text, the *Laojun bashiyi hua tushuo* (abbreviated as *Tushuo* in the discussion following), describes Lord Lao's deeds on earth with a heavy focus on the conversion in altogether eighty-one pictures accompanied by short descriptions.[2] Using these different variants of the story, the following discussion will point out its development within Daoism, its relation to the tales surrounding King Aśoka, and its wider meaning in terms of the quest of the hero.

Banquets and Ordeals

Going beyond the "floating sands" of the Taklamakan desert and passing through the lands of Central Asia, Lord Lao and Yin Xi reach northern India and settle to practice the Dao in the mountains of Kashmir.

---

[2] For editorial and historical details on these texts, see chapters 1 and 2 above.

Here the local ruler finds them. According to the *Huahu jing*, he is hostile at first but softens when the Daoists invite him to a banquet (*SDZN* 9.18a). In the contemporaneous *Wenshi neizhuan* version, the king at once shows a positive interest in the Daoist teaching and invites the two sages to a banquet. However, Lord Lao accepts only after first hosting the king and all his subjects (*SDZN* 9.12a). The *Tushuo* states that the king discovers them while hunting and, together with his seven sons, is immediately converted (nos. 27–28; Reiter 1990, 29). Only when they return for more detailed instructions are the banquet invitations offered. According to the *Hunyuan shengji*, the king was a relative of Lord Lao from a former life but has forgotten his true karma and has to be taught anew (4.5b). In all cases, the god explicitly warns the king that his followers are exceedingly numerous and will be hard to satisfy.

Soon the banquets begin. The Daoists, equipped with magical powers, have no problem entertaining hordes of barbarians in great splendor:

> Laozi hung silky curtains made from the cloud-energy of the five phases: white in the west of the valley, black in the north, green in the east, red in the south, and yellow in its center.
>
> He invited everyone in the kingdom, from the king above to the common folk below. The king in addition summoned several million people from the thirty-six barbarian countries to come to the big feast. Laozi, in the middle of the five-colored cloud-curtains, feasted them for seven days and seven nights. There were plenty of magnificent delicacies—and no trace of strain or lack. (*Huahu jing*, *SDZN* 9.18a; *Hunyuan shengji* 4.9a)

The return invitation, however, proceeds less smoothly, since Lord Lao's human and celestial followers arrive in ever larger numbers for days and weeks together. The king, seeing his treasury increasingly depleted, begins to worry and doubt the good intention of his visitors.

> Suddenly an evil thought arose in his mind. "Maybe," he thought, "the old man is really a demon and not a wise man at all. Let us capture him right away! Set up a stake in the marketplace and burn him to death! That will soon prove it." (*Wenshi neizhuan*, *SDZN* 9.12b; *Hunyuan shengji* 4.9b)

The two Daoists are duly taken to the stake and burned. Sitting serenely in the lotus posture, they chant the *Daode jing* and remain entirely unharmed—until, after forty days, all the wood in the kingdom is exhausted (see Fig. 16). The king, exasperated, has them thrown into a deep pool, but several dragons appear to support the Daoists and keep them safe. The *Hunyuan shengji* and the *Tushuo* have two additional ordeals, one in which the Daoists are boiled in hot water and saved by

Fig. 16. The barbarians burn Lord Lao at the stake.
Source: Laojun bashiyi hua tushuo, no. 31

lotus blossoms rising from the bottom of the cauldron, and the other in which millions of soldiers assembled by the king try to kill them with swords and spears, knives and lances. The Daoists, however, are aided by heavenly troops who use thunder and lightning against their foes.[3]

Eventually the king is forced to surrender. Lord Lao has won his kingdom, overcome the trials and revealed the power of the Dao. Whether withdrawn in the solitude of the mountains, placed in an active social environment, or subjected to deadly ordeals, the Dao conquers all and will always survive.

Read in this fashion as a purely Daoist myth, the story integrates many tales and symbols to present the powers of the Dao on earth. Just as during the banquet the god has an inexhaustible supply at his disposal and can entertain large numbers of people over several weeks, the Dao, too, is inexhaustible and will forever give of its riches. Just as the king is both attracted to the strangers and reluctant to follow their teachings, so common people have initial reservations about the Dao and often hesitate to trust it. Just as Lord Lao and Yin Xi undergo the barbarian ordeals but are constantly supported by the Dao, people have to suffer in their lives but can always count on the Dao to see them through. Even the tortures of hell—where sinners are burned at the stake, thrown into cauldrons of boiling water, drowned in deep pools, and impaled on a mountain of swords and a tree of knives (see Goodrich 1981)—hold no more terror when the Dao is there.

Historically, a clear line of expansion can be observed among the different versions of the conversion, making Lord Lao go ever farther and convert more people with increasingly magical means. As a result, by the thirteenth century, he destroys heretical teachings in the Indian city of Śrāvastī, conceals the sun and the moon to convert the population of the Buddha's birthplace of Kapilavastu, moves a large, obstructive mountain in the country of the Seleukids, and successfully converts Khotan, Sogdia, Parthia, and large parts of the Indian subcontinent (*Tushuo*, nos. 27–44).

In terms of Buddhist influence, the banquets in this story are a mythical representation of the *pañcavārsika*, the great quinquennial festival, a "frenzy of alms-giving" during which the king invites the entire Buddhist community to a banquet and showers them with gifts. Setting up huts on an open plain, the king gives gold and silver, cloth

---

[3] The first two ordeals are specified in all texts and occur first in the *Huahu jing* (*SDZN* 9.18b–19a) and the *Wenshi neizhuan* (*SDZN* 9.12b–13a). The remaining two are found in *Hunyuan shengji* 4.10a and *Tushuo* nos. 31 and 33 (Reiter 1990, 30–31).

and utensils, and vast quantities of food to the sangha. Stripping himself utterly, he even presents, as Aśoka says in the *Aśokavadāna* (Legends of King Aśoka), "the whole earth, surrounded by the ocean, to the community of the Buddha's disciples."[4] The barbarian king in the story, put to the Buddhist test of the quinquennial festival, thus fails because he gets worried about his earthly possessions and reacts with anger and fear. He is not a true *cakravartin*, the royal "turner of the wheel" and supporter of the faith.

The Daoist sages, on the other hand, succeed in maintaining and demonstrating their divine powers, following the Buddhist model of Samudra, the monk who converts King Aśoka (Strong 1983, 73). Originally despised, he languishes in the king's prison and undergoes torture but cannot be harmed. As the *Aśokavadāna* says, the jailer

> threw Samudra into an iron cauldron full of water, human blood, marrow, urine, and excrement. He lit a great fire underneath, but even after much firewood had been consumed, the cauldron did not get hot. Once more, he tried to light the fire, but again it would not blaze. He became puzzled and, looking into the pot, he saw the monk seated there, cross-legged on a lotus. (Strong 1983, 216)

Terrified, the jailer runs to King Aśoka who, upon arriving at the prison, sees Samudra "fly up to the firmament and, wet from the water like a swan, start to display various magical feats" (Strong 1983, 216). He promptly experiences conversion and later grows into the powerful Buddhist monarch he is known as thereafter.

The very same motifs of being boiled but surviving by sitting in meditation supported by lotus blossoms are thus found in both the ancient Indian and medieval Chinese stories. Symbolizing the evil nature of the king and the unceasing power of the religion even in the most terrifying circumstances, these motifs also represent the symbolic renewal one undergoes through contact with, and acceptance of, a religious faith; they are an essential feature not only of conversion stories but also of shamanic initiations.

In Buddhism, the ordeal motifs occur also as a form of *dāna* or offerings. In one story about Aśoka, the king is not satisfied by giving up

---

[4] For a discussion of this festival, see Strong 1983, 92–95; 1990, 109–12. Banquets for the sangha were in fact performed by rulers in both India and China. The Chinese traveler Xuanzang describes one he experienced in northern India, and Emperor Wu of the Liang held one in his capital (Strong 1990, 115–16). I am indebted to John Strong for sending me his comments on this section together with a copy of his 1990 article.

his wealth, ministers, and family, but even offers himself. Preparing his body as if for cremation, he lights himself but, being deeply absorbed in his devotion to the Three Jewels, he does not burn. Even after being in the flames for an entire week he emerges unscathed from the ordeal. Here, as in the conversion stories and in shamanic initiations, the ordeal is a symbol for death and rebirth, signifying the transition from non-believer to devotee, from worldly king to saintly ruler, from novice to initiate.[5]

The conversion of the barbarians in its initial episodes thus shows Lord Lao as the pure Dao who suffers without harm and is transformed into a subduer of kings. His role in the story contrasts sharply with that of the worldly monarch, who falls short of being the ideal ruler by not supporting the religious community to his last shirt, never mind the sacrifice of his own body. Lord Lao is not only the master of the world, he is also the pure force of life—and the power of perfect enlightenment—that withstands all assault and conquers death in any form. The Dao is stronger than any suffering on earth or in hell; the Dao is eternal life and survives forever. Ostensibly about the spread of the Dao throughout western countries, the conversion story also displays the Dao's powers in all possible situations, giving solace and confidence to its believers. Joined with the Dao, everyone is invincible; with heaven at one's side, what harm can come?

Lord Lao the King

Harming the Dao with malice aforethought, on the other hand, has dire consequences. The barbarian king, despairing of the situation, surrenders to Lord Lao and wishes to learn from him. The god, however, to show that one does not cross the Dao lightly, first punishes him by sending down celestial troops that wipe out half the kingdom's population:

> Demons and spirits poured in from all the heavens. On horseback and on foot, they descended—fourteen feet tall and numbering in the millions. Wielding iron sticks in their hands, they flooded the kingdom. Every day there were more of them, with no end in sight.

---

[5] This interpretation of the events follows Strong 1990, 112. For shamanism and its initiation, see Eliade 1964. For more on rebirth and its various forms, see Eliade 1958.

> They killed the barbarians to get at their king. Growing ever more alarmed, he saw how in all of the thirty-six barbarian countries people died left and right. Throwing his head and face to the earth, he begged for mercy. He did not dare face Laozi.[6]

The king having defied the Dao faces death. Whoever turns his back on the pure power of eternal life, the story says, is bound to suffer. Only through his heartfelt, sincere repentance can he avoid this fate; only his complete surrender to the Dao and utter openness to its guidance will avert disaster.

Lord Lao, seeing the king grovel and give up even the last bit of egoistic resistance, stops the slaughter and reveals his true stature.

> He transformed into a great man of gold and diamonds, brilliantly radiating in five colors. He was sixteen feet tall and endowed with the seventy-two auspicious signs. His face and eyes glittered purple, and he could be seen floating freely in mid-air. Left he appeared and right he disappeared; up he went and down he came. This was his true body of the emptiness of the ten directions. (*Huahu jing*, *SDZN* 9.19b)

Installing Yin Xi as his representative and teacher of the barbarians, the god then proceeds to establish formal rules, which closely resemble the basic precepts and behavioral restraints of Buddhists. The barbarians must not

> plunder nests, destroy birds' eggs, or in any way harm the myriad living beings. Stealing and robbery or any assaults on the orphaned and weak are prohibited. So are cursing, reviling, sexual intercourse, drinking wine, eating meat, or uttering any slander or lie.
>
> Moreover, the barbarians are not allowed to ride in carriages or on horseback, nor must they wear shoes. When walking they must always carry a staff to startle the worms of the earth out of their way lest they harm them. (*Huahu jing*, *SDZN* 9.20ab)

In addition, Laozi orders the barbarians to wear the *kasāya* or Buddhist monk's robe, a reddish-brown garment of "five colors" that leaves the right shoulder bare, and to obtain their food by begging for it, as well as to observe a rigid schedule of obeisance and fasting.[7] Having passed on

---

[6] This story is contained first in the sixth-century *Huahu jing* (*SDZN* 9.19a), then reappears in *Hunyuan shengji* 4.10b–11a; *Tushuo*, no. 33 (Reiter 1990, 31).

[7] See *Wenshi neizhuan*, *SDZN* 9.14b; *Hunyuan shengji* 4.12b–13b. For a description of the *kasāya*, see Hurvitz 1956, 47.

this code of laws to ensure his rule in the barbarian countries, Lord Lao sets off again to spread the Dao in further regions.

In the Belaturgh Mountains, he saves the people from dangerous dragons who have taken up residence in a local lake. In the Central Asian state of Khotan, he gives precepts and teachings to the people and appears to them in his luminous divine body. In the countries of the Sakas and the Seleukids, he suppresses heretic teachings and swats away a mountain that houses a nasty wizard. In Kapilavastu, the birthplace of the Buddha, he takes the sun and the moon in his hands and creates darkness until the local king is converted and vows to abstain from killing. In Udayana, he creates the *vinaya* rules while sitting under a tree. In Magadha, he establishes the Buddhist teaching among the higher castes. In Śrāvastī, finally, he descends as the Buddha, preaches the dharma, and wins numerous followers. In addition, he extirpates all the ninety-six heretic practices (*waidao*), many of which are ascetic techniques of ancient India, like walking about naked, immolating the body, and the like.[8]

Lord Lao thus uses his divine and magical powers to extirpate all opposition and heresy. In its stead he installs a worldwide code of rules and regulations that ensures his complete supremacy. Once his power is fully established, he presides over a rather uneventful rule, then leaves Yin Xi in charge and departs without much fanfare, ascending once again into heaven. From there he reappears in different transformations and delivers revelations to the Chinese people.

Throughout, this episode shows strong Buddhist influence. Lord Lao's code of rules and regulations clearly consists of the basic moral and behavioral rules of the Buddhists, while his continued wanderings imitate the activities of the Buddha in both content and location. The clearest link on this score is established in the *Hunyuan shengji*, according to which Lord Lao lives the full life of the Buddha even after his various conversion activities (5.5a–6b; 5.11b–16a). Adopting these motifs and tales from Buddhism, the Daoist story thus shows how the god fulfills the worldwide mission of the Dao, appearing in many guises and places as the representative of the omnipotent Dao on earth.

Still, not all versions of the *Huahu jing* give all the episodes involving banquets, ordeals, and the subduing of the barbarian king. Some, such as the first chapter of the eighth-century version recovered from Dunhuang, describe Lord Lao going west and setting himself up in Khotan, where

---

[8] The latter are listed in *Youlong zhuan* 4.7b–8b. The other conversion efforts of the deity are found in *Hunyuan shengji* 4.15a–18a; *Tushuo* nos. 38–44 (Reiter 1990, 31–34).

he summons all his followers and the people of the world. Even the barbarians and their kings arrive and accept the teaching without a murmur.[9] Similarly, the eighth chapter (P. 3404) presents a lengthy dialogue between the god and the king on the correct understanding of the Dao and its efficacy for government. Here, too, the king is willing and asks ever more questions, begging Lord Lao for proper guidance. In these cases the conversion story serves less as a myth that charts the progress and power of the Dao on earth than as a framework narrative in which to present the political and moral teachings of the religion, evoking the mythical content without spelling it out in detail.

Quest and Culmination

In a wider comparative context, the conversion of the barbarians can also be linked with the story of the hero, in this case paralleling his quest and its culmination. The hero typically passes the threshold to actively pursue the destiny he now has clearly before him. He "journeys through a world of unfamiliar yet strangely intimate forces, some of which severely threaten him (tests), some of which give magical aid (helpers). When he arrives at the nadir of the mythological round, he undergoes a supreme ordeal and gains his reward" (Campbell 1949, 246). He has a sense of struggle, of forging ahead, of pushing for a goal outside himself that will provide his fullest realization (Biallas 1986, 164).

Still he meets with numerous obstacles—monsters, demons, and enemies to fight and overcome—and undergoes serious ordeals. As part of this struggle, the hero has to confront evil and death, may even be killed, dismembered, or castrated. The suffering of the hero is felt throughout the world as darkness and infertility; it shows that even with his enormous supernatural powers, evil and death are real dangers that must be actively confronted.[10]

However, the hero remains true to himself and surrenders fully to his destiny. He undergoes the ordeals and puts his faith in the divine power that upholds and supports him. Thus he passes through the danger and emerges not only unscathed but newly resurrected. Having witnessed the torments of the underworld and defeated death, he is a living example of true immortality, documenting in his own experience

---

[9] This chapter is found in S. 1857, reprinted in T. 2139, 54.1266b–67b, and translated in Kohn 1993, 73. The same version also appears in the *Youlong zhuan* (4.5a–7a).

[10] See Leeming 1973, 217; Biallas 1986, 216.

the power and mercy of the divine absolute embodied in him (Leeming 1973, 265). Like the shaman or the newly initiated, he has died, been dismembered, suffered torture, and yet has come together again. He has risen from the dead and is now a new and higher person, more powerful and stronger than before (see Eliade 1958). He can realize his true potential, show his true power to the world, and eventually rise up to heaven as the celestial being he truly is (Leeming 1973, 315). As Joseph Campbell puts it:

> The triumph may be represented as the hero's sexual union with the goddess mother of the world (sacred marriage), his recognition by the father-creator (father atonement), his own divinization (apotheosis), or again—if the powers have remained unfriendly to him—his theft of the boon he came to gain (bride-theft, fire-theft); intrinsically it is an expansion of consciousness and therewith of being (illumination, transfiguration, freedom). (1949, 246)

While Lord Lao's western exploits conform only in part to the hero pattern, it is instructive to look at them from this comparative perspective since it illuminates certain mythic elements that otherwise remain obscure. The banquet invitations, for example, initially show the hesitant yet powerful reaction of people to the Dao when it becomes manifest in the world. Their equivalent is found in hero tales when the young man is first admired for his looks and strength, and his good conduct places him above the princes and other local contenders. Only gradually and after he has been accepted as a person in his own right is his full identity revealed, but then the struggle for the throne begins. Similarly, relations between the barbarian king and the Daoist intruders are initially of a friendly and hospitable nature, manifested in mutual invitations and in an open appreciation of the foreign visitors. Only after their strange powers have become clear and unexpectedly large numbers of followers have become a burden do relations turn hostile and the ordeals begin. The banquets, clearly imitative of the Buddhist quinquennial festivals, even imitating them in their details, are thus mythologically a forum in which the hero pattern of initial friendliness and later hostility is acted out. In both cases, the turning point is the uncovering of the true identity of the key protagonists, who are found to be a great deal more powerful than originally assumed.

Next, the various ordeals the Daoists must undergo are not only the typical punishments associated with hell—again a Buddhist notion adapted in medieval Daoism—but also closely parallel the trials of the hero as he suffers death and descent to the underworld, dismemberment and utter destruction, and yet rises victorious, having proven his mettle by overcoming even death. Looked at mythologically, the ordeals symbolize the power of the Dao over key elements of the world, such as water and fire, heat and cold, human hatred and military weapons. In addition, their very severity contrasts significantly with the previous friendliness during the banquets, just as the lowly position and suffering of Lord Lao and Yin Xi during the ordeals is the exact opposite of their divine splendor and enjoyment during the banquets. The rebirth symbolism, moreover, clearly present in the hero tale and ritually enacted in shamanistic practice, links the conversion story once again with the transformations of Lord Lao, who is forever appearing in different forms and under different names, but never loses his divinity as the essence of the Dao.

Having survived the ordeals, the hero wins a decisive victory over the ruling king (Raglan 1990, 151). Lord Lao also does this, accepting the groveling monarch's apologies with hesitation, and eventually acknowledging his surrender and taking over his rule. This takeover in the classical hero story often involves marriage to the old king's daughter, symbolizing, as Alan Dundes points out, the successful union between the old rule and the new, between the male and the female (1990, 193). Lord Lao does not marry anyone; on the contrary, he even prohibits marriage among his new subjects, instituting instead the Buddhist rule of celibacy. This shows how his rule, unlike that of the hero, constitutes a complete break with the old regime, how radically different religious dispensation and saintly pursuits are from mundane rule and ordinary life.[11] Here, the hero pattern, this time by contrast, helps to reveal a deeper level of mythological meaning in the conversion story.

And finally, the reign of the newly made hero-king tends to be uneventful, the only major feature noted in the stories being his new law code. After several decades on the throne—moving on to another great rite of passage—the hero-king may lose favor and be driven from the throne, and meet with a mysterious death, often at the top of a hill (Raglan 1990, 154). Or again, as Campbell points out, he may return, blessed by divine powers and acting as their emissary (1949, 246). This ending, too, has only partial validity for the conversion of the barbarians. Like the hero, Lord Lao issues a set of new rules to his followers and leads them for a number of years. However, he is not driven out nor

---

[11] The same holds true for the careers of the other two great religious founders, the Buddha and Christ. They are also born virginally, go out to win their kingdoms, overcome an ordeal of death, and establish a radically new rule in the world that is in no way married to the old. See Pye 1979; Dundes 1990.

does he die, mysteriously or otherwise. Rather, after the mighty of the world have submitted to him fully, his departure for heaven marks the beginning of further salvific activities on behalf of all, a continued mission for the sake of humanity. Here the religious tale emphasizes the divine nature of its protagonist, who is forever highly esteemed and leaves voluntarily when his time has come. The god, unlike the hero, never dies but resides forever in heaven from where he continues to descend when humanity needs his help.

Yin Xi as Hero

The conversion of the barbarians is both the conclusion and the culmination of Lord Lao's sojourn on earth, which began with his birth, virginal and supernaturally blessed, and continued through his employment at the Zhou court and his transmission of the *Daode jing* on the pass. All three parts of the god's worldly career have elements in common with the mythical birth and quest of the hero, and the latter two parts in particular can be described as phases of the deity's quest: the threshold phase when he crosses the pass and teaches Yin Xi; and the kingship phase when he converts the western countries to the Dao. The former can be seen as a vertical effort to connect the celestial Dao with the mundane reality on earth, bringing the adept closer to the Dao. The latter may be described as a horizontal conquest of the earth, bringing wide reaches and many lands under the salvific influence of the Daoist teaching. In both, Lord Lao as the Dao is not alone but interacts and joins with Yin Xi, his primary disciple and most active follower. The quest of Lord Lao is thus also the quest of Yin Xi, and through him, of all humanity.

Seen from this angle, the first phase of the quest, set symbolically and spatially on the threshold of the pass, sees the development of Yin Xi into a true follower of the Dao. It begins with his encounter with Lord Lao, continues with his formal instruction, and ends with his full acceptance as the god's companion. The four parts of this phase—examination, dedication, transmission, and attainment—constitute the complete path of Yin Xi's Daoist realization and in exemplary form narrate the ordination process of medieval Daoists.

Only when Lord Lao leaves his homeland does he become accessible to human followers. Similarly, only when the Dao leaves its pure and empty serenity in the celestial spheres can it be encountered, transmitted, learned, and perfected on earth. The threshold imagery of this phase of the sage's quest is symbolic of the situation facing all active Daoists and the necessary condition for the transmission of one of its central texts, the *Daode jing*. The openness between the worlds provides the framework for each individual's pursuit of the Dao. Lord Lao in this phase is the Dao, the master, the preceptor, and the chief of ordination.

Still, although he dominates the setting and is the center around which the narrative develops, the real hero of this part of the story is Yin Xi, the disciple. Undaunted by the Dao's efforts at concealment, passing one test after another—even willing to decapitate his family—Yin Xi pushes forward, pleads with the Dao and pursues it, and eventually attains acceptance. Dedicating himself fully to selfless service and showing compassion and understanding for the weakness of others, he proves himself worthy of the deity's teaching. He obeys all instructions, gives up his worldly career, and learns whatever there is to learn. Yin Xi never allows himself to be distracted from his goal even when the Dao leaves him on his own to find perfection. Instead, he patiently and persistently follows the set path. He is there at the appointed place and the appointed time, and even then, though he does not find the Dao immediately, he persists and ultimately succeeds.

Yin Xi is the key protagonist of this phase as he searches for the Dao, pursuing it without hesitating for an instant and eventually attaining full realization. The texts that focus on him recognize this fact and provide him with the signs of the true hero: supernatural birth, wondrous signs, and unusual childhood abilities, just as the hagiographies do for the deity. Lord Lao's crossing the threshold of the pass, one phase in the heroic quest for the Dao, is therefore Yin Xi's chance to grow, the prime opportunity to pursue his own quest and become a hero in his own right. As both sages travel to their meeting place in Sichuan, their quests begin to merge. The black sheep shop accordingly becomes the starting point for the conquest of both their kingdoms.

Once they have set off for the lands of the barbarians, both sages are equally involved. Although Lord Lao takes the lead and is often the main spokesman of the Dao, Yin Xi is always at his side and becomes king in his own right when the god passes governance on to him. Lord Lao, this story says, guides and issues rules and may even govern for a time, but he will not stay. In this worldly manifestation, the Dao is ongoing, changing continuously, forever moving—rising to heaven or traveling to new places on earth. If its active consolidating power is to remain, it must be realized in a human representative, a person of perfect Daoist stature who is at the same time the true ruler of the state.

Thus Lord Lao, after winning the kingdom and setting up his law, does not entrust the government to the barbarian king, however devout he may be. Just believing in the Dao, the story says, is not sufficient to be a ruler among men; to rise that high, one must be perfected in the Dao. Thus Yin Xi, the fully perfected Daoist, takes over the government. Doing so, he mediates between the pure, otherworldly Dao represented by Lord Lao, who has conquered but cannot stay, and the defiled existence in the world represented by the barbarian king, who is converted but cannot rule. Expanding this image mythologically, Yin Xi becomes the ideal human being, the true *Mensch* who stands between gross material nature and the celestial purity of the Dao. Overcoming the former by following the latter, Yin Xi attains the earth as his true kingdom and becomes ruler in place of Lord Lao. He lives with and refines the gross, uncouth, material aspects of mundane existence while at the same time incorporating and representing the pure celestial being of the Dao.

13

Revelations of the Dao

After the successful conclusion of his conversion of the world, Lord Lao ascends again to heaven; from there he continues to return to China in new transformations. By teaching and revealing the Dao to various historical and legendary figures, he shapes the development of Chinese culture as he travels extensively through heaven and on earth and supervises the immortal administration. Since these activities are given precise dates in the hagiographies—dates that coincide with generally accepted historical events, such as the political upheaval under King You of Zhou or Confucius' meeting with Lao Dan (see Table 19)—a particularly Daoist vision of Chinese history emerges. This typically takes historically held worldviews and reinterprets them as worldly manifestations of the Dao; it makes historical thinkers and founders into recipients of Lord Lao's grace and adds tales in which legendary personages play a role in the establishment and legitimization of major Daoist institutions. Through this combination of accepted fact, religious legend, and Daoist doctrine, the myth creates a powerful vision of history as the purposeful manifestation of the deity's teachings.

The *Youlong zhuan* devotes six entire sections to the revelations of Lord Lao in Chinese history.[1] The *Hunyuan shengji* details the same revelations in its sixth and seventh scrolls (6.12b–24b; 7.1a–42b), but also adds accounts of a number of lesser Daoist sages (such as Gengsang Chu and Yangzi Ju from the *Zhuangzi*) and major patriarchs (such as the Mao brothers) as recipients of Lord Lao's inspiration. Both texts describe how the god appeared as:

---

[1] These sections are: "Explaining the Rites to Confucius" (sect. 22, 4.9b); "Appearing as the Master on the River" (23, 4.16a); "Giving the *Taiping jing* to Gan Ji" (24, 4.17b–19a); "Delivering the Celestial Masters under the Han" (25, 5.1a); "Revealing Rites to Ge Xuan" (26, 5.7a); "Bestowing a Daoist Title on the Wei Emperor [through Kou Qianzhi]" (27, 5.9a–10b).

—Lao Dan to Confucius around 500 B.C.E.;
—Heshang gong to the Han Emperor Wen in 160 B.C.E.; Dongfang Shuo to Emperor Wu about 100 B.C.E.; Lord Lao to Emperor Huan in 165 C.E.;
—the Yellow Venerable Lord to Gan Ji, the founder of the Great Peace movement around the beginning of the Common Era;
—Lord Lao to Zhang Daoling, the first Celestial Master, in 142;
—Lord Lao to Ge Xuan, the legendary originator of the Numinous Treasure school, around the year 200;
—Lord Lao once again to Kou Qianzhi, the new Celestial Master under the Northern Wei, in 415 and 423.

All of these, to the believer, are revelations in which Lord Lao in different forms descends from his heavenly abode to present a suitable form of the Daoist teaching to an influential person of the time. As times change, so do the teachings, so that the instances of revelation covered in this chapter can be divided into three distinct types: philosophical, millenarian, and salvational.

Table 19
Lord Lao's travels and revelations after the conversion

Date (B.C.E.)	Location/Event
994 (Mu 4)	At Fusang tree: holding an assembly of immortals
895 (Yi 1)	Mianzhu (Sichuan): revelation to Li Zhenduo
860 (Li 21)	Louguan: revelation to Song Lun
784 (Xuan 43)	Near River Wei: prophecy of Zhou decline under King You
781 (You 2)	Great earthquake: prophecy coming true
743 (Ping 23)	Second western journey and conversion
502 (Jing 17)	Zhou capital: meeting with Confucius as Lao Dan
425 (Weilie 2)	Qin capital: prophecy as Historiographer Dan
360 (Xian 8)	At Fusang tree: holding an assembly of immortals
305 (Nan 9)	Kunlun: residence in Purple Tenuity; temples erected by Duke Zhao of Qin
218 (Qin dyn. 28)	Mount Tai: supporting Feng and Shan sacrifices; shrine to Lord Lao in Louguan
179 (Han Wendi 1)	Yellow River: presenting Heshang gong commentary to Emperor Wen

Source: Hunyuan shengji 1.24a–34b; also in Laojun nianpu yaolüe (Chronology of Lord Lao, DZ 771)

The first set of revelations is of a philosophical nature. Here Lord Lao reveals theoretical insights into the Dao to a leading thinker, to Confucius, or to a philosophically engaged emperor, such as Emperor Wen of the Han. In either case his teaching has an impact on the government of the time. It encourages the ruler to act with nonaction and in harmony with the Dao and at the same time dazzles the worldly partner, a humble seeker of divine inspiration, with the splendor of the Dao. The next set describes Lord Lao as a messianic god who appears in ecstatic trances to Gan Ji and Zhang Daoling, the founders of the first two Daoist movements. Matching his own divinity, Lord Lao's earthly partner is no longer merely a seeker, but an active religious leader and practitioner of meditation, alchemy, and immortality techniques. Rather than helping to shape the existing political order of the world, these revelations of the Dao propose complete renewal in a millennium of Great Peace and spur the organization of religious cults. The last set of revelations shows Lord Lao as a benevolent deity who descends to earth out of concern for the salvation of humanity. Providing more detailed rules and instructions to the adepts Ge Xuan and Kou Qianzi, he reforms existing religious communities with the goal of making them a model for the state and thus transforming the entire world into an empire of the Dao.

In its presentation of these revelations of the god and their various teachings, the *Youlong zhuan* transforms Chinese history into a purposeful development caused and guided by the Dao. No longer considered isolated events in a series of arbitrary or accidental occurrences, certain philosophies, millennial movements, and organized Daoist schools become part of the intelligent and intentional push of the Dao toward salvation. The text thus describes Chinese religious history as a series of sacred events, standing the traditional historiographic vision on its head. Rather than the cyclical Mandate of Heaven model, in which a new dynasty inevitably follows the path of its predecessors toward decline and destruction, it proposes a linear and progressive evolution of the Dao on earth.

Confucius and the Han Emperors

The meeting of Lao Dan and Confucius is, as described earlier, the key scenario in the legend surrounding the ancient philosopher and alleged author of the *Daode jing*. At first, among students of the Confucian school, it illustrated the untiring efforts of the Master in his search for knowledge; among Daoists it showed the elevated stature of the thinker Lao Dan. In the religious vision, however, it points to the divinity of Lord Lao who, although present in the midst of humanity, is an agent of the sacred and bringer of immortal wisdom to Confucius who then figures as one of his prophets.

In presenting these events, the Song hagiographies cite four ancient sources: *Kongzi jiayu* (ch. 11), *Shiji* (ch. 63), *Zhuangzi*, and *Liezi* (ch. 4).[2] The first, in accordance with Confucian doctrine, shows Confucius' insatiable hunger for learning by telling how he travels to Lao Dan, from whom he receives the advice that "only one who is without greed can be like a son to others; only one who is without evil can be a true minister to his ruler" (11.1b). This tallies with the story in Laozi's biography in the *Shiji* where, as already mentioned, Lao Dan tells Confucius to let go of his "prideful airs and manifold desires," encouraging him to embrace the Daoist virtues of humility and tranquility. This, in turn, follows the original tale in the *Zhuangzi*, in which Lao Dan says:

> He who takes wealth to be good is unable to let go of his income; whoever takes worldly fame to be good is unable to let go of his good name; and whoever takes political influence to be good is unable to pass his rule on to others. Grasping these things tightly, people are filled with anxiety. Forced to give them up, they are utterly inconsolable. Never once do they look in the mirror to examine themselves or stop to think. They are people condemned by heaven. (ch. 14; see also Watson 1968, 162)

The message in all these versions, as well as in the other variants contained in the *Zhuangzi*, is basically the same: Lao Dan encourages Confucius to be more of a Daoist, to partake in the purity of heaven and earth, and to let go of worldly involvement. Confucius is suitably awed and develops great admiration, and even veneration, for the god. This veneration is clearest in the *Liezi*, according to which the chief minister of the Shang presses Confucius to name a sage. After some evasion,

> Confucius grew impatient and changed color. He said nothing for a moment. "Among the people of the western lands," he answered at last, "there is a sage. He does not actively rule, and yet there is no disorder. He does not actively teach, and yet there is faith in him. He does not actively transform things, and yet there is progress. He is so magnificent—people do not have a proper name for him. Still, I am not sure that he is a sage. Really, whether he truly is a sage or not, I cannot tell."[3]

---

[2] The *Kongzi jiayu* dates from the third century C.E. and takes up the earliest reference to the story from the *Lüshi chunqiu* (9.4; 17.8). It also appears in the Confucian works *Zengzi wen* and *Shuoyuan* (Garden of Stories; Graham 1990, 112). The *Shiji* was discussed earlier (see ch. 1). In the *Zhuangzi*, the story appears seven times 30/12/41–45, 35/13/45–53, 38/14/44–56, 39/14/56–60, 39/14/74–82, 55/21/24–38, 58/22/28–43. For the *Liezi* version, see below.

[3] *Liezi* 4.4b–5a. See also Graham 1960, 78. The story also appears in *Youlong zhuan* 4.15b–16a; *Hunyuan shengji* 6.23b.

This story, sometimes interpreted as showing Buddhist influence on the reconstituted *Liezi*, links Confucius with the cosmic Laozi after his conversion of the western countries. Presented as part of the encounter with Confucius in the Song hagiographies, it raises the meeting to a revelation. Lao Dan is no mere archivist and Confucius is not simply a seeker. Lao Dan is Laozi and therefore Lord Lao and the personified Dao; as such he does not teach, he reveals. Confucius is the honored master of the Confucian school and the leading thinker of China in this phase of history; as such he does not learn for himself, but only transmits the words of the divine Dao. The meeting thus becomes a revelation whose teachings match the need of the historical period in their advice of simplicity and humility. It raises the leading philosopher to a worldly representative of the Dao, which at this time is primarily concerned with transforming society toward greater harmony, using principles such as spontaneity, nonaction, and freedom from desires.

A similar match with contemporary thinking emerges in Lord Lao's second revelation. In it he appears as Heshang gong before the Han Emperor Wen (r. 179–156), hovering magically in mid-air, then floating down to earth to present the governmental teachings of Huang-Lao as they are contained in the Heshang gong commentary to the *Daode jing*.[4] Historically, this commentary was compiled only in the second century C.E., but both the legend and many of its teachings go back to the early Han, when the Huang-Lao master Yue Jugong, also known as Master Anqiu, propagated the political theories he learned from a certain legendary figure, known only as the Elder on the River (Chan 1991, 94; Kusuyama 1979, 6). Mythologically, the story shows that worldly rule can only prosper with the help of the Dao and that the way of the world is ultimately directed by the divine. History in its course is meant to be, and the ideal ruler accepts this and arranges his government accordingly. Just as Confucius learns that the individual has no power over the flow of life and death and must find his place by moving smoothly along with it, so Emperor Wen comes to understand that the political and social development of the empire are nothing in and of themselves but must fit in with the cosmic rhythm of the Dao.

---

[4] These teachings involve the practice of self-cultivation as the key to perfect government. See Peerenboom 1991; Chan 1991; Major 1993. The Heshang gong legend is first recorded in the *Shenxian zhuan* (Güntsch 1988, 93; Chan 1991, 90). In the Song, it appears in *Youlong zhuan* 4.16b–17a; *Hunyuan shengji* 7.4a. On the date of the commentary, see Kusuyama 1979, 18 and 160; Kobayashi 1990; Chan 1991, 108.

The Song hagiographies drive home this point by additionally identifying Lord Lao with Dongfang Shuo, the trickster and magical adviser of Emperor Wu of the Han (r. 140–87 B.C.E.), who tells the emperor about the true scope and amazing marvels of the universe.[5] They further detail the Daoist aspirations of this emperor by stating that the Highest Lord Lao

> sent down the Queen Mother of the West and the Lady of Highest Prime [Shangyuan furen] to bestow upon the emperor five silver statues with the explanation that they are the likeness of the Venerable Lord. The two emissaries were also to give the emperor the *Shangqing jing* [Scripture of the Realm of Highest Clarity] and the *Wuyue zhenxing tu* [Chart of the True Shape of the Five Sacred Mountains]. (*Youlong zhuan* 4.17a; *Hunyuan shengji* 7.5b)

This account integrates the stories of Emperor Wu's divine contacts that appear in the *Han Wudi neizhuan* (Essential Biography of Han Emperor Wu, DZ 293), according to which the emperor is given much divine help but in the end fails to achieve immortality.[6] Merging this text with Lord Lao's hagiography, the Song works change the story again to make the ruler into a successful Daoist monarch who has the revealed images formally installed for worship and who, like the Yellow Emperor before him, proceeds to found Daoist institutions in over thirty locations.

After visiting Emperor Wu, according to the *Youlong zhuan*, Lord Lao appears again to an emperor, but this time in a dream, to instruct him to renew the active sacrifices at Bozhou (4.17b). This account integrates Emperor Huan's sacrifice to Laozi in 165 C.E., a well-known historical event documented in the *Laozi ming*, into the mythical exploits of the god. By making the sacrifice an event instigated by the deity—in imitation of Emperor Ming's dream of the Buddha in 50 C.E., which marks the official introduction of Buddhism to China[7]—the myth again raises the reign of an emperor to a supernatural level and gives it the formal sanction of the Dao.

In these stories, both official doctrines and imperial politics of the Han dynasty are transformed into manifestations of the Dao. The Dao

---

[5] *Youlong zhuan* 4.17a. Dongfang Shuo has various biographies (Kaltenmark 1953, 137; Giles 1948, 47–51). In Daoist sources, he appears as an adviser of Emperor Wu (*Han Wudi waizhuan* [Outer Biography of the Han Emperor Wu], DZ 293; see Smith 1992), to whom he describes the world of the immortals (*Shizhou ji* [Record of the Ten Continents], DZ 598; see Smith 1990).

[6] For translations and studies, see Schipper 1965; Smith 1992; Cahill 1993.

[7] For more on this story, see Zürcher 1959, 22; Ch'en 1964, 29–31; Tsukamoto and Hurvitz 1985, 41–50.

uses different semblances to make the best course of history known to humankind. Lord Lao may appear as a hermit who teaches Daoist ideas to an emperor, as a celestial who orders a goddess to descend with sacred scriptures and divine talismans, or in a dream that points the ruler in the right direction. The revelations at this stage, although still philosophical in content, are highly religious in style. Lord Lao is no longer a human philosopher, however insightful, but a divine essence. As the status of the god rises and the means of revelation widens, the addressees become higher in rank—no longer mere philosophers, they include emperors who become divine kings of the Dao.

Gan Ji and Zhang Daoling

In his second set of revelations, Lord Lao brings a new vision of the Dao to the ecstatic seekers Gan Ji and Zhang Daoling, who in turn become the founders of the schools of Great Peace and the Celestial Masters. The first such manifestation of the deity, according to the Song hagiographies, involved the revelation of the *Taiping jing* under Emperor Cheng of the Former Han (r. 28–25 B.C.E.; see Fig. 17). At this time,

> Chaos Prime [Lord Lao] split off a bodily form and descended to wander in Langye, where he bestowed the *Taiping jing* in 170 scrolls to Gan Ji.
> Its central teaching is that human life is endowed by heaven with spirit, by earth with essence, and by the center with energy. If people preserve essence, love spirit, and harbor energy, their bodies live long and the world reaches Great Peace. (*Youlong zhuan* 4.17b–18a; *Hunyuan shengji* 7.16a–17a)

This recounts the orthodox understanding of the first appearance of the *Taiping jing*, an event that cannot be corroborated from historical sources.[8] However, it does describe correctly the ideology of the early movements, which saw their activity as conducive to achieving a state of Great Peace, defined as an openness and harmony between heaven, earth, and humanity, and developed in continuation of Han dynasty Huang-Lao thought (Kaltenmark 1979, 21).

---

[8] Its recipient Gan Ji is an entirely legendary figure (see Maeda 1985a; Petersen 1989, 169), while the text itself was submitted to the throne in the second century, then destroyed during the Yellow Turban rebellion and reconstituted in 572 by Zhou Zhixiang. See Boardman 1962; Kandel 1979; Mansvelt-Beck 1980; Seidel 1983, 335–37; Petersen 1989; 1992; Robinet 1997, 70–71; Bokenkamp 1997, 32–34. A current edition is found in DZ 1101 and Wang 1960.

Fig. 17. Lord Lao wanders in Langye and bestows the *Taiping jing* on Gan Ji.
Source: Laojun bashiyi hua tushuo, no. 56

In contrast to the historical view of the *Taiping jing*, the hagiographies expand the account of its transmission, reporting a second descent of the deity in 85 C.E. At this time,

> Laozi again passed Langye and gave Gan Ji the 180 precepts of the Dao, which were to help the libationers [community leaders] preserve their bodies and cultivate perfection.
>
> "The sages and worthies of old," Laozi told him, "all followed these precepts to attain the Dao. The Dao originally had no precepts, but by following these as your teacher you can realize it. The Dao must never be lost; the teacher must never be taken lightly." (*Youlong zhuan* 4.18a; also *Hunyuan shengji* 7.18b–19a)

These 180 precepts are today found in a text of the southern Celestial Masters dated to the fourth century and linked by its later preface to Gan Ji and the *Taiping jing*.[9] Although these rules appear later historically, the myth places them at the first appearance of the *Taiping jing*, albeit in the second stage of its revelation, and marks them as the means to strengthen the growing Daoist community. Moving still further to encompass the Chinese state as a whole, the myth as formulated in the *Youlong zhuan* records a third stage of this revelation. In it Lord Lao descends again in the early second century and orders Gong Chong to present the *Taiping jing* and its precepts formally to Emperor Xun (r. 126–144). This event, noted also in historical sources, is one of the earliest official mentions of the text.

Lord Lao's revelation of the *Taiping jing*, his first appearance as messianic savior, thus evolves in three steps: first, in the transmission of a sacred text to a chosen master who assembles a small group of followers; second, about a century later, as instruction for the group in moral and behavioral rules to intensify community cohesion; third, after another fifty years, as the order to present the model to the ruler in order to reform the empire at large. The revelation as a whole thus expands the vision of the Daoist *oikumene* from individual instruction through community organization to the government of all China. Its goal is to spread the path of perfection throughout the country and raise the Chinese world as a whole to a celestial level.

This goal, however, is only partly accomplished by the *Taiping jing*, which turns out to be a difficult scripture to follow and meets massive resistance from the unenlightened Han rulers. As a result, the deity soon reappears in another part of the empire to give a similar revelation to

---

[9] The text is the *Laojun shuo yibai bashi jie*. For a discussion, see chapter 4 above.

Zhang Daoling, one that also proceeds in several stages and presents detailed guidelines for the practice of the Dao.

Zhang Daoling, as described in the Song hagiographies, is a disappointed literatus who withdraws to Mount Gaosong, the central of the five sacred mountains, to meditate and concoct an elixir of immortality. There, in 93 C.E., Lord Lao presents him with a first revelation by sending a "spirit personage" to transmit the *Huangdi jiuding danshu* (Book of the Yellow Emperor's Nine Tripod Elixir, DZ 885) and the *Wuyue zhenxing tu* (DZ 1223).[10] Following these texts' instructions, Zhang refines himself and attains a high level of purity in the Dao. To procure optimal conditions for his elixir, he later proceeds to Mount Heming in Sichuan where he successfully produces the divine drug. Instead of taking the final step, however, he decides not to ascend. As he explains to his disciple Wang Chang, he has no right to do so unless he first serves the state and helps the people.[11]

Lord Lao, moved by this selfless attitude, responds by granting him a second revelation which, according to the myth, occurs sometime in the 120s. He sends down the Jade Maiden of Purity and Harmony (Qinghe yunü) to instruct Zhang in breathing and energy exercises. Practicing faithfully for one thousand days—the standard three years—Zhang attains such powers that he can see his bodily organs within and control the myriad spirits without. He is thus enabled to cure diseases, harmonize the seven planets, and control nasty demons. Helping people with these powers, he assembles a first group of followers. In addition, he takes a first dose of the elixir to become a highly potent member of the spirit world (*Youlong zhuan* 5.2a; *Hunyuan shengji* 7.23b).

This success results in Lord Lao's first personal descent, recounted in a story dated to the summer solstice of 142 C.E. This date matches the official date of the founding of the Celestial Masters. Zhang, sitting in deep meditation in a mountain cave, sees the god "descend in the company of a thousand chariots and a myriad horsemen, riding in a golden carriage covered by a canopy of feathers and drawn by a team of four dragons and four tigers, and accompanied by an entourage numerous

---

[10] On the role of these two texts in Daoist history, see Pregadio 1991; Schipper 1967.

[11] *Youlong zhuan* 5.1b; *Hunyuan shengji* 7.22b. The account integrates descriptions of Zhang Daoling as a Daoist faith-healer and community leader (*Hanshu* 65; *Sanguo zhi* [Record of the Three Kingdoms] 8), as a practitioner of immortality (*Shenxian zhuan* 4; *YJQQ* 109.19a), and as the first Celestial Master (*Han Tianshi shijia* [Geneaology of the Han Celestial Masters], DZ 1463, 2.1b; *Zhenxian tongjian* 18.1a–4a; *Soushen ji*, DZ 1746, 2.12b–13a). For a study of his legend, see Imbault-Huart 1884. See also Bokenkamp 1997, 34.

beyond count." The god establishes the formal covenant of Orthodox Unity and transmits a series of sacred scriptures to Zhang, who from then on is known as the first Celestial Master. By venerating the scriptures, Zhang attains eternal life; for making the right efforts, he is invited on an ecstatic journey with the god. "The Highest Lord riding in a cloudy dragon chariot with Zhang on a white crane," they reach heaven where Lord Lao is seated on a jade throne while Zhang kneels at his feet to receive the highest teachings (*Youlong zhuan* 5.2ab; *Hunyuan shengji* 7.23b–24a).

This successful encounter is followed by another revelation first recorded in the *Nandou duren jing* (Scripture of Salvation with the Help of the Southern Dipper, DZ 624), a tenth-century text on spells and talismans of the Southern Dipper.[12] The hagiographies, absorbing this tradition, describe how Lord Lao descends in 144 (on the fifteenth day of the tenth month) to present Zhang with scriptural instructions for the establishment of a formal ritual cycle, and again one last time in 155 (on the seventh day of the first month) to take him to Mount Kunlun where he feasts him for three days, then gives him orders to vanquish the demonic Six Heavens, make the country prosperous, and give it peace (*Youlong zhuan* 5.3ab; *Hunyuan shengji* 7.24b).

According to the Laozi myth, the revelations to Zhang Daoling are responsible not only for the organization of the community and parishes of Orthodox Unity Daoism as historically documented in the early period, but also for the annual purification schedule, established much later and under Buddhist influence.[13] Having established all these successfully, Zhang decides to ascend, departing in 157 (on the ninth day of the ninth month) from the Yuntai guan (Cloud Terrace Monastery) in Liangzhou. The heavenly host awaits him with a formal entourage and a dragon chariot. His son and grandson, Zhang Heng and Zhang Lu, continue his good work (*Youlong zhuan* 5.5b; *Hunyuan shengji* 7.25a).

These revelations of Lord Lao again occur through a sequence of appearances to a senior Daoist master who is first trained to perfect the Dao himself, then guided to establish its harmony among a growing group of followers. Its stages show (1) how the god becomes more and more personally involved—from sending an anonymous envoy to feasting Zhang on Mount Kunlun; (2) how his message becomes more practical—from scriptures through rules to ritual instructions; and (3) how his benefits

---

[12] For a discussion of this and related texts, see chapter 4 above.

[13] On the early communities, see Stein 1963; Ōfuchi 1985; 1985a; for the ritual calendar, see Soymié 1977.

spread ever farther—from Zhang's individual perfection to peace in the world. His cause is urgent because the current cosmic cycle is drawing to a close and the salvation of humanity through the Dao must happen in the here and now before the decline advances much further. Zhang Daoling, depicted as a selfless servant of humanity and the divine, is the vehicle through which Lord Lao sets up precepts and purifications as measures against impending disaster. Here again, events in Chinese history are reinterpreted to allow for a purposeful intervention of the Dao. Instead of unfolding spontaneously, they reveal Lord Lao's well-directed effort to turn all of China into a divine community.

Ge Xuan and Kou Qianzhi

The last two medieval revelations also work toward this end, deepening and widening the divine community on earth. They provide the more sophisticated forms of Daoist practice found in the Numinous Treasure scriptures, open a road to the heavens in the ecstatic excursions of the Highest Clarity school, and lead to the establishment of the theocracy under the Northern Wei.

In structure, these revelations conform to the pattern described above. Their recipients, Ge Xuan and Kou Qianzhi, each practice various Daoist arts and establish themselves as recluses on a sacred mountain. Over several occasions of divine descent, they are granted scriptures and instructions that will bring the world closer to Great Peace. Both then proceed to transmit their teachings, establishing religious organizations and bringing the new revelations to the attention of their rulers. Lord Lao's continued efforts to save the world in the purity of the Dao result in further practical measures of harmony on earth.

According to the Song hagiographies, Ge Xuan was born in 164 C.E. (on the eighth day of the fourth month, the Buddha's birthday) and showed himself an eager Daoist from an early age. Meditating in solitude on Mount Tiantai, he was visited by Lord Lao and saw the deity "enveloped by a bright halo and riding in a jade carriage of the Eight Luminants covered with a jeweled canopy" (*Youlong zhuan* 5.8a; *Hunyuan shengji* 7.28b). On the festival of Upper Prime (the seventh of the first month) in the year 179, Ge Xuan received the complete Numinous Treasure scriptures in thirty-six scrolls from the deity, together with a number of essential Highest Clarity materials, again in thirty-six scrolls.

Encouraged by this vision, Ge Xuan subsequently established a new set of methods linked with both groups of texts. The Highest Clarity methods include ecstatic excursions to the otherworld, an individual form of purification (*zhai*), and formal community rituals to support ancestors and the family. Numinous Treasure methods consist of various communal purifications, including the Golden Register and Mud and Ashes ceremonies (*Youlong zhuan* 5.8a; *Hunyuan shengji* 7.29a). Having established these, Ge Xuan is granted the celestial title "Immortal Lord of Great Ultimate on the Left" (Taiji zuo xiangong) in 238; then in 244, he ascends to take his proper place in the hierarchy above (*Youlong zhuan* 5.8b; *Hunyuan shengji* 7.30b).

This account turns history on its head. Neither the Numinous Treasure scriptures nor those of the Highest Clarity school go back to Ge Xuan, an immortality seeker and alchemist of around 200 C.E., who is first mentioned in the works of his grandnephew Ge Hong. He was styled an early recipient of Numinous Treasure scriptures only in the late fourth century by his descendant Ge Chaofu, the compiler of the first text of this school. As the Numinous Treasure school came to flourish in the fifth century, Ge Xuan's status rose among the celestials, and he duly became the leading supernatural figure of one of its major branches. As for the Highest Clarity doctrines, they originated in a series of revelations from various divine figures to the medium Yang Xi in the 360s, and had nothing to do with either Lord Lao or Ge Xuan.[14]

Although the myth correctly describes the teachings associated with the two schools, by linking them with a single recipient and a single divine source, it proposes a degree of doctrinal integration that never existed in history. At the same time, by placing the teachings around 200 C.E., the myth implicitly establishes their priority vis-à-vis Buddhism, whose practices in historical fact played a key role in shaping Numinous Treasure doctrine and ritual (see Zürcher 1980). Its massive downplaying of the Highest Clarity scriptures also reflects the restructuring of Daoism in the Song, when this school lost its leading role and a greater emphasis was placed on ritual and magic rather than on personal ecstatic excursions. In accordance with its aim to show Lord Lao's impact on the growth of Daoist life on earth, the myth thus concentrates more on the communal organization of the religious life than on the advanced spiritual practices of Daoism as undertaken by Highest Clarity adherents.

---

[14] For Ge Xuan's legend, see *Shenxian zhuan* (ch. 7; Güntsch 1988, 223); *Baopuzi* (DZ 1185; chs. 4, 6, 8; Ware 1966). Later accounts are found in *Zhenxian tongjian* 23.1a and in the *Taiji Ge Xuan gong zhuan* (Biography of Ge Xuan, Lord of the Great Ultimate, DZ 450) of the year 1246. On the development of the Numinous Treasure scriptures, see Ōfuchi 1974; Bokenkamp 1983; Kobayashi 1990. For an early history of the Highest Clarity tradition, see Strickmann 1978; 1981; Robinet 1984.

The same basic principle holds true for Lord Lao's sixth revelation, presented to Kou Qianzhi in the early fifth century. But there the account is much closer to historical sources, especially the *Weishu*. According to that work, Kou Qianzhi was a recluse on Mount Gaosong, where he was visited by Lord Lao in 415. First he saw two immortal lads who announced the impending arrival of the god. Then the god himself descended to tell Kou that he had been chosen as the new Celestial Master and revealed to him a set of precepts commonly known as the "New Code."[15] The Song hagiographies summarize the long speech given by the deity in the *Weishu* but split the revelation into two occasions—one in 415, the other in 417—and the precepts into two texts: a nine-scroll work transmitted first, and the "New Code" bestowed second (*Youlong zhuan* 5.9b; *Hunyuan shengji* 7.38b). They concur with the *Weishu* again with regard to Kou's other major revelation, recorded in the year 423. At this time Lord Lao sent a divine messenger to give Kou four registers with detailed ritual instructions, a divine robe, the formal title "True Lord of Great Peace," and six pieces of divine fruit that convey magical powers. He also deputed twelve jade maidens to teach Kou essential longevity techniques that would ready him to present his dispensation at court and become the official leader of Daoism.[16]

According to historical sources, Kou Qianzhi did indeed experience a divine revelation on the mountain and went to the capital in 424, where he found favor with the Toba Emperor Shizu. Supported by the official Cui Hao, he established a formal Daoist theocracy, had Daoist institutions set up all over the country, and organized monthly community banquets for the people. Cui in the meantime rose to prime minister and became very influential at court. The theocracy reached its peak in 439, when the emperor became an ordained Daoist and chose the reign title True Lord of Great Peace (440–451), claiming the fulfillment of earlier wishes and prophecies. It declined with Kou's death in 448 and ended with the execution of Cui Hao in 450 (Mather 1979, 116–20).

In the myth, on the other hand, the revelations to Ge Xuan and Kou Qianzhi follow the standard pattern already established with Zhang Daoling. Set on a sacred mountain, in a cosmic power spot that can "receive energy from a universal source and transform it to planetary requirements" (Thompson 1990, 181), it begins with the appearance of the deity's messenger, followed by his first personal descent and the transmission of scriptures and precepts in a formal ceremony that

---

[15] They are today contained in the *Laojun yinsong jiejing*. Refer to discussion in chapter 4.

[16] *Weishu* 114; Ware 1933, 233; *Youlong zhuan* 5.9b; *Hunyuan shengji* 7.39b.

resembles Daoist ordination on earth. Next, the adept practices as ordered and is rewarded with a second and even a third revelation of texts, instructions, and immortality techniques. Thus empowered, the Daoist descends from his power spot—as the deity descended from heaven—and transmits his teachings to the community, establishing formal organizations that are simultaneously religious and political. The transformation of the people's daily lives through purification ceremonies and precepts coincides with their salvation in the Dao. The farther this transformation spreads, the more the world approaches the ideal state of Great Peace.

Time and Revelation

Altogether, Lord Lao's six revelations as presented in the Song hagiographies show the continuous progress of the Dao through its realization on earth. First addressing only a single philosopher, however influential, the Dao moves on to communicate with several Han emperors, then appears to religious leaders of various generations. Through its activities it creates first a single localized religious community, then a religious organization that spans the country, and finally a full-fledged, government-sponsored theocracy. The history of Chinese thought and religious organization, according to this vision, is transformed into the systematically widening presence of the Dao on earth.

Rewriting Chinese history in this way, the *Youlong zhuan* also departs from the dominant mode of Chinese historical thinking, where moral, social, and historical patterns of linearity exist but remain secondary to the cyclical vision of rising and falling dynasties, rituals, and the seasons.[17] The Daoist vision, unlike its mainstream counterpart, sees time as predominantly linear and places cyclicality in a lesser position. Lord Lao appears and reappears with regularity, the ritual schedule of the Dao adapts to the seasons, and much of Daoist practice focuses on the alignment of body and mind to the phases of yin and yang. Nevertheless, just as the original realm of the Dao exists before the world with its natural cycles comes into being, so the ultimate activity and purpose of its representative on earth is beyond the rhythms of ordinary existence. The cyclical patterns of life serve the Dao with its higher, linear sense of purpose, and not vice versa as in mainstream thought, where linear

---

[17] On the cyclical nature of time in China, see Sivin 1986; Wilhelm 1952. For more on its representation in mainstream myth, see Chen 1992. On modes of linearity, see Needham 1969.

interpretations and developments enhance cyclicality and ultimately aim at recovering harmony in cosmic cycles.

The Daoist myth thus presents an alternative vision to mainstream understanding although both are rooted in elementary temporal tensions created by the cyclicality of nature and the linear unfolding of human life and history. This tension is resolved through the cyclical vision in mainstream myth, which sees linearity as a form of alienation and wishes humanity to return to its natural home in the rhythms of cosmic harmony (Chen 1992, 124). The Daoist myth, in contrast, prefers the linear mode and envisions perfection as the ultimate realization of the Dao on earth and the complete transformation of the mundane into the divine, the natural into the heavenly.

This Daoist preference also goes hand in hand with the use of supernatural revelation as the key vehicle of the deity's presence in the world. Revelation, by general definition, is the unveiling of something mysterious and eternally hidden. It is at root irrational and, as Paul Tillich says, imparts "only what essentially is concealed and accessible by no mode of knowledge whatsoever."[18] This unveiling of the hidden is then accomplished through action, mediated by a proper time and place, and delivered via a sacred object or a sacred person (Leeuw 1938, 566).

Revelation can be either natural or supernatural. The former takes nature as the key to understanding life's mysteries and finds the sacred in the cyclicality and wondrous manifestations of the universe itself. Here nature is the visible manifestation of power, the "living garment of God," and through its cycles people can "think about the finitude of the world and our own existence and come thereby to know something of God's wisdom and creative power."[19]

Supernatural revelation, in contrast, sees the cause of nature and the world in an agent wholly other. According to this view, nature "is not our mother: Nature is our sister. We can be proud of her beauty, since we have the same father; but she has no authority over us" (Leeuw 1938, 576). Human beings, and particularly those to whom a deity reveals itself through signs, thereby become the special agents of that deity, the "chosen people." Through supernatural revelation, typically including clear directives such as prophecies about the future, codes for religious communities, and behavioral instructions, the deity enters into a covenant with humanity and gives history a particular purpose. Thus it

---

[18] Tillich 1927, 406, cited in Leeuw 1938, 565.

[19] Deninger 1987, 359. See also Leeuw 1938, 575; King 1954, 42; Guenther 1968, 279–80; Mensching 1976, 83.

provides for an overarching linear development from the beginning to the end of time, from mere existence to salvation.[20]

In the Daoist tradition, the philosophical understanding of the Dao as documented in the ancient texts can be described in terms of natural revelation. Like many ancient thinkers, Laozi and Zhuangzi find the divine mystery that reveals itself in the continuous cycles of the natural world. Beyond naming and yet omnipresent, the Dao stands behind all, to be recognized by anyone who uses the spirit rather than the senses and the intellect to see. Manifest in all aspects of the cosmos, it can be felt and realized if one leaves one's egoistic limits and cultural sophistication behind and joins the flow of life in its perfect simplicity and utter freedom.

This natural dimension is superseded in the Daoist religion where the Dao, personified as Lord Lao, has become an active supernatural deity who stands at the center of history and dispenses his salvific messages at regular intervals, creating a community of believers, moral codes of behavior, and Daoist forms of government. In addition, his activities give direction to the unfolding of history, emerging in an active eschatology of the Dao. Thus millenarianism, another feature typically associated with supernatural revelation, appears as a key characteristic of the early Daoist movements.

Millenarianism means the belief that the world will soon come to an end and a newer, and better and more permanent one will take its place.[21] It is accompanied by an eschatology and often linked with messianism, the belief that a divine savior will appear to pave the way to renewal. Typically arising in times of difficulty and crisis, millenarianism has a distinct notion of salvation as:

a. collective, in the sense that it is to be enjoyed by the faithful as a group;
b. terrestrial, in the sense that it is to be realized on this earth and not in some otherworldly heaven;
c. imminent, in the sense that it is to come both soon and suddenly;
d. total, in the sense that it will utterly transform life on earth, so that the new dispensation will be no mere improvement on the present but perfection itself;

---

[20] Leeuw 1938, 580; Deninger 1987, 360; Mensching 1976, 76–78.

[21] On millenarianism in general, see Cohn 1962; 1995; Shepperson 1962; Thrupp 1962; Worsley 1968; Schwartz 1987. Its sociological impact is discussed in Festinger et al. 1956. For millenarianism in China, see Naquin 1976; Shek 1987; Mollier 1990; Bokenkamp 1994; Kikuchi 1994. On early Daoist rebellions as expressions of millenarian hopes, see Eichhorn 1954; 1955; 1957; Levy 1956; Seidel 1984a.

e. accomplished by agencies that are consciously regarded as supernatural (Cohn 1962, 31).

In addition, its view of history is dominantly linear in that it believes the end of the world to be imminent, while its view of agency relies on the supernatural, typically a single creator god, to give guidance and support to the "chosen people." The deity, moreover, typically communicates directly with a special envoy or prophet and is believed to represent all the forces of good as they are locked in mortal combat—and thus often also in worldly struggle—with the demonic powers of evil. Scholars have convincingly shown that all this applies to the early Daoist movements, which supports my assertion here that they were oriented toward supernatural revelation and a linear concept of time.[22]

Based on the concept of a creative and guiding divinity, the account of Lord Lao's revelations in the major hagiographies is more than a retelling of history. By placing the major and minor revelations in one sequence and putting the god in their center, it transforms the natural revelation of the philosophers into a supernatural revelation through the deity, creating a vision of purposeful divine activity in the world. Laozi meets Confucius and Emperor Wen of the Han as a transcendent god, even if his message concerns the natural Dao and shows the way of wisdom and nonaction in going along with the rhythms of nature. More powerfully, Lord Lao appears to Gan Ji and Zhang Daoling, formally descending from heaven with an immortal entourage, and enters into a special covenant with them. The deity delivers detailed salvific instructions and practical methods for the organization of a community of chosen ones in preparation for the millennium. He does the same, driven by a concern for the religious transformation of the existing Chinese *oikumene*, in his revelations to Ge Xuan and Kou Qianzhi, showing himself to be a god who is beyond nature and rules all. He guides humanity toward a salvation in and through history—a history, moreover, that is no longer framed cyclically in eternal returns, but is linear and consists of ongoing growth toward celestial perfection.

---

[22] The contrast between the millenarian vision and traditional forms of Chinese thought is so radical that an outside, possibly Western influence cannot be completely ruled out. This is especially the case when one accepts Norman Cohn's recent understanding (1995) that millenarianism is not an inherently human response to situations of crisis but a clearly defined cultural pattern that emerged with Zoroastrianism in ancient Persia and flourished first and foremost in Judaism and early Christianity. For a discussion of the early Daoist movements in this light, see Kohn 1998d.

In addition, the typical revelation process in all its parts (preparation, physical setting, and threefold structure) closely resembles the ordination pattern of Daoists on earth. First, a gifted individual feels a longing for the Dao and purifies and humbles himself in preparation for following it. Second, he goes to a cosmic power spot (*fudi*), marked by a monastery or a sacred mountain where the Dao and its teachings can most easily be encountered.[23] Third, the god or his representative, the Daoist master, descends, often in three appearances, to bestow upon the devotee the scriptures, precepts, and practical methods of the Dao.

The recipient of the revelation—and the Daoist after full ordination—is elevated to celestial status. He is then allowed a glimpse of the heavens in an ecstatic journey with the deity, after which he returns to earth to become a religious leader, expounding the teaching in accordance with the divine covenant just sealed. The Dao trains its religious leaders and assistants on the heavenly plane just as a Daoist master trains his ordinands on earth. The transmission of the Dao from the deity to the religious leader is structurally identical with that from the Daoist master to his disciple, from leader to follower. Their descents are parallel and isomorphic: Just as the god descends from heaven to the mountain, so the master/leader descends from the mountain to the people.

Through the encounter with the god, the recipient of the revelation, moreover, becomes a full representative of the Dao on earth, just as his disciples and followers become his representatives in turn. The omnipresence and unlimited power of the deity are conferred on the leader, in whom they are manifest as magical powers over life and death and as the ability to freely interact with the celestials. From him, the deity's power is passed down to the chosen people who experience it as perfect health, long life, prosperity, and social stability. The more politically powerful the leader and the farther the spread of the Daoist community, the more concrete the Dao's manifestation on earth and the closer the world moves toward the culmination of history and the realization of Great Peace.

---

[23] Power spots exist all over the world and are very often mountains. As William Irwin Thompson says, "Power points are domains in which information can be stored. . . . [W]hen a 'sensitive' approaches or stumbles upon a domain or power point, the potential information becomes virtual information in his consciousness and passes over into sound, image, or an intuitive awareness with no sensory base" (1990, 182).

14

The Rule of the Perfect Dynasty

The culmination of history is reached, according to the Laozi myth, in the Tang dynasty, when intense and continuous personal interaction occurs between the deity and not only dedicated practitioners and emperors but also commoners and larger segments of the population. No longer the distant creator god or inspiring savior who relates only to select ecstatic seekers, Lord Lao is now the ancestor of the ruling house and as such not only takes an active interest in events on earth but is also accessible through prayers, temple worship, and encomia, and vigorously manifests himself in visions and through the granting of supernatural talismans.

While the myth uses the multiple appearances of Lord Lao to transform history into a continuous manifestation of the sacred, history itself forms its base, since the Tang—and to a lesser degree the Song—engaged in the active veneration of the god as the representative of cosmic harmony and protector of the state. In the case of the Tang, this began with its very inception. The ruling Li family claimed direct descent from Lord Lao and ascended the throne with the help of Daoist millenarian prophecies. Throughout their rule, moreover, they not only favored Daoism as a doctrine of unification but actively used the religion to control the country and spread Tang rule, reorganizing the ritual structure and establishing numerous Daoist temples for their support. The Song, too, especially under Emperor Zhenzong, claimed divine support through heavenly texts and offered various sacrifices and inscriptions to Lord Lao (see chapter 2 above).

The *Youlong zhuan* devotes its last three sections to this part of the god's career. Two sections deal with his role as "Sage Ancestor of the Great Tang" (sects. 28–29; 5.11a–6.10a) and a third supplementary section addresses his "Veneration by Emperor Zhenzong of the Song" (sect. 30; 6.10a–16a).[1] The pattern these sections establish is one of impulse and response (*ganying*), beginning with the Li family's quest for power (see Table 20). The first instance is Lord Lao's miraculous appearance in 617–618, when he sent first the god of Mount Huo, then the commoner Ji Shanxing of Mount Yangjiao to convey to Li Yuan the prophecy that he would indeed win the empire. In response to this, the emperor in 620 honored the god formally as "sage ancestor" (*shengzu*) of the dynasty and renamed the center at Louguan Zongsheng guan.

Table 20
Lord Lao's miracles and appearances under the Tang

Date	Place	Person(s)	Event	Du	YLZ	HYSJ
617	Mt. Huo	Mtn god	prophecy	4a	5.11a	8.3b
618	Mt. Yangjiao	Ji Shanxing	vision	4a	5.11a	8.4a
622	Mt. Yangjiao	Ji Shanxing	vision	—	5.13b	8.7b
662	Mt. Beimang	Xu Lishi	stone	5b	5.15b	8.12a
662	Luoyang	—	vision	5b	5.15b	8.12b
679	Mt. Beimang	Kou Yi	vision	—	5.18a	8.15a
684	Haozhou	Wu Yuanchong	vision	6a	5.19a	8.15b
721	Bozhou	—	tree bloom	—	5.21b	8.23a
720s	Buzhou	—	moon stone	7a	5.20b	8.23b
720s	Ruzhou	Zhang Qi	jade stone	7a	5.21a	8.23b
720s	Quzhou	—	fish stone	7ab	5.21a	8.24a
729	Yizhou	Zhang Jing-zhong	vision	8ab	5.22a	8.24b
729	Weibei	Xuanzong	dream	—	5.23b	—
741	Hangu Pass	Tian Tongxiu	talisman	8b	5.23b	8.35b
741	Chang'an Louguan	Xuanzong —	dream statue	9b —	5.24b —	8.31a —
741	Chang'an	Chen Xilie	vision	—	5.25a	—
746	Chang'an Mt. Taibai	Xuanzong —	dream talisman	10ab —	5.25b —	— —
746	Mt. Li	Xuanzong	vision	10b	5.25b	—
749	Ningzhou	—	statues	10b	5.26a	—
750	Mt. Taibai	Wang Yuanyi	vision	11b	5.26b	9.3b
754	Taiqing gong	Li Qi	vision	11b	6.1a	9.4b
756	Lizhou	Xuanzong	vision	11b	6.1b	9.4b
757	Tonghua jun	group	vision	12a	6.1b	9.7b
759	Chang'an	Suzong	dream	12b	6.2b	9.8b
763	Chuzhou	—	talisman	13a	6.3a	9.9a
794	Guozhou	Xie Ziran	teaching	13a	6.3a	9.9b
826	Taiqing gong	Zheng Yu	vision	13b	6.3b	9.11a
826	Taiqing gong	Qing Gong-quan	vision	13b	6.3b	9.11b

---

[1] In content, the two sections on the Tang largely follow Du Guangting's *Lidai chongdao ji* (DZ 593; see Verellen 1994). The same material is also covered in *Hunyuan shengji* 8.3b–9.25a.

Table 20—*continued*

Date	Place	Person(s)	Event	Du	YLZ	HYSJ
837	Langzhou	Gao Yuanyu	drawing	14a	6.4a	9.12b
841	Bozhou	crowd	vision	14b	6.4b	9.12b
869	Bozhou	rebels	repulsion	14b	6.4b	9.16b
872	Mt. Tiantai	Yao Hao	manuscript	15a	6.5a	—
881	Mt. Yangjiao	Wang Chong-ying	tree bloom	15b	6.5b	9.19a
884	Qingyang gong	Li Wuwei	talisman	17a	6.7a	9.19b

Note: The three sources indicated here are Du Guangting's *Lidai chongdao ji*, the *Youlong zhuan*, and the *Hunyuan shengji*.

The next divine impulse was the blossoming of a withered cypress in Bozhou, which in turn inspired Gaozu's successor Taizong in 633 to have the temple there restored. Similarly, under his successor, Gaozong, the deity in 662 sponsored the find of a wondrous stone, and upon its being honored with due ceremony, appeared to express his approval in a vision. Responding to this in turn, the emperor in 666 personally offered worship at Bozhou and gave Lord Lao the title "Sovereign Emperor of Mystery Prime" (Xuanyuan huangdi)—which was changed in 1014 to "Sovereign Emperor of Chaos Prime" (Hunyuan huangdi) because of a character taboo.

The principle at work here, impulse and response, is also rendered "resonance," "action and reaction," or "affect and effect." It is an old notion in mainstream Chinese thought, used in the Daoist context to show the active and tangible presence of the deity.[2] In addition, the various activities of god and emperors change the quality of the entire country. Daoist-inspired reign titles and new modes of ritual elevate worldly time to sacred time, and the founding of temples and renaming of mountains transform ordinary space into sacred space. By making his presence felt in such tangible forms and so frequently, the god turns Tang rule, at least in the mythic vision, into the realization of Great Peace on earth.

Lord Lao's divine manifestations in the Tang can be divided into two major types: the discovery of wondrous signs and talismans, typically material objects recovered from the earth; and his appearance in visions, either suspended in mid-air or visible on temple walls. The wondrous talismans tended to be hidden plaques or caskets, or stones of fabulous workmanship with strange inscriptions that were considered to be of

---

[2] For discussions of *ganying*, see Le Blanc 1985, 4; 1992, 94. For its role in the Daoist notion of miracle, see Verellen 1992.

marvelous origin. The appearance of these signs and their interpretation closely parallel mainstream traditions around celestial omens.

Visions of the god, on the other hand, can be divided into three kinds: first, Lord Lao appears as a celestial, standing on a cloud surrounded by a divine entourage (usually during ceremonies offered in his honor); second, the deity inscribes his likeness on a natural surface, such as a sheer cliff, or on a sacred enclosure, such as a temple wall; third, the god shows himself on special occasions, either in personal visions or in dreams, dispensing emergency aid as needed and taking humans on journeys to the otherworld. These correspond to what Western scholars have called theophanies, and in their fullest form involve not only verbal but also physical contact between the divine and human realms.[3]

Unearthed Treasures

Laozi's first support for the Tang takes the form of unusual stones or talismans that are dug up from the earth, sometimes upon his explicit request. The first such manifestation occurred in 618 at the beginning of Tang rule, when Laozi appeared in a vision to the commoner Ji Shanxing and ordered him to deliver an encouraging prophecy to the new emperor. As described earlier, the god overcame Ji's reluctance to mingle with the high and mighty by promising that when he arrived at court a stone turtle would be presented as a token of his supernatural integrity. This indeed happened,[4] and the appearance of both the stone and the prophecy made the emperor very happy. It had the twofold effect of providing legitimization for the dynasty and strengthening Daoist influence at court.

A series of finds under Emperor Xuanzong in the eighth century legitimated the reorganization of the court liturgy along Daoist lines. The first, found by locals in Bozhou in 723, was a half-moon-shaped piece of jade that showed a picture of a musician immortal. When struck, it made a marvelous sound. The emperor named it "Half-Moon Lithophone" and had it hung in the garden of the imperial ancestral temple to Lord Lao. Another sounding jade appeared on the grounds of an ancient monastery in Ruzhou; it, too, was hung in the same garden.

---

[3] See Eliade and Sullivan 1987, 315; Leeuw 1938, 569.

[4] The stone turtle bore the inscription: "All under heaven will be at peace, your descendants will flourish greatly, bringing forth thousands and ten thousands of sprouts, for thousands and ten thousands of generations" (*Youlong zhuan* 5.12ab). It is first recorded in the inscription of 723. See ch. 2 above.

Third, a metal fish from Quzhou was found when the foundations for a new Daoist monastery were dug. It was three feet long and of purple and blue-green coloring. "It looked like nothing ever done by man" and made a spectacular sound when struck. The emperor named it "Auspicious Fish Lithophone" and hung it in the Taiwei gong in Luoyang to be sounded during rituals or whenever a scripture was being chanted. All Daoist institutions hastened to imitate it in wood and stone (*Lidai chongdao ji* 7ab; *Youlong zhuan* 5.21a). Because of these divine musical inspirations, the emperor was moved to commission new liturgical dances, among them the famous "Dance of the Purple Culmen." First performed in honor of Lord Lao in the summer of 742, this work gave a highly Daoist flavor to court ritual (Schafer 1987, 56). The effect of these developments was again twofold: The dynasty received divine support and the Daoist position at court was strengthened. Still, what may appear from a political point of view to be a smooth move toward legitimating ritual change, in the Daoist myth becomes yet another instance in the progressing realization of the Dao on earth, a manifestation of the increased closeness of the heavenly and the mundane.

Two other important finds also brought changes to the realm: the "Heavenly Treasure" find on the Hangu Pass in 741, which caused the establishment of a new reign title; and the "Central Harmony" jade unearthed in Chengdu in 884, which precipitated the rise of the Qing-yang gong and was commemorated in Yue Penggui's inscription (see Fig. 18).[5] The stories of these finds are similar. An official or officiating Daoist going about his duties recognizes a sign of the god in the form of a purple cloud or red radiance and orders people to dig at the divinely indicated spot. There they find a wondrous talisman, often buried in a stone container with a golden box and in all cases inscribed with red characters in an obscure ancient script. Once the talisman is recovered from the earth, its divine powers are made accessible to the realm through the establishment of a new reign title and through the reorganization of ritual and the elevation of the status of its original location. Thus the "Heavenly Treasure" find presaged extensive reforms of court ritual and state organization along more Daoist lines. The "Central Harmony" talisman drew attention to Lord Lao's last Chinese station on his journey to the west, and encouraged a revival of Daoist practice while raising the location to a major Daoist center.

---

[5] On both of these events, see chapter 2.

Fig. 18. The miracle at Qingyang gong.
Source: Laojun bashiyi hua tushuo, no. 80

Because it effects a greater presence of the Dao on earth, the talisman is in each case treated formally. It is dug up, presented to the emperor, installed in a special place, and worshiped with proper pomp and ceremony. Sometimes its picture or replicas of it are made available to temples throughout the country. In this, and in its overall meaning, the wondrous Daoist find parallels the ideas and treatments that are associated with celestial omens in mainstream Chinese culture.

Celestial omens that first appeared at the end of the Former Han and during the reign of Wang Mang[6] generated omen lore critical to the fate of each dynasty in which they were manifest. They were considered the manifestation of divine support or criticism of the ruling house and were widely published. Wondrous Daoist finds clearly share the religio-political significance and special treatment that omens were accorded, and in this sense they are also similar to miraculous finds and the divine qualities of saints' relics worshiped in medieval Europe.

Visions of the God

The most important vision of Lord Lao occurs at the founding of the Tang dynasty to the commoner Ji Shanxing on Mount Yangjiao. The deity appears to him several times, dressed entirely in plain silk, with white hair and a black headdress. He rides a white horse with a red mane and red hooves and is attended by two jade lads in green garb with red shoes. In the first vision, he orders Ji to relay his message to the new emperor; he reappears when his messenger fails to carry out the order, and returns a third time after its successful completion both to hear Ji's report and to confirm his own identity as Li Er, the dynasty's ancestor. By that time, a good half year after the initial contact, the place of the original vision had been sanctified, renamed Mount Longjiao, and honored with a temple to the deity, the Qingtang guan (*Youlong zhuan* 5.11b–12b; *Hunyuan shengji* 8.4a–5b).

More numerous and similar visions follow, either inspired by Ji's devout worship at the temple or by Lord Lao's desire to have another message relayed to the emperor. Cumulatively, they illustrate the close-ness of the god to humanity, the heightened interest the god takes in the fate of his descendants on earth, and the efforts of worldly authorities to sanctify the location of the theophany. In addition, the physical appearance of the deity tallies with the colors used in the Tang campaign (red and

---

[6] For studies of Wang Mang and his use of omens, see Dull 1966, 152; Sargent 1977.

white). These colors were also common in statues of the god that appeared in growing numbers and enjoyed rising popularity during the late Six Dynasties, once Daoists overcame their reluctance to give visual form to the invisible and inaudible Dao (Chen 1975, 269; Kamitsuka 1993, 226). The most common depiction of the god shows him seated centrally on a high throne, dressed in official-style robes and a rectangular hat, with a beard and a fly whisk. Like his Buddhist counterpart he is framed by a flame-shaped mandorla, seated on a lotus throne, and accompanied by two attendants. The two attendants, dressed similarly in official robes, stand to his right and left. Usually they are not specifically identified, but in their positions and stance they imitate the bodhisattvas Vajragarbha and Avalokiteśvara.[7]

Aside from the vision's resemblance to surviving graphic representations of Lord Lao, the three steps of Ji's vision also have parallels in ritual. First, the ritual is prepared and the deity is invited; the main rite follows, consisting of an active interchange between humanity and the divine; third, the rite is concluded with a report of success, and the deity is sent off again. The first set of visions of Lord Lao at the beginning of Tang rule is therefore not only structured to imitate the pattern of Daoist ritual, it is also timed to coincide with important moves in the Tang campaigns. The visions thus create an atmosphere of divine approval—and even predestination—at the beginning of the dynasty.

This pattern continues throughout the Tang, with different types of visions occurring at regular intervals. Among the celestial visions, the most important occurred under Gaozong (in 662 and 679), toward the end of Xuanzong's reign (in 754), and under Jingzong (in 826). In each of those cases, the deity was seen at a major Daoist institution while services in his honor were in progress. He appeared just as he had to Ji Shanxing, corresponding to the classic depiction of immortals arriving on clouds with a formal entourage. He not only matched the statues of Lord Lao in his dress and appearance, but also showed his support of the dynasty by wearing the colors red and white.

Miraculous appearances of Lord Lao on cliffs or walls are reported for the years 726 and 837. In the first case, which occurred under Emperor Xuanzong, the official Zhang Jingzhong from Yizhou (Sichuan) reported that an image of the god had spontaneously appeared on a pillar in a local Buddhist temple. It showed the deity covered by a marvelous canopy, with auspicious clouds around his feet and celestial flowers hovering around him. Interpreting the manifestation as a sign of great

---

[7] For examples of such statues and a discussion, see Matsubara 1961, plates 307a and 307c; Kamitsuka 1993, 238; James 1986, 72.

good fortune, the emperor rewarded the institution and ordered the composition of a formal encomium (*Youlong zhuan* 5.22a; *Hunyuan shengji* 8.24a). In the second case (in 837), Gao Yuanyu, prefect of Langzhou, noticed a strange radiance on the cliff north of the district town. Approaching to inspect the light, he discovered that lines appearing spontaneously in the stone delineated an image of Lord Lao in formal attire, holding an incense burner, and accompanied by an attendant with a double topknot. Certain that this could not have been put there by human means, Gao offered a prayer, in response to which a purple cloud appeared above the cliff. Afterward his district was greatly blessed.[8]

Yet a third type of vision brings about an even closer interaction between god and man. Here the deity first appears in a clear manifestation, surrounded by his usual entourage; he then either invites his human partner on a celestial journey or aggressively interferes to dispel some danger to the faithful. The most famous celestial journey occurred in 759, when Emperor Daizong saw the god in a dream and was invited to join him on a journey that took them through all the heavens and to encounters with the gods. Even more miraculous, a painting of Lord Lao in full formal gear and surrounded by celestials that appeared spontaneously in the Guangtian guan (Radiant Heaven Monastery) in Chang'an, turned out to be identical to the emperor's vision in every detail.[9]

Another well-documented occurrence of this type happened in 684, the year of Empress Wu's usurpation. On the eighteenth of the second month, Lord Lao descended to appear to Wu Yuanchong in the Longtai guan (Dragon Terrace Monastery) in Haozhou. His coming was announced by six immortals who were clad in variegated gauze and descended from the northwest on multicolored clouds drawn by red dragons. The god himself arrived on a five-colored cloud, seated on a marvelous white horse with a red tail; he was clad in yellow garb and a flowery headdress, and had white hair and beard. Inviting Wu to join him on the divine cloud, he took him into the air, followed by the six immortals on their dragons, all splendid in their multicolored garb and shining head-dresses. While this immediate group around the deity was surrounded by brilliant light from all sides, behind it a large entourage of more immortals and celestials followed to the sounds of spheric music. On

---

[8] These events are recorded in *Daojiao lingyan ji* 6.4ab; *Youlong zhuan* 6.4b; *Hunyuan shengji* 9.12ab.

[9] This is described in *Daojiao lingyan ji* 6.1b; *Youlong zhuan* 6.2b; *Hunyuan shengji* 9.8b–9a.

earth, a large crowd assembled to observe the spectacle. Gradually the vision dimmed and Wu returned home.[10]

The hagiographies comment that Empress Wu, on hearing this report, was at first not pleased but could not find any harm in it either. She duly acknowledged the validity of the sign, changed the temple's name to Fengxian gong (Temple of Worship for the Immortals), and relaxed her strict measures against Daoism. In the political context of the time, the vision prevented harm to Daoists and their teaching and again showed the support of the deity for his people.[11]

Finally, emergency appearances occurred toward the end of the dynasty, when rebellions arose and even the sanctuaries of Lord Lao were at risk. He descended most often to protect his temple in Bozhou, but also appeared to help faithful commoners escape from marauding troops. The most memorable incident of the first sort is Huang Chao's attempt to take over the Bozhou temple around the year 880. Various nasty schemes of his were met with divine retaliation. The texts relate:

> Wantonly Huang Chao's men set fire to the temple, but a dark cloud rose and spread rain immediately so that the fire was extinguished. The rebels fled toward the river.
>
> Later they again haunted the area and surrounded and attacked Bozhou with knives drawn. A black vapor and heavy snow arose, leaving the invaders dead and frozen on the ground. As soon as the area was liberated, the vapor vanished.
>
> When the remainder of Huang Chao's troops attacked Bozhou yet again, spirit birds gathered around town with arrows in their beaks and another black cloud arose over the residence of the local official. Terrified, the rebels fled and were never seen again.[12]

---

[10] *Lidai chongdao ji* 6a; *Youlong zhuan* 5.19ab; *Hunyuan shengji* 8.15a-17b.

[11] A similar vision appeared under Emperor Xuanzong, in the ninth month of 742. Fourteen people, including the academician Chen Xilie, saw a purple cloud approaching the Taiqing men (Great Clarity Gate) in the capital. Recognizing the white-clad god with his two green-clad attendants, they bowed and received his message: "I am Laozi. Tell my descendant [Xuanzong] that he is a perfected in the upper realm. He is to stand next to me. I will dispatch various assistants to help him complete a statue of me. When it is finished, it will protect him from all harm and empower his rule. There will be no more disasters, and the empire will be at peace." See *Youlong zhuan* 5.25a; Benn 1987, 139.

[12] *Guangsheng yi* 2.15ab; *Daojiao lingyan ji* 1.9ab [Reiter 1983, 372–83]; see also *Youlong zhuan* 6.5b; *Hunyuan shengji* 9.17a. For more on Tang rebels, see Miyakawa 1964; 1974.

In all these cases, the visual manifestation of the god is in close accordance with standard images and paintings. Typologically, it follows the ancient tradition of shamanic visitations in which the shaman first made ready for contact with the deity by undergoing purification, then opened himself to the vision of the divine or allowed his soul to ascend. Eventually, he encountered the deity and bathed in its celestial splendor, only to part again and find himself alone and pining for the beauty and ease of divine life.[13] This experience is first described in the pre-Han work *Chuci* (Songs of the South), in which a deity descends for the greater good fortune of the community. The visions of Lord Lao thus integrate the ancient shamanic experience of receiving a god; moreover, when linked with a celestial journey, they hark back to shamanic ecstatic travels, which were later articulated in poetry and became part of the meditational excursions practiced by Highest Clarity Daoists.

Finds of sacred talismans and visions of the god under the Tang, sharing features with the ancient traditions of omen lore and shamanic exploits, transform the age in which they occur into one of divinity and holiness. Whenever the deity manifests himself, a new reign title is chosen and time becomes sacred; wherever a wondrous sign is unearthed or a vision appears, a new temple is built and its location becomes part of the holy. Through his repeated appearances in different forms, the deity thus gradually changes the nature of the Chinese empire, creating an ever more holy realm, a world of the Dao on earth.

Miracles

The pattern that underlies this understanding of the Lord Lao myth is, as noted earlier, the classical idea of impulse and response. Central to Chinese mainstream culture, it is based on the vision of an integrated cosmos, in which every good and bad deed has a response in auspicious or inauspicious signs from heaven. Human actions are thus a part of universal movements that are pervasive yet usually hidden from view. Conversely, heavenly activities and natural phenomena are also an immediate expression of the state of society and human life. The notion of impulse and response reflects a form of thinking that is acausal and nonlinear. Inductive and synthetic, it establishes "a logical link between two effective positions at the same time in different places in space." It is thus a Chinese version of the principle of synchronicity, the opposite of

---

[13] For studies of the earlier pattern, see Hawkes 1959, 42–44; 1967; Yü 1987; Cahill 1985.

causal thinking, which seeks links at the same place in different points of time.[14]

This mainstream thinking about cosmic and human activity means that the dominant Chinese understanding of miracles falls under what Western scholars call the supernatural attitude. According to this thinking, "miracles do not represent anything basically impossible, because the natural world is overshadowed by another and mightier supernatural reality" (Keller and Keller 1969, 17). In a nature-based, all-encompassing cosmology, everything is part of the same reality, only some parts are more obvious than others. This supernatural view is prevalent in so-called primitive cultures and plays a dominant role in the cultural complex of shamanism (Waida 1987, 9:542–43).

Not surprisingly then, the ancient Chinese word for miracle is *lingying*, "response of the numinous," or *lingyan*, "evidence of the numinous" (Verellen 1992, 227–28). Marvelous powers of individuals, such as levitation, omniscience, and multilocation, as well as exceptional healings and exorcisms, and even resurrections of the dead, are noted in the literature as "strange" but not impossible. Nor are they considered the work of some utterly alien divine power, as in the Christian tradition where such events make up ninety percent of all miracles (Rogo 1982, 111).

In contrast, the dominant Christian view of miracles is what is called the monotheistic attitude. It states that all supernatural events are due to the manifestation of a divine power that is fundamentally transcendent and beyond nature. Miracles in the Christian tradition are unusual and inexplicable events that create surprise and wonder and are linked with the belief in a causing deity. As Raglan points out, "mere surprise does not lead to a belief in miracles; it has first to be combined with certain definite religious beliefs" (1990, 173). The defining characteristic of a miracle in this view, moreover, is its revelatory content—an element that is ultimately more important than its rarity or amazing aspect.[15]

---

[14] For a discussion of synchronicity in Chinese thinking, see Porkert 1974, 1; as a psychological principle, see Jung 1955, 49; Koestler 1972, 82.

[15] See Keller and Keller 1969, 16; Leeuw 1938, 568; Waida 1987, 9:547; Ward 1982. For discussions of specific miracles in the West, see also Rogo 1982; Finucane 1977. To complete the picture, the third and most modern view of miracles is that of rational materialism, which claims that they do not exist and that all strange events have a natural explanation. See Kelsey 1987, 9:549; Lewis 1960, 100; Thompson 1990.

Seen from this perspective, the miracles worked by Lord Lao under the Tang represent a mixture of the two basic attitudes defined by Western scholars. Elements of the supernatural attitude are obvious in the traditional pattern of impulse and response, since finds of talismans or visions of gods confirm the rulers' actions or inspire them to greater veneration of the Dao. Because of these miracles, rulers make increased efforts to transform time and space into a realm of the sacred. Yet the visions also express the monotheistic attitude in that they are like divine revelations of the Dao, while the finds are repeatedly stated to be otherworldly and thus the signs of a transcendent power. Here again, the Daoist tradition perpetuates mainstream Chinese thinking yet also leads beyond it to a new dimension of religiosity and sacred life.

The ultimate goal, as far as the Daoist myth is concerned, is the creation of a form of heavenly life on earth, a goal achieved gradually through the sacralization of time and space. In terms of time, the most common means applied to this end—again borrowing from mainstream notions and practices—is the installation of a new, more divine reign title, such as "True Ruler of Great Peace" used by the Wei Emperor Taiwu under the theocracy. Under the Tang, the most celebrated reign title change was the choice of "Heavenly Treasure" for the period after the find of the sacred talisman in 741, but there were also many other, shorter reigns that indicated the effort to mark off sacred time. Reform of court ritual was another means through which time was transformed. Ritual reform had been central to creating the proper impulse and response relationship between heaven and humanity since the establishment of the Mingtang under the Zhou.[16] Under the Tang, and especially under Xuanzong, a Daoist court liturgy centering more on the stars than on humanity was established; it used a new type of costume and written texts instead of incantations (Schafer 1987, 50; Xiong 1996, 287).

Sacred space, on the other hand, was created by the establishment of imperial Daoist temples throughout the empire, beginning with the five sacred mountains. The imperial temple system grew through the reorganization of the two major ancestral temples in the capitals after the model of Daoist heavens, and through rich donations of land and gifts made to the central sanctuary of the god at Bozhou.[17] In addition, various

---

[16] On the Mingtang and ritual reform, see Soothill 1952; Maspero 1951; Mikami 1966; Bilsky 1975; Forte 1988; and Wechsler 1985, 195–211.

[17] For the practice of setting up imperial temples at cosmic locations, see Forte 1992, 217. On the transformation of the ancestral temples, see Ding 1979; 1980; Xiong 1996, 266–70. The many honors accorded to Bozhou and its impressive

mountains where a manifestation of the deity had been seen were transformed into divine locations by having their names changed and Daoist institutions established on them. For example, Mount Yangjiao was renamed Longjiao, and its district came to be called Shenshan (Divine Mountain); a Daoist temple was built there that later became known as the Qingtang guan (*Youlong zhuan* 5.14a). Similarly Mount Beimang became the location of annual sacrifices to Lord Lao after the god appeared there in 662 (*Youlong zhuan* 5.15b–16a; *Hunyuan shengji* 8.12ab). Finally, the vision of the god on Mount Taibai was honored with the title "Lord of the Numinous Response" (Lingying gong) and its district renamed Zhenfu (Perfect Talisman) after the god directed the emperor to a talisman hidden there in 746 (*Youlong zhuan* 5.25b).

The continued activities of Lord Lao as described in the myth bring the dynasty nearer to the realization of the ideal Daoist rule. Moving along in an active pattern of impulse and response, the transcendent Dao and the order of the world become ever closer and coincide at more and more points through the ongoing sacralization of time and space. The more the world matches the rhythm of the Dao and is filled with its rituals and sacred places, the more the Dao is present in it and the greater its realization of perfection. Through the multiple manifestations of Lord Lao in the latter part of his career, the Dao thus becomes an active participant in the world and the world a part of the Dao.

Visions and the Bones of Saints

On a further comparative note, the Chinese treatment of sacred talismans closely resembles the way in which the bones of saints and martyrs were worshiped by medieval Christians. In Europe, divine signs pointed to the resting place of holy remains, which were then recovered, cleansed, and removed to important basilicas or cathedrals. They were worshiped with great formality, and soon "miracles began to occur through the intercession of the newly found saints" (Rogo 1982, 15). Like Chinese talismans, the bones of the saints were considered treasures of pure power, alive in their own way. As Scott Rogo notes:

> Relics, especially the integral skeletons of widely known saints, emitted a kind of holy radioactivity which bombarded everything in the area, and as early as the sixth century it was believed that objects placed next to them

---

growth are described in *Guangsheng yi* 2.14b; *Youlong zhuan* 6.4b; *Hunyuan shengji* 8.23a. See also Ding 1980, 201–6; Benn 1987, 131.

would absorb some of their power and grow heavier. They affected oil in lamps which burned above them, cloths placed nearby, water or wine which washed them, dust which settled on them, fragments of the tomb which enclosed them, gems or rings which touched them, the entire church which surrounded them, and of course the hopeful supplicants who approached to kiss, touch, pray before and gaze upon them. (Rogo 1982, 26)

Similarly, Chinese talismans possessed concentrated Dao-power, which they radiated into the environment around them. Their primary impact was not to cure individuals, however, but to serve the Chinese *oikumene* and bestow order and harmony on the world. Although state-centered and worshiped in imperial rituals to the greater benefit of the empire, divine signs in China also promoted the interests of the Daoist religion, just as the miracles worked through the bones of the saints increased the church's impact in medieval Europe. Both religions also actively adapted preceding traditions, the Daoists drawing on mainstream omen lore and talismans of old (see Seidel 1983), the church linking their saints' bones with pagan wonder-working relics to such a degree that the true religion of the Middle Ages can be described largely as the worship of relics (Rogo 1982, 25; see also Brown 1978; 1981).

Not only is the Chinese worship of unearthed talismans close to the medieval European belief in the power of saints' bones, the form of Lord Lao's appearances under the Tang are also strongly reminiscent of Christian theophanies or "appearances of the sacred" (Eliade and Sullivan 1987, 315). Especially striking are visions of the Blessed Virgin Mary, noted for providing auspicious signs, making prophecies for the greater good, giving help to the people, and saving her faithful followers. There are numerous examples for her divine activities, one of which occurred in 1830:

> At the motherhouse of the Daughters of Charity in Paris, a young postulant named Zoe Catherine Laboure awoke to see the figure of a young child about four or five years old at her bedside. He beckoned Catherine to rise and follow him to the chapel. She obediently accompanied the apparition to the church, where at the altar stood a glowing figure of the Virgin Mary. Catherine threw herself to the floor, and the gentle apparition imparted a series of messages to her. Catherine was given to understand that some of these prophecies would be fulfilled shortly, while others would come to pass in 1870. After issuing its revelations, the apparition vanished "like a cloud that had evaporated," and Catherine returned to her room. (Rogo 1982, 206)

Although doubted by her father confessor, Catherine's predictions prove true, and a few months later she is visited a second time. This time the apparition floats above the altar of the chapel. The typical characteristics of this episode, also found commonly in other appearances of the Virgin, are strikingly similar to the Chinese cases: the witness is young and pure, an innocent and simple person; the visitation takes place in a sacred environment; and the apparition is concerned with worldly affairs and makes accurate predictions (Rogo 1982, 207–8).

The need for a pure witness and sacred environment, moreover, explains why, in many messages destined for the emperor, Lord Lao does not simply appear to his target audience directly. The emperor is too involved in affairs, too old, too impure, or again too far from a suitable place for celestial communication. He is neither personally sensitive enough to receive the divine message nor does he dwell in a sufficiently open and purified place to which the message could get through. The concern with worldly affairs, in addition, places the divine manifestations firmly into the context of mundane time and space. Both the Virgin's correct prophecies and Lord Lao's well-timed descents suggest that "the appearances are somehow at least partially generated by the culture itself" (Rogo 1982, 206).[18]

Typically such visions or theophanies are double-edged events. They "secure, renew, and strengthen one's own reality," but there is always the danger of total dissolution, of the annihilation of one's profane existence by being submerged in the divine (Eliade and Sullivan 1987, 315). The visionary, engulfed by a splendor beyond imagination, can never be the same; the place of the visitation, blessed by the divine presence, becomes part of a higher sphere of pure heavenly power and "continues to 'vibrate' with supernatural efficacy" (Turner and Turner 1982, 147). The political and social realities ordinarily governed by human efforts are raised to a level of providence and divine intervention, and politics turn into an aspect of soteriology. Time and space are transformed into a sacred realm in the West just as they are in China.

Corporeal visions of the deity both East and West, moreover, offer a glimpse of the otherworld, harkening back to times of purity in the beginning of history and presaging a beneficent age for the future. Thus Marian pilgrimages in the nineteenth century grew into popular movements and convinced "the people that biblical times were not dead." They showed the Blessed Virgin Mary as "an autonomous figure who

---

[18] Explanations include reactions to threats against the status quo, manifestations of cosmic archetypes, an overactive imagination or intentional manipulations for political ends. See Rogo 1982, 212; Wechsler 1985, 71.

takes initiatives on behalf of mankind, often intervening in the midst of economical and political crises" (Turner and Turner 1982, 153, 145). Lord Lao does something very similar. Both deities create a temporal wholeness that in a sacred moment overcomes the linearity of life and "an extended sacred family" that spans the "gap between the known and the unknown" (Hawley 1987, xix). Through their manifestations, political action and social interaction are no longer neutral but occur in an atmosphere of sacrality, a dimension of cosmic importance. Lord Lao's manifestations, therefore, are not simply the occasional descent of a high-ranking ancestor but become the focus of political unity and social integration. Even as an ancestor mediating between the emperor and Heaven, he is still the Daoist god, the personification of highest Heaven. This double role is also typical of the saints with their tremendous divine power, who still "are frequently conceived as a second echelon of holy beings, dependent for their own power upon their access through devotion to a more encompassing, higher divinity."[19]

Like European saints, Lord Lao interacts with the ruler and the people with the aim to transform the mundane into the divine and create an approximation of Great Peace in the world. This activity of the god follows a standardized pattern already established in his earlier revelations and closely similar to Western models. Typically a pure and humble seeker of the Dao or a lowly official or Daoist priest is given a heavenly sign—either an unusual radiance, a spontaneous drawing, or a full vision of the deity—in an unspoiled or sanctified environment. He responds with awe and exultation, accepting the god's presence without question. He is rewarded either with the find of a numinous talisman, which imparts Dao-radiance to the world, or with the revelation of an auspicious prophecy for the government. Transmitted by the proper procedure and brought to the attention of the emperor, the divine manifestation is greatly honored. Its appearance gives rise to a new sacralization of time and place and bolsters the establishment or consolidation of a sanctified political rule throughout the country.

As the dynasty proceeds, so Lord Lao's miracles and theophanies change in accordance with the needs of the time. Serious prophetic finds and visions are frequent at the beginning of Tang rule. These culminate in the reign of Xuanzong with the discovery of numerous sacred objects—musical stones that trigger reforms of court liturgy (sacred time), and talismans and statues that are placed in temples throughout the empire (sacred space). However, such events shift toward the periphery both

---

[19] Hawley 1987, xxi; see also Turner and Turner 1982, 146.

socially and physically toward the end of the dynasty, when the court is forced into exile in Sichuan and the major talismanic find occurs there.

This shift in the nature and location of manifestations can, moreover, be seen to parallel the career of the god. His birth in Bozhou signifies the active presence of the Dao on earth; the beginning of the Tang dynasty, in the miracle of the cypress, is equivalent to it, signaling the new arising of the Dao, the beginning of Great Peace. Lord Lao's emigration, including his meeting with Yin Xi on the Hangu Pass and the transmission of the *Daode jing*, is both the highlight of his earthly career and the point of his transition beyond it. It is parallel to the reign of Xuanzong who, more than any other Tang emperor, stood for the prosperity and glory of the times but also had to flee to Sichuan after the An Lushan Rebellion, thus coming to represent a threshold in Tang history. Finally, Lord Lao's second meeting with Yin Xi, the god's approval of his disciple, and their joint departure signify the end of the active presence of the Dao in China—at least for a time. In the same way, the year 884, when the government fled the central plain, marks the effective end of Tang rule.

Sacred space, determined by the locations of Lord Lao's major exploits, also corresponds to sacred time, and the god's life is mythically reenacted in the reign of the Tang dynasty. Just as Lord Lao comes and goes, is manifest in China then spreads his teaching in the west, so the ruling dynasty achieves perfection but loses it again. The god's continued efforts at establishing Great Peace for all of China give way, after the heyday of Tang prosperity, to the urge of the Dao for universal salvation. The shift of the political center to the periphery of the empire is, religiously speaking, the same as Lord Lao's emigration. The reconstitution of political forces under the Song, then, signals the return of the Dao, an opportunity for new signs and visions of the deity. The hagiographies present two principal signs: a radiance at Bozhou in 1098 (*Hunyuan shengji* 9.43a) and the transmission of the *Huming jing* to Liang Guangyin on Maoshan in 1112 (9.45b). However, the revelations by the Dark Warrior under the first Song emperors, heavenly texts appearing under Emperor Zhenzong, and the various Daoist projects during this dynasty all contributed to the creation of a newly harmonious state of Great Peace. Through them the rule of perfection continued, even if under a family of new rulers.

Conclusion to Part Two

From the creation of the universe to the establishment of Great Peace under the Tang, Lord Lao, the deified Laozi, supported the Chinese world and guided it toward the best possible developments. In all six phases of his integrated myth, Lord Lao gave shape to the Daoist vision of divinity and perfection. His stories are unique to the Chinese tradition and yet can be related to those found in other religions whose ideas they also integrate.

Thus, the Lord Lao creation myth in its inherent structure corresponds to the pattern found in origin myths all over the world. It borrows from mainstream Chinese visions of the emergence of the world from chaos, and also transforms the classical Daoist understanding of the immediate relation of the Dao to the world by adding to it a level of pure Dao-existence consisting of the heavens, the gods, and the scriptures. The god's role as the teacher of dynasties also matches the universal sacralization of the king and extends ancient Chinese rituals of rulership. Yet it also changes them, first to place the Dao between heaven and the ruler in the form of the sage adviser, then to recover the ancient identity of sage and ruler in the ideal of the Daoist-ordained emperor.

The birth and activities of Lord Lao on earth integrate the historical data on the philosopher Laozi, the birth of the Buddha, and the polemical legend of the conversion of the barbarians; they also closely tally with the birth and quest of the hero, motifs known from Western and other sources. Born of his own volition from a virgin under auspicious circumstances, the god appears as a divine child, able to walk and speak upon birth, and fully conscious of his celestial mission. After an uneventful childhood and a life of official service, he decides to emigrate and on his way, in a typical threshold situation, tests Yin Xi as his disciple and transmits the *Daode jing* together with oral instructions for its recitation. Meeting Yin Xi a second time, Lord Lao reconfirms his disciple's celestial status, and the two set out to convert the barbarians, fulfilling the quest of the hero and establishing the world as the recovered kingdom of the Dao. In the end, the god leaves his perfected disciple to govern in his stead and, after performing conversion miracles all over Asia, ascends to heaven.

The key scenario of the mythological complex surrounding the god closely matches the core hero myth; it also actively links mainstream Chinese ideas about the birth and deeds of sage rulers with Buddhist myths to shape religious Daoist visions of ordination and conversion. As models for the ideal life of the Dao on earth, Lord Lao and Yin Xi stand for every faithful Daoist follower; they represent the idealized roles of master and disciple, and show through their magical feats and ordeals that neither good nor bad fortune can ever diminish or hamper the powers of the Dao. Lord Lao's adventures on earth provide both guidelines and solace to the Daoist believer, showing how he can and should be alive in and through the Dao, how he can and should see life as an intermediate stage between one form of celestial existence and another.

Celestial existence, moreover, can be even more fully realized on earth when larger numbers of people, and especially the imperial government, follow the Dao. In the Lord Lao myth, the state of Great Peace, the Chinese ideal of societal perfection, was attained first among small groups as they received guidance in revelations from the deity, then in the empire at large, as the Tang house honored Lord Lao as their ancestor and followed the god's instructions. The god's revelations, to Confucius of the Eastern Zhou, Emperors Wen, Wu, and Huan of the Han, Gan Ji of the Great Peace movement, Zhang Daoling of the Celestial Masters, Ge Xuan of the Numinous Treasure school, and Kou Qianzhi of the Northern Wei theocracy, represent the continuous effort of the Dao to transform human society into a celestial community and change mundane into sacred history. History, never an accidental sequence of unconnected events, is no longer even a cycle of renewal and decline but, teleologically reoriented, demonstrates the ever-intensified presence of the Dao in the world.

Finally realized under the Tang, the state of Great Peace is blessed with frequent appearances of Lord Lao in miracles and theophanies. Their reception, building on traditional Chinese ideas linking omens and the relative virtue of the ruling house, are also similar to the sacrality and veneration of saints in medieval Europe. They inspire the emperor to actively undertake the transformation of his administration and realm into a sacred community, which he does by appointing Daoist officials, creating sacred time through new reign titles, and establishing sacred space through Daoist mountains and monasteries. The integrated mytho-

logical complex surrounding the god thus imparts a coherent and meaningful form to the development of the world and humanity, presenting
the active believer's history of the Dao.

Looked at from yet another perspective, the myth formulates various
ways in which the Dao relates to the world: how it realizes itself by
embodiment in the human realm, how it relates to its own creation, and
how it acts through this creation to realize its different aspects. The myth
thus always concerns a whole divided and made whole again, the
complementary parts of integrated oneness, the dividing and joining
aspects of the Dao in its various forms.

These central concerns of the myth can best be described in terms of
binary opposites as defined in structuralism. Although they cannot
exhaust the full depth of the individual stories, these opposites offer an
overall grasp of the myth's most essential aspects and provide another
way of examining the intricate mythological complex surrounding Lord
Lao. Three levels can be distinguished: cosmology, humanity, and action
in the world. And it is certainly no accident that even these most general
levels are grounded in a pair of binary opposites (cosmos and humanity)
and its resolution (cosmic action by humans).

Cosmologically, then, there are three major pairs: creation versus
return; the descent of the deity versus the ascent to immortality; and the
universal order of Great Peace versus eschatology, the decline of culture
and destruction of the world.

First, in the process of creation the god personifies the Dao in chaos
and thus resides as the seed of order in the swirling mists of the cosmic
sea. There he stimulates and guides the development of divine forces
that eventually create the world. The deity, both controlling and joining
creation, shows that the Dao, however primordial, remains forever part
of the world and supports every living being. Yet life is only one aspect
of reality, and all created beings have to die, to return to the chaos womb
they came from. Lord Lao mediates the opposition between creation and
return not only by his omnipresence in both states but also as a model
for the conscious, religious recovery of the primeval state. In this life,
going back to the root and attaining mystical oneness with the Dao, the
key aim of Daoist vision and practice, is expressed in the myth as the
omnipresence and creative power of the god, the living reality of the Dao
on earth.

Descent and ascent, too, are key Daoist goals that are associated with
the deity. The former is apparent in Lord Lao's transformations, his
ongoing appearances to rulers and practitioners, guiding them on their
way to the Dao. The latter is described in his successful ascension after

showing the way of immortality to the world. Mythically opposite, the two are nevertheless two sides of the same coin. Practitioners realize that only the descent of the divine enables the ascent of the human. Similarly, Great Peace, the state of perfect harmony that is permanent and stable, contrasts with eschatology, the belief in the continued decline and eventual end of the world, which characterizes the present as a state of fundamental impermanence and flux. As a permanent feature underlying and yet pervading the kalpa cycles of cosmic history, the deity never ceases to extend stability to an impermanent world, to provide Great Peace in the form of political and cultic perfection, giving every dynasty the opportunity to achieve its utmost realization.

In all three sets of cosmological opposites, the deity straddles both sides, mediating creation and return, descent and ascent, Great Peace and the decline of the world. The myth on this level demonstrates the ubiquity and omnipotence of the Dao, explaining through actions and narrated events something that would remain abstruse and vague if formulated only in abstract terms. The Dao contains all and supports all equally, it is there on all sides and in all aspects of reality, encouraging and helping, guiding and controlling, advancing and returning. Placed beyond all manifest reality, it is still never separate from it; controlling the world, it is still not free from it. The Dao is the ultimate power, and Lord Lao reveals it in action—creating the world and realizing immortality as the complementary manifestations of his greatness.

The second set of binary opposites focuses on humanity and shows a different side of the Dao. Here we have the sage adviser versus the ignorant ruler, the great man or hero versus the loser, and the potent helper versus the innocent victim.

In the first pair, Lord Lao appears as counselor to the mythical rulers, providing the wisdom of the Dao to kings who are helpless without him. This mythically represents the ideal relationship between the ritually centered ruler who is politically powerless and the withdrawn sage who inspires sound government policies. This ideal was most clearly formulated in Huang-Lao Daoism under the Han, where Laozi as the inspired sage guides the Yellow Emperor, the eternal learner and grateful disciple.

The contrast between the hero and the loser appears most obviously in the conversion of the barbarians, where the god wins his kingdom and reveals his supernatural powers, while the barbarian king grovels before him and accepts the restrictive Buddhist rules for himself and his people. The opposition of the potent helper versus the innocent victim is found in later miracle stories, where Lord Lao appears in time to rescue his faithful followers from poverty, civil war, and other calamities.

These sets of binary opposites make an active statement about the Dao as a part of humanity and as a force within the world. It supports good government and increases the ruler's benevolence; it lovingly helps those who believe and rescues them from harm. At the same time, it will not be mocked and ruthlessly puts down its enemies, reigning victorious even in the most desperate situations. The Dao, then, not only encompasses all aspects of the world when seen in cosmological perspective, it also mediates all movements and activities. Within the world of humanity, it also shows the power of good and stands for the civilizing, beneficent force that inspires rulers. It is the act of providence that saves the helpless from disaster, and the divine force that can smite all evil. The Dao to manifest its truth needs the existence of the learner, the loser, and the victim, through whom it can demonstrate its wisdom, power, and support. Mediating the basic cosmic-human opposition through divine action on earth, the god gives form and purpose to human existence.

In yet another set of contrasts, the Dao is wholly manifest as action. Here the oppositions are eternity versus life and death, life versus death, and perfected versus technical practices.

The first is present in the two roles of Lord Lao: a deity in the heavens, who is eternal and unchanging, resting forever at the root of continuous creation; and an incarnate person on earth, born as a human being and living the life of a man. This pair contrasts the Dao and humanity after the modes of formlessness and physical form, showing that the Dao although primarily eternal, can also be finite and ultimately is manifest in both modes—thus giving believers the comfort of belonging, of being part of something larger.

The second opposition, the contrast between life and death, is expressed in Lord Lao's journeys during the conversion episode, especially his (and Yin Xi's) ecstatic excursions to the heavens and the hellish tortures they undergo at the hands of the barbarians. This contrast, by extension, also vividly points to the opposition between heaven and hell, and powerfully conveys the message that the Dao has power over both realms and is not fazed by hell.

Third, the opposition of perfected and technical methods is mythically represented in the figures of Lord Lao's principal disciples. In the episode on the transmission of the *Daode jing*, Laozi's prime disciple Yin Xi vows to do everything to bring salvation to the world, while his servant Xu Jia gives up his Daoist inspiration for a large sum of money. The Dao, operating behind the scene, empowers and supports both, but there is a clear value judgment in favor of the former.

These three activities of Lord Lao as the Dao—resting quiescent as the principle of order in the cosmos then being born on earth, ecstatically traveling to the heavens and undergoing the tortures of hell, and supporting both the pure disciple and the greedy technician—not only make a statement about the encompassing nature of the Dao and its power on earth, but also establish important hierarchies and structures for practicing Daoists. While alive on earth, the first says, you are still a part of the Dao; you, like the incarnate god, can reach out and be with the Dao whenever you choose. There are heavens and hells in the world, the second explains, but they are yours to control; just as you can delight in the heavens, so you will also be able to overcome the hells. Being part of the Dao, you can work with them both, just remain steadfast and hold to the scriptures. Various methods, perfected and technical, the third says, serve the Dao on earth, and while each has its own value, they occupy different positions in the structure of the Daoist teaching. Encompassing all yet always supporting the good, the Dao establishes and supports structures within the world that clearly differentiate between good and evil but still in their entirety belong intimately to the creative and eternal Dao.

The mythological complex surrounding Lord Lao, with its cosmo-logical, human, and action-centered binary opposites, reveals the Dao in a vivid way unmatched by abstract discourse. It shows believers their rightful place in the larger scheme of things and fills them with hope and confidence in the ever-changing and almost but not quite perfect world of humanity.

Bibliography

Abe, Stanley. 1997. "Northern Wei Daoist Sculpture from Shaanxi Province." *Cahiers d'Extrême-Asie* 9:69–84.

Akioka Hideyuki 秋岡英行. 1994. "Jō Sanhō to jōdai dōkyō seiha" 張三丰と清代道教西派. *Tōhō shūkyō* 東方宗教 83:1–15.

Akizuki Kan'ei 秋月觀英. 1964. "Rikuchō dōkyō ni okeru ōhōsetsu no hatten" 六朝道教における應報說の發展. *Hirosaki daigaku jimbun shakai* 弘前大學人文社會 33:25–60.

——. 1965. "Sairon sangen shishō no keisei" 再論三元思想の形成. *Hirosaki daigaku bunkyō ronsō* 弘前大學文經論叢 1:437–56.

——. 1966. "Dōkyō to bukkyō no fubo enchō kyō" 道教と佛教の父母恩重經. *Shūkyō kenkyū* 宗教研究 39.4:23–54.

Allan, Sarah. 1972. "The Identities of T'ai-kung-wang in Chou and Han Literature." *Monumenta Serica* 29:57–99.

——. 1981. *The Heir and the Sage: A Structural Analysis of Ancient Chinese Dynastic Legends*. San Francisco: Chinese Materials Center.

——. 1991. *The Shape of the Turtle: Myth, Art and Cosmos in Early China*. Albany: State University of New York Press.

Allwohn, Adolf. 1959. "Der religionspsychologische Aspekt des sakralen Königtums." In *The Sacral Kingship—La regalita sacra*, 37–47. Supplement to *Numen IV*. Leiden: E. J. Brill.

Andersen, Poul. 1980. *The Method of Holding the Three Ones*. London and Malmo: Curzon Press.

——. 1991. "Taoist Ritual Texts and Traditions with Special Reference to *Bugang*, the Cosmic Dance." Ph.D. diss., University of Copenhagen.

——. 1994. "Talking to the Gods: Visionary Divination in Early Taoism." *Taoist Resources* 5.1:1–24.

Babcock, Barbara A., ed. 1978. *The Reversible World: Symbolic Inversion in Art and Society*. Ithaca: Cornell University Press.

Baldrian-Hussein, Farzeen. 1984. *Procédés secrets du joyau magique*. Paris: Les Deux Océans.

——. 1986. "Lü Tung-pin in Northern Sung Literature." *Cahiers d'Extrême-Asie* 2:133–70.

——. 1990. "Inner Alchemy: Notes on the Origin and the Use of the Term *neidan*." *Cahiers d'Extrême-Asie* 5:163–90.

Barrett, T. H. 1996. *Taoism Under the T'ang: Religion and Empire During the Golden Age of Chinese History*. London: Wellsweep Press.

Bauer, Wolfgang. 1956. "Der Herr vom gelben Stein." *Oriens Extremus* 3:137–52.

Baxter, William H. 1983. "A Look at the History of Chinese Color Terminology." *Journal of the Chinese Language Teachers Association* 19.1:1–25.

——. 1998. "Situating the Language of the *Lao-tzu*: The Probable Date of the *Tao-te-ching*." In *Lao-tzu and the* Tao-te-ching, edited by Livia Kohn and Michael LaFargue, 231–54. Albany: State University of New York Press.

Bell, Catherine. 1987. "Lu Hsiu-ching." In *Encyclopedia of Religion*, edited by Mircea Eliade, 9:50–51. New York: Macmillan.

——. 1988. "Ritualization of Texts and Textualization of Ritual in the Codification of Taoist Liturgy." *History of Religions* 27.4:366–92.

——. 1992. "Printing and Religion in China: Some Evidence from the *Taishang Ganying Pian*." *Journal of Chinese Religions* 20:173–86.

Bellah, Robert. 1970. "Religious Evolution." In *Beyond Belief*, edited by Robert Bellah, 20–50. New York: Harper and Row.

Benn, Charles D. 1977. "Taoism as Ideology in the Reign of Emperor Hsüan-tsung." Ph.D. diss., University of Michigan, Ann Arbor.

——. 1987. "Religious Aspects of Emperor Hsüan-tsung's Taoist Ideology." In *Buddhist and Taoist Practice in Medieval Chinese Society*, edited by David W. Chappell, 127–45. Honolulu: University of Hawaii Press.

——. 1991. *The Cavern Mystery Transmission: A Taoist Ordination Rite of A.C. 711*. Honolulu: University of Hawaii Press.

Biallas, Leonard J. 1986. *Myths: Gods, Heroes, and Saviors*. Mystic, Conn.: Twenty-third Publications.

Bilsky, Lester J. 1975. *The State Religion of Ancient China*. 2 vols. Taipei: Chinese Folklore Association.

Bingham, Woodridge. 1970. *The Founding of the T'ang Dynasty: The Fall of Sui and the Rise of T'ang*. 1941. Reprint, New York: Octagon Books.

Birrell, Anne. 1993. *Chinese Mythology: An Introduction*. Baltimore: Johns Hopkins University Press.

Boardman, Eugene P. 1962. "Millenary Aspects of the Taiping Rebellion (1851–64)." In *Millenial Dreams in Action: Essays in Comparative Study*, edited by Sylvia L. Thrupp, 70–79. The Hague: Mouton.

Bodde, Derk. 1942. "The Chinese View of Immortality: Its Expression by Chu Hsi and Its Relationship to Buddhist Thought." *Review of Religion* 6:364–82.

——. 1942a. "The New Identification of Lao-tzu Proposed by Professor Dubs." *Journal of the American Oriental Society* 62:8–13.

——. 1975. *Festivals in Classical China*. Princeton: Princeton University Press.

Bokenkamp, Stephen. 1983. "Sources of the Ling-pao Scriptures." In *Tantric and Taoist Studies*, edited by Michel Strickmann, 2:434–86. Brussels: Institut Belge des Hautes Etudes Chinoises.

——. 1986. "The Peach Flower Font and the Grotto Passsage." *Journal of the American Oriental Society* 106:65–79.

——. 1993. "Traces of Early Celestial Masters Physiological Practices in the *Xianger* Commentary." *Taoist Resources* 4.2:37–52.

——. 1994. "Time After Time: Taoist Apocalyptic History and the Founding of the T'ang Dynasty." *Asia Major* 7.1:59–88.

——. 1997. *Early Daoist Scriptures*. With a contribution by Peter Nickerson. Berkeley: University of California Press.

——. 1997a. "The Yao Boduo Stele as Evidence for the 'Dao-Buddhism' of the Early Lingbao Scriptures." *Cahiers d'Extrême-Asie* 9:55–68.

Boltz, Judith M. 1986. "In Homage to T'ien-fei." *Journal of the American Oriental Society* 106:211–52.

——. 1987. *A Survey of Taoist Literature: Tenth to Seventeenth Centuries*. Berkeley: University of California, China Research Monograph 32.

——. 1987a. "Lao-tzu." In *Encyclopedia of Religion*, edited by Mircea Eliade, 8:454–59. New York: Macmillan.

Brandon, S. G. F. 1958. "The Myth and Ritual Position Critically Considered." In *Myth, Ritual and Kingship*, edited by Samuel H. Hooke, 261–91. Oxford: Clarendon Press.

Brokaw, Cynthia. 1991. *The Ledgers of Merit and Demerit: Social Change and Moral Order in Late Imperial China*. Princeton: Princeton University Press.

Brown, Peter. 1978. *The Making of Late Antiquity*. Cambridge, Mass.: Harvard University Press.

——. 1981. *The Cult of the Saints*. Chicago: University of Chicago Press.

Bumbacher, Stephan Peter. 1995. "Cosmic Scripts and Heavenly Scriptures: The Holy Nature of Taoist Texts." *Cosmos* 11.2:139–54.

Burkert, Walter. 1979. *Structure and History in Greek Mythology and Ritual*. Berkeley: University of California Press.

Cahill, Suzanne. 1980. "Taoists at the Sung Court: The Heavenly Text Affair of 1008." *Bulletin of Sung and Yuan Studies* 16:23–44.

——. 1985. "Sex and the Supernatural in Medieval China: Cantos on the Transcendent Who Presides Over the River." *Journal of the American Oriental Society* 105:197–220.

——. 1986. "Reflections on a Metal Mother: Tu Kuang-t'ing's Biography of Hsi-wang-mu." *Journal of Chinese Religions* 13/14:127–42.

——. 1993. *Transcendence and Divine Passion: The Queen Mother of the West in Medieval China*. Stanford: Stanford University Press.

Campbell, Joseph. 1949. *The Hero with a Thousand Faces*. New York: Pantheon Books.

Carus, Paul, and D. T. Suzuki. 1973. *Treatise on Response and Retribution*. 1906. Reprint, LaSalle, Ill.: Open Court Publishing.

Cedzich, Ursula-Angelika. 1987. "Das Ritual der Himmelsmeister im Spiegel früher Quellen." Ph.D. diss., University of Würzburg,

Chan, Alan. 1991. *Two Visions of the Way: A Study of the Wang Pi and the Ho-shang-kung Commentaries on the Laozi*. Albany: State University of New York Press.

Chan Hok-lam. 1968. "Liu Chi and His Models: The Image-Building of a Chinese Imperial Adviser." *Oriens Extremus* 15:34–55.

———. 1973. "Chang Chung and His Prophesy: the Transmission of the Legend of an Early Ming Taoist." *Oriens Extremus* 20:65–102.

Chan, Wing-tsit. 1963. *A Source Book in Chinese Philosophy*. Princeton: Princeton University Press.

Chang, Kwang-chih. 1976. *Early Chinese Civilization: Anthropological Perspectives*. Cambridge, Mass.: Harvard-Yenching Institute Monograph Series 23.

———. 1980. *Shang Civilization*. New Haven, Conn.: Yale University Press.

———. 1983. *Art, Myth, and Ritual: The Path to Political Authority in Ancient China*. Cambridge, Mass.: Harvard University Press.

Chaves, Jonathan. 1977. "The Legacy of Ts'ang Chieh: The Written Word as Magic." *Oriental Art* 23.2:200–15.

Chen Guofu 陳國符. 1975. *Daozang yuanliu kao* 道藏源流考. Taipei: Guting.

Ch'en, Kenneth. 1945. "Buddhist-Taoist Mixtures in the *Pa-shih-i-hua t'u*." *Harvard Journal of Asiatic Studies* 9:1–12.

———. 1964. *Buddhism in China*. Princeton: Princeton University Press.

———. 1973. *The Chinese Transformation of Buddhism*. Princeton: Princeton University Press.

Chen, Robert S. 1992. *A Comparative Study of Chinese and Western Cyclic Myths*. New York: Peter Lang.

Chen Yuan 陳垣. 1962. *Nan Song chu Hebei xin daojiao kao* 南宋初河北新道教考. 1941. Reprint, Beijing: Zhonghua shuju.

Chen Yuan 陳垣, Chen Zhizhao 陳智超, and Zeng Qingying 曾慶瑛. 1988. *Daojia jinshi lue* 道家金石略. Beijing: Wenwu.

Ching, Julia. 1983. "The Mirror Symbol Revisited: Confucian and Taoist Mysticism." In *Mysticism and Religious Traditions*, edited by Steven T. Katz, 226–46. New York: Oxford University Press.

———. 1997. *Mysticism and Kingship in China*. Cambridge: Cambridge University Press.

Cleary, Thomas. 1991. *Vitality Energy Spirit: A Taoist Sourcebook*. Boston: Shambhala.

Cohn, Norman. 1962. "Medieval Millenarianism: Its Bearing on the Comparative Study of Millenarian Movements." In *Millenial Dreams in Action: Essays in Comparative Study*, edited by Sylvia L. Thrupp, 31–43. The Hague: Mouton.

———. 1995. *Cosmos, Chaos, and the World to Come: The Ancient Roots of Apocalyptic Faith*. New Haven, Conn.: Yale University Press.

Colavito, Maria M. 1992. *The New Theogony: Mythology for the Real World*. Albany: State University of New York Press.

Cook, Roger. 1974. *The Tree of Life: Image for the Cosmos*. New York: Avon.

Coyle, Michael. 1981. "Book of Rewards and Punishments." In *Chinese Civilization and Society: A Sourcebook*, edited by Patricia B. Ebrey, 71–74. New York: Free Press.

D'Aquili, Eugene G., and Charles D. Laughlin, Jr. 1979. "The Neurobiology of Myth and Ritual." In *The Spectrum of Ritual: A Biogenetic Structural Analysis,* edited by Eugene G. D'Aquili, Charles D. Laughlin, Jr., and John McManus, 152–82. New York: Columbia University Press.

Davis, Edward L. 1994. "Society and the Supernatural in Sung China." Ph.D. diss., University of California, Berkeley.

Dean, Kenneth. 1993. "Group Initiation and Exorcistic Dance in the Xinhua Regime." In *Minsu quyi,* edited by Wang Ch'iu-gui, 2:105-95. Beijing: Minsu yanjiu yuan.

Demiéville, Paul. 1987. "The Mirror of the Mind." In *Sudden and Gradual: Approaches to Enlightenment in Chinese Thought,* edited by Peter N. Gregory, 13–40. Honolulu: University of Hawaii Press.

Deninger, Johannes. 1987. "Revelation." In *Encyclopedia of Religion,* edited by Mircea Eliade, 12:356–62. New York: Macmillan.

Despeux, Catherine. 1986. "L'ordination des femmes taoïstes sous les Tang." *Etudes Chinoises* 5:53–100.

———. 1990. *Immortélles de la Chine anciénne: Taoïsme et alchimie féminine.* Paris: Pardés.

———. 1995. "L'expiration des six souffles d'après les sources du Canon taoïque: Un procédé classique du Qigong." In *Hommage à Kwong Hing Foon: Etudes d'histoire culturelle de la Chine,* edited by Jean-Pierre Diény, 129-63. Paris: Collège du France, Institut des Hautes Etudes Chinoises.

DeWoskin, Kenneth J. 1982. *A Song for One or Two: Music and the Concept of Art in Early China.* Ann Arbor: University of Michigan, Center for Chinese Studies.

———. 1983. *Doctors, Diviners, and Magicians of Ancient China.* New York: Columbia University Press.

Dibelius, Martin. 1935. *From Tradition to Gospel.* New York, n.p.

Dilworth, David A. 1989. *Philosophy in World Perspective: A Comparative Hermeneutic of the Major Theories.* New Haven: Yale University Press.

Ding Huang 丁煌. 1979. "Tangdai daojiao taiqing gong zhidu kao" 唐代道教太清宮制度考. Part I. *Lishi xuebao* 歷史學報 (Chenggong University) 6:275–314.

———. 1980. "Tangdai daojiao taiqing gong zhidu kao" 唐代道教太清宮制度考. Part II. *Lishi xuebao* 歷史學報 (Chenggong University) 7:177–220.

Doria, Charles, and Harris Lenowitz. 1976. *Origins: Creation Texts from the Ancient Mediterranean.* Garden City, New York: Anchor/Doubleday.

Doty, William G. 1986. *Mythography: The Study of Myths and Rituals.* University, Ala.: The University of Alabama Press.

Drexler, Monika. 1994. *Daoistische Schriftmagie: Interpretationen zu den Fu im Daozang.* Stuttgart: Franz Steiner, Münchener Ostasiatische Studien, 68.

Duara, Prasanjit. 1988. "Superscribing Symbols: The Myth of Guandi, Chinese God of War." *Journal of Asian Studies* 47:778–95.

Dubs, Homer H. 1941. "The Date and Circumstances of the Philosopher Laotzu." *Journal of the American Oriental Society* 61:215–21.

——. 1942. "The Identification of the Lao-dz: A Reply to Professor Bodde." *Journal of the American Oriental Society* 62:300–4.

Dudley, Paula. 1990. "Lao-tse: Tao-te-ching." Audio-cassette. Recorded by the Tao Alchemical Company.

Dull, Jack. 1966. "A Historical Introduction to the Apocryphal (*ch'an-wei*) Texts of the Han Dynasty." Ph.D. diss., University of Washington, Seattle.

Dumoulin, Heinrich. 1988. *Zen Buddhism: A History.* Vol 1: India and China. New York: Macmillan.

Dundes, Alan, ed. 1984. *Sacred Narrative.* Berkeley: University of California Press.

——. 1984a. "Earth-Diver: Creation of the Mythopoeic Male." In *Sacred Narrative*, edited by Alan Dundes, 270–94. Berkeley: University of California Press.

——. 1990. "The Hero Pattern and the Life of Jesus." 1976. Reprinted in *In Quest of the Hero*, edited by Robert A. Segal, 177–223. Princeton: Princeton University Press.

Durt, Hubert. 1996. "L'apparition du Buddha a sa mère après son nirvāna." In *De Dunhuang au Japon: Etudes chinoises et bouddhiques offertes a Michel Soymié*, edited by Jean-Pierre Drège, 1–24. Paris: Droz.

Duyvendak, J.J.L. 1947. "The Dreams of the Emperor Hsüan-tsung." *India Antiqua.*

Eberhard, Wolfram. 1933. *Beiträge zur kosmologischen Spekulation der Han-Zeit.* Berlin, n.p.

——. 1949. *Das Toba-Reich Nordchinas.* Leiden: E. J. Brill.

——. 1968. *The Local Cultures of South and East China.* Translated by Alide Eberhard. Leiden: E. J. Brill.

Ebrey, Patricia B., and Peter N. Gregory, eds. 1993. *Religion and Society in T'ang and Sung China.* Honolulu: University of Hawaii Press.

Edinger, Edward F. 1972. *Ego and Archetype: Individuation and the Religious Function of the Psyche.* Baltimore: Penguin.

Edsman, Carl-Martin. 1959. "Zum sakralen Königtum in der Forschung der letzten hundert Jahre." In *The Sacral Kingship—La regalita sacra*, 3–17. Supplement to *Numen* IV. Leiden: E. J. Brill.

Eichhorn, Werner. 1954. "Description of the Rebellion of Sun En and Earlier Taoist Rebellions." *Mitteilungen des Instituts für Orientforschung* 2.2:325–52 and 2.3:463–76.

——. 1955. "Bemerkungen zum Aufstand des Chang Chio und zum Staate des Chang Lu." *Mitteilungen des Instituts für Orientforschung* 3:291–327.

——. 1957. "T'ai-p'ing und T'ai-p'ing Religion." *Mitteilungen des Instituts für Orientforschung* 5:113–40.

Eliade, Mircea. 1957. *The Sacred and the Profane: The Nature of Religion.* Translated by William R. Trask. New York: Harcourt & Brace.

——. 1957a. "Time and Eternity in Indian Thought." *Eranos Jahrbuch* 1957:173–201.

——. 1958. *Birth and Rebirth: The Religious Meanings of Initiation in Human Culture.* New York: Harper and Brothers Publishers.

——. 1963. *Myth and Reality.* New York: Harper & Row.

——. 1964. *Shamanism: Archaic Techniques of Ecstasy.* Princeton: Princeton University Press, Bollingen Series.

——. 1965. *The Myth of the Eternal Return.* New York: Random House. Bollingen Series.

——. 1984. "Cosmogonic Myth and 'Sacred History.'" In *Sacred Narrative,* edited by Alan Dundes, 137–51. Berkeley: University of California Press.

Eliade, Mircea, and Lawrence E. Sullivan. 1987. "Hierophany." In *Encyclopedia of Religion,* edited by Mircea Eliade, 6:313–17. New York: Macmillan.

Engelhardt, Ute. 1987. *Die klassische Tradition der Qi-Übungen: Eine Darstellung anhand des Tang-zeitlichen Textes Fuqi jingyi lun von Sima Chengzhen.* Wiesbaden: Franz Steiner.

Erdberg Consten, Eleanor von. 1942. "A Statue of Lao-tzu in the Po-yün-kuan." *Monumenta Serica* 7:235–41.

Feeley-Harnik, Gillian. 1985. "Issues in Divine Kingship." *Annual Review of Anthropology* 14:273–313.

Festinger, Leon, Henry W. Ricken, and Stanley Schachter. 1956. *When Prophecy Fails: A Social and Psychological Study of a Modern Group that Predicted the Destruction of the World.* New York: Harper & Row.

Finucane, Ronald C. 1977. *Miracles and Pilgrims: Popular Beliefs in Medieval England.* Totowa, New Jersey: Rowman and Littlefield.

Forke, Alfred. 1972. *Lun-Heng: Wang Ch'ung's Essays.* New York: Paragon.

Forte, Antonino. 1973. "Deux études sur le manichéisme chinois." *T'oung-pao* 59:220–53.

——. 1988. *Mingtang and Buddhist Utopias in the History of the Astronomical Clock: The Tower, Statue and Armillary Sphere Constructed by Empress Wu.* Rome and Paris: Ecole Française d'Extrême-Orient.

——. 1992. "Chinese State Monasteries in the Seventh and Eighth Centuries." In *E Chō ō Go tenchiku koku den kenkyū* 慧超往五天竺國傳研究, edited by Kuwayama Seishin 桑山正進, 213–58. Kyoto: Kyoto University, Jimbun kagaku kenkyūjo.

Franke, Herbert. 1972. "Einige Drucke und Handschriften der frühen Ming-Zeit." *Oriens Extremus* 19:55–64.

——. 1977. "Bemerkungen zum volkstümlichen Taoismus der Ming-Zeit." *Oriens Extremus* 24:75-112.

——. 1990. "The Taoist Elements in the Buddhist *Great Bear Sutra* (*Pei-tou ching*)." *Asia Major* 3.1:75–112.

Frankfort, H. 1948. *Kingship and the Gods.* Chicago: University of Chicago Press.

Franz, Marie Luise von. 1972. *Patterns of Creativity Mirrored in Creation Myths.* Zürich: Spring Publications.

Frazer, James G. 1911–15. *The Golden Bough: A Study in Magic and Religion.* 12 vols. London: Macmillan.

——. 1984. "The Fall of Man." In *Sacred Narrative,* edited by Alan Dundes, 71–97. Berkeley: University of California Press.

Fukui Fumimasa 福井文雅. 1987. *Hannya shingyō no rekishiteki kenkyū* 般苦心經の歴史的研究. Tokyo: Shunjusha.

——. 1995. "The History of Taoist Studies in Japan and Some Related Issues." *Acta Asiatica* 68:1–18.

Fukui Kōjun 福井康順. 1951. "Shinsenden kō" 神仙傳考. *Tōhō shūkyō* 東方宗教 1:1–21.

———. 1962. "Bunshi naiden kō" 文始内傳考. *Tōhōgaku ronshū* 東方學論集, 15th Anniversary Volume, 276–89.

———. 1964. "Genmyō naihen ni tsuite" 玄妙内篇について. In *Iwai hakase koki kinen tenseki romshū* 岩井博士古稀記念典籍論集, 565–75. Tokyo: Dai'an.

Fukunaga Mitsuji 福永光司. 1973. "Dōkyō ni okeru kagami to ken" 道教における鏡と劍. *Tōhō gakuhō* 東方學報 45:59–120.

———. 1987. "Kōen jōtei to tennō taitei to genshi tenson" 昊天上帝と天皇大帝と元始天尊. In *Dōkyō shisōshi kenkyū* 道教思想史研究, edited by Fukunaga Mitsuji, 123–56. Tokyo: Iwanami.

Fung, Yu-lan and Derk Bodde. 1952. *A History of Chinese Philosophy*. 2 vols. Princeton: Princeton University Press.

Gauchet, L. 1941. "Le *Tou-jen king* des taoïstes: son texte primitif et sa date probable." *Bulletin de l'Université l'Aurore*, Third Series, 2:511.

———. 1949. "Recherches sur la triade taoïque." *Bulletin de l'Université l'Aurore* 3.10:326–66.

Geertz, Clifford, ed. 1977. "Centers, Kings, and Charisma: Reflections on the Symbolics of Power." In *Culture and Its Creators*, edited by Joseph Ben-David and Terry N. Clark, 150–71. Chicago: University of Chicago Press.

Gennep, Arnold van. 1960. *The Rites of Passage*. Chicago: University of Chicago Press.

Gesick, Lorraine, ed. 1983. *Centers, Symbols and Hierarchies: Essays on the Classical States of Southeast Asia*. New Haven, Conn.: Yale University Press, Southeast Asia Monograph, no. 26.

Getty, Alice. 1988. *The Gods of Northern Buddhism*. 1928. Reprint, New York: Dover.

Giles, Herbert A. 1906. "Lao-tzu and the *Tao-te-ching*." In *Adversaria Sinica*, edited by Herbert A. Giles, 58–78. Shanghai: Kelly & Walsh.

———. 1916. *Strange Stories from a Chinese Studio*. Shanghai: Kelly & Walsh.

Giles, Lionel. 1948. *A Gallery of Chinese Immortals*. London: John Murray.

Girardot, Norman. 1976. "The Problem of Creation Mythology in the Study of Chinese Religion." *History of Religions* 15:289–318.

———. 1983. *Myth and Meaning in Early Taoism*. Berkeley and Los Angeles: University of California Press.

———. 1985. "Behaving Cosmogonically in Early Taoism." In *Cosmogony and Ethical Order: New Studies in Comparative Ethics*, edited by Robin W. Lovin and Frank E. Reynolds, 67–97. Chicago: University of Chicago Press.

Goodrich, Anne S. 1981. *Chinese Hells*. St. Augustin, Germany: Monumenta Serica.

Gordon, R. L., ed. 1981. *Myth, Religion and Society: Structuralist Essays by M. Detienne, L. Gernet, J. P. Vernant and P. Vidal-Naquet*. Cambridge: Cambridge University Press.

Graham, A. C. 1960. *The Book of Lieh-tzu*. London: A. Murray.

———. 1981. *Chuang-tzu: The Seven Inner Chapters and Other Writings from the Book of Chuang-tzu*. London: Allen & Unwin.

———. 1986. *Yin-Yang and the Nature of Correlative Thinking*. Singapore: The Institute for East Asian Philosophies.

———. 1989. *Disputers of the Tao: Philosophical Argument in Ancient China*. La Salle, Ill.: Open Court Publishing Company.

———. 1990. "The Origins of the Legend of Lao Tan." 1981. Reprinted in *Studies in Chinese Philosophy and Philosophical Literature*, edited by A. C. Graham, 111–24. Albany: State University of New York Press.

Granet, Marcel. 1930. *Chinese Civilization*. London: Routledge & Kegan Paul.

Grootaers, Willem. 1952. "The Hagiography of the Chinese God Hsüan-wu." *Asian Folklore Studies* 11:139–82.

Grottanelli, Cristiano. 1987. "Kingship: An Overview." In *Encyclopedia of Religions*, edited by Mircea Eliade, 8:313–17. New York: Macmillan.

Gu Jiegang 顧頡剛. 1936. *Sanhuang kao* 三皇考. Beijing: Yenching Journal of Chinese Studies, Monograph 8.

Gu, Zhizhong, trans. 1992. *Creation of the Gods*. 2 vols. Beijing: New World Press.

Guenther, Herbert V. 1968. "Tantra and Revelation." *History of Religions* 7.4:279–301.

Güntsch, Gertrud. 1988. *Das Shen-hsien-chuan und das Erscheinungsbild eines Hsien*. Frankfurt: Peter Lang.

Hackmann, Heinrich. 1920. "Die Mönchsregeln des Klostertaoismus." *Ostasiatische Zeitschrift* 8:141–70.

———. 1931. *Die dreihundert Mönchsgebote des chinesischen Taoismus*. Amsterdam: Koninklijke Akademie van Wetenshapen.

Hadfield, P. 1949. *Traits of Divine Kingship in Africa*. London: Watts & Co.

Haloun, Gustav. 1925. "Die Rekonstruktion der chinesischen Urgeschichte durch die Chinesen." *Japanisch-deutsche Zeitschrift für Wissenschaft und Technik* 3.7:243–79.

Haloun, Gustav, and W. B. Henning. 1953. "The Compendium of the Doctrine and Styles of the Teaching of Mani, the Buddha of Light." *Asia Major* 3.2:184–212.

Hansen, Valerie L. 1990. *Changing Gods in Medieval China. 1127–1276*. Princeton: Princeton University Press.

Harper, Donald. 1978. "The Han Cosmic Board." *Early China* 4:1–10.

———. 1994. "Resurrection in Warring States Popular Religion." *Taoist Resources* 5.2:13–28.

Hartland, Edwin S. 1910. *Primitive Paternity: The Myth of Supernatural Birth in Relation to the History of the Family*. 2 vols. London: D. Nutt.

Hawkes, David. 1959. *Ch'u Tz'u: The Songs of the South*. Oxford: Clarendon Press.

———. 1967. "The Quest of the Goddess." *Asia Major* 13:71–94.

———. 1981. "Quanzhen Plays and Quanzhen Masters." *Bulletin d'Ecole Française d'Extrême Orient* 69:153–70.

Hawley, John S., ed. 1987. *Saints and Virtues*. Berkeley: University of California Press.

Hendrischke, Barbara. 1993. "Der Taoismus in der Tang-Zeit." *Minima Sinica* 1993/1:110–43.

Hendrischke, Barbara, and Benjamin Penny. 1996. "The 180 Precepts Spoken by Lord Lao: A Translation and Textual Study." Taoist Resources 6.2:17–29.

Henricks, Robert. 1989. Lao-Tzu: Te-Tao ching. New York: Ballantine.

Hervouet, Yves, ed. 1978. A Sung Bibliography; Bibliographie des Sung. Hong Kong: The Chinese University Press.

Hidding, K.A.H. 1959. "The High God and the King as Symbols of Totality." In The Sacral Kingship—La regalita sacra, 48–53. Supplement to Numen IV. Leiden: E. J. Brill.

Hocart, Arthur M. 1969. Kingship. 1927. Reprint, Oxford: Oxford University Press.

——. 1970. Kings and Councillors. 1936. Reprint, Chicago: University of Chicago Press.

Homann, Rolf. 1971. Die wichtigsten Körpergottheiten im Huang-t'ing-ching. Göppingen: Alfred Kümmerle.

Hooke, Samuel H., ed. 1933. Myth and Ritual. London: Oxford University Press.

——, ed. 1935. The Labyrinth. London: Society for Promoting Christian Knowledge.

——, ed. 1958. Myth, Ritual and Kingship. Oxford: Clarendon Press.

Hou Ching-lang. 1975. .Monnaies d'offrande et la notion de trésorerie dans la religion chinoise. Paris: College du France, Institut des Hautes Etudes Chinoises.

Huang Miaozhi 黃苗子. 1991. Wu Daozi shiji 吳道子事輯. Beijing: Zhonghua.

Huang, Paolos. 1996. Lao Zi: The Book and the Man. Helsinki: The Finnish Oriental Society.

Hucker, Charles O. 1985. A Dictionary of Official Titles in Imperial China. Stanford: Stanford University Press.

Hurvitz, Leon. 1956. Wei Shou on Buddhism and Taoism. Kyoto: Jimbun kagaku kenkyūjo.

——. 1961. "A Recent Japanese Study of Lao-tzu: Kimura Eiichi's Rōshi no shin kenkyū." Monumenta Serica 20:311–67.

Imbault-Huart, M.C. 1884. "La légende du premier pape des taoïstes." Journal Asiatique 8.4:389–461.

Inoue Yutaka 井上豐. 1992. "Rokutei-rokkajin no henyū" 六丁六甲の變容. Tōhō shūkyō 東方宗教 80:15–32.

Ishibashi Nariyasu 石橋成康. 1991. "Shinshutsu Nanatsudera zō Seijō hōgyō kyō kō" 新出七寺藏清淨法行經考. Tōhō shūkyō 東方宗教 78:69–87.

Ishida Hidemi 石田秀實. 1987. "Taijō rōkun setsu chōseijō kyō honbun kōtei oyobi ni nihongo yakushu" 太上老君說常清靜經本文校訂並ひに日本語譯注. Yawata daigaku ronshū 八幡大學論集 38:86–114.

——. 1987a. Ki: Nagareru shintai 氣─流れる身體. Tokyo: Hirakawa.

——. 1989. "Body and Mind: The Chinese Perspective." In Taoist Meditation and Longevity Techniques, edited by Livia Kohn, 41–70. Ann Arbor: University of Michigan, Center for Chinese Studies.

Ishida Kenji 石田憲司. 1995. "Taiwan nanbu no shinbujin shinkō ni tsuite" 台灣南部の眞武神信仰について. Tōhō shūkyō 東方宗教 85:24–40.

Ishii Masako 石井昌子. 1983. "Dōkyō no kamigami" 道教の神神. In *Dōkyō* 道教, edited by Fukui Kōjun 福井康順 et al., 1:121–88. Tokyo: Hirakawa.

Jagchid, Sechin. 1980. "Chinese Buddhism and Taoism During the Mongolian Rule of China." *Mongolian Studies* 6:61–98.

James, Edwin O. 1969. *Creation and Cosmology*. Leiden: E. J. Brill.

James, Jean M. 1986. "Some Iconographic Problems in Early Daoist-Buddhist Sculpture in China." *Archives of Asian Art* 42:71–76.

Japussy, Waldo. 1990. *The Tao of Meow*. Columbus, Ohio: Enthea Press.

Jaspers, Karl. 1962. *Socrates, Buddha, Confucius, Jesus: The Paradigmatic Individuals*. New York: Harcort, Brace & World.

Jing, Anning. 1994. "Yongle Palace: The Transformation of the Daoist Pantheon During the Yuan Dynasty." Ph.D. diss., Princeton University.

Johnson, David. 1985. "The City-God Cults of T'ang and Sung China." *Harvard Journal of Asiatic Studies* 45:363–457.

Johnson, T. W. 1974. "Far Eastern Foxlore." *Asian Folklore Studies* 33:35–68.

Jones, Ernest. 1951. "The Madonna's Conception Through the Ear." In *Essays in Applied Psychoanalysis*, edited by Ernest Jones, 266–357. London: The Hogarth Press.

Jung, C. G. 1949. "The Psychology of the Child Archetype." In *Essays on a Science of Mythology: The Myth of the Divine Child and the Mysteries of Eleusis*, edited by C. G. Jung and Karoly Kerenyi, 97–138. New York: Pantheon Books. Bollingen Series.

———. 1955. *The Interpretation of Nature and the Psyche: Synchronicity*. London: Routledge & Kegan Paul.

———. 1960. *On the Nature of the Psyche*. Princeton: Princeton University Press, Bollingen Series.

Kalinowski, Marc. 1983. "Les instruments astro-calendriques des Han et la méthode liu-jen." *Bulletin de l'Ecole Française d'Extrême-Orient* 72:309–420.

———. 1990. "La littérature divinatoire dans le *Daozang*." *Cahiers d'Extrême-Asie* 5:85–114.

Kaltenmark, Max. 1953. *Le Lie-sien tchouan*. Peking: Université de Paris Publications.

———. 1969. *Lao-tzu and Taoism*. Stanford: Stanford University Press.

———. 1979. "The Ideology of the *T'ai-p'ing-ching*." In *Facets of Taoism*, edited by Holmes Welch and Anna Seidel, 19–52. New Haven: Yale University Press.

———. 1980. "Chine." In *Dictionnaire des Mythologies*, 1–75. Paris: Flammarion.

Kamata Shigeo 鎌田茂雄. 1986. *Dōzō nai bukkyō shisō shiryō shūsei* 道藏内佛教思想資料集成. Tokyo: Daizō Publishers.

Kamitsuka Yoshiko 神塚淑子. 1993. "Nanbokuchō jidai no dōkyō zōzō" 南北朝時代の道教造像. In *Chūgoku chūsei no bunbutsu* 中國中世の文物, edited by Tonami Mamoru 礪波護, 225–89. Kyoto: Kyoto University, Jimbun kagaku kenkyūjo.

———. 1998. "Lao-tzu in Six Dynasties Sculpture." In *Lao-tzu and the Tao-te-ching*, edited by Livia Kohn and Michael LaFargue, 63–85. Albany: State University of New York Press.

Kandel, Barbara. 1979. *Taiping jing: The Origin and Transmission of the 'Scripture on General Welfare': The History of an Unofficial Text*. Hamburg: Gesellschaft für Natur- und Völkerkunde Ostasiens.

Karetzky, Patricia E. 1992. *The Life of the Buddha: Ancient Scriptural and Pictorial Traditions*. Lanham, Md.: University Press of America.

Karlgren, Bernhard. 1946. "Legends and Cults in Ancient China." *Bulletin of the Museum of Far Eastern Antiquities* 18: 199–365.

Katz, Paul R. 1993. "The Religious Function of Temple Murals in Imperial China: The Case of the Yung-lo Kung." *Journal of Chinese Religions* 21:45–68.

———. 1994. "The Interaction Between Ch'üan-chen Taoism and Local Cults: A Case Study of the Yung-lo Kung." *Proceedings of the International Conference on Popular Beliefs and Chinese Culture*. Taipei: Center for Chinese Studies, 201–50.

———. 1996. "Enlightened Alchemist or Immoral Immortal? The Growth of Lü Dongbin's Cult in Late Imperial China." In *Unruly Gods: Divinity and Society in China*, edited by Meir Shahar and Robert P. Weller, 70–104. Honolulu: University of Hawaii Press.

———. 1997. "Temple Inscriptions and the Study of Taoist Cults: A Case Study of Inscriptions at the Palace of Eternal Joy." *Taoist Resources* 7.1:1–22.

Keightley, David N. 1978. "The Religious Commitment: Shang Theology and the Genesis of Chinese Political Culture." *History of Religions* 17:211–25.

Keller, Ernst, and Marie-Luise Keller. 1969. *Miracles in Dispute: A Continuing Debate*. Philadelphia: Fortress Press.

Kelsey, Morton. 1987. "Miracles: Modern Perspectives." In *Encyclopedia of Religion*, edited by Mircea Eliade, 9:548–52. New York: Macmillan.

Kikuchi Noritaka 菊地章太. 1994. "Rokuseiki chūgoku no kyuseishu shinkō" 六世紀中國の救世主信仰. In *Dōkyō bunka e no tembō* 道教文化への展望, edited by Dōkyō bunka kenkyūkai 道教文化研究會, 320–41. Tokyo: Hirakawa.

Kimura Eiichi 林村英一. 1959. *Rōshi no shin kenkyū* 老子の新研究. Tokyo: Sō bunsha.

King, Winston L. 1954. *Introduction to Religion: A Phenomenological Approach*. New York: Harper & Row.

Kirk, Geoffrey S. 1970. *Myth: Its Meaning and Function in Ancient and Other Cultures*. Cambridge, Eng.: Sather Classical Lectures 40.

Kirkland, J. Russell. 1986. "The Last Taoist Grand Master at the T'ang Imperial Court: Li Han-kuang and T'ang Hsüan-tsung." *T'ang Studies* 4:43–67.

———. 1997. "The Historical Contours of Taoism in China: Thoughts on Issues of Classification and Terminology." *Journal of Chinese Religions* 25:57–82.

Kleeman, Terry F. 1993. "The Expansion of the Wen-ch'ang Cult." In *Religion and Society in T'ang and Sung China*, edited by P. B. Ebrey and P. N. Gregory, 45–74. Honolulu: University of Hawaii Press.

Knaul, Livia. 1981. *Leben und Legende des Ch'en T'uan*. Frankfurt: Peter Lang.

———. 1985. "The Winged Life: Kuo Hsiang's Mystical Philosophy." *Journal of Chinese Studies* 2.1:17–41.

Kobayashi Masayoshi 小林正美. 1990. *Rikuchō dōkyōshi kenkyū* 六朝道教史研究. Tokyo: Sōbunsha.

———. 1992. "The Celestial Masters Under the Eastern Jin and Liu-Song Dynasties." *Taoist Resources* 3.2:17–45.

———. 1995. "The Establishment of the Taoist Religion (*Tao-chiao*) and Its Structure." *Acta Asiatica* 68:19–36.

Koestler, Arthur. 1972. *The Roots of Coincidence*. London: Hutchinson.

Kohn, Livia. 1987. *Seven Steps to the Tao: Sima Chengzhen's Zuowanglun*. St. Augustin/Nettetal, Germany: Monumenta Serica.

———. 1987a. "The Teaching of T'ien-yin-tzu." *Journal of Chinese Religions* 15:1–28.

———, ed. 1989. *Taoist Meditation and Longevity Techniques*. Ann Arbor: University of Michigan, Center for Chinese Studies.

———. 1989a. "Guarding the One: Concentrative Meditation in Taoism." In *Taoist Meditation and Longevity Techniques*, edited by Livia Kohn, 123–56. Ann Arbor: University of Michigan, Center for Chinese Studies.

———. 1989b. "Taoist Insight Meditation: The Tang Practice of *Neiguan*." In *Taoist Meditation and Longevity Techniques*, edited by Livia Kohn, 199–222. Ann Arbor: University of Michigan, Center for Chinese Studies.

———. 1989c. "The Mother of the Tao." *Taoist Resources* 1.2:37–113.

———. 1989d. "Die Emigration des Laozi: Mythologische Entwicklungen vom 2. bis 6. Jahrhundert." *Monumenta Serica* 38:49–68.

———. 1990. "Chen Tuan in History and Legend." *Taoist Resources* 2.1:8–31.

———. 1991. *Taoist Mystical Philosophy: The Scripture of Western Ascension*. Albany: State University of New York Press.

———. 1991a. "Taoist Visions of the Body." *Journal of Chinese Philosophy* 18:227–52.

———. 1992. *Early Chinese Mysticism: Philosophy and Soteriology in the Taoist Tradition*. Princeton: Princeton University Press.

———, ed. 1993. *The Taoist Experience: An Anthology*. Albany: State University of New York Press.

———. 1993a. "Quiet Sitting with Master Yinshi: Medicine and Religion in Modern China." *Zen Buddhism Today* 10:79–95.

———. 1994. "The Five Precepts of the Venerable Lord." *Monumenta Serica* 42:171–215.

———. 1995. *Laughing at the Tao: Debates Among Buddhists and Taoists in Medieval China*. Princeton: Princeton University Press.

———. 1995a. "Two New Japanese Encyclopedias of Taoism." *Journal of Chinese Religions* 23: 155–62.

———. 1996. "Laozi: Ancient Philosopher, Master of Longevity, and Taoist God." In *Religions of China in Practice*, edited by Donald Lopez, 52–63. Princeton: Princeton University Press.

———. 1996a. "The Looks of Laozi." *Asian Folklore Studies* 55.2:193–236.

———. 1997. "Yin Xi: The Master at the Beginning of the Scripture." *Journal of Chinese Religions* 45:83–139.

———. 1997a. "The Taoist Adoption of the City God." *Ming Qing Yanjiu* 5:68–106.

——. 1998. "The Lao-tzu Myth." In *Lao-tzu and the* Tao-te-ching, edited by Livia Kohn and Michael LaFargue, 41–62. Albany: State University of New York Press.

——. 1998a. "The *Tao-te-ching* in Ritual." In *Lao-tzu and the* Tao-te-ching, edited by Livia Kohn and Michael LaFargue, 143–61. Albany: State University of New York Press.

——. 1998b. "Rōshi shukkan no monogatari to dōshi no jokai" 老子出關の物語と道士敘階. In *Dōkyō no rekishi to bunka* 道教の歷史と文化, edited by Yamada Toshiaki 山田利明 and Tanaka Fumio 田中文雄, 69–90. Tokyo: Hirakawa.

——. 1998c. "Steal Holy Food and Come Back as a Viper: Conceptions of Karma and Rebirth in Medieval Daoism." *Early Medieval China* 4:1–34.

——. 1998d. "The Beginnings and Cultural Characteristics of East Asian Millenarianism." *Japanese Religions* 23.1:29–51.

——. 1998e. "Taoist Scholasticism: A Preliminary Inquiry." In *Scholasticism: Cross-Cultural and Comparative Perspectives*, edited by José Ignacio Caiesón, 115–40. Albany: State University of New York Press.

Kohn, Livia, and Michael LaFargue. 1998. *Lao-tzu and the* Tao-te-ching. Albany: State University of New York Press.

Kominami Ichirō 小南一朗. 1974. "Shinsenden no fukugen" 神仙傳の复元. In *Iriya kyōju, Kogawa kyōju taikyū kinen Chūgoku bungaku gengogaku ronshū* 入矢教授古稀記念中國文學言語學論集, 301–14. Tokyo, n.p.

——. 1991. *Seiōbo to tanabata denshō* 西王母と七夕傳承. Tokyo: Hirakawa.

——. 1997. *Kazō shiryō o chūshin to shita shinsen shisō no kenkyū* 畫像資料を中心とした神仙思想研究. Kyoto: Kyoto University, Jimbun kagaku kenkyūjo.

Krappe, Alexander. 1944. "Far Eastern Foxlore." *California Folklore Quarterly* 3:124–47.

Kroll, Paul W. 1996. "Body Gods and Inner Vision: *The Scripture of the Yellow Court*." In *Religions of China in Practice*, edited by Donald S. Lopez, Jr., 149–55. Princeton: Princeton University Press.

Kubo, Noritada 窪德忠. 1968. "Prolegomena on the Study of the Controversies Between Buddhists and Taoists in the Yuan Period." *Memoirs of the Research Department of the Tōyō Bunko* 26: 39–61.

——. 1972. "Rōshi hachijuichi ka zusetsu ni tsuite" 老子八十一化圖說について. *Tōyō bunka kenkyūjo kiyo* 東洋文化研究所紀要 58:1–74.

——. 1986. *Dōkyō no kamigami* 道教の神神. Tokyo: Hirakawa.

Kusuyama Haruki 楠山春樹. 1976. "Rōkunden to sono nendai" 老君傳とその年代. *Tōhō shūkyō* 東方宗教 47:12–30. Reprinted in Kusuyama 1979, 371–92.

——. 1976a. "Rōshi ketsukai kō" 老子節解考. *Nihon chūgoku gakkai hō* 日本中國學會報 28. Reprinted in Kusuyama 1979, 199–238.

——. 1977. "Taijō kongen shinroku kō" 太上混元眞錄考. In *Yoshioka Yoshitoyo hakase kanri kinen Dōkyō kenkyū ronshū* 吉岡義豐博士還曆記念道教研究論集, 457–76. Tokyo: Kokusho kankōkai. Reprinted in Kusuyama 1979, 393–422.

——. 1978. "Seiyōshi densetsu kō" 青羊肆傳說考. *Tōhō shūkyō* 東方宗教 52:1–4 Reprinted in Kusuyama 1979, 423–35.

——. 1979. *Rōshi densetsu no kenkyū* 老子傳說の研究. Tokyo: Sōbunsha.

———. 1992. *Dōka shisō to dōkyō* 道家思想と道教. Tokyo: Hirakawa.

LaFargue, Michael, and Julian Pas. 1998. "On Translating the *Tao-te-ching*." In *Lao-tzu and the Tao-te-ching*, edited by Livia Kohn and Michael LaFargue, 277–300. Albany: State University of New York Press.

LaFleur, William R. 1987. "Biography." In *Encyclopedia of Religion*, edited by Mircea Eliade, 2:220–24. New York: Macmillan.

Lagerwey, John. 1981. *Wu-shang pi-yao: Somme taoïste du VIe siècle*. Paris: Publications de l' Ecole Française d'Extrême-Orient.

———. 1991. *Der Kontinent der Geister: China im Spiegel des Taoismus*. Olten: Walter-Verlag.

———. 1992. "The Pilgrimage to Wu-tang Shan." In *Pilgrims and Sacred Sites in China*, edited by Susan Naquin and Chün-fang Yü, 293–332. Berkeley: University of California Press.

———. 1997. "A propos de la situation actuélle des pratiques religieuses traditionelles en Chine." In *Renouveaux religieux en Asie*, edited by Catherine Clémentin-Ojha, 3–16. Paris: Ecole Française d'Extrême-Orient.

Lai, Whalen. 1979. "Ch'an Metaphors: Waves, Water, Mirror, Lamp." *Philosophy East and West* 29:243–55.

———. 1980. "Toward a Periodization of Chinese Religion." *Society for the Study of Chinese Religions Bulletin* 8:79–90.

———. 1986. "Dating the *Hsiang fa chüeh i ching*." *Annual Memoirs of the Ōtani University Shin Buddhist Comprehensive Research Institute* 4:61–91.

———. 1987. "The Earliest Folk Buddhist Religion in China: *T'i-wei Po-li Ching* and Its Historical Significance." In *Buddhist and Taoist Practice in Medieval Chinese Society*, edited by David W. Chappell, 11–35. Honolulu: University of Hawaii Press.

Lamotte, Etienne. 1987. *History of Indian Buddhism: From the Orgins to the Śāka Era*. Translated by Sara Webb-Boin. Louvain: Peeters Press.

Larre, Claude, Isabelle Robinet, and Elisabeth Rochat de la Vallée. 1993. *Les grands traités du Huainan zi*. Paris: Editions du Cerf.

Lau, D. C. 1963. *Lao-tzu: Tao Te Ching*. Harmondsworth: Penguin Books.

———. 1982. *Chinese Classics: Tao Te Ching*. Hong Kong: Hong Kong University Press.

Layard, John. 1972. *The Virgin Archetype: Two Essays*. Zurich: Spring Publications.

Le Blanc, Charles. 1985. *Huai-nan-tzu: Philosophical Synthesis in Early Han Thought*. Hong Kong: Hong Kong University Press.

———. 1987. "From Ontology to Cosmogony: Notes on the *Chuang-tzu* and the *Huai-nan tzu*." In *Chinese Ideas About Nature and Society: Studies in Honor of Derk Bodde*, edited by Charles Le Blanc and Susan Blader, 117–29. Hong Kong: Hong Kong University Press.

———. 1992. "Résonance: une interprétation chinoise de la réalité." In *Mythe et philosophie à l'aube de la Chine impérial: Etudes sur le Huainan zi*, edited by Charles Le Blanc and Rémi Mathieu, 91–111. Montreal: Les Presses de l'Université de Montréal.

Le Blanc, Charles, and Rémi Mathieu, eds. 1992. *Mythe et philosophie a l'aube de la Chine imperial: Etudes sur le Huainan zi*. Montreal: Les Presses de l'Université de Montréal.

Ledderose, Lothar. 1984. "Some Taoist Elements in the Calligraphy of the Six Dynasties." *T'oung-pao* 70:246–78.

Leeming, David A. 1973. *Mythology: The Voyage of the Hero*. Philadelphia: J.B. Lippincott Company.

———. 1990. *The World of Myth*. New York: Oxford University Press.

Leeuw, Gerardus van der. 1938. *Religion in Essence and Manifestation*. London: Allen & Unwin.

Legge, James. 1885. *Li Ki*. Oxford: Clarendon Press, Sacred Books of the East, III–IV.

Levy, Howard S. 1956. "Yellow Turban Rebellion at the End of the Han." *Journal of the American Oriental Society* 76:214–27.

Lewis, C. S. 1960. *Miracles: A Preliminary Study*. New York: Macmillan.

Lewis, Mark E. 1990. *Sanctioned Violence in Early China*. Albany: State University of New York Press.

Li Yangzheng 李養正. 1993. *Daojiao yu zhuzi baijia* 道教與諸子百家. *Daojiao wenhua congshu* 道教文化叢書, vol. 10. Beijing: Yanshan chubanshe.

———. 1993a. *Dangdai zhongguo daojiao* 當代中國道教. Beijing: Zhongguo shehui kexue chubanshe.

Li Yuanguo 李遠國. 1985. *Sichuan daojiao shihua* 四川道教事話. Chengdu: Sichuan Renmin.

———. 1987. *Qigong jinghua ji* 氣功精華集. Chengdu: Bashu shushe.

———. 1988. *Daojiao qigong yangsheng xue* 道教氣功養生學. Chengdu: Sichuan Academy of Social Sciences.

———. 1991. *Zhongguo daojiao qigong yangsheng daquan* 中國道教氣功養生大全. Chengdu: Sichuan cishu chubanshe.

Lieu, Samuel N. C. 1985. *Manichaeism in the Later Roman Empire and Medieval China: A Historical Survey*. Manchester: Manchester University Press.

Lin, Paul J. 1977. *A Translation of Lao-tzu's Tao-te-ching and Wang Pi's Commentary*. Ann Arbor: University of Michigan, Center for Chinese Studies.

Lincoln, Bruce. 1975. "The Indo-European Myth of Creation." *History of Religions* 15:121–45.

———. 1986. *Myth, Cosmos, and Society: Indo-European Themes of Creation and Destruction*. Cambridge, Mass.: Harvard University Press.

Liu Chenghuai 劉城淮. 1988. *Zhongguo shanggu shenhua* 中國上古神話. Shanghai: Wenyi.

Liu Guojun 劉國鈞. 1934. "Laozi shenhua kaolue" 老子神化考略. *Jinling xuebao* 金陵學報 4:61–78.

Liu, Laurence. 1989. *Chinese Architecture*. New York: Rizzoli.

Liu Lizhen 劉理眞. 1988. "Laozi quanzhen qigong" 老子全眞氣功. *Baijia gongfa* 百家功法 1988.8:2–5.

Liu Shouhua 劉守華. 1993. *Daojiao yu minsu wenxue* 道教與民俗文學. Beijing: Yanshan chubanshe.

Liu Ts'un-yan. 1962. *Buddhist and Taoist Influences on Chinese Novels*. Wiesbaden: Harrassowitz.

——. 1973. "The Compilation and Historical Value of the *Tao-tsang*." In *Essays on the Sources of Chinese History*, edited by Donald Leslie, 104–20. Canberra: Australian National University Press.

Liu Xiaogan. 1994. *Classifying the Zhuangzi Chapters*. Translated by William E. Savage. Ann Arbor: University of Michigan, Center for Chinese Studies.

——. 1998. "Naturalness (*Tzu-jan*), the Core Value in Taoism: Its Ancient Meaning and Its Significance Today." In *Lao-tzu and the* Tao-te-ching, edited by Livia Kohn and Michael LaFargue, 211–28. Albany: State University of New York Press.

Long, Charles H. 1963. *Alpha: The Myths of Creation*. New York: G. Braziller.

——. 1987. "Cosmogony." In *Encyclopedia of Religion*, edited by Mircea Eliade, 3:93–100. New York: Macmillan.

Loon, Piet van der. 1984. *Taoist Books in the Libraries of the Sung Period*. London: Oxford Oriental Institute.

Lovin, Robin, and Frank E. Reynolds, eds. 1985. *Cosmogony and Ethical Order*. Chicago: University of Chicago Press.

Lu Gong 陸恭. 1982. "Daojiao yishu de zhenpin: Ming Liaoning kanben Taishang laojun bashiyi hua tushuo" 道教藝術的珍品: 明遼寧刊本太上老君八十一化圖說. *Shijie zongjiao yanjiu* 世界宗教研究 2:51–55.

Maeda Ryōichi 前田良一. 1989. "Kyu kyu nyo ritsurei o saguru" 急急如律令をさくる. In *Dōkyō to higashi Ajia* 道教と東アジア, edited by Fukunaga Mitsuji, 101–25. Kyoto: Jimbun shoin.

Maeda Shigeki 前田繁樹. 1985. "Rōkun setsu ippyaku hachiju kaijo no seiritsu ni tsuite" 老君說一百八十戒序の成立について. *Tōyō no shisō to shūkyō* 東洋の思想と宗教 2:81–94.

——. 1985a. "Rikuchō jidai ni okeru Kan Kichi den no hensen" 六朝時代における干吉傳の變遷. *Tōhō shūkyō* 東方宗教 65:44–62.

——. 1995. "The Evolution of the Way of the Celestial Master: Its Early View of Divinities." *Acta Asiatica* 68:54–68.

Major, John S. 1984. "The Five Phases, Magic Squares, and Schematic Cosmography." In *Explorations in Early Chinese Cosmology*, edited by Henry Rosemont, 133–66. Chico, Calif.: Scholars' Press.

——. 1986. "New Light on the Dark Warrior." *Journal of Chinese Religions* 13/14:65–87.

——. 1993. *Heaven and Earth in Early Han Thought: Chapters Three, Four, and Five of the* Huainanzi. Albany: State University of New York Press.

Malinowski, Bronislaw. 1926. *Myth in Primitive Psychology*. London: Kegan Paul, Trench, Trubner & Co.

Mansvelt-Beck, B.J. 1980. "The Date of the *Taiping jing*." *T'oung-pao* 66:149–82.

Maspero, Henri. 1924. "Légendes mythologiques dans le Chou King." *Journal Asiatique* 20:1–101.

——. 1951. "Le *Ming-t'ang* et la crise religieuse chinoise avant les Han." *Mélanges chinoises et bouddhiques* 9:1–71.

——. 1981. *Taoism and Chinese Religion*. Translated by Frank Kierman. Amherst: University of Massachusetts Press.

Masuo Shin'ichirō 増尾伸一郎. 1994. "Nihon kodai ni okeru Tenchi hachiyō shinshūkyō no joyū" 日本古代における天地八陽神咒經の受容. In *Dōkyō bunka e no tembō* 道教文化への 展望, edited by Dōkyō bunka kenkyūkai 道教文化研究會, 342–60. Tokyo: Hirakawa.

——. 1998. "Nihon kodai no dōkyō shoyū to gigi kyōten" 日本古代の道教 受容と疑偽經典. In *Dōkyō no rekishi to bunka* 道教の歴史と文化, edited by Yamada Toshiaki 山田利明 and Tanaka Fumio 田中文雄. Tokyo: Hirakawa.

Mather, Richard B. 1979. "K'ou Ch'ien-chih and the Taoist Theocracy at the Northern Wei Court 425–451." In *Facets of Taoism*, edited by Holmes Welch and Anna Seidel, 103–22. New Haven: Yale University Press.

Mathieu, Rémi. 1992. "Une création du monde." In *Mythe et philosophie à l'aube de la Chine impérial: Etudes sur le Huainan zi*, edited by Charles Le Blanc and Rémi Mathieu, 69–88. Montreal: Les Presses de l'Université de Montréal.

Matsubara Sanburō 松原三郎. 1961. *Chūgoku bukkyō chōkokushi kenkyū* 中國佛教 調刻史研究. Tokyo: Yoshikawa Kōbunkan.

Matsumoto Kōichi 松本浩一. 1997. "Taihokushi no shimyō to reido hōkai" 臺北 市の祠廟と禮斗法會. *Tōhō shūkyō* 東方宗教 90:22–44.

McMullen, David L. 1987. "Bureaucrats and Cosmology: The Ritual Code of T'ang China." In *Rituals of Royalty: Power and Ceremonial in Traditional Societies*, edited by D. Cannadine and S. Price, 181–236. Cambridge: Cambridge University Press.

Mensching, Gustav. 1976. *Structures and Patterns of Religion*. Translated by Hans-Joachim Klimkeit and C. Srinivasa Sarma. Delhi: Motilal Banarsidass.

Mercatante, Anthony S. 1978. *Good and Evil: Mythology and Folklore*. New York: Harper and Row.

Mikami Jun 三上順. 1966. "Meidō to iegata haniwa" 明堂と家形埴輪. *Tōhō shūkyō* 東方宗教 28:35–49.

Min Zhiting 閔智亭. 1990. *Daojiao yifan* 道教儀範. Beijing: Zhongguo daojiao xueyuan.

Mitamura Keiko 三田村圭子. 1994. "Taijō rōkun setsu chō seijōkyō chu ni tsuite" 太上老君說常清靜經注について. In *Dōkyō bunka e no tembō* 道教文化への 展望, edited by Dōkyō bunka kenkyūkai 道教文化研究會, 80–98. Tokyo: Hirakawa.

Miura Kunio 三浦國男. 1983. "Dōten fukuchi shō ron" 洞天福地小論. *Tōhō shūkyō* 東方宗教 61:1–23.

——. 1989. "The Revival of *Qi*: *Qigong* in Contemporary China." In *Taoist Meditation and Longevity Techniques*, edited by Livia Kohn, 329–58. Ann Arbor: University of Michigan, Center for Chinese Studies.

Miyakawa Hisayuki 宮川尚志. 1964. *Rikuchōshi kenkyū: Shūkyōhen* 六朝史研究 宗教篇. Kyoto: Heirakuji

——. 1974. "Legate Kao P'ien and a Taoist Magician, Lu Ying-chih, in the Time of Huang Ch'ao's Rebellion." *Acta Asiatica* 27:75–99.

Miyake Hitoshi 宮家準. 1993. "Shugendō to dōkyō" 修驗道と道教. *Tōhō shūkyō* 東方宗教 81:22–42.

Miyazawa Masayori 宮澤正順. 1994. "Kyu kyu nyo ritsurei ni tsuite" 急急如律令 について. *Girei bunka* 儀禮文化 20:14–35.

———. 1994a. "Dōkyō to ningengaku: Sō Zō to kōteikyō" 道教と人間學——曾造 と黃庭經. *Taishō daigaku kenkyū ronsō* 大正大學研究論叢 2:155–90.

Mochizuki Shinkō 望月信享. 1936. *Bukkyō daijiten* 佛教大辭典. Tokyo: Sekai seiten kankō kyōkai.

Möller, Hans-Georg. 1996. *Laotse: Tao Te King. Nach den Seidentexten von Mawang-dui.* Frankfurt: Fischer.

Mollier, Christine. 1990. *Une apocalypse taoïste du Ve siècle: Le livre des incantations divins des grottes abyssales.* Paris: Collège du France, Institut des Etudes Chinoises.

———. 1997. "La méthode de l'empereur du nord du mont Fengdu: une tradition exorciste du taoïsme médiévale." *T'oung-pao* 83:329–85.

Morgan, Evan. 1934. *Tao, the Great Luminant.* Shanghai: Kelly and Walsh.

Mori Yuria 森由利亞. 1994. "Zenshinkyō ryūmonha keizu kō" 全眞教龍門派 系譜考. In *Dōkyō bunka e no tembō* 道教文化への展望, edited by Dōkyō bunka kenkyūkai 道教文化研究會, 180–211. Tokyo: Hirakawa.

Morinaga, Sōkō. 1988. "My Struggle to Become a Zen Monk." In *Zen: Tradition and Transition*, edited by Kenneth Kraft, 13–29. New York: Grove Press.

Mugitani Kunio 麥谷邦夫. 1982. "Kōtei naikeikyō shiron" 黃庭內景經試論. *Tōyō bunka* 東洋文化 62:29–61.

———. 1989. "Dōkyō yiseki sanhōki" 道教遺跡參訪記. *Tōhō shūkyō* 東方宗教 73:63–81.

Murray, Henry A., ed. 1968. *Myth and Mythmaking.* Boston: Beacon Press.

Nakajima Ryūzō 中島隆藏. 1984. "Taijō gyōhō innenkyō ni okeru ōhōron" 太上業報因緣經における應報論. In *Makio Ryōkai hakase shoju kinen ronshū Chūgoku no shūkyō shisō to kagaku* 牧尾良海博士頌壽記念論集中國の宗教思想と科學, 335–54. Tokyo: Kokusho kankōkai.

Naquin, Susan. 1976. *Millenarian Rebellion in China: The Eight Trigrams Uprising of 1813.* New Haven: Yale University Press.

———. 1992. "The Peking Pilgrimage to Miao-feng Shan: Religious Organizations and Sacred Sites." In *Pilgrims and Sacred Sites in China*, edited by Susan Naquin and Chün-fang Yü, 333–77. Berkeley: University of California Press.

Nattier, Jan. 1992. "The Heart Sutra: A Chinese Apocryphal Text?" *Journal of the International Association of Buddhist Studies* 15.2:153–223.

Needham, Joseph. 1969. "Time and Eastern Man." In *The Grand Titration: Science and Society in East and West*, lectures by Joseph Needham, 218–98. London: George Allen & Unwin.

———, et al. 1983. *Science and Civilisation in China*, vol. V.5. *Spagyrical Discovery and Invention—Physiological Alchemy.* Cambridge: Cambridge University Press.

Nickerson, Peter. 1994. "Shamans, Demons, Diviners, and Taoists: Conflict and Assimilation in Medieval Chinese Ritual Practice." *Taoist Resources* 5.1:41–66.

——. 1996. "Abridged Codes of Master Lu for the Daoist Community." In *Religions of China in Practice*, edited by Donald S. Lopez, Jr., 347–59. Princeton: Princeton University Press.

——. 1996a "Taoism, Death, and Bureaucracy in Early Medieval China." Ph.D. diss., University of California, Berkeley.

——. 1997. "The Great Petition for Sepulchral Plaints." In *Early Daoist Scriptures*, by Stephen Bokenkamp, 230–74. Berkeley: University of California Press.

Nikaidō Yoshihiro 二階堂善弘. 1998. "Gentenjōtei no henyū" 玄天上帝の變容. *Tōhō shūkyō* 東方宗教 91:60–77.

Noguchi Tetsurō 野口鐵郎, Sakade Yoshinobu 坂出祥伸, Fukui Fumimasa 福井文雅, and Yamada Toshiaki 山田利明, eds. 1994. *Dōkyō jiten* 道教事典. Tokyo: Hirakawa.

O'Brien, Joan, and Wilfred Major. 1982. *In the Beginning: Creation Myths from Ancient Mesopotamia, Israel and Greece*. Chico, Calif.: Scholars' Press.

Ochiai, Toshinori. 1991. *The Manuscripts of Nanatsudera*. Kyoto: Italian School of East Asian Studies.

Ōfuchi Ninji 大淵忍爾. 1964. *Dōkyōshi no kenkyū* 道教史の研究. Okayama: Chūgoku Insatsu.

——. 1974. "On *Ku Ling-pao ching*." *Acta Asiatica* 27:33–56.

——. 1979. *Tonkō dōkei: Zuroku hen* 敦煌道經 — 圖錄篇. Tokyo: Kokubu shoten.

——. 1979a. "The Formation of the Taoist Canon." In *Facets of Taoism*, edited by Holmes Welch and Anna Seidel, 253–68. New Haven: Yale University Press.

——. 1985. "Kokan matsu goto beidō no soshiki ni tsuite" 後漢末五斗米道の組織について. *Tōhō shūkyō* 東方宗教 65:1–19.

——. 1985a. "Dōkyō ni okeru sangensetsu no seisei to tenkai" 道教における三元說の生成と展開. *Tōhō shūkyō* 東方宗教 66:1–21.

Ōfuchi Ninji 大淵忍爾, and Ishii Masako 石井昌子. 1988. *Dōkyō tenseki mokuroku, sakuin* 道教典籍目錄, 索引. Tokyo: Kokusho kankōkai.

Onozawa Seiichi 小野澤精一, ed. 1978. *Ki no shisō* 氣の思想. Tokyo: Tokyo University.

Orzech, Charles D. 1989. "Seeing Chen-yen Buddhism." *History of Religions* 29.2:87–114.

Ōzaki Masaharu 尾岐正治. 1979. "Kō Kenshi no shinsen shisō" 寇謙之の神仙思想. *Tōhō shūkyō* 東方宗教 54:52–69.

——. 1995. "The History of the Evolution of Taoist Scriptures." *Acta Asiatica* 68:37–53.

Parkes, Graham. 1984. "Unter dem Augenblick: Der Abgrund der Ewigkeit." *Zen Buddhism Today* 2:47–59.

Paul, Diana. 1979. *Women in Buddhism*. Stanford: Stanford University Press.

Peerenboom, R. P. 1991. *Law and Morality in Ancient China: The Silk Manuscripts of Huang-Lao*. Albany: State University of New York Press.

Penny, Benjamin. 1996. "Buddhism and Daoism in *The 180 Precepts Spoken by Lord Lao*." *Taoist Resources* 6.2:1–16.

Perry, John Weir. 1966. *Lord of the Four Quarters: Myths of the Royal Father.* New York: George Braziller.

Petersen, Jens O. 1989. "The Early Traditions Relating to the Han-dynasty Transmission of the *Taiping jing.*" *Acta Orientalia* 50:133–71 and 51:165–216.

———. 1992. "The *Taiping jing* and the A.D. 102 Clepsydra Reform." *Acta Orientalia* 53:122–58.

Pontynen, Arthur. 1980. "The Deification of Laozi in Chinese History and Art." *Oriental Art* 26:192–200.

———. 1980a. "The Dual Nature of Laozi in Chinese History and Art." *Oriental Art* 26:308–13.

———. 1983. "The Early Development of Taoist Art." Ph.D. diss., University of Iowa, Iowa City.

Porkert, Manfred. 1961. "Untersuchungen einiger philosophisch-wissenschaftlicher Grundbegriffe und –beziehungen im Chinesischen." *Zeitschrift der deutschen morgenländischen Gesellschaft* 110:422–52.

———. 1974. *The Theoretical Foundations of Chinese Medicine.* Cambridge, Mass.: MIT Press.

Porter, Bill. 1993. *The Road to Heaven: Encounters with Chinese Hermits.* San Francisco: Mercury House.

Pregadio, Fabrizio. 1991. "*The Book of the Nine Elixirs* and Its Tradition." In *Chūgoku kodai kagakushi ron* 中國古代科學論, edited by Yamada Keiji 山田慶兒, 539–636. Kyoto: Jimbun kagaku kenkyūjo.

Preston, James J., ed. 1982. *Mother Worship: Theme and Variations.* Chapel Hill: University of North Carolina Press.

Proudfoot, Wayne. 1985. *Religious Experience.* Berkeley: University of California Press.

Pye, Michael. 1979. *The Buddha.* London: Duckworth.

Pyysiainen, Ilkka. 1987. "The Buddha: A Biographical Image in Relation to Cosmic Order." In *Mythology and Cosmic Order*, edited by René Gothoni and Juha Pentikainen, 115–21. Helsinki: Suomalaisen Kirjallisuuden Senru, Studia Fennica, vol. 32.

Qing Xitai 卿希泰. 1988. *Zhongguo daojiao shi* 中國道教史. Chengdu: Sichuan renmin.

Raglan, F.R.S. 1934. "The Hero of Tradition." *Folklore* 45:212–31.

———. 1990. "The Hero: A Study in Tradition, Myth, and Drama, Part II." 1936. Reprinted in *In Quest of the Hero*, edited by Robert A. Segal, 87–175. Princeton: Princeton University Press.

Rank, Otto. 1952. *The Trauma of Birth.* New York: Robert Brunner.

———. 1990. "The Myth of the Birth of the Hero." 1909. Reprinted in *In Quest of the Hero*, edited by Robert A. Segal, 3–86. Princeton: Princeton University Press.

Rao Zongyi 饒宗頤. 1991. *Laozi xianger zhu jiaojian* 老子想爾注校牋. 1956. Reprint, Shanghai: Guji chubanshe.

Reiter, Florian C. 1983. "Some Observations Concerning Taoist Foundations in Traditional China." *Zeitschrift der deutschen morgenländischen Gesellschaft* 133:363–76.

———. 1985. "Der Name Tung-hua ti-chün und sein Umfeld in der taoistischen Tradition." In *Religion und Philosophie in Ostasien: Festschrift für Hans Steininger*, edited by G. Naundorf, K. H. Pohl, and H. H. Schmidt, 87–101. Würzburg: Königshausen und Neumann.

———. 1988. "The Visible Divinity: The Sacred Image in Religious Taoism." *Nachrichten der deutschen Gesellschaft für Natur– und Völkerkunde Ostasiens* 144:51–70.

———. 1988a. *Grundelemente des religiösen Taoismus: Das Spannungsverhältnis von Integration und Individualität in seiner Geschichte zur Chin-, Yüan- und frühen Ming-Zeit.* Stuttgart: Franz Steiner Verlag, Münchener Ostasiatische Studien 48.

———, ed. 1990. *Leben und Wirken Lao-Tzu's in Schrift und Bild: Lao-chün pa-shih-i-hua t'u-shuo.* Würzburg: Königshausen und Neumann.

———. 1990a. *Der Perlenbeutel aus den drei Höhlen. Arbeitsmaterialien zum Taoismus der frühen T'ang-Zeit.* Asiatische Forschungen, vol. 12. Wiesbaden: Otto Harrassowitz.

Ren Farong 任法融. 1983. *Taishang laojun zuo shisizi yangsheng jue shiyi* 太上老君作十四字養生訣釋義. Beijing: Chinese Taoist Association.

Ren Jiyu 任繼愈. 1990. *Zhongguo daojiao shi* 中國道教史. Shanghai: Renmin.

Ren Jiyu 任繼愈, and Zhong Zhaopeng 鐘肇鵬, eds. 1991. *Daozang tiyao* 道藏提要. Beijing: Zhongguo shehui kexue chubanshe.

Reynolds, Frank E. 1976. "The Many Lives of the Buddha: A Study of Sacred Biography and Theravāda Tradition." In *The Biographical Process: Studies in the History and Psychology of Religion*, edited by Frank E. Reynolds and Donald Capps, 37–61. The Hague: Mouton.

Reynolds, Frank E., and Donald Capps, eds. 1976. *The Biographical Process: Studies in the History and Psychology of Religion.* The Hague: Mouton.

Robinet, Isabelle. 1977. *Les commentaires du Tao to king jusqu'au VIIe siècle.* Paris: College du France, Institut des Hautes Etudes Chinoises.

———. 1979. "Metamorphosis and Deliverance of the Corpse in Taoism." *History of Religions* 19:37–70.

———. 1979a. "Introduction au *Kieou-tchen tchong-king*." *Journal of Chinese Religions* 7:24–45.

———. 1983. "Le *Ta-tung chen-ching*: Son authenticité et sa place dans les textes du Shang-ch'ing." In *Tantric and Taoist Studies*, edited by Michel Strickmann, 2:394–433. Brussels: Institut Belge des Hautes Etudes Chinoises.

———. 1983a. "*Chuang-tzu* et le taoïsme religieux." *Journal of Chinese Religions* 11:59–109.

———. 1984. *La révélation du Shangqing dans l'histoire du taoïsme.* 2 vols. Paris: Publications de l'Ecole Française d'Extrême-Orient.

———. 1986. "The Taoist Immortal: Jester of Light and Shadow, Heaven and Earth." *Journal of Chinese Religions* 13/14:87–106.

———. 1990. "The Place and Meaning of the Notion of Taiji in Taoist Sources Prior to the Ming Dynasty." *History of Religions* 29:373–411.

———. 1993. *Taoist Meditation*. Translated by Norman Girardot and Julian Pas. Albany: State University of New York Press.

———. 1994. "Le rôle et le sens des nombres dans la cosmologie et l'alchimie taoïstes." *Extrême-Orient, Extrême-Occident* 16:93–120.

———. 1994a. "Primus movens et creation récurrente." *Taoist Resources* 5.1:29–69.

———. 1995. *Introduction a l'alchimie intérieure taoïste: De l'unité et de la multiplicité*. Paris: Éditions du Cerf.

———. 1997. *Taoism: Growth of a Religion*. Translated by Phyllis Brooks. Stanford: Stanford University Press.

———. 1998. "Later Commentaries: Textual Polysemy and Syncretistic Interpretations." In *Lao-tzu and the* Tao-te-ching, edited by Livia Kohn and Michael LaFargue, 119–42. Albany: State University of New York Press.

Rogo, D. Scott. 1982. *Miracles: A Parascientific Inquiry into Wondrous Phenomena*. New York: The Dial Press.

Roth, Harold D. 1995. "Evidence for Meditative Stages in Early Taoism." Paper presented at the First American-Japanese Taoist Studies Conference, Tokyo.

———. 1996. "The Inner Cultivation Tradition of Early Daoism." In *Religions of China in Practice*, edited by Donald S. Lopez, Jr., 123–48. Princeton: Princeton University Press.

Sailey, Jay. 1978. *The Master Who Embraces Simplicity: A Study of the Philosophy of Ko Hung (A.D. 283–343)*. San Francisco: Chinese Materials Center.

Sakade Yoshinobu 坂出祥伸. 1985. "Hōso densetsu to Hōsokyō" 彭祖傳説と彭祖經. In *Chūgoku shinhakken kagakushi shiryō no kenkyū* 中國新發見科學史資料の研究, edited by Yamada Keiji 山田慶兒, 2:405–62. Kyoto: Kyoto University, Jimbun kagaku kenkyūjo.

———, ed. 1994. *Dōkyō no daijiten* 道教の大事典. Tokyo: Shin jimbutsu ōrai sha.

———. 1994a. "Ki to dōkyō shinzō no keisei" 氣と道教神像の形成. *Bungei ronsō* 文藝論叢 42:256–93.

Sakade Yoshinobu 坂出祥伸, and Masuo Shin'ichirō 增尾伸一郎. 1991. "Chūsei nihon no shintō to dōkyō" 中世日本の神道と道教. In *Nihon, Chūgoku no shū kyō bunka no kenkyū* 日本・中國の宗教文化の研究 53–80. Edited by Sakai Tadao 酒井忠夫, Fukui Fumimasa 福井之雅, and Yamada Toshiaki 山田利明. Tokyo: Hirakawa.

Sakauchi Shigeo 坂内榮夫. 1988. "Ō Kika to sono jidai" 王棲霞とその時代. *Tōhō shūkyō* 東方宗教 72:1–19.

Samuels, Mike, and Nancy Samuels. 1975. *Seeing with the Mind's Eye: The History, Technique, and Uses of Visualization*. New York: Random House.

Sargent, Clyde Bailey, trans. 1977. *Wang Mang: A Translation of the Official Account of His Rise to Power as Given in the History of the Former Han Dynasty*. 1947. Reprint, Westport, Conn.: Hyperion Press.

Sargent, Galen E. 1957. "T'an-yao and His Time." *Monumenta Serica* 16:363–96.

Saso, Michael. 1995. *The Gold Pavilion: Taoist Ways to Peace, Healing, and Long Life*. Boston: Charles E. Tuttle.

Schafer, Edward H. 1955. "Notes on Mica in Medieval China." T'oung-pao 43:165–286.

———. 1973. The Divine Woman. Berkeley: University of California Press.

———. 1980. Mao-shan in T'ang Times. Boulder, Colo.: Society for the Study of Chinese Religions, Monograph 1.

———. 1987. "The Dance of the Purple Culmen." T'ang Studies 5:45–68.

———. 1997. "The Scripture of the Opening of Heaven by the Most High Lord Lao." Taoist Resources 7.2: 1–20.

Schipper, Kristofer M. 1965. L'Empéreur Wou des Han dans la légende taoïste. Paris: Publications de l'Ecole Française d'Extrême-Orient 58.

———. 1967. "Gogaku shingyōzu no shinkō" 五嶽眞形圖の信仰. Dōkyō kenkyū 道教研究 2:114–62.

———. 1975. Concordance du Tao Tsang: titres des ouvrages. Paris: Publications de l'Ecole Française d'Extrême-Orient.

———. 1975a. Concordance du Houang-t'ing king. Paris: Publications de l'Ecole Française d'Extrême-Orient.

———. 1978. "The Taoist Body." History of Religions 17:355–87.

———. 1979. "Le Calendrier de Jade: Note sur le Laozi zhongjing." Nachrichten der deutschen Gesellschaft für Natur– und Völkerkunde Ostasiens 125:75–80.

———. 1984. "Le monachisme taoïste." In Incontro di religioni in Asia tra il terzo e il decimo secolo d. C., edited by Lionello Lanciotti, 199–215. Firenze: Leo S. Olschki.

———. 1985. "Vernacular and Classical Ritual in Taoism." Journal of Asian Studies 65:21–51.

———. 1985a. "Taoist Ordination Ranks in the Tun-huang Manuscripts." In Religion und Philosophie in Ostasien: Festschrift für Hans Steininger, edited by G. Naundorf, K. H. Pohl, and H. H. Schmidt, 127–48. Würzburg: Königshausen und Neumann.

———. 1994. The Taoist Body. Translated by Karen C. Duval. Berkeley: University of California Press.

———. 1994a. "Purity and Strangers: Shifting Boundaries in Medieval Taoism." T'oung-pao 80:61–81.

Schmidt, Hans-Hermann. 1985. "Die hundertachtzig Vorschriften von Lao-chün." In Religion und Philosophie in Ostasien: Festschrift für Hans Steininger, edited by G. Naundorf, K. H. Pohl, and H. H. Schmidt, 151–59. Würzburg: Königshausen und Neumann.

Schmidt-Glintzer, Helwig. 1986. Die Identität der buddhistischen Schulen und die Kompilation buddhistischer Universalgeschichten in China. Wiesbaden: Franz Steiner.

Schwartz, Hillel. 1987. "Millenarianism: An Overview." In Encyclopedia of Religion, edited by Mircea Eliade, 9:521–32. New York: Macmillan.

Seaman, Gary. 1987. Journey to the North: An Ethnohistorical Analysis and Annotated Translation of the Chinese Folk Novel "Pei-you chi." Berkeley: University of California Press.

Segal, Robert A., ed. 1990. *In Quest of the Hero*. Princeton: Princeton University Press.

Seidel, Anna. 1969. *La divinisation de Lao-tseu dans le taoïsme des Han*. Paris: Ecole Française d'Extrême Orient.

———. 1969a. "The Image of the Perfect Ruler in Early Taoist Messianism." *History of Religions* 9:216–47.

———. 1970. "A Taoist Immortal of the Ming Dynasty: Chang San-feng." In *Self and Society in Ming Thought*, edited by Wm. Th. DeBary, 483–531. New York: Columbia University Press.

———. 1978. "Der Kaiser und sein Ratgeber." *Saeculum* 29:18–50.

———. 1978a. "Das neue Testament des Tao." *Saeculum* 29:147–72.

———. 1983. "Imperial Treasures and Taoist Sacraments: Taoist Roots in the Apocrypha." In *Tantric and Taoist Studies*, edited by Michel Strickmann, 2:291–371. Brussels: Institut Belge des Hautes Etudes Chinoises.

———. 1984. "Le sutra merveilleux du Ling-pao suprême, traitant de Lao tseu qui convertit les barbares." In *Contributions aux études du Touen-houang*, edited by Michel Soymié, 3:305–52. Geneva: Ecole Française d'Extrême-Orient.

———. 1984a. "Taoist Messianism." *Numen* 31:161–74.

———. 1985. "Geleitbrief an die Unterwelt. Jenseitsvorstellungen in den Graburkunden der späteren Han-Zeit." In *Religion und Philosophie in Ostasien: Festschrift für Hans Steininger*, edited by G. Naundorf, K. H. Pohl, and H. H. Schmidt, 161–84. Würzburg: Königshausen und Neumann.

———. 1987. "Traces of Han Religion in Funeral Texts Found in Tombs." In *Dōkyō to shūkyō bunka* 道家と宗教文化, 21–57. Tokyo: Hirakawa.

———. 1990. "Chronicle of Taoist Studies in the West 1950–1990." *Cahiers d'Extrême-Asie* 5:223–347.

Shahar, Meir, and Robert P. Weller, eds. 1996. *Unruly Gods: Divinity and Society in China*. Honolulu: University of Hawaii Press.

Shek, Richard. 1987. "Chinese Millenarian Movements." In *Encyclopedia of Religion*, edited by Mircea Eliade, 9:532–36. New York: Macmillan.

Shepperson, George. 1962. "The Comparative Study of Millenarian Movements." In *Millenial Dreams in Action: Essays in Comparative Study*, edited by Sylvia L. Thrupp, 44–52. The Hague: Mouton.

Shimomi Takao 下見高雄. 1974. "Katsu Kō 'Shinsen den' ni tsuite" 葛洪神仙傳について. *Fukuoka joshi tandai kiyō* 福岡女子短筒紀要 8:57–75.

Sickman, Laurence. 1980. *Eight Dynasties of Chinese Painting: Collections of the Nelson Gallery-Atkins Museum, Kansas City and the Cleveland Museum of Art*. Cleveland: Cleveland Museum of Art.

Sivin, Nathan. 1969. "On the 'Pao-p'u-tzu nei-p'ien' and the Life of Ko Hung." *Isis* 40:388–91.

———. 1986. "On the Limits of Empirical Knowledge in the Traditional Chinese Sciences." In *Time, Science, and Society in China and the West*, edited by J. T. Frazer, N. Lawrence, and F. C. Haber, 151–72. Amherst: University of Massachusetts Press.

——. 1988. *Traditional Medicine in Contemporary China*. Ann Arbor: University of Michigan, Center for Chinese Studies.

——. 1991. "Change and Continuity in Early Cosmology: *The Great Commentary to the Book of Changes.*" In *Chūgoku kodai kagakushi ron, zokuhen* 中國古代科學史論續篇, edited by Yamada Keiji 山天慶兒 and Tanaka Tan 田中炎, 3–43. Kyoto: Kyoto University, Jimbun kagaku kenkyūjo.

Skar, Lowell. 1997. "Administering Thunder: A Thirteenth-Century Memorial Deliberating the Thunder Rites." *Cahiers d'Extrême-Asie* 9:159–202.

Smith, Thomas E. 1990. "The Record of the Ten Continents." *Taoist Resources* 2.2:87–119.

——. 1992. "Ritual and the Shaping of Narrative: The Legend of the Han Emperor Wu." Ph.D. diss., University of Michigan, Ann Arbor.

——. 1994. "The Ritual of Scriptural Transmission as Seen in the *Han wudi neizhuan.*" Paper presented at the 46th Annual Meeting of the Association for Asian Studies, Boston.

Soothill, William E. 1952. *The Hall of Light: A Study of Early Chinese Kingship*. New York: Philosophical Library.

Soothill, William E., and Lewis Hudous. 1937. *A Dictionary of Chinese Buddhist Terms*. London: Kegan Paul.

Soymié, Michel. 1977. "Les dix jours du jeune taoïste." In *Yoshioka Yoshitoyo hakase kanri kinen Dōkyō kenkyū ronshū* 吉岡義豐博士還歷記念道教研究論集, 1–21. Tokyo: Kokusho kankōkai.

Sproul, Barbara C. 1979. *Primal Myths: Creating the World*. San Francisco: Harper & Row.

Staal, Julius. 1984. *Stars of Jade: Calendar Lore, Mythology, Legends and Star Stories of Ancient China*. Decatur, Geor.: Writ Press.

Stein, Rolf A. 1963. "Remarques sur les mouvements du taoïsme politico-religieux au IIe siècle ap. J.-C." *T'oung-pao* 50:1–78.

Strickmann, Michel. 1978. "The Mao-shan Revelations: Taoism and the Aristocracy." *T'oung-pao* 63:1–63.

——. 1981. *Le taoïsme du Mao chan: chronique d'une révélation*. Paris: Collège du France, Institut des Hautes Etudes Chinoises.

——. 1993. "The Seal of the Law: A Ritual Implement and the Origins of Printing." *Asia Major*, 3rd s. 6.2:1–84.

Strong, John. 1983. *The Legend of King Aśoka: A Study and Translation of the Aśokavadāna*. Delhi: Motilal Barnasidass.

——. 1990. "Rich Man, Poor Man, *Bhikkhu*, King: Aśoka's Great Quinquennial Festival and the Nature of *Dana*." In *Ethics, Wealth, and Salvation: A Study in Buddhist Social Ethics*, edited by Russell Sizemore and Donald Swearer, 107–23. Columbia: University of South Carolina Press.

Sun, K'o-k'uan. 1981. "Yü Chi and Southern Taoism During the Yüan Period." In *China Under Mongol Rule*, edited by John D. Langlois, 212–53. Princeton: Princeton University Press.

Sunayama Minoru 沙山稔. 1984. "Lingbao duren jing sizhu daji" 靈寶度人經四注答記. *Shijie zongjiao yanjiu* 世界宗教研究 1984.2:30–48.

Sung, Z. D. 1971. *The Text of Yi King*. Taipei: Chengwen.

Takeuchi Yoshio 武内義雄. 1978. *Takeuchi Yoshio zenshū* 武内義雄全集. 12 vols. Tokyo: Kadokawa.

Tang Yongtong 湯用彤. 1981. *Han Wei liang Jin nanbei chao fojiao shi* 漢魏兩晉南北朝佛教史. 1938. Reprint, Beijing: Zhonghua.

Tang Yongtong 湯用彤, and Tang Junyi 湯君毅. 1961. "Kou Qianzhi de zhuzuo yu sixiang" 寇謙之的著作與思想. *Lishi yanjiu* 歷史研究 1961.5:64–77.

Ten Broeck, Janet R. T., and Tong Yiu. 1950. "A Taoist Inscription of the Yüan Dynasty: *The Tao-chiao pei*." *T'oung-pao* 40:60–122.

Tetsui Yoshinori 鐵井慶紀. 1970. "Kōtei densetsu ni tsuite" 黄帝傳說について. *Shinagaku kenkyū* 支那學研究 34:78–89.

———. 1972. "Kōtei to Shiyo no tosō setsuwa ni tsuite" 黄帝と蚩尤の鬥爭說話について. *Tōhō shūkyō* 東方宗教 39:50–64.

———. 1975. "Konron densetsu ni tsuite isshiron" 崑崙傳說について. *Tōhō shūkyō* 東方宗教 45:33–47.

———. 1990. *Chūgoku shinwa no bunka jinruigaku teki kenkyū* 中國神話の文化人類學的研究. Edited by Ikeda Suetoshi 池田末利. Tokyo: Hirakawa.

Thiel, Josef. 1961. "Der Streit der Buddhisten und Taoisten zur Mongolenzeit." *Monumenta Serica* 20:1–81.

Thomas, Edward. 1927. *The Life of the Buddha*. London: Kegan Paul & Rutley.

Thompson, Laurence. 1985. "Taoism: Classic and Canon." In *The Holy Book in Comparative Perspective*, edited by Frederick M. Denny and Rodney F. Taylor, 204–23. Columbia: University of South Carolina Press.

Thompson, William Irwin. 1981. *The Time Falling Bodies Take to Light: Mythology, Sexuality, and the Origins of Culture*. New York: St. Martin's Press.

———. 1990. *At the Edge of History: Passages about Earth*. Great Barrington, Mass: Lindisfarne Press.

Thrupp, Sylvia L. 1962. "Millenial Dreams in Action: A Report on the Conference Discussion." In *Millenial Dreams in Action: Essays in Comparative Study*, edited by Sylvia L. Thrupp, 11–30. The Hague: Mouton.

Tillich, Paul. 1927. "Die Idee der Offenbarung." *Zeitschrift für Theologie und Kirche* 8:400–24.

Tsai Chih Chung, Koh Kok Kiang, and Wong Lit Khiong. 1989. *The Sayings of Lao Zi*. Singapore: Asiapak Comic Series.

Tsui, Bartholomew P. M. 1991. *Taoist Tradition and Change: The Story of the Complete Perfection Sect in Hong Kong*. Hong Kong: Christian Study Centre on Chinese Religion and Culture.

Tsukamoto, Zenryū 塚本善隆. 1961. *Gisho shakurōshi no kenkyū* 魏書釋老志の研究. Tokyo: Bukkyō bungaku kenkyūjo.

Tsukamoto Zenryū, and Leon Hurvitz. 1985. *A History of Early Chinese Buddhism*. 2 vols. Tokyo: Kodansha.

Turner, Victor. 1969. *The Ritual Process: Structure and Anti-Structure*. Chicago: Aldine.

Turner, Victor, and Edith Turner. 1982. "Postindustrial Marian Pilgrimage." In *Mother Worship: Theme and Variations*, edited by James J. Preston, 145–73. Chapel Hill: University of North Carolina Press.

Verellen, Franciscus. 1989. *Du Guangting (850–933)—taoïste de cour à la fin de la Chine médiévale*. Paris: Collège du France, Institut des Hautes Etudes Chinoises.

———. 1992. "Evidential Miracles in Support of Taoism: The Inversion of a Buddhist Apologetic Tradition in Tang China." *T'oung-pao* 78:217–63.

———. 1994. "A Forgotten T'ang Restoration: The Taoist Dispensation After Huang Ch'ao." *Asia Major* 7.1:107–53.

———. 1995. "The Beyond Within: Grotto-Heavens in Taoist Ritual and Cosmology." *Cahiers d'Extrême-Asie* 8:265–90.

Wädow, Gerd. 1992. *Tien-fei hsien-sheng lu: Die Aufzeichnungen von der manifestierten Heiligkeit der Himmelsprinzessin. Einleitung, Übersetzung, Kommentar*. St. Augustin/Nettetal, Germany: Steyler Verlag, Monumenta Serica.

Waida, Manabu. 1987. "Miracles: An Overview." In *Encyclopedia of Religion*, edited by Mircea Eliade, 9:542–48. New York: Macmillan.

Waley, Arthur. 1934. *The Way and Its Power: A Study of the Tao Te Ching and Its Place in Chinese Thought*. London: Allen & Unwin.

———. 1963. *Travels of an Alchemist*. 1931. Reprint, London: Routledge & Kegan Paul.

Wang Deyou 王德有. 1991. *Rōshi den* 老子傳. Translated by Xu Hai 徐海. Tokyo: Chiyusha.

Wang Jing 王景, and Du Jiehui 杜節會, eds. 1991. *Qianjia miaogong xu* 乾家妙功序. Beijing: Kexue jishu chubanshe.

Wang Ka 王卡. 1989. "Yuanshi tianzun yu Pangushi kaitian pidi" 元始天尊與盤古氏開天闢地. *Shijie zongjiao yanjiu* 世界宗教研究 1989.3:61–69.

Wang Ming 王明. 1960. *Taiping jing hejiao* 太平經合校. Beijing: Zhonghua.

———. 1984. *Daojia he daojiao sixiang yanjiu* 道家和道教思想研究. Chongqing: Zhongguo shehui kexue chubanshe.

Wang Weicheng 王維誠. 1934. "Laozi huahu shuo kaozheng" 老子化胡說考證. *Guoxue jikan* 國學季刊 4.2:1–122.

Ward, Benedicta. 1982. *Miracles and the Medieval Mind*. Philadelphia: University of Pennsylvania Press.

Ware, James R. 1933. "The *Wei-shu* and the *Sui-shu* on Taoism." *Journal of the American Oriental Society* 53:215–50.

———. 1966. *Alchemy, Medicine and Religion in the China of A.D. 320*. Cambridge, Mass.: MIT Press.

Watson, Burton. 1968. *The Complete Works of Chuang-tzu*. New York: Columbia University Press.

Wayman, Alex. 1957. "Contributions Regarding the Thirty-two Characteristics of the Great Person." In *Liebenthal Festschrift*, edited by Kshitis Roy, 243–60. Santiniketan: Visvabharati.

Wechsler, Howard. 1985. *Offerings of Jade and Silk: Ritual and Symbol in the Legitimation of the T'ang Dynasty*. New Haven: Yale University Press.

Weizsäcker, C. F. von. 1964. *The Relevance of Science: Creation and Cosmogony.* London: Collins.

Wen Yiduo 文一多. 1956. *Shenhua yu shi* 神話與詩. Beijing: Zhonghua.

Wheatley, Paul. 1971. *The Pivot of the Four Quarters: A Preliminary Enquiry into the Origins and Character of the Ancient Chinese City.* Chicago: Aldine.

White, William Charles. 1940. *Chinese Temple Frescoes: A Study of Three Wall-paintings of the Thirteenth Century.* Toronto: University of Toronto Press.

Whitehead, Alfred N. 1927. *Religion in the Making.* Cambridge: Cambridge University Press.

Widengren, Geo. 1961. *Mani and Manichaeism.* New York: Hold, Reinhart and Winston.

Wile, Douglas. 1992. *Art of the Bedchamber: The Chinese Sexology Classics Including Women's Solo Meditation Texts.* Albany: State University of New York Press.

Wilhelm, Hellmut. 1952. "Der Zeitbegriff im Buch der Wandlungen." *Eranos Jahrbuch* 20:321–48.

———. 1971. *Frühling und Herbst des Lü Bu-wei.* Düsseldorf: Diederichs.

Williams, Michael A., ed. 1982. *Charisma and Sacred Biography.* Chico, Calif.: Scholars' Press.

Wong, Eva. 1992. *Cultivating Stillness: A Taoist Manual for Transforming Body and Mind.* Boston: Shambhala.

———. 1997. *Teachings of the Tao.* Boston: Shambhala.

Worsley, Peter. 1968. *The Trumpet Shall Sound: A Study of 'Cargo' Cults in Melanesia.* New York: Schocken Books.

Wright, Arthur F. 1959. *Buddhism in Chinese History.* Stanford: Stanford University Press.

———. 1978. *The Sui Dynasty.* New York: Knopf.

Wu, Hung. 1986. "Buddhist Elements in Early Chinese Art." *Artibus Asiae* 47:263–352.

Wu, K. C. 1982. *The Chinese Heritage.* New York: Crown Publishers.

Xie Mingling 謝明玲. 1984. "Butsu setsu fubo enshōkyō to Taijō rōkun setsu hō fubo enshō kyō to sono kankei ni tsuite" 佛說父母恩重經と太上老君說報父母恩重經とその關係について. *Tōyō daigaku kenkyū seiyin kiyō* 東洋大學研究生院紀要 21:219–32.

Xiong, Victor. 1996. "Ritual Innovations and Taoism Under Tang Xuanzong." *T'oung-pao* 82:258–316.

Yamada Takashi 山田俊. 1992. *Kōhon Shōgenkyō* 稿本昇玄經. Sendai: Tōhoku daigaku.

Yamada Toshiaki 山田利明. 1974. "Taihei kōki shinsenrui kentei hairetsu no ikkōsatsu" 太平廣記神仙類卷第配列の一考察. *Tōhō shūkyō* 東方宗教 43:30–50.

———. 1982. "Bunshi sensei mujō shinjin kanrei naiden no seiritsu ni tsuite" 文始先生無上眞人關令内傳の成立について. In *Rekishi ni okeru minshū to bunka* 歴史における民習と文化, 221–35. Tokyo: Hirakawa.

——. 1989. "Longevity Techniques and the Compilation of the *Lingbao wufuxu*." In *Taoist Meditation and Longevity Techniques*, edited by Livia Kohn, 97–122. Ann Arbor: University of Michigan, Center for Chinese Studies.

——. 1989a. "Dōbō shinson shikō" 洞房神存試考. *Tōhō shūkyō* 東方宗教 74:20–38.

——. 1995. "The Evolution of Taoist Ritual: K'ou Ch'ien-chih and Lu Hsiu-ching." *Acta Asiatica* 68:69–83.

——. 1995a. "Dōkyō shinzō no chūhai" 道教神像の崇拜. *Chūgoku tetsugaku bungakka kiyō* 中國哲學文學科紀要 3:17–33.

Yamada Toshiaki 山田利明, and Yūsa Noboru 遊左昇, eds. 1984. *Taijō dōgen shinshūkyō goi sakuin* 太上洞淵神咒經語彙索引. Tokyo: Sōundō.

Yan Lingfeng 嚴靈峰. 1983. *Jinzi congzhu* 經子叢著. Taipei: Xuesheng.

Yan Weibing 嚴威丙. 1989. *Shiyong daojia qigong fa* 實用道家氣功法. Guangxi: Minzu chubanshe.

Yang Liansheng 楊聯陞. 1956. "Laojun yinsong jiejing jiaoshi" 老君音誦誡經校釋. *Chongyang yanjiu yuan lishi yanyu yanjiu suo jikan* 中央研究院歷史言語研究所集刊 28:17–54.

Yao, Tao-chung. 1980. "Ch'üan-chen: A New Taoist Sect in North China During the Twelfth and Thirteenth Centuries." Ph.D. diss., University of Arizona, Tucson.

——. 1986. "Ch'iu Ch'u-chi and Chinggis Khan." *Harvard Journal of Asiatic Studies* 46:201–19.

Yetts, Percifal. 1916. "The Eight Immortals." *Journal of the Royal Asiatic Society* 1916, 773–807.

——. 1922. "More Notes on the Eight Immortals." *Journal of the Royal Asiatic Society* 1922, 397–426.

Yokote Hiroshi 横手裕. 1990. "Zenshinkyō no henyū" 全眞教の變容. *Chūgoku tetsugaku kenkyū* 中國哲學研究 2:23–92.

Yoshikawa Tadao 吉川忠夫. 1990. "Ō Genshi kū" 王遠知考. *Tōhō gakuhō* 東方學報 62:69–98.

——. 1997. "Reihi sanpō denshinroku no shūhen" 靈飛散方傳信錄の週邊. *Tōhō shūkyō* 東方宗教 90:1–21.

Yoshioka Yoshitoyo 吉岡義豐. 1955. *Dōkyō kyōten shiron* 道教經典史論. Tokyo: Dōkyō kankōkai.

——. 1959. *Dōkyō to bukkyō* 道教と佛教. Vol. 1. Tokyo: Kokusho kankōkai.

——. 1967. "Zaikairoku to Chigonsō" 齋戒籙と至言總. *Taishō daigaku kenkyūjo kiyō* 大正大學研究所紀要 52:283–302.

——. 1979. "Taoist Monastic Life." In *Facets of Taoism*, edited by Holmes Welch and Anna Seidel, 220–52. New Haven: Yale University Press.

Yu, David C. 1981. "The Creation Myth and Its Symbolism in Classical Taoism." *Philosophy East and West* 31:479–500.

Yu Gongbao 虞功保. 1991. *Zhongguo gudai yangsheng shu baizhong* 中國古代養生術白種. Beijing: Tiyu xueyuan chubanshe.

Yü, Ying-shih. 1964. "Life and Immortality in the Mind of Han-China." *Harvard Journal of Asiatic Studies* 25:80–122.

——. 1987. "O Soul, Come Back: A Study of the Changing Conceptions of the Soul and Afterlife in Pre-Buddhist China." *Harvard Journal of Asiatic Studies* 47:363–95.

Yuan Ke 袁珂. 1985. *Zhongguo shenhua chuanshuo cidian* 中國神話傳說詞典. Shanghai: Wenyi.

——. 1986. *Zhongguo shenhua chuanshuo* 中國神話傳說. Beijing: Zhongguo minjian wenyi.

——. 1988. *Zhongguo shenhua shi* 中國神話史. Shanghai: Wenyi.

Yūsa Noboru 遊左昇. 1986. "Seito seiyōkyū seijōsan oyobi hisen ni okeru dōkyō kenkyū no genshō" 成都青羊宮清城山及ひ四川における道教研究の現壯. *Tōhō shūkyō* 東方宗教 68:86–98.

——. 1989. "Tōdai ni mirareru kyukutenson shinkō ni tsuite" 唐代に見られる救苦天尊信仰について. *Tōhō shūkyō* 東方宗教 73:19–40.

Zhang Weiling 張煒玲. 1990. "Guanling Yin Xi shenhua yanjiu" 關令尹喜神化研究. *Daojiao xue tansuo* 道教學探索 3:21–74.

——. 1991. "Beichao zhi qian louguan daojiao xiuxingfa de lishi kaocha" 北朝之前樓觀道教修行法的歷史考察. *Daojiao xue tansuo* 道教學探索 4:67–117.

Zhu Yueli 朱越利. 1992. *Daojiao yaoji gailun* 道教要籍概論. In *Daojiao wenhua congshu* 道教文化叢書, vol. 2. Beijing: Yenshan chubanshe.

Zhuang Hongyi 莊宏誼. 1986. *Mingdai daojiao zhengyi pai* 明代道教正一派. Taipei: Xuesheng.

Zito, Angela. 1996. "City Gods and Their Magistrates." In *Religions of China in Practice*, edited by Donald S. Lopez, Jr., 72–81. Princeton: Princeton University Press.

——. 1997. *Of Body and Brush: Grand Sacrifice as Text/Performance in Eighteenth Century China*. Chicago: University of Chicago Press.

Zürcher, Erik. 1959. *The Buddhist Conquest of China: The Spread and Adaptation of Buddhism in Early Medieval China*. 2 vols. Leiden: E. J. Brill.

——. 1980. "Buddhist Influence on Early Taoism." *T'oung-pao* 66:84–147.

——. 1982. "Prince Moonlight: Messianism and Eschatology in Early Medieval Buddhism." *T'oung-pao* 68:1–75.

Glossary-Index

absolute, the, 194–95; and hero, 284–85
Adams, D., 213
alchemy: Laozi in, 3n9, 78–79; methods of, 15
Amoghavajra, 100
Ānanda, 18
A 'nan tongxue jing 阿難同學經, 114, 116
animals: celestial, 185, 200; exercises based on, 80
An Lushan 安錄山, 27, 328
Anmo tongjing jing 按摩通精經, 219
Anqi guan 安期觀, 145
Anqiu Sheng 安丘生, 295
An Shigao 安世高, 116
antiquity: lower, 210; middle, 214
Anzhai bayang jing 安宅八陽經, 141, 148, 161
apocalypse. *See* Li Hong
archivist: Laozi as, xi, 9, 256
art: iconography in, 142. *See also* Lord Lao, paintings of, statues of; trinity
Aśoka, 276, 280–81
Aśokavadāna (Legends of King Aśoka), 280
Avalokiteśvara, 318

Badi jing 八帝經, 161
Baibu congshu 百部叢書, 75n24, 121n14
Baihe guan 白鶴觀, 144, 145
Baiyuan 白元, 72

Bai Yuchan 白玉蟾, 66
Baiyun guan 白雲觀, 109
Bamboo *Laozi*, 9n6
banquets, 275, 276–77, 280–81; interpretation of, 285
Bao fumu enzhong jing 報父母恩重經, 115, 128, 128n27, 162
Baopuzi 抱朴子, *Daode jing* recitation in, 267; Ge Xuan in, 303n14; Laozi in, 226; *Taisu jing* in, 64n3; talismans in, 148n10; text of, 11n11; visualization in, 69–70, 71n16, 187, 247n18
Baoxuan jing 寶玄經, 24
barbarians: conversion of, 11, 18n19, 20, 24–28, 152, 173, 275–90; creation of, 16; in Daoist myth, 279; destruction of, 281–82; and hero myth, 284–87; king of, 275, 276, 279–81, 284, 285; texts on, 276. *See also* Huahu jing
Beidi yansheng bijue 北帝延生秘訣, 100n11
beidou 北斗. *See* Dipper
Beidou changsheng jing 北斗長生經, 92, 98, 161
Beidou ershiba zhangjing 北斗二十八章經, 115, 136n41, 161
Beidou jing 北斗經, 100, 100n12
Beidou yansheng jing 北斗延生經, 92, 98, 161
Beidou zhang 北斗章, 162
beiji 北極. *See* Pole Star